CHINA
IN THE NEW MILLENNIUM

CHINA
IN THE NEW MILLENNIUM

MARKET
REFORMS
and SOCIAL
DEVELOPMENT

edited by James A. Dorn

CATO
INSTITUTE
Washington, D.C.

Library of Congress Cataloging-in-Publication Data

China in the new millennium : market reforms and social development /
    edited by James A. Dorn.
        p.   cm.
    Includes bibliographical references and index.
    ISBN 1-882577-60-4. — ISBN 1-882577-61-2
    1. China—Economic policy—1976–   2. Economic stabilization—
China.   3. China—Foreign economic relations.   4. Social change—
China.   5. China—Forecasting   I. Dorn, James A.
HC427.92.C464447   1998
338.951—dc21   98-34592
                                          3SKS0003012155   CIP

Printed in the United States of America.

CATO INSTITUTE
1000 Massachusetts Ave., N.W.
Washington, D.C. 20001

Contents

ACKNOWLEDGMENTS

This book is an outgrowth of the Cato Institute's June 1997 conference in Shanghai, "China as a Global Economic Power: Market Reforms in the New Millennium," which was cosponsored with Fudan University's Center for American Studies. That conference would not have been possible without the generous support of the Atlas Economic Research Foundation, Arthur and Johanna Cinader, Federal Express, William Melton, R. J. Reynolds Tobacco Company, the Starr Foundation, and the Ford Foundation. Their generosity is much appreciated.

Madame Xie Xide, director of the Center for American Studies and former president of Fudan University, was instrumental in paving the way for the Shanghai conference. Professor Zhou Dun Ren also deserves high marks for the outstanding job he did in helping to organize the event.

Cato president Ed Crane's moral support during this project and his vision for a more open society in China have been very helpful. Many others have helped to make the book a reality, but special thanks go to the authors for their cooperation in what was a very complex undertaking. Finally, I wish to thank David Lampo for never letting me forget that books have deadlines and Lee Koehler, my summer intern, for his efficiency in helping me meet at least some of my deadlines.

1. Introduction—China in the New Millennium

James A. Dorn

> There is no general rule to ensure that all countries or regions should reach the same level of economic attainment or the same rate of progress at any given time or over any given period. Economic achievement and progress depend largely on human aptitudes and attitudes, on social and political institutions and arrangements which derive from these, on historical experience, and to a lesser extent on external contacts, market opportunities and on natural resources. And if these factors favourable to material progress are present, persons, groups and even societies will not stagnate, so that it is the absence of the favourable determinants, and not poverty, which is the causal factor in prolonged stagnation.
>
> —P. T. Bauer
> *Dissent on Development*

China's Market Experiment

China's daring experiment with markets and prices, which began in 1978, has propelled China into the top 10 trading nations in the world. Over the past two decades, China has achieved the fastest economic growth of any national economy, averaging nearly 10 percent per year. If that growth continues, China could become the world's largest economy during the first half of the 21st century.

The continued success of China's journey to prosperity, however, will depend critically on whether its leaders are willing to allow a true market system to develop, in which individuals can hold secure title to their property and are held accountable for their mistakes, or whether China remains a "socialist market economy," in which

---

James A. Dorn is Vice President for Academic Affairs at the Cato Institute and Professor of Economics at Towson University.

the state plays a dominant role. The question is, Will China follow the path of Hong Kong and adopt market liberalism or continue on the road of market socialism and risk ending the Chinese economic miracle?

The reality is that, unless China can insulate economic life from the state, future economic and social development will be on shaky ground. Indeed, if China is to escape the crippling effects of crony capitalism, now evident in much of East Asia, the institutional clash between markets and socialism in China must be resolved in favor of greater economic freedom. The model for China should be Hong Kong, with its market-supporting institutions. Hong Kong's strict adherence to the principle of nonintervention and the rule of law has allowed it to become the freest economy in the world, and that freedom has produced tremendous wealth and a strong civil society. China cannot afford to ignore those truths.

At the heart of both Kong Kong's success and China's has been the spontaneous nature of wealth creation that takes place within the confines of market exchange. All rational people want a better life for themselves and their children. Free markets provide an opportunity to make the best use of nature's scarce resources and to discover and take advantage of one's talents. Central planning denies people that opportunity and is contrary to human nature. That is why, in the end, it has failed wherever and whenever it has been tried.

The idea of a spontaneous market order—a natural order that benefits individuals and society—is a direct threat to the Chinese Communist Party (CCP), which has a strong interest in maintaining its monopoly of power. The growth of the nonstate, market sector of the Chinese economy has undermined the power of the communist state. Yet, if the market sector is curtailed, the economy will slow and there could be social unrest.

That Chinese puzzle is not easily resolved. China has been moving along in the right direction—markets have been opening, living standards have improved (per capita incomes have quadrupled since 1978), and civil society has grown—but China is still burdened with inefficient state-owned enterprises (SOEs), a banking system riddled with nonperforming loans, and massive poverty, especially in rural areas. Moreover, the Chinese people, now over 1.2 billion strong, have never experienced real freedom.

2

One of the key features of this book is its emphasis on the relation between the free market, personal autonomy, and social development. Most people now understand that a market economy fosters wealth creation, but they too often fail to perceive how the spontaneous market process promotes individual freedom and human and social progress. This book shows how China's opening to the outside world has enhanced personal freedom and promoted civil society—that is, the nonpolitical space in which individuals voluntarily develop human relations apart from the state.

China's continuing transition from a planned economy to a market economy, as a way to organize economic life, has spilled over into everyday life and added immeasurably to human progress—people are freer to travel, to go into business, to change jobs, to work outside the state sector, to talk with foreigners, to use the Internet, to read foreign literature, and to enjoy themselves than ever before. Although many freedoms are still curtailed, no honest observer would say that China has less freedom today than 20 years ago. This side-effect of material progress is an important part of the Chinese economic miracle that is too often forgotten.

The genesis of this book was the Cato Institute's second Shanghai conference, "China as a Global Economic Power: Market Reforms in the New Millennium," cosponsored with Fudan University's Center for American Studies, June 15–18, 1997. That conference, like the historic September 1988 conference at which Nobel laureate economist Milton Friedman spoke, brought together a group of distinguished scholars and policy experts to discuss the state of China's reforms and China's future. The difference, of course, is that in the interim between the two conferences, communism collapsed in Eastern Europe and the Soviet Union, which no longer exists; the prodemocracy movement in China was quashed in Tiananmen Square; Deng Xiaoping died; Hong Kong reverted to Chinese jurisdiction; and the 15th Party Congress put its stamp of approval on the new leadership going into the next century.

Those events, and the further economic liberalization that occurred after 1988, made the set of issues to be addressed at the 1997 conference different in degree but not in substance. The issue of state versus private ownership remains unresolved; the financial condition of SOEs is bleaker than in 1988, but the causes are much the same; the Asian financial crisis has alerted China to the dangers inherent in state-led investment planning, but those dangers derive from Soviet-style central planning and have been criticized for some time by Western observers; and, most important, the notion that markets can be grafted onto socialist institutions to produce a vibrant "socialist market economy" is a dream that is sure to become a nightmare as China confronts economic reality.

The issue of planning versus the market—that is, of a planned order versus a spontaneous order—remains at the center of the debate over China's future. That issue receives substantial attention in this volume. How it is decided will determine whether private capital markets develop in China or whether investment decisions remain politicized.

The book is divided into five parts: "The Future of China's Market Economy" (Part I), "Lessons for China from Hong Kong" (Part II), "China's Place in the Global Trading Order" (Part III), "Social Development in China" (Part IV), and "Institutional Choice and China's Development" (Part V). A brief summary of each section follows.

The Future of China's Market Economy

Topics covered in Part I include the prospect of China becoming a global "economic superpower," a term Charles Wolf Jr. finds vacuous; the current state of China's economic reforms and the steps needed to make China a true market economy; the problem of whether SOE reform should be gradual or radical; the tensions inherent in a socialist market economy and how those tensions may work themselves out; and the notion of a spontaneous market order and how that order is consistent with ancient Chinese thought, as found in the writings of Lao Tzu.

Lessons for China from Hong Kong

In Part II, attention shifts to Hong Kong and the lessons that China can learn from the world's freest economy. The importance of free trade, sound capital markets, a stable currency, low taxes, and a legal system that protects persons and property against the arbitrary and heavy hand of government are shown to be essential to Hong Kong's success and to China's future.

China's Place in the Global Trading Order

Part III examines the issue of whether China should be admitted to the World Trade Organization and, if so, when and on what terms. Other issues dealing with China's status as a global trading power are considered, including whether China will abide by the rules of a liberal trading order (e.g., with regard to the recent telecom regulatory principles); whether China will further liberalize its foreign exchange regime; and how the U.S.-China relationship may evolve as China gains in economic stature.

Social Development in China

Part IV considers the effects of economic liberalization on the course of human rights and social development in China. Under central planning and state ownership, all economic decisions become political decisions. China's opening to the outside world and the development of a large and dynamic nonstate sector have lessened the power of the central government and provided new opportunities for the Chinese people. Cato Institute president Edward H. Crane explains why China is at a crossroads and must choose between political society and civil society—that is, between coercion as society's organizing principle and freedom. The information revolution comes squarely down on the side of freedom. If China resists that change, it will fail to develop to its fullest.

Minxin Pei and Kate Xiao Zhou provide a rich variety of examples of how greater economic freedom in China has led to a widening and deepening of civil society. An important part of that process, as Tom G. Palmer shows, involves the rise of business enterprise. The millions of individuals who run the small businesses that have mushroomed in China, especially in the coastal areas, comprise a new class that has put a brake on government activism.

Under central planning, the idea of equal shares—the "iron rice bowl" mentality—weakened work incentives and elevated equality to a national virtue. But using the force of government to achieve greater equality is not a virtue, it is a vice. There is nothing virtuous in taking property and income from those who are productive and redistributing it to those who are not. With the onset of reform in 1978, things began to change, albeit slowly, as people recognized the importance of linking effort and reward. Today, the freedom to sell in the open market has increased living standards, but it has also produced a greater disparity of incomes, especially between the fast growing coastal areas and the rest of China. That inequality, however, is not necessarily bad—it represents greater liberty and

5

opportunity to search for profit than has existed in the past. In the future, China will be richer than it would have been if it had stuck fast to the "iron rice bowl" mentality.

The danger is that China will become overly concerned with income inequality and use the power of government to create a large redistributive state modeled after the European welfare states. Such a decision would be a step backwards and slow the market-driven growth that has lifted millions of Chinese out of poverty since 1978.

In his chapter, "Getting over Equality," P. J. O'Rourke equates the quest for equality—in terms of equalizing outcomes—with collectivism and shows why that quest is not only detrimental to wealth creation but immoral as well. Leveling the incomes of rich people, in either the East or the West, is not the way to prosperity or morality.

What China needs to do, argues José Piñera, is to empower people by privatizing assets and allowing people to invest their own money to provide for their own future. That is why he warns China against adopting a national pay-as-you go pension system and, instead, advocates learning from Chile's success with a privately funded pension system. As Michael Tanner points out, the best mechanism for creating a secure retirement income and adequate health-care coverage is the market, not the plan.

Institutional Choice and China's Development

Part V deals with the constitutional, fiscal, and regulatory changes needed to keep China on the road to a freer and more prosperous nation. It is important for China to have "simple tax rules," as Stephen Moore recommends, and to follow Hong Kong's example by adopting a low, flat-rate tax. But it is even more important for China to incorporate any tax change into a constitution that limits government power to tax and to spend and protects individual rights to life, liberty, and property. China's transition from plan to market will not be complete until there is a legal and constitutional framework that protects those natural human rights.

That is why Roger Pilon advocates a "constitution of liberty" for China. "If China is to preserve and expand upon its recent achievements," argues Pilon, "it will need a constitution that institutionalizes, not simply tolerates, the forces that have led to improvements there." The fact that the government has recently allowed F. A.

Hayek's classic 1960 book, *The Constitution of Liberty*, to be published, circulated, and discussed in China is a positive sign.

In the final chapter, Jerry Taylor criticizes the idea of "sustainable development," as it is commonly used by environmental planners. Command-and-control schemes to protect the environment by limiting economic growth are misguided, according to Taylor. The best way for China to achieve a clean environment and a healthier nation is not to hamper markets by overregulation but to harness markets by privatization.

New Thinking

Mao Zedong once said, "Who controls a man's ideas controls the man" (quoted in the *Wall Street Journal* 1998: A14). In 1999, China will celebrate its 50th anniversary under communism. For much of that time, the state had total control over people's lives and that control was exercised, in large part, by controlling the economy. State ownership and central planning meant that almost everyone worked for the government and depended on the government for survival. As such, people had to be political; they had to toe the party line. Civil society, in effect, was outlawed.

With the opening that has occurred since 1978, the idea of economic freedom has been planted on Chinese soil and the tree of liberty has been allowed to grow. Whether that growth will continue will depend on how far China's leaders are willing to go in allowing the Chinese people to explore new ideas and to be free to choose— not only in the marketplace but in all aspects of life. The debate that still needs to be aired in China is the debate over the proper role of government. That debate is now just beginning.

In March 1998, the governor of Qinghai province, Bai Enpei, in a speech before China's legislature, stated, "Things the government shouldn't manage, or can't manage, or manages badly, should be given to enterprises, society, and relevant institutions to manage themselves" (Forney 1998). That attitude, if widespread, will invigorate China.

Difficult issues remain for China; the problem of privatizing SOEs and the question of constitutional reform are perhaps the most fundamental. The future of China as a global economic power will depend on how they are resolved. One thing is clear: without a better understanding and appreciation of the nature of the spontaneous market order, the institutional infrastructure necessary to support that order will not evolve in China. And, if that occurs, social development will also suffer.

References

Bauer, P.T. (1976) *Dissent on Development.* Revised ed. Cambridge, Mass.: Harvard University Press.

Forney, M. (1998) "Voice of the People." *Far Eastern Economic Review*, 7 May 1998.

Hayek, F.A. (1960) *The Constitution of Liberty.* Chicago: University of Chicago Press.

Wall Street Journal (1998) "China's Road from Serfdom." *WSJ*, 12 May: A14.

PART I

THE FUTURE OF CHINA'S MARKET ECONOMY

2. China: An Emerging "Economic Superpower"?

Charles Wolf Jr.

This chapter is divided into three sections: a prologue focusing on terminology—in particular, on what the term "economic superpower" means and whether it is applicable to China; a summary of selected global economic and military trends and a description of China's place in relation to them; and an epilogue with concluding observations about China's role in the world economy based on the preceding data and discussion.

Terminology

Some words acquire a cachet and a currency vastly exceeding their informational content. They acquire a sort of life of their own, despite a degree of obscurity bordering on vacuity. Many years ago an insightful analyst of the media, Stuart Chase, labeled this phenomenon "the tyranny of words." An example is provided by the word "superpower," or "economic superpower."

The term "superpower" is a legacy of the Cold War of the 1970s and 1980s. The term was invented to describe what was presumed to be the overwhelming preponderance of both military and economic power of the United States and the Soviet Union, compared with any other countries or independent coalition of countries. In retrospect, and in light of what we now know about the state of the Soviet economy apart from its military industry and technology, the economic power that had been attributed to the Soviet Union was vastly overrated.

Moreover, even if the assumed combination of military and economic power possessed by the Soviet Union and the United States

---

Charles Wolf Jr. is Senior Economic Advisor and Corporate Fellow in International Economics at RAND.

warranted the "superpower" designation during the Cold War, its relevance to the current and future multipolar world is dubious. In this world, the measurement of effective military as well as economic power has become more complicated, and its effective use has become sharply limited by a variety of political, economic, technical, and societal constraints—some of which are domestic and others international in character. These constraints, which typically are associated with specific, scenario-dependent circumstances, reduce the willingness and ability of individual countries or coalitions of countries, to influence events in various arenas. For example, the ingredients of economic power that may be relevant in trade negotiations between governments or disputes (such as a U.S. threat to apply sanctions to countries that trade with or invest in Iran or Libya) may be irrelevant in negotiations between multinational corporations (for example, between Boeing and Airbus); and the ingredients of military power that may be relevant in an East Asian contingency (for example, in Korea) may be quite irrelevant in Bosnia.

Reflecting these complexities, there have been numerous attempts—misguided, in my opinion—to separate the military and economic components of "superpowerdom." For example, sometimes Russia is characterized as "still a *military* superpower," and sometimes Japan is characterized as an "*economic* superpower" (despite its virtual economic stagnation during the 1990s), and sometimes China is referred to as "an emerging economic superpower."

In the midst of this semantic confusion, one fundamental difference between the economic and military components of power should be emphasized. The components of military power are essentially *centralized* in the hands of governments. Thus, governments typically have exclusive command over military forces—conventional, nuclear, surface, air, naval forces, C³I, and so on. This prerogative is, within the boundaries of the state, a non-contested monopoly. (The phenomenon of national and international terrorism is a distracting exception to this fundamental characterization of military power as centralized, monopolized, and exclusive.)

In contrast, the components of economic power tend to be predominantly *decentralized*, rather than residing within the exclusive purview of governments. If and when these components are centralized, or substantial movement is attempted in the direction of centralization, economic power tends to diminish as a result. Thus, the components of economic power, while partly in the hands of governments to an extent that varies across countries and over time, are largely in the hands of private, quasi-private, provincial, township and village enterprises (TVEs), and joint ventures and corporate alliances across national boundaries that may encompass public and private entities as well as joint multinational entities. In sum, economic power tends to be centrifugal, while military power is centripetal. Moreover, unless the components of economic power remain largely decentralized, I hypothesize that they will weaken and atrophy.

From this abbreviated discussion of terminology, I conclude that it is misleading to use the term "economic superpower" to describe China, or the United States for that matter, for several reasons: first, the constraints that limit the exercise of that power, and its various components, sharply deflate the meaning of "super"; second, the principal components of economic power have to be decentralized to be maintained, let alone to grow, and hence these components should not properly be viewed as coterminous with governments or government policies; and finally, attempts to centralize these various components of economic power in the hands of governments will very likely backfire and diminish them in the process.

Long-Term Economic and Military Trends

To assess the economic as well as military dimensions of China's present and prospective power, it is useful to compare them with those of other countries, and thereby to place China in the context of the unfolding global economic and security environment. Toward this end, I will begin by drawing on a recent RAND study of economic and military trends from the present through 2015, for China, the United States, Japan, Korea, India, and several other countries, as well (Wolf, Yeh, Kennedy, et al. 1995).

The RAND study focused on three key indicators of the future economic and military positions of these countries: gross domestic product (GDP), per capita GDP, and military capital stocks (representing the accumulation of spending by each country on procurement of military equipment and military R & D, *minus* depreciation of the previously accumulated stock of military capital).

13

These indicators provide useful benchmarks for assessing China's growing economic and military power. However, it should be noted that numerous qualifications, controversies, and limitations are associated with this study. For example, the underlying economic growth model used in the study and applied to all of the countries included in it, is a highly aggregative and simplified macroeconomic model that includes both quantitative and qualitative (i.e., judgmental) elements (e.g., a key parameter in the model relates to "total factor productivity," whose estimation is based on econometric analysis of historical data modified by explicit judgments by the RAND analysts who worked on the study concerning future prospects). Also, this study used purchasing power parity (ppp) or real exchange rates reflecting the buying-power of each country's own currency, rather than nominal current foreign exchange (FX) rates or averages of those rates over several years. The use of ppp rates rather than nominal FX rates to convert Chinese yuan to dollars has the effect of boosting China's GDP estimates by a factor of six or seven, while having the reverse effect of reducing Japan's GDP estimates by about 40 or 50 percent compared to what they would be if FX rates were used instead. Another source of controversy in the RAND estimates arises from the fact that the figure we used for China's GDP in yuan is somewhat higher than that presented in some of the official data, due principally to the increased imputed value of health and housing services that we allowed for in the RAND calculations.

In the course of this work, we formulated several different scenarios for China as well as for some of the other countries included in the study. In the GDP estimates presented in Figure 1, those for China represent the average of two China scenarios— a "sustained-growth" scenario and a "disrupted-growth" scenario. For the other countries, the Figure 1 estimates reflect the base-line cases used for each country, rather than averages where more than one scenario was used.

Note that the data in Figure 1 are expressed in terms of the relative buying-power (i.e., purchasing power) of the respective country currencies converted to 1997 U.S. dollars. This has a major effect on the *levels* of the corresponding estimates for each country, compared to what these estimates would be if instead the GDP figures were based on nominal FX rates. As noted above, if FX rates were used for the conversion into U.S. dollars, the GDP estimates for China

FIGURE 1
GDP Estimates for China and Other Countries, 1997–2015

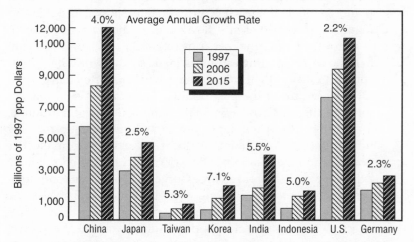

SOURCE: Wolf, Yeh, Kennedy, et al. (1995), updated using U.S. GDP deflator (annual average, 1993–96 4 2.27 percent) to express estimates in 1997 dollars.

would be only one-sixth of those shown in Figure 1, while the estimates for Japan would be about 80 percent higher than shown in Figure 1.

It can be expected that, over the next two decades, these large discrepancies between the ppp exchange rates and nominal FX exchange rates will narrow if and as the respective countries become more open to trade and capital flows. Consequently, the ppp-based estimates for China will probably turn out to be somewhat less than what is shown in Figure 1, while the corresponding FX-based estimates would be somewhat more than the one-sixth ratio mentioned above. Conversely, the GDP estimates for Japan will very likely turn out to be higher than the levels shown in Figure 1, while the corresponding FX-based estimates for Japan would be somewhat lower than that cited earlier.

With these caveats in mind, several important points can be inferred from Figure 1 with respect to sizing the economy of China in relation to the global economy and to the economies of other countries:

15

- China's GDP, like that of the United States, will be about one quarter of the global gross product in 2015. It is also worth pointing out that the GDP growth rate shown for China in Figure 1, which represents the average of the estimated growth rates for the two China scenarios referred to earlier, is less than half the corresponding estimates made by the World Bank, and considerably less than half of what China's reported real growth rates were during the past decade. There are several reasons for expecting this slowdown in the coming decade: for example, a probable rise in the aggregate capital-output ratio for new infrastructure investments including transportation, electric power, and other major public works, such as the enormously expensive multi-purpose Three Gorges project; large continuing construction costs in Pudong and elsewhere; probably rising energy costs; the need to reduce or reverse the environmental effects of water and atmospheric pollution; continued costs and losses associated with state-owned enterprises (SOEs)[1]; and perhaps increased military spending.
- By 2015, China's GDP in ppp dollar equivalents will be more than twice that of Japan, while Japan's GDP will be about twice that of Korea.
- The five principal Asian economies (China, Japan, India, Korea, and Indonesia) will constitute about 45 percent of the global economy, on the assumption that Germany's GDP remains about 40 percent of that of the entire European Union, whose combined GDP will shrink to about 15 percent of the global product. The United States GDP will be about 25 percent of the global product (about the same proportion as at present).
- Finally, the economy of India in 2015 would be about 60 percent as large as that of the entire European Union, according to the estimates shown in Figure 1.

Another way of scaling China's economy, is to show its per capita GDP estimates in relation to those of other countries, as indicated in Figure 2.

The estimates in Figure 2 are based on the same GDP figures shown in Figure 1, combined with current population estimates for

---

[1] These drains may well be reduced to the extent that reform and privatization of the SOEs succeeds.

FIGURE 2
Per Capita GDP Estimates, 1997–2015

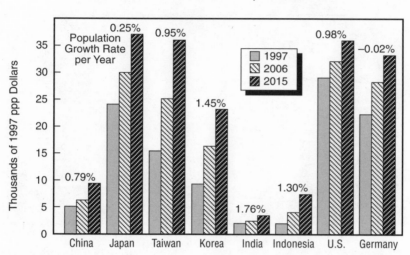

Sources: Wolf, Yeh, Kennedy, et al. (1995); Wolf and Kennedy (1995).

the respective countries and population growth rates drawn from the World Health Organization and other sources described in the referenced RAND study.

Figure 2 presents a strikingly different picture from that of Figure 1 in terms of how the Chinese economy fits into the global economy.

c The per capita estimates for the United States, Japan, Germany, and Taiwan are about equal as of 2015—between $33,000 and $37,000.

c The per capita figure for each of these "rich" countries is about four times that of China, while the per capita figure for Korea (about $23,000 for the reunified country) reaches about two-thirds that of the rich countries.

c Of the countries shown in Figure 2, the lowest per capita figures are those of China, Indonesia, and India—China's per capita GDP will be about $9,000, while that of India will be about one-third and Indonesia about three-quarters that of China.

It is also useful to place China in relation to another dimension of the international power balance—namely, that relating to the accumulation of military capital (through procurement of new

17

FIGURE 3
MILITARY CAPITAL ESTIMATES, 1997–2015

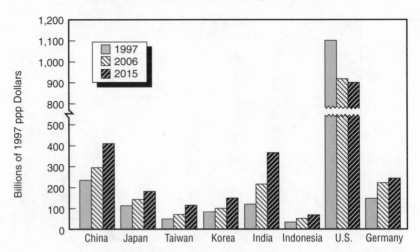

SOURCES: Wolf, Yeh, Kennedy, et al. (1995) updated to 1997 dollars using U.S. GDP deflator; Wolf and Kennedy (1995).

weapon systems either from domestic production or through imports of military equipment, *minus* the depreciation on the previously accumulated military capital stock). These estimates are shown in Figure 3.

Before commenting on the significance of the Figure 3 estimates, several cautionary observations about these calculations should be noted. One caution arises from the fact that it may be less appropriate to use ppp exchange rates rather than nominal FX rates to make the military capital comparisons across countries, than for the GDP and per capita GDP comparisons shown in Figures 1 and 2. To the extent that acquisitions of military capital are procured at world market prices, clearly the FX rates would represent the appropriate conversion metric. On the other hand, it can be argued that, to the extent that China acquires new military equipment from its own defense industries at yuan-based prices, or through its quasi-barter transactions with Russia, the ppp exchange rate still retains validity.

In any event, military capital itself—even if the estimates shown in Figure 3 are valid—is a highly imperfect and incomplete indicator of military capabilities, let alone intentions relating to their use. Even if the estimates in Figure 3 were accurate, military capital is only one of the inputs affecting military capabilities, and the effect of capital on military capabilities depends heavily on many other inputs. These other inputs include training and morale; command, communications, control, and intelligence; military leadership and doctrine; and maintenance and logistic support. These other ingredients are not readily inferred from the estimates of military capital accumulations, and they are ones in which China's effectiveness and competitive position are relatively weak. The pace at which they will be upgraded in the coming years is a key issue which is beyond the scope of this chapter.

Mindful of the limitations mentioned above, some interesting inferences can be drawn from the data shown in Figure 3:

- Between the present and 2015, the military capital stocks of China and Japan will approximately double, while India's military capital will nearly quadruple over the same period.
- While the U.S. military capital stock still predominates in the global balance, its relative weight decreases for two reasons: first, the U.S. military capital estimate for 2015 is actually about 25 percent less than the current level, because annual depreciation of its large existing military capital stocks exceeds new military procurement in the intervening years; second, the build-up of military capital by the other countries shown in Figure 3 increases their absolute and hence relative stocks of military capital. (Of course, the estimates shown in Figure 3 are based on an estimating methodology that begs the crucial question of technology and quality embodied in the dollar figures. Whether the so-called "revolution in military affairs" will enable the U.S. to maintain or even enhance its qualitative advantage over other countries, notwithstanding a smaller relative dollar value, is an important matter that is not adequately reflected in the estimating methodology used here.)

There is a final point linking the military capital issues discussed above and reflected in Figure 3 with China's growing economic and technological capabilities. This link relates to the $25 to $30 billion annual global arms market, in which China figures as both a buyer (principally from Russia) and a seller to countries in South Asia, the Middle East, and East Asia. Asia as a whole has become the principal

FIGURE 4
ASIAN AND GLOBAL TRADE: MERCHANDISE EXPORTS, 1995–96

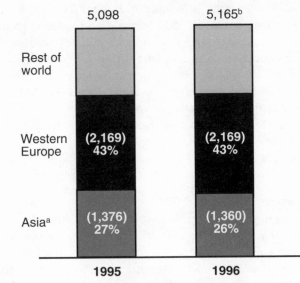

[a]Asia includes Taiwan ("province of China") and India.
[b]Estimated from data for three quarters.
SOURCE: International Monetary Fund (1997).

regional focus of this global arms trade. China is thus an important player in the arms market, and an even more important and rising player in nonmilitary merchandise trade.

China's large and growing prominence in the global economy is one of the factors accounting for the growing role of the entire Asian region in international trade and long-term capital markets. As indicated in Figure 4, Asia's merchandise exports account for slightly more than one quarter of total world exports.[2]

Although Western Europe's merchandise exports are considerably larger than those of Asia, European exports are concentrated within the European region to a much greater extent than is the case with regional concentration of Asia's exports. One reflection of this fact is that U.S. trade with Asia exceeds that with Europe, and is growing

[2]This statement, as well as prior and subsequent ones, do not reflect the impact of Asia's financial crisis in 1997 and thereafter.

TABLE 1
MERCHANDISE EXPORTS OF SELECTED COUNTRIES, 1995–96
(BILLIONS OF CURRENT DOLLARS)

	1995	1996
U.S.	585	625
Germany	524	521
Japan	443	411
Hong Kong	174	181
China	149	151
Korea	125	130
Taiwan	112	102[a]

[a]Estimated from data for first half of 1996.
SOURCE: International Monetary Fund (1997).

faster than the latter. It should be noted that the data shown in Figure 4 are confined to merchandise exports. Exports of services represent an additional 30 percent on top of the merchandise export figures for the global economy as a whole; in the case of the U.S. services exports represent about a 40 percent addition to U.S. merchandise exports.

Table 1 shows the merchandise exports of selected individual countries. Several points are worth noting about the data in Table 1:

- While China's exports are large and growing, even including Hong Kong its merchandise exports are less than those of Japan.
- Because China's exports tend to be oriented toward global markets, China is likely to encounter increasing competition from other globally oriented Asian exporters—including Korea, Taiwan, and the Southeast Asian countries—which are also targeted on those markets including that of the United States.
- The further growth of China's exports is likely to depend on the rates of GDP growth and of per capita GDP growth both outside and within the Asia-Pacific region, as well as the extent and pace at which China's trade policy increases the economic "openness" of its own markets.

Another indication of China's major role in the global economy is its prominence in international capital markets. In 1995 and 1996,

21

net flows of long-term private capital (covering foreign direct investment, portfolio equity investment, and long-term private nonguaranteed debt) have been about $200 billion annually, of which the share going to China has been about 20–25 percent.[3] These large and continuing flows, combined with China's somewhat anomalous surpluses in its trade account and its current account in recent years, have contributed to the growth of China's foreign exchange reserves to over $130 billion in 1997. This sum represents the largest foreign exchange reserves held by any emerging market country, and is second only to that of Japan ($221 billion) in the global economy as a whole.

Concluding Observations

It is clear from the numerous indicators and trends discussed in this chapter, that China is, and increasingly will be, a major "player" in the global economy. This conclusion follows whether one looks at the prospective size and growth of its GDP (even allowing for some reduction in the dramatic growth rates of the past decade), its prominence in international trade and export markets, and its conspicuous role as a recipient of long-term capital flows and their associated transfers of advanced management and high technology.

While the indicators and trends are clear in conveying this message, nevertheless several caveats should be emphasized. China's continued growth in international trade markets will depend on both the openness of those markets and the increased openness of its own markets. Also, China's ability to maintain its large share of net global private capital flows, and the valuable technology and management transfers associated with them, will depend on the extent to which it is able to maintain substantial rates of economic growth in the future, and to improve the broad investment "climate" prevailing in China. The types of private capital flows mentioned above, which comprise two-thirds to three-quarters of all net flows of long-term capital, are likely to be turned on or off depending on certain specific policies adopted by China compared with those of other emerging markets that are competing with it for long-term capital inflows. These policies include the predictability of property

---

[3]For a discussion of the different types and trends of private and public long-term capital flows, see Wolf (1995, chap. 6).

rights and the rule of law, fiscal and monetary policies that affect the rate of inflation and expectations about it, regulatory policies, and the general outlook for political stability. Within this matrix of broad policy influences, the enforceability of contractual obligations by local and central governments will be a critically important conditioning influence affecting future flows and destinations of long-term capital.

As a major player in the global economy, China can and should be expected to have a prominent role in such multilateral organizations as the WTO (although the notion that is sometimes expressed that China cannot be a major player in the global economy until it becomes a WTO member is plainly false), in APEC, in the G-6 Asian Summit (and eventually in the G-8 as well), in the ASEAN Regional Forum, the Asian Development Bank, and in other multilateral and international organizations. Moreover, the agendas of these organizations for moving toward a greater degree of economic openness in transactions for goods, services, and capital, should complement and reinforce China's own agenda for moving in similar directions. (A specific example of such complementarity is perhaps provided by China's township and village enterprises, which have been key elements in China's recent and prospective future growth. Sustaining the further development and growth of this novel form of quasi-private ownership can be greatly facilitated by a wider opening of the equity markets in Shanghai and in Shenzhen-Guangzhou.)

So, my answer to the question originally posed in the title of this paper—whether China will become a major economic power in the global economy—is partly concurring, and partly demurring. China is already a major economic power, and will become more so in the years ahead. At the same time, I demur from the notion that its continued rise as an economic power will make it an economic "superpower." The reasons for this demurral are numerous. One reason, previously alluded to, is that economic power and performance depend on multiple, decentralized entrepreneurial initiatives and innovations. The notion of economic "superpowerdom" is erroneous and misleading. If, for example, China were to make a strong effort to centralize and "command" these initiatives, they would be likely to atrophy, and to erode the economic performance they were designed to advance. Another reason is that there will be numerous other major economic powers in the global economy, and they and the decentralized entrepreneurial entities within them will tend to act as strong counterweights to China or any other country aspiring to a position as an economic "superpower." These counterweights include ones in Asia—for example, Japan, India, and to a lesser extent Korea, Indonesia, and the Southeast Asian countries—as well as the United States and the European Union. An Asia-Pacific region, as well as a global economy, in which multiple economic powers compete with one another should be advantageous to them as well as to China.

References

International Monetary Fund (1997) *International Financial Statistics.* Washington, D.C.: International Monetary Fund.

Wolf, C. (1997) *The Economic Pivot in a Political Context.* New Brunswick, N.J.: Transaction Books.

Wolf, C., and Kennedy, M. (1995) "Long-Term Economic and Military Trends, 1994–2015: Russia, Germany and Indonesia." Unpublished manuscript, RAND.

Wolf, C.; Yeh, K.C.; Kennedy, M.; et al. (1995) *Long-Term Economic and Military Trends, 1994–2015: The United States and Asia.* MR-627. Santa Monica, Calif.: RAND.

3. China's Unfinished Economic Experiment

Nicholas R. Lardy

By a number of important criteria China's economic transformation has been more successful than that of any other transition economy. These include several dimensions of China's economic growth performance and its rapid integration into the world economy. The latter is reflected not only in vastly increased trade flows but also in record levels of inward foreign direct investment and unparalleled access to international capital markets.

Yet in certain other critical respects, despite its relatively early start on economic reform, China lags far behind other transition economies. Most obviously, it lags in the transformation of its ownership structure. The share of manufactured goods produced in state-owned firms has declined significantly over the past decade and a half. But this has come primarily from the expansion of nonstate firms, such as township and village enterprises, rather than the privatization of state-owned enterprises. In more recent years the decline has occurred because state-owned firms have been "corporatized" and their output reassigned to a new category of "shareholding firms."

However, not all of these collective firms operate very differently from state-owned firms (Walder 1995). Many nonstate firms, for example, have been created by village, township, and city governments rather than by true entrepreneurs. While these firms do not have much access to budget funds or bank loans, they are frequently supported with extra-budgetary funds available to local governments. Thus like most state-owned enterprises, they are not subject to much financial discipline. Moreover, the most recent estimate of

Nicholas R. Lardy is a Senior Fellow in the Foreign Policy Studies Program at the Brookings Institution.

trends in total factor productivity in collective (i.e., nonstate) industry also raise doubts about its success. Whereas earlier estimates suggested that total factor productivity growth in collective industry was about twice as rapid as in state-owned firms, a new estimate based on improved data suggests that collectively owned firms are only marginally ahead of state-owned firms in terms of factor productivity growth (Jefferson, Rawski, and Zheng 1996). Similarly, the 9,200 firms that have adopted the corporate form of ownership laid out by the 1994 Company Law have a governance structure that makes it difficult to distinguish them from traditional state-owned enterprises. Most of them, for example, have become wholly state-owned limited liability companies. Under this form of organization there are no shareholders and thus no shareholder meetings; the board of directors is appointed by the state; and the authority of the board is severely limited.[1]

Equally important, although the share of output they produce has been falling, state-owned firms have not been fading away. Employment in the state-owned sector expanded from about 72 million to about 109 million or about 50 percent between year-end 1977 and year-end 1993 (State Statistical Bureau 1994: 83). Also significant, state-owned firms continue to absorb a disproportionately large share of investment resources. For example, state-owned firms absorbed two-thirds of all investment in manufacturing in 1994, virtually the same share as in the mid-1980s. This occurred despite a sharp drop in the state-owned share of manufacturing output, from about two-thirds in 1985 to only 40 percent in 1994 (Naughton 1995: 1091).

China's financial reform, particularly the transformation of its banks, also has been largely deferred. The four major state-owned banks, the so-called specialized banks, still are the dominant source of credit in the economy. Although three new policy banks were established in 1994 in order to pave the way for the commercialization of the specialized banks, this process has not really begun for a number of reasons that will be explored below.

---

[1]For example, the boards of wholly state-owned companies have no power to approve mergers, break-ups, dissolutions, increases, or decreases in a firm's capital, or the issuance of bonds. All of these powers are specifically reserved for the state.

China's transition remains an unfinished experiment. It represents an attempt to raise the efficiency of resource use without either a substantial transformation of ownership arrangements or the imposition of hard budget constraints. The evidence reviewed in this paper suggests that completing the economic transformation will require a costly recapitalization of the financial system and a fundamental change in the relationship between firms and financial institutions.

Economic Growth

China's economic growth record appears clearly superior to all other transition economies on several grounds. First, Chinese growth accelerated from the very beginning of economic reform, a distinct contrast from other transition economies where real output fell sharply in the early years of reform. In Russia, for example, real output in 1995 was only half that of 1989.[2] Of the countries of the former Soviet Union, only Estonia and Uzbekistan, had real output declines of less than 40 percent within two years of the time intense reform started. Real output in the transition economies of Eastern Europe generally declined less, probably because the size of the military-industrial sector in these economies was substantially smaller than in the former Soviet Union. Nonetheless two years after the year of the most intense economic reform, real output in Slovakia, the Czech Republic, Bulgaria, and Romania had declined by about one-fourth. Even Poland, which in many ways has had the most successful transition, after initiating economic reform in 1990 suffered a cumulative real output decline of more than 15 percent before economic growth turned positive in 1992.

Second, China's rate of growth has been far more rapid than other transition economies that have passed through the contraction phase and are now expanding. Official Chinese data show real average annual growth from 1978 through 1995 of 9.5 percent.[3] In Poland,

[2]The data on economic growth in the former Soviet Union and in Eastern Europe are from European Bank for Reconstruction and Development (1995), as cited in Aslund, Boone, and Johnson (1996). It should be noted that most observers believe that these data, which are based on official data from each of the countries in question, overstate the decline in real output.

[3]State Statistical Bureau, various statistical communiques. Note, however, that many Western studies suggest that the official data overstate the rate of growth, perhaps by as much as 1 to 2 percentage points per year.

27

which has the longest record of positive economic growth after its initial fall, economic growth since 1992 has averaged 6 percent. Elsewhere in Eastern Europe economic growth resumed only in 1995 and at rates that can only be described as anemic, in the low single digits. The extent to which growth rates will increase in the future remains to be seen.

Finally, China's growth has been very broadly based. Both rural and urban areas have experienced significant real economic expansion. The expansion of output and real incomes in rural areas is particularly important since the overwhelming share of the population living in absolute poverty as reform began was concentrated there. Estimates of the World Bank show that in 1978 fully one-third of China's rural population, or 260 million persons, lived below the absolute poverty line.[4] The rapid growth of rural income, even in China's poorest rural areas, meant that the number of persons living in absolute poverty in rural areas had fallen by more than half to 123 million, or 15.2 percent of the rural population, by 1983. The decline in rural poverty in the balance of the 1980s was much slower. Nonetheless by 1990 only 97 million or 11.5 percent of the rural population lived below the poverty line had. By 1994 the number had dropped further to less than 80 million.

Inland regions with initially lower levels of per capita output may be falling behind some more developed coastal areas. But this is not because they have not participated in the economic growth process. On average their growth rates have been above the national average. They are falling behind in absolute terms temporarily because they are starting from a much lower initial level of development.

Integration into the World Economy

Trade

China's total trade, which totaled $290 billion in 1996, has grown by about 15 percent per annum since reform began in 1978. Since this pace of expansion has been much greater than the growth of world trade, China's share of world trade more than quintupled

[4]The income level below which a person is said to be living in absolute poverty is based initially on the income necessary to purchase a subsistence diet of 2,150 calories per day. It is further assumed that in rural areas expenditure on food absorbs three-fourths of all income (World Bank 1992).

between 1977 and 1995.[5] Particularly since the mid-1980s China's trade patterns have been increasingly in conformity with its underlying comparative advantage (Lardy 1992). This is especially obvious on the export side where China's sales into the international market increasingly have consisted of labor intensive manufactures such as apparel, textile yarn and fabrics, footwear and other leather goods, and toys rather than the crude oil and other natural resource products that comprised a large share of total exports in the early 1980s.

Foreign Direct Investment

China's rapid integration into the world economy is also reflected in record amounts of inward foreign direct investment. By the end of 1996 cumulative foreign direct investment actual used totaled more than $175 billion. It is frequently said that China's economic reforms since 1978 have placed it on a trajectory of development similar to that of other East Asian economies. While this is certainly true in some dimensions, China's extensive use of foreign direct investment bears much more similarity to Southeast Asian countries than to those in East Asia where foreign direct investment has played a much more modest role. In short, foreign direct invest is far more significant in China's economic transformation than it was in those of Japan, South Korea, or Taiwan. Indeed, in the first half of the 1990s China attracted more foreign direct investment than have Japan, South Korea, and Taiwan combined in the entire post-World War II period.

International Capital Markets

Finally, China enjoys better access to international capital markets than other transition economies. China was the first transition economy to earn an investment grade credit rating from the international ratings agencies on its sovereign external debt. Through the end of

[5]China's share of world trade in 1977 was six-tenths of 1 percent (Lardy 1994: 2). Chinese exports of $148.77 billion were 3.3 percent of 1995 world exports of $4,475 billion dollars.

1996 China had issued about \$12 billion in debt instruments on international markets (International Monetary Fund 1995: 42).

Institutional Transformation

State-Owned Sector

Evaluation of the degree of success of economic reforms in the state-owned sector is a controversial subject. On the one hand numerous studies suggest that total factor productivity in this sector has increased significantly since 1978.[6] Authors of these studies argue that enterprise managers have responded positively to new economic incentives, in the process raising productivity significantly even in the absence of significant changes in the ownership of state firms.

On the other hand, the financial performance of state-owned firms has deteriorated dramatically, particularly since the mid-1980s. The rate of return on assets in the state sector fell from 15 percent in 1987 to 5 percent in 1994. As a result profits and government tax revenue generated by state-owned firms have fallen, leaving the state with insufficient resources to finance its fiscal expenditures. That, in turn, has led to a nonfinancial public sector deficit that has averaged more than 10 percent annually since 1987. Most of this has been financed through the banking system rather than by selling bonds to the public or borrowing from foreigners (World Bank 1997: 14).

Another manifestation of the declining financial performance of state-owned firms is their growing financial losses and the large fiscal subsidies the state provides to keep these enterprises afloat. Data on losses in the manufacturing sector are shown in Table 1. The long-term trend in the share of enterprises making financial losses is upward, from about one-fourth as reform was getting underway in the late 1970s to almost half by the mid-1990s. As shown in Table 1, the share of state-owned industrial enterprises losing money fell in the early years of reform, reaching a low of less than 10 percent in 1985 before starting a steady rise to reach a third of all enterprises by the mid-1990s. Roughly the same trend is evident

---

[6]For a survey of the work completed on this topic through the early 1990s, see Harrold (1993).

TABLE 1
LOSSES IN STATE-OWNED INDUSTRIAL ENTERPRISES, 1978–96

Year	Percentage	Billions of RMB	Year	Percentage	Billions of RMB
1978	na	4.2	1988	10.9	8.2
1979	na	3.6	1989	16.0	11.8
1980	22.9	3.4	1990	27.6	34.9
1981	20.8	4.6	1991	25.8	36.7
1982	12.8	4.8	1992	23.4	36.9
1983	10.2	3.2	1993	30.3	45.3
1984	10.2	2.7	1994	na	48.3
1985	9.6	3.2	1995	na	54.1
1986	13.1	5.4	1996	37.5	69
1987	13.0	6.1			

NOTE: These data cover state-owned enterprises with independent financial accounting. At year-end 1995 there were 118,000 industrial state-owned enterprises, of which 87,900 practiced independent financial accounting.
SOURCE: State Statistical Bureau (1996: 429) and *China Daily* (1997: 4).

in the data on the absolute size of these losses. These dropped from RMB 4.2 billion in 1978 to a low of RMB 2.7 billion in 1983 before beginning a seemingly inexorable upward climb to RMB 69 billion in 1996.

Initially it was believed that a large share of the enterprises losing money could be explained by distortions in China's price system that required some enterprises to sell a large share of their output at state controlled prices that were far below those prevailing on the market. For example, losses were concentrated in the grain, coal, petroleum and natural gas, and imported timber and wool sectors (Broadman 1995: 12). Thus, financial losses were not necessarily considered to be an indication of economic inefficiency and were expected to disappear as price controls were eliminated.

This explanation may be roughly consistent with the declining share of loss-making enterprises and the decline in the monetary value of losses in the first half of the 1980s, when more and more product prices were liberalized. However, it is not consistent with the rising share of loss-making enterprises after 1985, when price

TABLE 2
FISCAL SUBSIDIES TO LOSS-MAKING ENTERPRISES, 1985–96

Year	Billions of RMB	Percentage of State Budget	Percentage of GDP
1986	32.5	17	3.4
1987	37.6	16	3.3
1988	44.6	17	3.2
1989	59.9	12	3.7
1990	57.9	17	3.3
1991	51.0	14	2.5
1992	44.5	11	1.8
1993	41.1	8	1.3
1994	36.6	6	0.8
1995	32.8	5	0.6
1996	35.3	4	0.5

NOTES: Subsidies are listed in the Chinese budget as a negative revenue. Column 3 shows the subsidies as a percent of state budgetary revenue. These losses do not include the value of government price subsidies provided to enterprises responsible for the procurement, processing, and distribution of grain, cotton, edible vegetable oils, meat, and other consumer goods provided to urban consumers.
SOURCES: State Statistical Bureau (1996: 222) and Liu (1997: 30).

liberalization continued. But the precise cause or causes of these losses remain unclear.[7]

Table 2 shows Chinese data on fiscal subsidies to loss-making enterprises. Its scope is both broader and narrower than Table 1. It is broader since it is not restricted to manufacturing firms. It is narrower since not all losses are necessarily covered by fiscal subsidies. These data show subsidies rose from about RMB 32 billion in 1986 to a peak of about RMB 60 billion in 1989 and then declined to about RMB 35 billion in the mid-1990s. Measured as a percent of the budget and as a percent of gross domestic product the trends were similar, but the decline in the 1990s was more dramatic. By 1996 fiscal subsidies absorbed only 4 percent of budget expenditures

[7]Two main explanations have been advanced. One is that enterprises systematically understate (overstate) their profits (losses) in order to avoid taxes. Another is that enterprise managers authorize wage increases far in excess of the growth of labor productivity, undermining the financial position of these firms.

and were the equivalent of only 0.5 percent of gross domestic product.

The numbers in Tables 1 and 2 are sometimes used to support the view that China's state-owned industry is not a significant impediment to reform. State-owned industrial enterprises may incur rising losses but even the record level of RMB 69 billion in 1996 represents only 0.9 percent of gross domestic product. Fiscal subsidies to all money losing enterprises are even smaller, suggesting that they do not impose much of a burden on the economy.

The core argument of this paper is that the data in Tables 1 and 2 are very partial and thus that the arguments summarized immediately above are misplaced.

The value of data on financial losses is limited because many state-owned enterprises do not pay interest on their loans from banks and they appear not to fully include unpaid interest as a cost of doing business. Thus, they vastly understate their losses or overstate their profits.

This conclusion is based on an examination of some basic dimensions of the finance of Chinese state-owned enterprises. Most of them are very heavily leveraged. On average, their ratio of liabilities to assets in 1995 was 85 percent, up from only 55 percent in 1989. The vast majority of the liabilities of firms are loans from state-owned banks. Many, if not most, enterprises fail to earn a return on their assets sufficient to pay interest on their loans. That is perhaps not surprising since return on assets of state-owned enterprises has been falling for years, reaching only 5 percent in 1994. Since nominal interest rates on loans average about 12 percent, it is not surprising that many highly leveraged enterprises are unable to pay interest on their cumulated borrowing.

One Chinese author has estimated that, as of the end of 1994, the state would need to write off RMB 1,215 billion in loans to reduce the debt of enterprises to the point where it could be serviced at current levels of profitability (Zhou 1995). That figure, which is equal to more than a quarter of gross domestic product, dwarfs the data shown in Tables 1 and 2. The tentative conclusion is that many enterprises fail to fully reflect the interest due on their loans as a cost of business and thus understate (overstate) their losses (profits).

The data in Table 2 also are misleading since most enterprise losses are no longer covered by grants from the state budget but by

TABLE 3
BANK LOANS OUTSTANDING AT YEAR-END, 1978–96

Year	Billions of RMB	Percentage of GDP
1978	185	52
1980	241	54
1985	591	69
1990	1,517	85
1991	1,804	89
1992	2,162	89
1993	2,681	85
1994	3,305	75
1995	4,054	70
1996	4,907	74

SOURCE: People's Bank of China (various years).

loans from state banks. Beginning in 1994 the Ministry of Finance was required to finance its entire budget deficit by the sale of bonds.[8] When the option of simply borrowing from the central bank (i.e., printing money) was foreclosed, the Ministry of Finance simply reduced subsidies to loss-making enterprises, forcing these institutions to increase their direct borrowings from the specialized banks rather than relying on funds channeled through the budget.

Banking

As already suggested, problems in the Chinese banking system mirror those in the state-owned industrial and commercial sector. This is largely because state-owned banks have been forced to extend an ever growing volume of loans to state enterprises. The magnitude of support that has been forthcoming from the banking system is suggested by the data in Table 3, which shows the volume of bank loans outstanding grew from RMB 185 billion in 1978, when reform began, to RMB 5 trillion by the end of 1996. Loans as a share of output expanded from 20 percent at the beginning of reform to

---

[8]Report on 1993 Final Accounts and the 1994 State Budget.

almost 74 percent by the end 1996.[9] The rapid growth of bank loans in the 1990s, just when fiscal subsidies to money-losing enterprises were being phased out, is particularly noticeable.

The vast majority of these bank loans flows to state-owned enterprises. Throughout the early and mid-1990s loans outstanding to collective enterprises in both urban and rural areas, to individual proprietors, and to agriculture combined never exceeded one-fifth of bank loans outstanding. Loans to individual proprietors were especially restricted. At year-end 1994 they stood at only RMB 15.59 billion, less than 4 percent of all bank loans outstanding (People's Bank of China 1994: 95).

Because of the weakness of the state-owned sector, a large share of the loans extended by the banks are currently nonperforming. Although there has been no survey of the quality of bank assets, several Chinese sources have suggested that one-third or more of all bank loans are nonperforming.[10] If banks ultimately recover as much as half of these loans upon the liquidation of the borrowers, the magnitude of losses faced by the banks would be RMB 670 billion.[11]

---

[9]The decline in the share of bank loans as a percent of GDP since 1991–92 is due to the rapid rise of lending by nonbank financial intermediaries. These institutions lie outside the scope of this study. Their loans expanded from about RMB 5 billion in 1978 to RMB 1.2 trillion by 1996. In 1996 total loans outstanding, by banks and nonbank financial institutions combined, were the equivalent of almost 90 percent of GDP.

[10]Chen Yuguang (1995) places enterprise bad loans and dead accounts in 1993 at RMB 400–500 billion, 30 percent of the loans outstanding at the end of that year. Wang Xiaozhong (1995: 4) places bad debts at nearly RMB 1 trillion in 1994, 40 percent of the country's total bank loans. These estimates are roughly consistent with the estimate mentioned earlier that RMB 1,215 billion in loans to state-owned enterprises would have to be forgiven to reduce the debt to a level that could be financed with present levels of profitability.

[11]Ultimate recovery from the liquidation of enterprises may well be less than one-half of the value of loans. A survey of firms that had been declared bankrupt and liquidated in eight provinces by the end of June 1995 showed that their total liabilities were two and one-half times their assets. In the eight provinces there were a total of 130 firms that had declared bankruptcy, of which 70 had been liquidated. The survey covered 59 bankrupt enterprises, of which 38 had been liquidated (Zhonggu 1995: 62). Moreover, it is likely that the real situation is much worse since in China measured liabilities of enterprises usually exclude unfunded pension liabilities for both current workers and those that have already retired. The slow pace of bankruptcy in China, in part, reflects the inability to allocate the proceeds of liquidation among competing claims, especially banks and retirees.

Losses of this magnitude would be catastrophic for China's banking system. The total capital of Chinese banks at year-end 1994 was only 227 RMB billion so a write-off of this magnitude would leave the banks technically insolvent (People's Bank of China 1994: 90).

Three possible solutions to the potential banking crisis are debt-equity swaps, in which the banks forgive loans to enterprises in exchange for ownership of all or part of the enterprise; privatization of the banks, which would provide an injection of new private capital into the banking system; and state recapitalization of the banks. Debt-equity swaps do not appear to be a viable option under present circumstances in China. They are sometimes a feasible alternative to bankruptcy for heavily indebted individual enterprises. They are a less feasible alternative to bankruptcy when a large portion of the entire state-sector has debts exceeding its assets.

Privatization, which has been used as a method of recapitalizing banks in some transition economies in Eastern Europe, also would not appear to be viable since the quality of bank assets is so uncertain. The state would appear to have little choice but to recapitalize the banking system.

Recapitalization is likely to entail writing off nonperforming loans and providing banks with government bonds to replace the assets that are written off. A quick calculation of the cost to the government if such a recapitalization had occurred in 1995 is most instructive. Assume that the write off of bad loans is in the range of RMB 800 billion to RMB 1,000 billion. Placing bonds of this amount with banks would more than triple the stock of government internal debt outstanding. In 1995 government bonds yielded about 15 percent interest. Thus, the annual cost to the government of recapitalizing the banks would be RMB 120 billion to RMB 150 billion. That amounts to 2.1 to 2.6 percent of gross domestic product or about one-fifth to one quarter of the combined fiscal revenues of central and local governments.

Recapitalization, however, is only part of the necessary institutional transformation. Banks must be transformed to operate on commercial terms, meaning lending would be based on evaluation of risk and rate of return considerations rather than undertaken at the behest of political leaders. Those enterprises that cannot survive in such an environment must go bankrupt rather than being propped up with government support from the budget or the banks.

Conclusion

The central conclusion of the above analysis is that it is far from clear that China's more gradual approach to economic reform is superior to the more rapid transformations attempted in some of the states of Eastern Europe. Those states absorbed the costs of restructuring quickly and were able to put in place systems for allocating investment resources more efficiently. That provides the most promising basis for sustaining long-term economic growth.

China's deferral of industrial restructuring had the obvious political advantage of allowing the Chinese Communist Party to maximize support for economic reform. No industrial restructuring meant no layoffs and low unemployment, particularly in urban areas. However, a decade and a half of investment decisions that largely reinforced the preexisting industrial structure almost certainly makes the long-term costs of restructuring much greater than if the process had started much earlier. The reason is simple—many of the industries that may not be viable in the long run now employ more workers and have a substantially larger stock of fixed assets than they did in the early 1980s. More importantly, China does not appear to have made much progress in creating systems to allocate capital more efficiently. That will make it extremely difficult to sustain rapid economic growth in the years ahead.

Even if the banks are recapitalized and converted to operate on commercial principles and enterprises are subject to hard budget constraints, one would expect a sustained period in which growth in China is lower than in the past decade. The government must reduce the real rate of investment in order to accommodate the flow of interest payments to the banks in a noninflationary manner. And banks, once they begin operating on a commercial basis, will curtail the growth of their lending in order to raise their capital adequacy.

References

Aslund, A.; Boone, P.; and Johnson, S. (1996) "How to Stabilize: Lessons from Post-Communist Countries." *Brookings Papers on Economic Activity*, No. 1: 217–91.

Broadman, H. (1995) "Meeting the Challenge of Enterprise Reform." World Bank Discussion Paper No. 283. Washington, D.C.: World Bank.

Chen, Y. (1995) "Banking Enterprise Debt Crisis and Inflation." *Caimao jingji (Finance and Trade Economics)*, No. 6 (June). In FBIS-Chi 95–158.

China Daily (1997) "State Firms Need Reform," 22 April.

European Bank for Reconstruction and Development (1995) *Transition Report 1995*. London: European Bank for Reconstruction and Development.

Harrold, P. (1993) "China: Enterprise Reform Strategy." Unpublished manuscript, 27 August.

International Monetary Fund (1995) *International Capital Markets: Developments, Prospects, and Policy Issues*. Washington, D.C.: International Monetary Fund.

Jefferson, G.; Rawski, T.; and Zheng, Y. (1996) "Chinese Industrial Productivity: Trends, Measurement Issues, and Recent Developments." *Journal of Comparative Economics* 23(2) (October): 146–80.

Lardy, N. (1992) "China's Foreign Trade." *The China Quarterly*, No. 131 (September): 691–720.

Lardy, N. (1994) *China in the World Economy*. Washington, D.C.: Institute for International Economics.

Liu, Z. (1997) "Report on the Implementation of the Central and Local Budgets for 1996 and on the Draft Central and Local Budgets for 1997." *Beijing Review* (7–13 April): 30.

Naughton, B. (1995) "China's Macroeconomy in Transition." *The China Quarterly*, No. 144 (December): 1083–1104.

People's Bank of China (various years) *Almanac of China's Finance and Banking*. Beijing: China Financial Publishing House.

People's Bank of China (1994) *China Financial Outlook 1995*. Beijing: China Financial Publishing House.

People's Bank of China (1994) *China Financial Outlook 1994*. Beijing: China Financial Publishing House.

State Statistical Bureau (1994) *Chinese Statistical Yearbook 1994*. Beijing: Statistical Publishing House.

State Statistical Bureau (1996) *Chinese Statistical Yearbook 1996*. Beijing: Statistical Publishing House.

Walder, A. (1995) "Local governments as Industrial Firms: An Organizational Analysis of China's Transition Economy." *American Journal of Sociology* 101(2) (September): 263–301.

Wang, X. (1994) "Bold, New Moves Needed to Make Headway." *China Daily*, 9 January: 4.

World Bank (1992) *China: Strategies for Reducing Poverty in the 1990s*. Washington, D.C.: World Bank.

World Bank (1997) Resident Mission in China , *Economic Note* (February).

Zhonggu, X. (1995) Survey in She, 18 December. In FBIS-CHI, 19 December: 62.

Zhou, T. (1995) "Debt Restructuring During the Ninth Five Year Plan Feasible." *Gaige* (September): 30–36. In FBIS-CHI, 8 December.

4. The Current State of China's Economic Reforms

Justin Yifu Lin

China's economic performance before the reform in 1979, like other socialist economies, was dismal. However, after the reform started, economic growth has been a miracle, similar to that of the "four small Asian dragons"—Taiwan, Hong Kong, Singapore, and South Korea.

Before the 1960s, no economy in the world had ever grown at an annual rate exceeding 6 or 7 percent for one or two decades. Influenced by this historical experience, a popular view in the economics profession was that there was a growth ceiling of 6 to 7 percent, called "the natural rate of growth," above which no economy could go for any prolonged period. Nevertheless, in the 1960s and 1970s, Taiwan, Hong Kong, Singapore, and South Korea all had annual growth rates near 10 percent, and they became "Newly Industrialized Economies." Because of this empirical evidence, the popular view changed to one that said a 10 percent annual growth rate was possible for a small economy if it adopted an export-oriented development strategy to take advantage of international markets. However, for large agrarian economies, like China and India, it was thought impossible to achieve such a high rate of growth. That assertion, however, was broken again by China's experience in the 1980s.

From 1978 to 1996, the annual growth rate of China's gross domestic product was 9.8 percent, which was as good as the performance of the four small Asian dragons in the 1960s and 1970s. In the five coastal provinces—Shandong, Jiangsu, Zhejiang, Fujian, and

Justin Yifu Lin is Founding Director of the China Center for Economic Research at Peking University and Professor of Economics at the Hong Kong University of Science and Technology. This chapter draws on Lin, Cai, and Li (1996a, 1996b).

Guangdong—where performance was above the average—the annual growth rate was as high as 12 percent, outperforming the four small dragons in their best years. The population in these five provinces was four times the combined population of the four small dragons, and the land area was five times the size of the small dragons. Such rapid growth in such a large area with such a big population had never occurred in human history.

The main driving forces for economic growth in an economy are capital accumulation, and improvements of incentives, resource allocation, and technology. China has one of the highest rates of capital accumulation in the world, reaching around 35 percent of GDP per year. In the transition from a planned economy to a market economy, room for improvement in incentives and resource allocation is still very substantial. More important, the current technological level in China is very low. For a technological latecomer like China, the prospect for low-cost technological catch-up is very good. Currently, the United States is the largest economy in the world. China's population is about five times that of the United States. Because of China's large population and as long as China's productivity level reaches one-fifth of the U. S. level, the Chinese economy will become the largest in the world. Many studies have projected that China will continue its current dynamic growth and become the largest economy in the world early in the next century. If that projection proves true, China will also provide the largest market for the exports of other countries.

However, in spite of the achievements obtained thus far, the Chinese economy also has encountered a number of serious problems. The major ones are as follows: (1) the recurrence of a "boom-and-bust" cycle; (2) the emergence of widespread corruption and rent seeking; (3) the deterioration of the financial performance of state-owned enterprises (SOEs)[1]; (4) the stagnation of farm income and the widening of regional income disparities; and (5) the decline in the growth rate of grain output, which averaged 4.7 percent per year in 1978–84, but declined and stagnated thereafter. If China

---

[1]Currently, about one-third of SOEs incur explicit losses, one-third have implicit losses, and only one-third make some profits. The subsidies to SOEs have become a heavy fiscal burden and deter reforms in the financial sectors.

cannot find solutions to these five problems, its long-term growth and stability may be threatened.

In the remainder of this chapter, I will analyze why China's economic growth was so dismal before the reform; why the reform has created such miraculous growth; why, despite the remarkable overall growth, many serious problems exist; and what reforms are necessary for continuing the dynamic growth. I will argue that the poor performance in the planned economy before the reform was caused by the institutional arrangements that were designed to facilitate the implementation of a heavy-industry-oriented development strategy in a capital-scarce economy. The problems after the reform arose from the incompatibility between the reformed market-economy institutional arrangements and the unreformed planned-economy institutional arrangements. The way out is to change the unreformed institutional arrangements so as to complete the transition from the planned economy to a market economy.

China's Development Strategy and Major Pre-Reform Problems

Most economic problems in China before and after the reforms can be traced to the adoption of a heavy-industry-oriented development strategy (HIODS) in the early 1950s. China's pre-reform economic structure had three integrated components: (1) a distorted macro-policy environment that featured artificially low interest rates, overvalued exchange rates, low nominal wage rates, and low prices for basic necessities and raw materials; (2) a planned allocation system for credit, foreign exchange, and raw materials; and (3) a traditional micro-management system for state enterprises and agricultural collectives. These three components were endogenous to the choice of a capital-intensive HIODS in a capital-scarce agrarian economy— although the specific institutional arrangements that were actually adopted in China were also shaped by socialist ideology, the Chinese Communist Party's experience during the revolution, and the Chinese government's political capacity.[2]

---

[2]Perkins and Yusuf (1984: 4) noted that a unique feature of China's economic development under socialism was the government's capacity to implement village-level programs nationwide through bureaucratic and party channels. Therefore, the Chinese government was able to impose certain institutional arrangements in the economy, deemed as important by ideology or by economic rationality, which may not be feasible in other economies (Perkins 1966).

41

At the founding of the People's Republic in 1949, the Chinese government inherited a war-torn agrarian economy in which 89.4 percent of the population resided in rural areas and industry consisted of only 12.6 percent of the national income. At that time, a developed heavy-industry sector was the symbol of the nation's power and economic achievement. Like government leaders in India and in many other newly independent developing countries, Chinese leaders certainly intended to accelerate the development of heavy industries. After China's involvement in the Korean War in 1950, with its resulting embargo and isolation from Western nations, catching up to the industrialized powers further became a necessity for national security. In addition, the Soviet Union's outstanding record of nation-building in the 1930s, contrasted with the Great Depression in Western market economies, provided the Chinese leadership with both inspiration and experience for adopting a HIODS. Therefore, after recovering from wartime destruction in 1953, the Chinese government planned to set up heavy industry as the priority sector. The goal was to build, as rapidly as possible, the country's capacity to produce capital goods and military materials. This development strategy was shaped through a series of five-year plans.[3]

Heavy industry is a capital-intensive sector. The construction of a heavy-industry project has three characteristics: (1) it requires a long gestation; (2) most equipment for a project, at least in the initial stage, needs to be imported from more advanced economies; and (3) each project requires a lump-sum investment. When the Chinese government initiated this strategy in the early 1950s, the Chinese economy had three characteristics: (1) capital was limited, and, consequently, the market interest rate was high; (2) foreign exchange was scarce and expensive because exportable goods were limited and primarily consisted of low-priced agricultural products; and (3) economic surplus was small and scattered due to the nature of a poor agrarian economy. Because these characteristics of the Chinese economy were mismatched with the three characteristics of a heavy-industry project, spontaneous development of capital-intensive

---

[3]The five-year plan was disrupted from 1963–65, the period immediately after the agricultural crisis of 1959–62. The first to the seventh five-year plans covered the periods from 1952–57, 1958–62, 1966–70, 1971–75, 1975–80, 1981–85, and 1986–90.

industry in the economy was impossible. Therefore, a set of distorted macro-policies was required for the development of heavy industry.

At the beginning of the first five-year plan, the government instituted a policy of low interest rates and overvalued exchange rates to reduce both the costs of interest payments and of importing equipment.[4] Meanwhile, in order to secure enough funds for industrial expansion, a policy of low input prices—including low nominal wage rates for workers and low prices for raw materials, energy, and transportation—evolved alongside the adoption of this development strategy. The assumption was that the low prices would enable the enterprises to create profits large enough to repay the loans or to accumulate enough funds for reinvestment. If the enterprises were privately owned, the state could not be sure whether the private entrepreneurs would reinvest the policy-created profits on the intended projects.[5] Therefore, private enterprises were soon nationalized,[6] and new key enterprises were owned by the state to secure control over profits for heavy-industry projects. Meanwhile, to make the low nominal-wage policy feasible, the government had to provide urban residents with inexpensive food and other necessities, including housing, medical care, and clothing. The low interest rates, overvalued exchange rates, low nominal wage rates, and low prices for raw materials and living necessities constituted the basic macro-policy environment of the HIODS.

The above macro-policies induced a total imbalance in the supply and demand for credit, foreign exchange, raw materials, and other

[4]For example, the interest rate on bank loans was officially reduced from 30 percent per year to about 5 percent per year. For each dollar borrowed at the beginning of a 7-year project, the principal and interest payment at the time that the project was completed would be reduced from $6.27 to $1.41.

[5]Even with all the above price distortions that facilitate the heavy-industry development in China, the time period required by a heavy-industry project to earn back the capital investment was, on average, about 4 to 5 times longer than the period required by a light-industry project (Li 1983: 37). Therefore, a profit-maximizing private owner would have higher incentives to invest in a light-industry project.

[6]Under the New Democracy Policy, adopted by the Communist Party in the late 1940s, private enterprises were supposed to coexist with SOEs for an extended period after the revolution. However, the enterprises were soon nationalized after 1952 when the government adopted the HIODS. The attempt to secure profits for the heavy-industry projects was the motivation for the government's change in position toward private enterprises.

basic necessities. Because nonpriority sectors would be competing with the priority sectors for the low-priced resources, plans and administrative controls replaced markets as the mechanism for allocating scarce credit, foreign reserves, raw materials, and basic necessities, ensuring that limited resources would be used for the targeted projects. Moreover, the state monopolized banks, foreign trade, and material distribution systems.[7]

In this way competition was suppressed, and profits ceased to be the measure of an enterprise's efficiency.[8] Because of the lack of market discipline, managerial discretion was potentially a serious problem. Managers of SOEs were deprived of autonomy to mitigate this problem.[9] The production of state enterprises was dictated by mandatory plans, and SOEs were furnished with most of their material inputs through an administrative allocation system. Product prices were determined by the pricing authorities. Government agencies controlled the distribution of products. The wages and salaries of workers and managers were determined not by their performance but by their education, age, position, and other criteria according to a national wage scale. Investment and working capital were mostly financed by appropriations from the state budget or loans from the banking system according to state plans. The SOEs remitted all of their profits, if any, to the state, and the state budget would also cover all losses incurred by the enterprises. In short, SOEs were like puppets. They did not have any autonomy over the

[7]In the literature in China and other socialist countries, many authors presumed that the distorted policy environment and the administrative controls were shaped by socialist doctrines. The socialist ideology might play a role in the formation of these policies, however, the existence of these policies and controls also have an economic rationale. They facilitate the implementation of a HIODS in a capital-scarce economy. This explains why nonsocialist developing economies such as India also had a similar policy environment and administrative controls when they adopted the same development strategy.

[8]An enterprise is bound to be loss-making if its outputs happen to be inputs to the other sectors, for example, energy and transportation, because the prices of its outputs are suppressed. On the contrary, an enterprise is bound to be profit-making if its outputs are at the low end of the industrial chain, because the enterprise can enjoy low input prices and high output prices at the same time.

[9]The state enterprises were granted some autonomy after the reforms in the late 1970s. As expected, one of the results of this reform was a rapid increase in wages, bonuses, and fringe benefits at the expense of the enterprise's profits.

employment of workers, the use of profits, the plan of production, the supplies of inputs, and the marketing of their products.

The development strategy and the resulting policy environment and allocation system also shaped the evolution of farming institutions in China. In order to secure cheap supplies of grain and other agricultural products for urban low-price rationing, a compulsory procurement policy was imposed in the rural areas in 1953. This policy obliged peasants to sell set quantities of their produce, including grain, cotton, and edible oils, to the state at government-set prices (Perkins 1966: chap. 4).

In addition to providing cheap food for industrialization, agriculture was also the main foreign-exchange earner. In the 1950s, agricultural products alone made up over 40 percent of all exports. If processed agricultural products are also counted, agriculture contributed to more than 60 percent of China's foreign-exchange earnings up to the 1970s. Because foreign exchange was as important as capital for the HIODS, the country's capacity to import capital goods for industrialization in the early stage of development clearly depended on agriculture's performance.

Agricultural development required resources and investment as much as industrial development. The government, however, was reluctant to divert scarce resources and funds from industry to agriculture. Therefore, alongside the HIODS, the government adopted a new agricultural development strategy that would not compete for resources with industrial expansion. The core of this strategy involved the mass mobilization of rural labor to work on labor-intensive investment projects such as irrigation, flood control, and land reclamation, and to raise unit yields in agriculture through traditional methods and inputs such as closer planting, more careful weeding, and the use of more organic fertilizer. The government believed that collectivization of agriculture would ensure these functions. The government also viewed collectivization as a convenient vehicle for procurring grain and other agricultural products at artificially low prices (Luo 1985). Income distribution in the collectives was based on each collective member's contribution to agricultural production. However, monitoring a member's effort in agricultural production is extremely difficult. The remuneration system in the collectives was basically egalitarian (Lin 1988).

The distorted macro-policy environment, planned allocation system, and micro-management institutions all made the maximum

45

mobilization of resources for developing heavy industry possible in a capital-scarce economy. Since most private initiative in economic activities was prohibited, the pattern of the government's investment was the best indicator of the bias in the official development strategy. Despite the fact that more than three-quarters of China's population subsisted on agriculture, agriculture received less than 10 percent of state investment in the period 1953–85, while 45 percent went to heavy industry. Moreover, heavy industry received a lion's share of the investments that fell under the heading "other," including workers' housing and infrastructure. As a result, the value of heavy industry in the combined total value of agriculture and industry grew from 15 percent in 1952 to about 40 percent in the 1970s.[10]

Judging from China's sector composition, the trinity of the traditional socialist economic structure—a distorted macro-policy environment, a planned allocation system, and a puppet-like micro-management institution—reached its intended goal of accelerating the development of heavy industry in China. However, China paid a high price for such an achievement. The economy is very inefficient due to two factors: (1) low *allocative* efficiency because of the deviation of the industrial structure from the pattern dictated by the comparative advantages of the economy, and (2) low *technical* efficiency due to managers' and workers' low incentives to work.

1. *Low allocative efficiency.* In the current stage of China's economic development, capital is relatively scarce and labor is relatively abundant. If prices were determined by market competition, capital would be relatively expensive and labor relatively inexpensive. Therefore, the comparative advantages of the Chinese economy lie

[10]When the reforms started in 1979, the government initially planned to increase agriculture's share in the state's fixed-capital investment from 11 percent in 1978 to 18 percent in the following 3 to 5 years. Due to the rapid agricultural growth brought about by the rural reforms, agriculture's share in the state's fixed-capital investment actually declined sharply to only about 3 percent in the late 1980s and early 1990s. However, the share of total fixed-capital investment in agriculture in the nation as a whole did not decline so much as the figures suggest, because part of the decline in state investment was compensated by an increase in farmers' investment (Feder, et al. 1992). Similarly, the share of heavy industry in the state's fixed-capital investment did not decline after the reforms in 1979. However, the state's share in the total investment declined from 82 percent in 1980 to 66 percent in 1990. Investments in the nonstate sectors are mostly on projects that are less capital intensive. Therefore, the share of heavy industry in the nation's fixed-capital investment is less than the share in state investment.

in labor-intensive sectors. If investments had been guided by market forces, profit incentives would have induced entrepreneurs to adopt capital-saving and labor-using technologies and to allocate resources more efficiently by shifting them to labor-intensive industries.

The loss of national income due to allocative inefficiency implies the reduction of surplus available for investment and a slower growth of the whole economy.[11] To maintain the growth rate, the accumulation rate must be raised, resulting in insufficient consumption and long-lasting low living standards.[12]

2. *Low technical efficiency.* Because profits ceased to be a measure of efficiency and the planned allocation system often failed to distribute materials in time, managers were forced to keep large reserves and had no incentive for utilizing resources economically. Overstaffing, underutilization of capital resources, and overstocking of inventories are all characteristics of puppet-like state enterprises.[13] Moreover, managers had no authority over workers' wage rates and bonuses. Workers' wages were not related to their efforts or to their enterprises' profits. Hence, the remuneration system invited low work

[11]Desai and Martin (1983) and Whitesell and Barreto (1988) estimated the misallocation of capital and labor among the sectors of the Soviet economy, which also adopted the heavy-industry-oriented development strategy. Desai and Martin find losses from misallocation in the range of 3 to 10 percent—possibly up to 15 to 17 percent of the inputs employed in industry. Whitesell and Barreto find that in the early 1980s output gains equivalent to 4 to 6 percent could have been achieved by a reallocation of capital and labor among the sectors of Soviet industry.

[12]The average annual rate of accumulation was raised from 24.2 percent of national income in the first five-year plan up to 33.0 percent and 33.2 percent in the fourth and fifth five-year plans, whereas the average annual growth rate of national income dropped from 8.9 percent to 5.5 percent and 6.1 percent. As a result, wages for state employees were held almost constant between the years 1952–78. As Deng Xiaoping admitted to a group of overseas Chinese who visited China in October 1974, wages were low, the living standard was not high, and workers only had enough clothing and a full stomach (Cheng 1982: 248).

[13]The State Economic System Reform Commission in a recent report estimated that the total number of overstaffing in China's state enterprises was more than 30 million, about 30 percent of the total labor force in the state sectors (*Zhonghua Zhoumo Bao* 1995). The World Bank (1985a) shows that, for the production of per unit GDP, energy, steel, and transportation consumption in China were, respectively, 63.8 percent to 229.5 percent, 11.9 percent to 122.9 percent, and 85.6 percent to 559.6 percent greater than those of other developing countries. In the structure of total capital, the working capital accounted for the largest share in China and was 4.8 to 25.7 percentage points higher than that of other countries. These figures imply that inventories of inputs and outputs were larger and inventories were kept longer in China than in other countries.

incentives. Similarly, in the agricultural collectives, the farm workers' incentives to work were low because the link between reward and effort was weak.[14] Losses resulting from these technical inefficiencies mean that actual production will be less than maximum—that is, production will occur inside the economy's production possibility frontier (see Lin, Cai, and Li 1996b: 210).

Because of low allocative efficiency and low technical efficiency, the Chinese economy was very inefficient. The most important indicator that reflected this inefficiency was the extremely low rate of total factor productivity growth in China. A World Bank study shows that, even calculated at the most favorable assumptions, the growth rate was merely 0.5 percent between 1952 and 1981, only a quarter of the average growth rate of 19 developing countries included in the study (World Bank 1985a). Moreover, the total factor productivity of China's state enterprises was in a state of stagnation or even negative growth between 1957 and 1982 (World Bank 1985b).

An Analytical Review of China's Economic Reforms

As Dwight Perkins (1988: 601) pointed out, "It is unlikely that China's leaders have a worked-out blueprint in mind when they set out to reform the economic structure." However, retrospectively, China's reforms followed a logical process that is predictable. The trinity of the traditional economic structure is endogenous to the adoption of a HIODS in a capital-scarce economy. The main fault in this economic structure was low economic efficiency arising from structural imbalance and incentive problems. Before the late 1970s, the government had made several attempts to address the structural problems by decentralizing the allocative mechanism from the central to the local government.[15] However, the administrative nature of the allocative mechanism was not changed and the policy environment and managerial system were not altered, and thus the attempts failed to rectify the structural imbalance and improve economic incentives. The goals of the reform in late 1978 were also to rectify the structural imbalance and improve incentives. However, that

[14]Lin (1992) estimates that losses due to low incentives in the agricultural collectives were as much as 20 percent of total factor productivity. For a theoretical model of the monitoring problems regarding incentives in a collective farm, see Lin (1989a).

[15]The first attempt was made in 1958–60, the second in 1961–65, and the third in 1966–76 (Wu and Zhang 1993: 65–7).

reform effort was set apart from previous attempts by the micro-management system reforms that made farmers and managers and workers in state enterprises partial residual claimants. This small crack in the trinity of the traditional economic structure caused it to be pried apart, which led to the gradual dismantlement of the traditional system.

The Micro-Management System Reforms

The most important change in the micro-management system was the replacement of collective farming by a household-based system, now known as the household responsibility system. The change in farming institutions had not been intended by the government at the beginning of the reforms. Although it had been recognized in 1978 that solving managerial problems within the collective system was the key to improving farmers' incentives, the official position at that time was still that the collective was to remain the basic unit of agricultural production. Nevertheless, a small number of collectives, first secretly and later with the blessing of local authorities, began to test a system of leasing a collective's land and dividing the obligatory procurement quotas to individual households in the collective. A year later these collectives brought out yields far larger than those of other teams. The central authorities later acknowledged this new form of farming, but required that it be restricted to poor agricultural regions, mainly to hilly or mountainous areas, and to poor collectives where people had lost confidence in the collective system. However, this restriction was ignored in most regions. Production performance was improved after a collective, regardless of its relative wealth or poverty, adopted the new system. The household responsibility system as a nationally acceptable farming institution was eventually given full official recognition in late 1981, exactly two years after the initial price increases. By that time, 45 percent of the collectives in China had already dismantled and instituted the household responsibility system. By the end of 1983, 98 percent of agricultural collectives in China had adopted this new system. When the household responsibility system first appeared, the land lease was only one to three years. However, the short lease reduced farmers' incentives for land-improvement investment. The lease contract was allowed to be extended up to 15 years in 1984. In 1993,

49

the government allowed the lease contract to be extended for another 30 years after the expiration of the first contract.

Unlike the spontaneous nature of farming institution reform, the reform in the micro-management system of the state enterprises was initiated by the government. These reforms have undergone four stages. The first stage (1979–83) emphasized several important experimental initiatives that were intended to enlarge enterprise autonomy and expand the role of financial incentives within the traditional economic structure. These measures included the introduction of profit retention and performance-related bonuses and permitted the SOEs to produce outside the mandatory state plan. The enterprises involved in exports were also allowed to retain part of their foreign exchange earnings for use at their own discretion. In the second stage (1984–86), the emphasis shifted to a formalization of the financial obligations of the SOEs to the government and exposed enterprises to market influences. From 1983, profit remittances to the government were replaced by a profit tax. In 1984, the government allowed SOEs to sell output in excess of quotas at negotiated prices and to plan their output accordingly, thus establishing the dual-track price system. During the third stage (1987–92), the contract responsibility system, which attempted to clarify the authority and responsibilities of enterprise managers, was formalized and widely adopted. The last stage (1993–present) has attempted to introduce the modern corporate system to SOEs. In each stage of the reform, the government's intervention was reduced further and the state enterprises gained more autonomy.

The reform of the micro-management system has achieved its intended goal of improving technical efficiency. Empirical estimates show that almost half of the 42.2 percent growth of output in grain and other crops in the years 1978–84 was driven by productivity change brought about by the reforms. Furthermore, almost all of the above productivity growth was attributable to the changes resulting from the introduction of the household responsibility system (Fan 1991; Huang and Rozelle 1996; Lin 1992; McMillan, Whalley, and Zhu 1989; Wen 1993). Production function estimates in several studies find that for industry the increase in enterprise autonomy increased productivity in the state enterprises (Chen et al. 1988; Gordon and Li 1989; Dollar 1990; Jefferson, Rawski, and Zheng 1992; Groves et al. 1992). Therefore, the reforms of the micro-management system in both agriculture and industry have created a flow of new resources, an important feature of China's reforms.

The increase in enterprise autonomy under a distorted macro-policy environment, however, also invited managers' and workers' discretionary behavior. Despite an improvement in productivity, the profitability of SOEs declined and the government's subsidies increased—due to both a faster-than-expected increase in wages, fringe benefits, and other unauthorized expenditures (Fan and Schaffer 1991) and the competition from autonomous township and village enterprises (TVEs) (Jefferson and Rawski 1995). Reducing or revoking enterprise autonomy was not politically viable (it would be too costly), so the government was forced to try other measures that further increased the autonomy of SOEs, in the hope that the new measures would make the enterprises financially independent.

Resource Allocation System Reform

The increase in enterprise autonomy put pressure on the planned distribution system. Because SOEs were allowed to produce outside the mandatory plans, the enterprises needed to obtain additional inputs and to sell the extra outputs outside the planned distribution system. Under pressure from the enterprises, material supplies were progressively delinked from the plan, and retail commerce was gradually deregulated. At the beginning, certain key inputs remained controlled. However, the controlled items were steadily reduced. Centralized credit rationing was also delegated to local banks at the end of 1984.

An unexpected effect of relaxing the resource allocation system was the rapid growth of nonstate enterprises, especially the TVEs.[16] Rural industry already existed under the traditional system as a result of the government's decision to mechanize agriculture and to develop rural processing industries to finance the mechanization in 1971. In 1978 the output of TVEs consisted of 7.2 percent of the total value of industrial output in China. Before the reforms, the growth

---

[16]Nonstate enterprises include TVEs, private enterprises, joint-venture enterprises, overseas Chinese enterprises, and foreign enterprises. Among them, the TVEs are the most important in terms of output share and number of enterprises. It is noteworthy that TVEs, although different in many aspects from state enterprises, are public enterprises that are funded, owned, and supervised by the township or village governments.

TABLE 1
GROWTH RATE OF OUTPUT AND TOTAL FACTOR PRODUCTIVITY
(AVERAGE ANNUAL PERCENTAGE CHANGE)

	1980–88	1980–84	1984–88
State Sector			
Output	8.49	6.77	10.22
TFP	2.40	1.80	3.01
Collective Sector			
Output	16.94	14.03	19.86
TFP	4.63	3.45	5.86

SOURCE: World Bank (1992).

of TVEs was severely constrained by access to credits, raw materials, and markets. The reforms created two favorable conditions for the rapid expansion of TVEs: (1) a new stream of surpluses brought about by the household responsibility reform provided a resource base for new investment activities, and (2) the relaxation of the traditional planned allocation system provided access to key raw materials and markets. In the period 1981–91, the number of TVEs grew at an average annual rate of 26.6 percent, employment grew by 11.2 percent, and total output value grew by 29.6 percent. The annual growth rate of the total output value of TVEs was three times that of SOEs in the same period. In 1993, TVEs accounted for 38.1 percent of the total industrial output in China. Nonstate enterprises increased their share of industrial output from 22 percent in 1978 to 56.9 percent in 1993 (State Statistical Bureau 1995: 73).

The rapid entry of TVEs and other types of nonstate enterprises produced the following two unexpected effects on the reforms:

First, nonstate enterprises were the product of markets. Being outsiders to the traditional economic structure, nonstate enterprises had to obtain energy and raw materials from competitive markets, and their products could be sold only to markets. They had hard budget constraints and they would not survive if their management was poor. Their employees did not have an "iron rice bowl" and could be fired. As a result, the nonstate enterprises were more productive than the state enterprises, as the comparisons of growth rate in output and total factor productivity between the state and collective sectors in Table 1 shows.

The dynamism of nonstate enterprises exerted a pressure on the state enterprises and triggered the state's policy of transplanting the micro-management system of the nonstate enterprises to the state enterprises and of delegating more autonomy to the state enterprises. Reform measures for improving the micro-management system of state enterprises—such as replacing profit remittance by a profit tax, establishing the contract responsibility system, and introducing the modern corporate system to state enterprises—were responses to competitive pressure from TVEs and other nonstate enterprises (Jefferson and Rawski 1995).

Second, the development of nonstate enterprises significantly rectified the misallocation of resources. In most cases, nonstate enterprises had to pay market prices for their inputs, and their products were sold at market prices. The price signals induced nonstate enterprises to adopt more labor-intensive technology and to concentrate on more labor-intensive small industries than in state enterprises.[17] Therefore, the technological structure of nonstate enterprises was more consistent with the comparative advantages of China's endowments. The entry of TVEs mitigated the structural imbalance caused by the HIODS. The improvement in resource allocation also leads to a faster growth in the reform.

Macro-Policy Environmental Reform

In the trinity of the traditional economic structure, the distorted macro-policy environment was linked most closely to the development strategy, and its effects on allocative and technical efficiency were indirect. The reforms on the macro-policies were thus the most sluggish. Most economic problems that appeared during the reforms—for example, the cyclic pattern of growth and the rampant rent seeking—could be attributed to the inconsistency between the distorted policy environment and the liberalized allocation and enterprise system. Therefore, the Chinese government constantly faced a dilemma: to make the macro-policy environment consistent with the liberalized micro-management and resource allocation system or to recentralize the micro-management and resource allocation

[17]For example, in 1986 an average industrial enterprise in China had 179.9 workers, and the fixed investment per worker was 7,510 yuan (State Statistical Bureau 1987b: 3); whereas an average TVE in the same year had 28.9 workers, and the fixed investment per worker was 1,709 yuan (State Statistical Bureau 1987a: 205).

system and maintain the internal consistency of the traditional economic structure. Ending enterprise autonomy, however, would meet with the resistance of employees of state enterprises, and returning to the traditional economic structure would mean the reappearance of economic stagnation. Therefore, no matter how reluctant the government might be, the only sustainable choice is to reform the macro-policy environment and make macro-policies consistent with the liberalized allocation and micro-management system.

Changes in the macro-policy environment started in the commodity price system. After introducing profit retention, the enterprises were allowed to produce outside the mandatory plan. The enterprises first used an informal barter system to obtain the outside-plan inputs and to sell the outside-plan products at premium prices. In 1984, the government introduced the dual-track price system, which enabled SOEs to sell their output in excess of quotas at market prices and to plan their output accordingly. The aim of the dual-track price system was to reduce the marginal price distortion in the SOEs' production decisions while leaving the state a measure of control over material allocation. By 1988 only 30 percent of retail sales were made at plan prices, and SOEs obtained 60 percent of their inputs and sold 60 percent of their outputs at market prices (Zou 1992).

The second major change in the macro environment occurred in the foreign exchange rate policy. In the years 1979–80, the official exchange rate was roughly 1.5 yuan per U.S. dollar. The rate could not cover the costs of exports, as the average cost of earning one dollar was around 2.5 yuan. A dual rate system was adopted at the beginning of 1981. Commodity trade was settled at the internal rate of 2.8 yuan per dollar; the official rate of 1.53 yuan per dollar continued to apply to noncommodity transactions. After 1985, the yuan was gradually devalued. Moreover, the proportion of retained foreign exchange, which was introduced in 1979, was gradually raised, and enterprises were allowed to swap their foreign exchange entitlement with other enterprises through the Bank of China at rates higher than the official exchange rate. Restrictions on trading foreign exchanges were further relaxed when a "foreign exchange adjustment center" was established in Shenzhen in 1985, in which enterprises could trade foreign exchanges at negotiated rates. By the late 1980s, such centers were established in most provinces in China and more than 80 percent of the foreign exchange earnings was swapped in such centers (Sung 1994). The climax of foreign exchange rate policy reform was the establishment of a managed floating system and unification of the dual rate system on January 1, 1994.

Interest-rate policy is the least affected area of the traditional macro-policy environment. Under the HIODS, the interest rate was kept artificially low to facilitate the expansion of capital-intensive industries. After the reforms started in 1979, the government was forced to raise both the loan rates and the savings rates several times.[18] However, the rates were maintained at levels far below the market-clearing rates throughout the reform process. In late 1993, the government announced a plan to establish a development bank with the function of financing long-term projects at subsidized rates and to turn the existing banks into commercial banks. It is unclear whether after the reform is completed the interest rate will be regulated or will be determined by markets. The mentality of the HIODS is deeply rooted in the mind of China's political leaders. To accelerate the development of capital-intensive industry in a capital-scarce economy, a distorted macro-policy environment—at the very least in the form of a low interest-rate policy—is essential. Quite likely, administrative interventions in the financial market will linger for an extended period.

The Achievements of China's Reform

The subject of why China's reforms have been so successful has been widely discussed, especially when compared with the reforms in Eastern Europe and the former Soviet Union (Chen, Jefferson, and Singh 1992; Qian and Xu 1993; Harrold 1992; McMillan and Naughton 1992; Gelb, Jefferson, and Singh 1993; McKinnon 1994). Except for the desirability of gradualism, the studies emphasized China's initial industrial structure (China has a large agricultural sector) or China's decentralized regional economic structure. If China's success was mainly the result of the country's unique initial conditions, then that success does not have any implications for

---

[18]To stop bank runs, the savings rates were indexed to inflation rates in October 1988. But the policy was revoked in 1991. In May 1993, the interest rate for a one-year time deposit was 9.18 percent, and for a one-to-three-year basic investment loan it was 10.80 percent (State Statistical Bureau 1993: 670–71). However, the market rate for a commercial loan was between 15 and 25 percent.

other economies, where the initial conditions may be different. Nevertheless, the economic problems in pre-reform China—namely, the structural imbalance and the low incentives—are common to all socialist economies, because they all adopted a similar economic development strategy and they all have a similar macro-policy environment, planned allocation system, and puppet-like state enterprises. Empirical evidence shows that, as in pre-reform China, Eastern European and Soviet economies were all overindustrialized with oversized state enterprises, their service sectors and light industries were underdeveloped, and employees' incentives were low (Newbery 1993, Brada and King 1991, Sachs and Woo 1993).

When China started its reforms in the late 1970s, the political leadership did not question the feasibility or desirability of the traditional economic structure. Its attempt was simply to improve incentives in the state enterprises and collective farms by giving agents in state enterprises and collective farms some autonomy so that a closer link between personal rewards and individual efforts could be established. The empirical studies already cited show that the attempt was successful and a new stream of resources was created by the micro-management system reform. The granting of partial microautonomy was only a small crack in the traditional economic structure. However, the partial autonomy also implies that entrepreneurs gain partial control over the allocation of the newly created stream of resources. The suppressed sectors in the traditional economy are the sectors that are consistent with the comparative advantages of the economy. The unexpected results of the micro-management reform are that, driven by profit motivation, the autonomous entrepreneurs allocated the new stream of resources under their control to the more profitable suppressed sectors. Since the planned allocation system and distorted macro-policy environment were preserved, the state still had control over the old stream of resources and guaranteed that these resources would be allocated to the priority sectors. Therefore, throughout the reform process, the economy enjoys continuous growth. Moreover, as the economy grew, the proportion of resources that was allocated according to the planned prices became increasingly small. Therefore, by the time the price for a commodity was liberalized, the shock was much smaller than the gap between the market price and plan price would have suggested.

If the above descriptions are a reasonable explanation of why China was able to enjoy continuous economic growth during the reform process, we can expect the following: first, the expansion of the suppressed sectors would not result in a decline in the priority sectors because the expansion of the suppressed sectors was supported by a new stream of resources; and, second, the economy should reach a higher rate of economic growth than the rate before the reforms because the new stream of resources was allocated to the more efficient sectors. Both assertions are confirmed by the empirical evidence. Table 2 shows the indexes and the growth rates of the major sectors in the national economy. It can be seen that no sector has declined since the reforms started and, except for the state enterprises, each sector's growth has accelerated.

The Problems of China's Reform

Because the reforms in macro-policies, especially those regarding the interest rate, lagged behind the reforms in the allocation system and micro-management institutions, the institutional arrangements of the macro-policy environment, resource allocation system, and micro-management governance are incompatible. There were several economic consequences arising from the institutional incompatibility.

The Boom-and-Bust Cycle

The policy of interest-rate suppression has not been eliminated so far. Because of the below market-clearing rate, the enterprises have incentives to obtain more credits than the supply permitted. Before the reforms, the excess demands for credit were suppressed by restrictive central rationing. Therefore, inflation was under the state's control. After the reforms in 1979, especially after the banking system reform in 1984, whenever the central government's direct control of credit rationing was relaxed, an investment rush ensued. On the one hand, because the expansion in credit during the investment rush is not supported by the increase in savings, the bank has to finance the credit expansion by creating additional high-powered money. On the other hand, the rush leads to an investment-led growth and a bottleneck in transportation, energy, and construction materials supply. Therefore, the high growth rate that is fuelled by credit expansion and money supply inevitably results in a high

57

TABLE 2
INDEX AND GROWTH RATE OF NATIONAL INCOME IN SELECTED SECTORS

| Year | Total | Agriculture | Industry[a] | | Construction | Transportation | Commerce |
			Total	State			
1952	100.0	100.0	100.0	100.0	100.0	100.0	100.0
1978	453.4	161.2	1,438.9	3,345.3	573.5	546.9	296.4
1992	1,473.2	332.9	7,011.2	9,825.7	2,455.0	1,888.5	749.2
Average Annual Growth Rate (percent)							
1952–78	6.0	1.9	10.8	14.5	6.9	6.8	4.3
1978–92	8.8	5.3	13.2	8.0	10.9	9.2	6.9

[a]Gross value of industrial output measured at constant prices.
SOURCE: State Statistical Bureau 1993: 34, 413.

inflation rate. Since the government is reluctant to increase the interest rate as a way to check the investment thrust and high inflation,[19] it had to resort to the traditional way of centralized rationing of credits and direct control of investment projects.

The rationing and controls gives the state sector a priority position. The pressure of inflation is reduced, but a slower growth follows. As mentioned earlier, although the reforms in the micro-management system have improved the productivity of the state sector, the deficits of the state sector increase due to the discretionary behavior of the managers and workers in the state enterprises. Therefore, the increase of the government's fiscal income depends more and more on the expansion of nonstate sectors. During the period of tightened state control, the growth rates of the nonstate sectors declines because the nonstate sectors' access to credits and raw materials are restricted. Such a slowdown in the growth rate become fiscally unbearable. Therefore, the state is forced to liberalize the administrative controls in order to make some room for the growth of the nonstate sectors. A period of faster growth will follow. Nevertheless, conflicts between the distorted macro-policy environment and the liberalized allocation and micro-management system will arise again. This cyclic pattern of growth and inflation has occurred three times since 1984 (see Figure 1).

Delegating credit approval authority to local banks in the autumn of 1984 resulted in a rapid expansion of credits and an investment thrust that resulted in an investment-led overheating in 1984–85. As a result, the money supply increased 49.7 percent in 1984 compared with its level in 1983, which caused the inflation rate to jump from less than 3 percent in the previous years to 8.8 percent in 1985. The government implemented a retrenchment program at the end of 1985 to control investment and inflation. Both the rates of growth and inflation dropped in 1986. The government's attempt to liberalize prices in early 1988 caused a high inflation expectation. The real interest rates for savings and loans turned negative because the nominal interest rates were not adjusted. Therefore, panic buying and a mini-bank run occurred. As a consequence, the money supply increased by 47 percent in 1988, and the inflation rate reached 18

---

[19]The low interest-rate policy is necessary for the survival of capital-intensive and other policy-induced loss-making state enterprises.

FIGURE 1
ECONOMIC GROWTH AND INFLATION IN CHINA

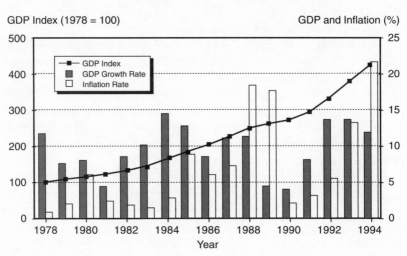

GDP Index (1978 = 100) GDP and Inflation (%)

SOURCE: State Statistical Bureau (1995: 4, 8, 45).

percent. Fearing that inflation might be out of control, the government introduced a retrenchment program in October 1988 to directly control credits and investment.

The inflation rate declined significantly after 1989. However, partly due to the retrenchment program and partly due to the aftermath of the Tiananmen incident, the rate of economic growth dropped to less than 5 percent in 1989 and 1990, which was the lowest rate since the beginning of reform in 1979. Encouraged by Deng Xiaoping's trip to southern China in the spring of 1992, the government reoriented its policy toward economic growth. The control of bank credit was relaxed and an investment rush reappeared. The growth rates of GDP reached 13.6 percent in 1992 and 13.5 percent in 1993. The overheating of the economy had already become apparent in the spring of 1993. The government attempted to introduce another round of retrenchment in June 1993. Nevertheless, fearing that the growth momentum might be stiffened, the government leaders had difficulty reaching a consensus about the desirability of a retrenchment program, and the implementation of the program was softened. As a consequence, the growth rate still reached

11.8 percent in 1994, but the inflation rate escalated to 21.7 percent. The inflation rate was brought down after 1994, but the growth rate also slowed.

This review shows that, whenever the interest rate is artificially fixed at a below market-clearing level, the existence of a tradeoff between growth and inflation is unavoidable during the transition process. To control the expansion of the money supply and inflation, the government needs to tightly control credits and investments. Slower growth will be the result. Relaxing controls on credit and investment, however, will lead to faster economic growth. But the consequence will be a rapid expansion of the money supply and high inflation.

The only real solution to the boom-and-bust cycle is to let the interest rate to be determined by market forces—that is, by the demand for and supply of credit. When the demand for investment, and thus the demand for credit, increases (decreases), the interest rate will rise (fall). An increase (drop) in the interest rate will dampen (stimulate) investment and credit demands, on the one hand, and encourage (suppress) saving and reduce (encourage) current consumption, on the other hand. Consequently, the economy will not overheat (overcool). The liberalization of financial markets and the freeing of interest rates would provide a built-in mechanism for stabilizing the economy.

The Rise of Corruption and Rent Seeking

A second consequence of the inconsistency between the distorted macro-policy environment and the liberalized allocation system and micro-management institutions was rampant corruption and rent seeking. After the reforms, market prices existed, legally or illegally, along with planned prices for almost every kind of input and commodity that the state controls. The difference between the market price and the planned price is an economic rent. It is estimated that economic rents from controlling commodity prices, the interest rate, and the exchange rate amounted to at least 200 billion yuan, about 21.5 percent of China's national income in 1988. In 1992, the economic rent from bank loans alone reached 220 billion yuan (Hu 1994).[20]

---

[20]The total credit of state banks was 2,161.6 billion yuan ($248.5 billion at the swap-market exchange rate). The difference between the official interest rate and the market rate was about 10 percent. The rents from bank loans alone were as high as 216 billion yuan.

The nonstate enterprises as well as the autonomous SOEs certainly have incentives to engage in rent-seeking activities through bribes and other measures to obtain the underpriced resources from the state allocation agencies. It is reported that under the competitive pressure, the SOEs in the heavy industries, which are given priorities in obtaining the state-controlled resources, also need to give certain side payments to the banks and other allocation agencies in order to secure the earmarked loan and materials or to obtain them promptly.

Because of the rent-seeking activities of other types of enterprises, SOEs are often unable to obtain the credits and materials earmarked to them in the plans. The rent-seeking activities also cause widespread public resentment and become a source of social instability. To guarantee the survival of SOEs and to check social resentment, the government attempted to reinstitute tight controls on the allocation system during the retrenchment programs of 1986, 1988, and 1993. However, the controls were later relaxed to enable faster growth.

The root of the rent-seeking activities is the gap between the artificially set government prices and market-clearing prices. Therefore, the way to eliminate rent seeking is to remove the remaining distortions in the macro-policy environment—that is, to free interest rates and other prices.

The Poor Performance of SOEs[21]

The problems of SOEs stem from the separation of ownership and control. Because of the separation, the incentives of the manager and the owner (i.e., the state) are potentially incompatible. The owner is not fully involved in the management process. The owner's information about the costs and revenues of the enterprise is incomplete. Therefore, managerial discretion may become a serious problem. The success of an enterprise depends on designing an institutional arrangement that will make the incentives of manager and owner become compatible, which in turn depends on the existence of a simple, low-cost, sufficient information indicator of managerial performance to overcome the information asymmetry.

An enterprise's profit in a fair, competitive market is a sufficient information indicator of managerial performance. As already argued, the macro-policy environment was distorted and the market

[21]This section draws heavily on Lin, Cai, and Li (1997).

competition was suppressed in the traditional planned economy. Under that condition, the profits or losses of an enterprise were determined mainly by its policy-determined prices of outputs and costs of inputs. Enterprise profit ceased to be a sufficient information indicator of managerial performance. To prevent managerial discretion, ending of managerial autonomy was a second-best institutional arrangement.

When the reform began, most policymakers and researchers attributed the SOEs' problems to the lack of managerial autonomy and incentives. As a result, the reform measures focused on increasing the autonomy of SOEs and improving incentives. The emergence of TVEs, joint ventures, and other nonstate enterprises also affected SOE performance by subjecting SOEs to greater competition in product and factor markets. Moreover, the decentralization of the managerial system in state enterprises has increased the linkage between the employees' rewards and enterprise efficiency and has induced SOEs to improve their management and efficiency. However, SOEs still face many policy-induced losses, which means that the profit or loss of an SOE still does not accurately reflect managerial performance. Finally, a SOE can use its policy-determined burden as an excuse to cover up its operational losses and other unproductive expenditures and to press the government for subsidies or low-interest bank loans. Because of its soft-budget constraint, a SOE has little incentive to improve efficiency (see Kornai 1990).

The major policy-induced losses of SOEs can be grouped into the following three categories:

First, some SOEs' capital intensity is too high and cannot survive without implicit or explicit subsidies because capital is still relatively scarce in China. The HIODS produced an extremely biased industrial structure. A substantial portion of SOEs, especially large-size SOEs, have an extremely high capital intensity, which is incompatible with China's endowment structure of abundant labor and scarce capital. At the same time, labor-intensive industries, which were compatible with China's comparative advantage, were suppressed. Since the reform, the adjustment of industrial structure has been achieved by the growth of nonstate enterprises, which allocate the newly available resources into the industries that are underdeveloped. Meanwhile, the SOEs maintain their capital structure. For instance, for the industrial enterprises in 1993, the per capita original value of fixed assets in SOEs was 42.4 thousand yuan, while the same value in collective enterprises was only 23.8 thousand yuan.

Compared with labor-intensive industry, capital-intensive industry has a longer construction period, longer production cycle, requires more working capital, and needs more funds for technical innovation. Hence, capital-intensive industry bears higher capital costs and does not have a comparative advantage in China. Although this problem already existed in the traditional economic system, the SOEs were set up to meet the state's strategic goals. The SOEs could obtain free-investment appropriations and low-interest loans, and were not concerned about the financial costs. Moreover, they were shielded from international competition. When the SOEs obtained autonomy, especially after the policy for investment funding changed "from appropriations to loans," the SOEs started to shoulder the interest costs, and the use of bank credits had an opportunity cost. Meanwhile, the SOEs started to be faced with international competition. The investments in heavy industries were the state's policy. When the SOEs were confronted with competition domestically and internationally, they would press the state to recognize their losses as the legacy of the state's investment policies and demand the state to cover their losses by subsidies.

Second, after nearly two decades of reform, the prices of most products have already been liberalized. However, the prices of infrastructure products and services—energy, raw materials, and communication, and so on—are still controlled. Since these products and services are the inputs of most sectors in the economy, their price increase has a widespread cost-push effect. To prevent the negative effects on other industries, the state is reluctant to liberalize infrastructure prices. Moreover, the price increases that were allowed by the state were insufficient to cover the increases in production costs. As a result, infrastructure industries are put into an unfavorable price structure. Since their losses are policy-determined, the state is obliged to cover them.

Third, SOEs bear a heavy burden of retirement pensions. During the pre-reform period, for the purpose of speeding up the construction of heavy industry, the traditional development strategy distorted the macroeconomic policy environment. One of the macro-policies was to institute low wages with in-kind benefits for the employees of SOEs. Under the low-wage policy, a SOE was responsible for its workers' medical care, retirement pension, housing, and all other needs. Other things being equal, one enterprise would have less profits if it had more retired personnel. This relationship did not pose any problem before the economic reform, because all revenues of a SOE were remitted to the state and the state would cover all of the expenditures of the SOE. However, starting with the economic reform, SOEs obtained a certain degree of autonomy and had independent interests. The difference in the retirement burden on a SOE and on a non-SOE became one of the major causes of unfair competition.

The longer a SOE has been set up, the more serious the problem. Many large- and medium-size SOEs were set up shortly after, or even before the socialist takeover. Their proportion of retired employees is quite large, which becomes a heavy burden. Nevertheless, the non-SOEs, which were set up after the economic reform, do not have this problem, so competition between SOEs and non-SOEs is unfair.

This disparity makes it difficult to tell whether a SOE's losses arise from the pension problem or from managerial discretion and mismanagement. Moreover, it makes it hard to blame the SOEs for their inefficient operation, and it gives SOEs a legitimate claim for subsidies from the state. The solution to the SOEs' problem is to remove the policy-determined burdens, which are legacies of the planned economy, so that the SOEs can compete fairly with other types of enterprises in the market and the SOEs' profits can serve as an indicator of managerial performance.

The Stagnation of Farm Income and the Widening Disparity of Regional Income

The stagnation of farm income and the widening disparity of regional income have the same root. China's reform started in the rural sector. In 1979–84, the per capita income of the farm population grew at an unprecedented rate of 13 percent per annum, which was faster than the growth of the national economy. As a result, the ratio of the urban population's income to that of the rural population dropped from 2.4:1 in 1978 to 1.7:1 in 1984. The growth of the peasants' income slowed down and became stagnant after 1984. The average annual growth rate in 1985–88 was only 2 percent; in 1989–91, after adjusting for price increases, the annual average growth rate fell to only 0.7 percent. While the national economy was growing rapidly, the slowdown in the growth of the peasants' income caused the widening of the urban-rural income gap. Because of the stagnating rural income, the income ratio rose to 2.5:1 in 1993, which was higher than that of 1978. Because the economic activities in the central and western regions of China are predominantly agricultural, the slowdown in the growth of farm income also caused disparities between the coastal provinces—which have better opportunities to develop TVEs and other nonfarm activities—and the hinterland provinces. In 1978, the ratio of per capita rural income in the eastern region to that in the central and western regions was 1.25:1 and 1.26:1. In 1992, the ratios rose to 1.89:1 and 1.62:1.

A comparison between developed and poorer provinces shows an even more striking gap. For instance, the average farmer's annual per capita income in the Sichuan province was only one-fifth, one-sixth, and one-seventh of that of urban residents in Beijing, Shanghai, and Quangdong, respectively. The expanding disparities have resulted in a large exodus of farm laborers from the poor hinterland provinces to the prosperous coastal cities. According to incomplete data, the number of migrant peasant laborers surged to 80 million in 1994. Because of the boom-and-bust cycles, many of the floating population may lose their jobs during recessionary periods. If a substantial portion of the floating population becomes unemployed in the urban area, maintaining social order and stability may become a serious problem.

The stagnating farm income and the widening regional income disparities cannot be attributed to a crisis in agricultural production. Since 1978, China's agricultural production has grown rapidly. The average annual growth rate in 1978–96 reached 6 percent per year. Even during the 1984–88 trough, the average annual growth rate of agriculture was 4.1 percent. According to international and historic experiences, if a country's agriculture can achieve an average growth rate of 3 percent, or can outgrow population by 1 percentage point over a long period, the achievement is admirable. While the growth of peasant income stagnated in 1989–92, agricultural production was the most rapid in recent years. In contrast, in 1994 the growth of peasant income was the most rapid in recent years while agricultural production fell from the previous year. These facts suggest that, from both negative and positive sides, agricultural production cannot be the cause of the stagnation of peasants' income and the increase of regional income gaps.

The fundamental cause of the stagnating farm income and the widening urban-rural income gaps and regional disparities is the continuous suppression of prices, including the prices of grain, cotton, and other natural resources, which is a heritage of the planned economy. Grain, cotton, and other products of natural resources are the main source of income for farmers in the central and western provinces. Suppressing those product prices hinders the growth of peasants' income. In addition, the more rapidly the eastern region develops, the more it demands grain, cotton, and other natural resources from the central and western regions. Because the prices of those goods are suppressed, the more the eastern region develops and acquires those goods, the more hidden subsidies the richer eastern region obtains from the poorer central and western regions. Therefore, the regional disparities widen during a period of rapid growth in the national economy.

From the above analysis, we can conclude that the fundamental way to increase farmers' income and to reduce the regional disparities is to remove the remaining controls on the prices of grain and other agricultural products and to establish an integrated national market.

The Grain Issue

With only 7 percent of the world's arable land, China has reared a population that accounts for 22 percent of the world total. This achievement is amazing. Yet the fact remains that the amount of cultivated land per capita in China is much lower than the world average. With the increase of population and the development of the economy, the amount of cultivated land per person in China tends to shrink further while grain demand, especially demand for feed grain, steadily increases. As a large country with one-quarter of the world's population, China cannot hope to rely totally on imports for its grain needs. This reality is reflected in China's political wisdom—"no grain, no stability." The stagnation of grain output after 1984 caused many concerns in China. The concerns became especially acute after the market price of grain surged by 30 percent in 1993, 51 percent in 1994, and 36 percent in 1995.

The price hikes seem to indicate that a crisis in China's grain economy is looming. However, grain production was not the cause of the price surges. In fact, 1993 saw a record grain harvest, output in 1994 was only 2.5 percent below the record, and 1995 set another new record.

Grain output fell in 1985 and stagnated for several years because the government cut prices by 10 percent, liberalized prices of other agricultural products, and farmers shifted their production to more profitable crops and activities. The main reason for the increase in grain prices in 1993, when grain output was at a historical peak, was also a result of the government's policy. In 1992, the government ended the state monopoly for the purchase and marketing of grain in the rural areas and abolished the grain coupon schemes in the cities. In response to these major reform steps, some coastal provinces that do not have a comparative advantage in grain production—such as Guangdong, Fujian, Zhejiang, and Jiangsu—reduced production in order to lower their subsidy payments to grain farmers. The demand for grain produced in the central region consequently increased, pushing up grain prices in that region. In order to procure sufficient quantities of grain under the policy of "deregulating prices but ensuring procurement quantities" at low cost, local governments in the central region blocked local markets, thus hoping to stabilize local grain prices. That, in turn, led to a shortage of grain and higher prices in the eastern region. When the peasants in the central and other regions learned of this, they became unwilling to sell grain locally. As a result, in the marketplace there was a relative supply shortage against the background of record grain yields.

In 1994, China's grain output fell by 2.5 percent from the previous year. Weather is still a major determinant of the supply of grain— a 2 to 3 percent fluctuation in grain output is quite normal. In typical situations, the government can iron out fluctuations in grain prices, resulting from temporary output reduction, by mobilizing the grain reserve. In view of this, the reduction in the growth rate of grain output in 1994 was not the main cause of the rise in grain prices that year. Rather, the higher prices were due to the government controls over grain prices and the state monopoly over the purchase and marketing of grain. The opportunity cost of grain production in the coastal areas was already very high. To ensure grain-sown acreage and to increase output, local governments in those areas had no other option but to raise procurement prices for grain. The central region was faced with consequent pressure from these actions. In order to stop the outflow of grain to the high-price coastal region and to ensure the procurement of grain, the governments in the central region had to raise grain procurement prices as well. The repeated government action of raising grain prices induced peasants to form an expectation that there was a severe grain shortage and that prices would go up further. That price expectation was further fueled by the overall inflation in the economy. In response, the peasants began to hoard grain, which led grain prices to shoot up once again. As a result, a phenomenon occurred that, while grain prices in the marketplace spiraled, peasants' grain stocks were piling up. The price spike in 1995 was again fueled by the inflation expectation in the economy.

The trend is inevitable that the demand for grain will increase and the cultivated land available for grain will decrease in the process of economic development. The way to increase grain output for meeting the increased demand is to raise the unit yield, which depends on the government's investments in yield-improvement and other related researches and farmers' incentives to adopt new high-yielding technologies. Studies show that grain crops in China still have a vast yield potential (Lin, Shen, and Zhou 1996c). If the government makes sufficient investments in yield-improvement research and liberalizes the grain market, allowing the price of grain to bring market supply and demand into balance, China will be able to produce enough grain to feed its population in the future.

Technically, China has the potential to be self-sufficient in grain production. However, China is a land-scarce economy and grain is a land-intensive crop. As China's economy develops and the comparative advantage of the Chinese economy changes, the costs to maintain grain self-sufficiency will become increasingly high. It will be economically sensible for China to revise the self-sufficiency policy and increase the import of grain as a way to meet part of domestic grain demand in the future.

Conclusion

Even though China's leaders did not have a blueprint in mind when reforms started, China's reforms have followed a path that can be explained by the theory of induced institutional innovation (Lin 1989, North 1990). The traditional economic structure was itself a product of institutional innovation induced by the government's attempt to pursue a HIODS in a capital-scarce economy. The traditional system made the mobilization of resources for building up the strategy-determined priority sectors possible. However, its economic efficiency was low. Therefore, when the integrity of the traditional economic system was cracked by introducing enterprise autonomy and the household responsibility system, institutional changes occurred in a way that were self-propelling toward the replacement of the traditional system with a more efficient market system. The household responsibility system greatly improved the farmers' incentive and agricultural productivity (Lin 1988). Moreover, the efficiency of the SOEs was also improved through greater autonomy and by meeting competition from the nonstate sectors. However, the dynamism of the economy came mainly from the swift entry of new, small, nonstate enterprises. The old planned allocation system and distorted macro-policy environment gradually became unsustainable and were discarded. During the reform process, the state, the enterprises, and the people have had sufficient time to make adjustments to the new market system. The reforms benefit the majority of people as the economy has maintained strong growth throughout the whole process.

The overall performance of China's gradual approach to transition is remarkable, but China has paid a price for the achievement. Because the reform of the macro-policy environment—especially the policies regarding interest rates, grain prices, and prices of raw materials—has lagged behind reforms of the micro-management institution and resource allocation mechanism, institutional arrangements in the economic system have become internally inconsistent. As a result of the institutional incompatibility, a boom-and-bust cycle, rent-seeking, a deterioration of SOEs' profits, a widening disparity in regional incomes, and the threat of future grain shortages have become internalized issues in the transitional process and threaten the sustainability of future growth.

From the preceding analysis we find that, although the existing problems are chronic and complicated, the cause of the problems is simple and clear. They are all caused by the institutional incompatibility due to the gradual, incremental approach to reform. For ensuring a sustained and smooth growth path, it is imperative for China to complete the reform of the macro-policy environment so as to complete the transition to a market economy. Since the macro-policy environment is endogenous to the state's development strategy, the government must give up its anti-comparative advantage HIODS— or, in modern terms, its capital-intensive, high-tech, industry-oriented development strategy—and shift to a strategy that focuses on capitalizing on China's comparative advantages. In addition, as the Chinese economy becomes a more mature market economy and is more integrated with the world economy, it is essential for the continuous growth of the Chinese economy to establish a transparent, rule-based, legal system that protects property rights so as to encourage innovations, technological progress, and domestic as well as foreign investments in China.

References

Brada, J.C., and King, A.E. (1991) "Sequencing Measures for the Transformation of Socialist Economies to Capitalism: Is There a J-Curve for Economic Reform?" Research Paper Series No. 13. Washington, D.C.: Socialist Economies Reform Unit, World Bank.

Chen, K.; Jefferson, G.; and Singh, I.J. (1992) "Lessons from China's Economic Reform." *Journal of Comparative Economics* 16(2) (June): 201–25.

Chen, K.; Wang, H.; Zheng, Y.; Jefferson, G.; and Rawski, T. (1988) "Productivity Change in Chinese Industry: 1953–1985." *Journal of Comparative Economics* 12(4) (December): 570–91.

Cheng, C.-Y. (1982) *China's Economic Development: Growth and Structural Change.* Boulder, Colo.: Westview Press.

Desai, P., and Martin, R. (1983) "Efficiency Loss from Resource Misallocation in Soviet Industry." *Quarterly Journal of Economics* 98(3) (August): 117–29.

Dollar, D. (1990) "Economic Reform and Allocative Efficiency in China's State-Owned Industry." *Economic Development and Cultural Change* 39(1) (October): 89–105.

Fan, Q., and Schaffer, M.E. (1991) "Enterprise Reforms in Chinese and Polish State-Owned Industries." Research Paper Series No. 11. Washington, D.C.: Socialist Economies Reform Unit, World Bank.

Fan, S. (1991) "Effects of Technological Change and Institutional Reform on Production Growth in Chinese Agriculture." *American Journal of Agricultural Economics* 73(2) (May): 265–75.

Feder, G.; Lau, L.; Lin, J.; and Luo, H.X. (1992) "The Determinants of Farm Investment and Residential Construction in Post-Reform China." *Economic Development and Cultural Change* 41(1) (October): 1–26.

Gelb, A.; Jefferson, G.; and Singh, I. (1993) "Can Communist Economies Transform Incrementally?" In O.J. Blanchard and S. Fisher (eds.) *NBER Macroeconomics Annual 1993.* Cambridge, Mass.: MIT Press.

Gordon, R., and Li, W. (1989) "Chinese Enterprise Behavior under the Reforms." *American Economic Review: Papers and Proceedings* 81(2) (May): 202–6.

Groves, T.; Hong, Y.; McMillan, J.; and Naughton, B. (1992) "Autonomy and Incentives in Chinese State Enterprises." Mimeo. San Diego: University of California, Graduate School of International Relations and Pacific Studies.

Harrold, P. (1992) "China's Reform Experience to Date." World Bank Discussion Paper, 180. Washington, D.C.: World Bank.

Hu, X.L. (1994) "1994: Reforms Have No Romantic Melody." *Gaige (Reform)* No. 1 (January).

Huang, J., and Rozelle, S. (1996) "Technological Change: The Re-Discovery of the Engine of Productivity Growth in China's Rural Economy." *Journal of Development Economics* 49(2)(May): 336–69.

Jefferson, G., and Rawski, T. (1995) "How Industrial Reform Worked in China: The Role of Innovation, Competition, and Property Rights." *Proceedings of the World Bank Annual Conference on Development Economics 1994.* Washington, D.C.: World Bank: 129–56.

Jefferson, G.; Rawski, T.; and Zheng, Y. (1992) "Growth, Efficiency and Convergence in China's State and Collective Industry." *Economic Development and Cultural Change* 40(2) (January): 239–66.

Kornai, J. (1990) *The Road to a Free Economy.* New York: Norton.

Li, Y. (1983) *Zhongguo Gongye Bumen Jiegou (The Structure of Chinese Industry).* Beijing: China People's University Press.

Lin, J.Y. (1988) "The Household Responsibility System Reform in China's Agricultural Reform: A Theoretical and Empirical Study." *Economic Development and Cultural Change* 36 (3, suppl.) (April): S199–S224.

Lin, J.Y. (1989) "An Economic Theory of Institutional Change: Induced and Imposed Change." *Cato Journal* 9(1) (Spring/Summer): 1–33.

Lin, J.Y. (1992) "Rural Reforms and Agricultural Growth in China." *American Economic Review* 82(1) (March): 34–51.

Lin, J.Y.; Cai, F.; and Li, Z. (1996a) *The China Miracle: Development Strategy and Economic Reform.* Hong Kong: Chinese University Press.

Lin, J.Y.; Cai, F.; and Li, Z. (1996b) "The Lessons of China's Transition to a Market Economy." *Cato Journal* 16 (2) (Fall): 201–31.

Lin, J.Y.; Shen, M.; and Zhou, H. (1996c) *Agricultural Research Priorities in China: A Supply and Demand Analysis of Seed Improvement Research for Major Grain.* Beijing: China Agricultural Press.

Lin, J.Y.; Cai, F.; and Li, Z. (1997) *Sufficient Information and State-owned Enterprise Reform.* Shanghai: Sanlian Press and People's Press. (Also published in Hong Kong by Chinese University Press for overseas distribution in English, 1998.)

Luo, H.X. (1985) *Economic Changes in Rural China.* Beijing: New World Press.

McKinnon, R.I. (1994) "Gradual versus Rapid Liberalization in Socialist Economies: Financial Policies and Macroeconomic Stability in China and Russia Compared." *Proceedings of the World Bank Annual Conference on Development Economics 1993.* Washington, D.C.: World Bank: 63–94.

McMillan, J., and Naughton, B. (1992) "How to Reform A Planned Economy: Lessons from China." *Oxford Review of Economic Policy* 8(1) (Spring): 130–43.

McMillan, J.; Whalley, J.; and Zhu, L. (1989) "The Impact of China's Economic Reforms on Agricultural Productivity Growth." *Journal of Political Economy* 97(4) (August): 781–807.

Newbery, D.M. (1993) "Transformation in Mature versus Emerging Economies: Why Has Hungary Has Been Less Successful Than China?" Paper presented to the International Symposium on the Theoretical and Practical Issues of the Transition towards the Market Economy in China, 1–3 July. Hainan, China: China Institute of Economic Reform and Development.

North, D.C. (1990) *Institutions, Institutional Change, and Economic Performance.* Cambridge, Mass.: Cambridge University Press.

Perkins, D.H. (1966) *Market Control and Planning in Communist China.* Cambridge, Mass.: Harvard University Press.

Perkins, D.H. (1988) "Reforming China's Economic System." *Journal of Economic Literature* 26(2) (June): 601–45.

Perkins, D.H., and Yusuf, S. (1984) *Rural Development in China.* Baltimore: Johns Hopkins Press.

Qian, Y., and Xu, C. (1993) "Why China's Economic Reforms Differ: The M-Form Hierarchy and Entry/Expansion of the Non-state Sector." *The Economics of Transition* 1(2) (June): 135–70.

Sachs, J.D., and Woo, W.T. (1993) "Structural Factors in the Economic Reforms of China, Eastern Europe and the Former Soviet Union," Paper presented at the Economic Policy Panel Meeting, 22–23 October. Brussels, Belgium.

State Statistical Bureau (1995) *Zhongguo Tongji Zaiyao, 1995 (A Statistical Survey of China, 1995).* Beijing: Zhongguo Tongji Chubanshe.

State Statistical Bureau (1987a, 1993, 1994) *Zhongguo Tongji Nianjian, 1993, 1994 (China Statistical Yearbook, 1987, 1993, 1994).* Beijing: Zhongguo Tongji Chubanshe.

State Statistical Bureau (1987b) *Zhongguo Gongyejingji Tongji Ziliao, 1987 (China Industrial Economy Statistical Material , 1987)* Beijing: Zhongguo Tongji Chubanshe.

Sung, Y.-W. (1994) "An Appraisal of China's Foreign Trade Policy, 1950–1992." In T.N. Srinivasan (ed.) *The Comparative Experience of Agricultural and Trade Reforms in China and India, 109–53.* San Francisco: International ICS Press.

Wen, G.J. (1993) "Total Factor Productivity Change in China's Farming Sector: 1952–1989." *Economic Development and Cultural Change* 42(1) (October): 1–41.

Whitesell, R., and Barreto, H. (1988) "Estimation of Output Loss from Allocative Inefficiency: Comparisons of the Soviet Union and the U.S." Research Memorandum RM-109. MA: Center for Development Economics, Williams College.

World Bank (1992) *Reform and Role of the Plan in the 1990s*. Washington, D.C: World Bank.

World Bank (1985a) *China: Economic Structure in International Perspective, Annex to China: Long-Term Issues and Options*. Washington, D.C.: World Bank.

World Bank (1985b) *China: Long-Term Issues and Options*. Oxford: Oxford University Press, published for the World Bank.

Wu, J., and Zhang, Z., eds. (1993) *Zhongguo Jingji Jianshe Baikequanshu (The Encyclopedia of China's Economic Construction)*. Beijing: Beijing Gongye Daxue Chubanshe.

Zhonghua Zhoumo Bao (China Weekend Newspaper) (1995) "The Over- staffing in the State Enterprises is over 30 Millions." 21 January.

Zou, G. (1992) "Enterprise Behavior under the Two-Tier Plan/Market System." Mimeo. Los Angeles, CA: IBEAR/SBA, University of Southern California.

5. Development of the Nonstate Sector and Reform of State Enterprises in China

Fan Gang

The so-called gradual or incremental approach to reform refers to the way of institutional transition in which the first step toward the market economy is not restructuring the existing old economic sectors, but developing the new system outside the old ones through economic growth. That is actually the case of China. The main achievement of two decades of gradual economic reform in China has not been the reform of the state sector, but the development of a dynamic nonstate sector that consists of community-owned township and village enterprises, joint ventures, shareholding companies, private firms, and self-employed businesses (see Table 1). While state enterprises are suffering growing financial losses, the nonstate sector has grown rapidly and has become the main contributor to the growth and development of China's emerging market economy.

The key question about gradualism is not whether it involves huge efficiency losses because of the distortions caused by the continuous existence of old sectors.[1] The high cost for maintaining the inefficient state enterprises may be justified by the opportunity costs of social unrest and reduction of GDP caused by radical changes. The key issue is whether the growth of new sectors and the economy as a whole will lead to the reform of the old system and prevent the economy from collapsing, which might be caused by the delay of

---

Fan Gang is Director of the National Economic Research Institute and the China Reform Foundation in Beijing, and a Professor of Economics at the Graduate School of the Chinese Academy of Social Sciences.

[1]Even if one can prove that the state sector gained some improvement compared to its previous situation, it is easy to show that it is inefficient to locate so many resources in the state sector.

TABLE 1
DEVELOPMENT OF THE NONSTATE SECTORS

Nonstate Sector	1980	1985	1986	1987	1988	1989	1990	1991	1992	1993	1994	1995
Output value of industry (OVI) as % of total OVI	24.0	35.2	37.7	40.3	43.2	43.9	45.4	47.1	51.9	56.9	64.1[a]	69.1
Employment as % of total employment	81.1	82.0	81.8	81.7	81.6	81.7	81.7	81.9	81.8	–	–	–
As % of total non-agricultural labor force[b]	na	–	–	–	–	–	42.5	42.6	44.4	47.7	47.0	–
State budgetary revenue from the nonstate sector as % of total state revenue	18.0	29.6	25.4	28.6	31.6	33.2	33.6	36.1	37.2	39.4	34.3	–
Retail sale as % of social total	48.6	59.6	60.6	61.4	60.5	60.9	60.4	59.8	58.7	60.1	68.1	–
As % of total fixed investment	na	33.9	–	36.9	38.6	38.7	34.4	34.1	32.9	38.5	43.1	–
As % of bank credit[c]	na	18.0	–	–	–	19.8	–	21.1	21.2	19.3	–	–

[a]1994 figure includes output (of 460 billion yuan) by shareholding companies controlled by state-owned entities.
[b]Including "urban collective workers" and workers in rural township and village enterprises, private enterprises, and self-employed individuals in nonagricultural undertakings.
[c]Including all loans to agriculture.

SOURCE: *China Statistical Yearbook* (various years).

the reform. The incremental approach to reform not only requires the development of new sectors, but also requires the eventual termination of the old system. This chapter analyzes the relation between the development of the nonstate sector and the reform of state-owned enterprises (SOEs) during the economic transition.

Decreasing Profitability of the State Sector

The reforms in the state sector have been for a long time mainly in the direction of decentralization of decisionmaking powers and managerial administration without any change of ownership. These reforms have resulted in "decentralized SOEs" and "autonomous" local governments playing an increasing role in determining resource allocation and income distribution within the unchanged ownership framework. Despite some improvement in productivity, the profitability of SOEs has been continuously deteriorating (see Table 2). Market competition from nonstate firms has forced the monopoly profits down. Wage payments, bonuses, fringe benefits, and "publicly financed consumption" (which are often disguised as costs) have increased more rapidly than the output, resulting in also the decline of returns to capital (Fan and Woo 1993). The percentage of loss-making SOEs increased to 51 percent by the end of June 1996 according to official data.

Due to the fiscal and financial reforms in the 1980s, SOEs now receive less and less subsidies from the state budget.[2] But they receive "quasi-subsidies" from the state banks in the form of "policy loans" and nonperforming debts. The main reason behind the delay of financial sector reform is the need for the state to mobilize financial resources to maintain the SOEs. With much higher access to bank credit, the average debt-to-asset ratio of SOEs has increased to over 80 percent in recent years. Nonperforming loans were estimated officially as 25 percent at the end of June 1996. Meanwhile, inter-enterprise debt (IED)—also known as "triangle debt"—has increased rapidly in recent years, and the IED-GDP ratio has risen to nearly 43 percent, which is among the highest in the world (Fan 1996).

[2]The nominal amount of total budgetary subsidies to loss-making enterprises was 36.6 billion yuan in 1994, only slightly more than that in 1985 (32.4 billion yuan), without discounting for inflation.

TABLE 2
FINANCIAL PERFORMANCE OF MAJOR STATE ENTERPRISES

State Enterprises[a]	1978	1980	1985	1988	1989	1990	1991	1992	1993	1994
Profit rates[b]	15.5	16	13.2	10.4	7.2	3.2	2.9	2.7	2.2	–
Profits and taxes as % of total assets value[c]	24.2	24.8	23.5	20.6	17.2	12.4	11.8	9.7	9.68	9.77
Profits and taxes as % of output value	24.9	24.1	21.8	17.8	14.9	12	11.6	11.4	11.1	11.37
Revenues from state sector as % of total revenue	na	–	82	70.4	68.4	66.8	66.4	63.9	60.6	65.7
Total losses (billions of yuan)	4.2	3.4	3.2	8.1	18	34.9	36.7	36.9	45.3	48.2
Total losses as % of total profits	8.2	5.8	4.3	9.1	24.2	89.8	91.3	69	55.3	58.1
Subsidies for losses (billions of yuan)	na	–	32.5	44.6	59.9	57.9	51	44.4	41.1	36.6
Loss-subsidies as % of budgetary revenues	na	14.3	17	20.3	17.4	14.1	10.7	8.1	7	–

[a]Large and medium-sized state enterprises with independent accounting.
[b]The State Statistical Bureau stopped providing the "profit rate" in 1994.
[c]The definition of "profits and taxes" is different from "pre-tax profits" because it includes all sales taxes or value-added taxes, not just the income tax.

SOURCE: *China Statistical Yearbook* (various years).

Growth of the Nonstate Sector

The most important "dual-track transition" has been the change in the ownership structure of the economy. China's progress in developing a market system and achieving rapid economic growth has been mainly due to the dynamic expansion of the nonstate sector. It is this development that makes the Chinese economy a "dual-track economy."

Rural Industries

The ownership reform actually started from the very beginning of the reform when the collective "commune" system was replaced by household farming (1979–83). That single reform made agriculture, which accounted for 30 percent of GDP but 80 percent of the labor force, de facto private and the least state controlled sector. When farmers became able to decide not only what they wanted to do on their "contracted land" but also what they wanted to do about their surplus labor, small private businesses (e.g., private transportation, retailing, and crafts) and community-owned industrial enterprises (so-called township and village enterprises [TVEs]) started to develop. TVEs are still a transitional form of ownership and are undergoing dramatic institutional changes,[3] but they have already become the major competitor against state enterprises, and account for over 40 percent of total industrial output.

Joint Ventures

Two other important factors underpinning the changes in ownership structure are the increasing capital inflows and the growing number of foreign joint ventures, especially those made by overseas Chinese who have ready access to Chinese markets and invest mostly in the labor-intensive nonstate sector. From 1979 to the end of 1995, foreign direct investment amounted to $137 billion in 330,000 projects, with $37.8 billion of foreign direct investment in 1995 alone. Of the total foreign direct investment, 67.5 percent came from Hong Kong, Macao, and Taiwan. A considerable percentage of investment

[3] A major institutional change has been the recent development of a collective or cooperative shareholding system in TVEs, which involves the distribution or sale of property rights in the form of shares of which up to 50 percent go to workers of the firms or members of the community (Chen 1994).

from the United States and Japan, which are the third and fourth largest sources of foreign investment, is also made by overseas Chinese in the countries concerned. In 1995, foreign-funded Chinese companies produced 14.6 percent of total industrial output and about 50 percent of manufactured consumer goods on the domestic market, and accounted for nearly 39 percent of China's international trade.

The Regional Factor

The nonstate sector developed more rapidly in those regions where reform occurred earlier and faster than in other regions. Four southern coastal cities, including Shenzhen and Xiamen, were chosen to be special economic zones (SEZs) in 1980, and Hainan province became the fifth in 1988. In addition, 20 other cities were approved to be "economic and technological development areas" (ETDAs). These SEZs and ETDAs have been the experimental fields for new institutions and reform policies. In most of these regions, the nonstate sector already accounts for more than 70 percent of production.

Development of the Nonstate Sector and the Reform of the State Sector

The growth of the nonstate sector has been fundamentally changing the environment of the state sector and therefore providing new and favorable conditions for reforming SOEs:

- The expanding nonstate sector has increased national income and "economic surplus," which has enabled the government to compensate some groups that face losses in the reform process, and thus has reduced the resistance and the possible pains that SOE reform might bring to some state employees.
- The growth of national income in general and the financial capability of the nonstate firms in particular have provided financial means for the capital restructuring of SOEs. At last, in the 1990s, the Chinese people started to be financially capable of purchasing state assets and state enterprises (at least the small ones) on a meaningful scale.
- The development of the nonstate sector has provided an increasing number of new job opportunities and helped reallocate state workers. This is even more significant for reducing the pain of and resistance to SOE reform. With the deterioration of the

financial situation of SOEs and the dynamic growth of the non-state sector, plus progress in reforming the social security system, more and more state employees are realizing that the state is no longer reliable, and that leaving SOEs may not be a bad choice.

- The growth of the nonstate sector has led to the emergence of new types of enterprises and entrepreneurs. Thus, it has become possible to reform SOEs through more peaceful and natural ways such as acquisition and merger, and reforms may be more likely to generate immediate improvement.

- The growing nonstate sector has forced SOEs to face market competition. Their original monopoly and the planning system have been broken by the entry of nonstate entities. With the increase of market competition, the institutional weakness of SOEs has been increasingly revealed.

- The dynamic growth of the nonstate sector has provided a "domestic institutional example" for the reform of the state sector. In the same macroeconomic environment, the fact that SOEs cannot do what nonstate firms can makes it more evident that reform is necessary.

It has been proven in many cases that, in those areas where the nonstate sector has a higher share in output and employment, the reform of SOEs is easier. In the coastal areas where the nonstate sector has become predominant in recent years, the SOEs have already entered the stage of "naturally phasing away."

In summary, the problems inside the SOEs are getting worse on one hand; on the other hand, the development of the nonstate sector is improving the outside conditions for reform. So the reform of SOEs naturally has been put on the policy agenda and is slowly progressing.

In 1992, the share of the nonstate sector in the total industrial output value exceeded 50 percent for the first time. In October 1993, the Third Plenary Session of the 14th Central Committee of the Communist Party of China adopted a new comprehensive reform plan—the Decision on Economic Reform—which for the first time announced that: (1) the objective of reform is to create a "socialist market economy"; (2) the nonstate sector should be encouraged to develop along with the state sector; (3) the reform of "property

rights" of SOEs and sales of state assets should be allowed; and
(4) the "corporatization" of SOEs is taken as the main way for the
immediate target of institutional change.

The 1993 decision was a major breakthrough for the reform agenda
of the top leadership. For the first time, the central committee mentioned that the reform of SOEs should include "property rights
reforms." This occurrence was not a coincidence, but rather a demonstration of economic logic. Using the same logic, one could predict
the occurrence of other events. For example, when the share of the
financial revenue provided by SOEs falls below 50 percent (today
SOEs contribute about 60 percent), the reform of the SOEs will be
further deepened. Recent progress in restructuring the state sector
also shows that there may be a good possibility that China will solve
the problems of state enterprises through ongoing incremental
changes.

Recent Progress in Ownership Reform of SOEs

There is no centrally promoted program of "mass privatization"
in China. Public ownership is still the central part of the official
formula for a "socialist market economy." Ownership reform, however, has already been under way but at a slow pace. The necessity
of ownership change is being realized by more and more people
who learn economics from their own daily life. When so little has
been achieved after almost all measures have been tried except the
reform of ownership, people naturally turn to the ownership issues.
More pragmatically, as SOEs become more and more of a financial
burden, rather than a source of revenue, the government becomes
more and more willing to remove them from its fiscal account.

Corporatization

Shareholding began to be used as a way to reform some SOEs in
1984, and it has accelerated since 1988 when stock exchanges were
opened in Shanghai and Shenzhen. Shares of firms have been sold
to private owners though so far mainly involving only "new shares."
The corporate form of ownership structure is widely used in newly
established companies or joint ventures. By the end of 1994, 25,800
companies were formally registered as shareholding corporations;
among them, 290 were listed in the market (323 listed companies at
the end of 1995), with 3.8 million individual shareholders. The

national average of private shares as a proportion of total shares of shareholding companies is about 30 percent, with the remainder consisting of "state shares" and "shares of state-owned entities." The high percentage of state shares makes the current shareholding companies more like conventional SOEs.[4] However, several points should be made: (1) as long as there is no big crisis, the ownership reform in China will be gradual; (2) owners will seek greater control when there is "market pressure" and owners "vote by foot"; and (3) it will take some time (years) for ownership to play a full role in improving management and performance. (How could one expect the performance of SOEs to change completely overnight after half-way corporatization and to behave the same way a private corporation does in a free-market system that has developed for hundreds of years?)

Sales of Small Local SOEs

Although the government is still trying every means to "revive" or "strengthen" SOEs (this policy is formally announced in every government statement), it has become more and more difficult for the government to maintain them. This is reflected in the recent wave of privatizations of small-sized, local SOEs.

The sales of existing assets of SOEs have been nominally permitted since late 1993, but such sales have been very restricted by official policy. Local governments (at county and city levels) began to act, however, after 1993 when they found it would be beneficial to get rid of the financial and fiscal burden of SOEs on the local economy. Besides forming joint ventures, an increasing number of small-sized SOEs have been sold to private owners, TVEs, and foreign investors. While it is difficult to find investors to buy the equities of existing SOEs, selling the securitized "net equities" (total value of assets minus total debt) to workers of the enterprises became a popular way for SOE restructuring at the local levels of the economy. This so-called cooperative shareholding (CSH) was first developed in TVEs, and by the end of 1995 three million TVEs had been converted

---

[4]In China's official statistics, when an SOE has turned into a shareholding company, it is no longer listed as an SOE. So any improvement by "corporatization" will not show up in the statistical performance of the SOE sector, but only be reflected in the overall situation.

into CSH companies (*China Information Daily* 1996).[5] In some counties of Shandong province up to 70 percent of small-sized SOEs have been privatized this way. The results of such a restructuring so far are quite positive and encouraging. Most firms have improved their financial situation. Those that turned out to be unprofitable have gone into bankruptcy with little government intervention. Finally, the transfer and resale of shares is occurring, meaning that the concentration of ownership is gradually under way.

The central government did not give the privatization of small SOEs formal approval until early 1997. But for more than three years it did not stop the process, meaning it actually liked to see the process going forward without taking political responsibility (this is quite typical of central government's behavior in regard to reforms in recent years). More formally, since 1995 the central leadership has adopted a new policy of "improving large SOEs while liberalizing small ones" (*zhua da fang xiao*). Although the question of how to "liberalize" the small SOEs has remained ambiguous in the formal document, that ambiguity encourages the local process of privatization. As for reforming the large SOEs, it seems that conditions are not yet ready for real reform.

Progress with the "bottom-up" small SOE reform that has occurred during the last several years indicates that China is now ready for restructuring small SOEs because of the emergence of new conditions. If things continue to go in the same direction, similar reform of medium and large SOEs may take place in 5 to 10 years. The whole process will take a long time and there will be a lot of problems during the transition, but there may be a way out—and the "two tracks" may hopefully converge in 20 years with a much improved ownership structure. That reform path may not be a "better solution" than other solutions, but at least we may hope there will be a solution that is better than doing nothing.

Conclusion

The preceding analysis may shed some light on the question of whether China will be able to get out of its current problems, especially the problem of money-losing SOEs by continuing its incremental reform. The answer seems to be, "yes, with good chance." Recent

---

[5]Cooperative shareholding is a special form of shareholding with characteristics of public ownership. The shares of the firm are owned by employees individually, but no matter how different the amount of shares held, everyone in the firm has equal voting rights and dividends are distributed equally among the employees.

progress has shown that the development of the nonstate sector has led to a decline in the relative importance of SOEs and an improvement in the conditions for restructuring the state sector. As long as the economy as a whole can continue grow and the nonstate sector in particular can continue to outgrow the state sector, China may eventually grow out of the problems related to the state sector.

References

Chen, X. (1994) "Rural Reform: Household Farming and Township and Village Enterprises." In *The Road of China: Reform and Development* (in Chinese). Edited by China Reform Foundation. Beijing: China's Economic and Financial Press.

China Information Daily (1996) 13 July.

China Statistical Yearbook (various years) Compiled by the State Statistical Bureau, People's Republic of China. Beijing: China Statistical Publishing House.

Fan, G. (1996) "Interenterprise Debt and Macroeconomic Performance in China" (in Chinese). *Jingji Yanjiu (Journal of Economic Research)*, March and April. Also available as a Working Paper in English, No. 96003, National Economic Research Institute of China, Beijing.

Fan, G., and Woo, W.T. (1993) "Decentralized Socialism and Macroeconomic Stability: Lessons from China." Working Paper No. 112, World Institute for Development Economics Research, United Nations University, July.

Comment

From Plan to Market: China's Gradualist Approach

Barry Naughton

Fan Gang (1998) has written a short but eloquent and important contribution to the literature on transition. He argues that gradualism was an appropriate policy for Chinese reform heretofore, and is also a good, and possibly the preferred approach, to future reforms. Particularly striking is Fan's advocacy of continued gradualism with respect to ongoing and future reform of the troubled state sector. Indeed, so complete is Fan's identification with gradualism that there was a typographical error in an early draft of his paper, an error that perhaps reflects a Freudian slip: instead of the Graduate School of the Chinese Academy of Social Sciences, Fan gives his affiliation as "Gradual School" of the Academy.

To those familiar with the debate on gradualism in the United States, Fan's position may seem surprising. He has collaborated on a number of papers with Wing Thye Woo, who has been a prominent critic of gradualist interpretations of Chinese economic success, along with Jeff Sachs. Some of Fan's insights have in the past been incorporated into papers by Woo and Sachs, and understandably, they have been interpreted in line with the framework adopted by Woo and Sachs. Here, however, Fan lays out his own overall framework, and it is of considerable interest.

The Transition Debate

The extensive literature in Chinese on the nature of transition is still relatively unknown in the West. In part, that is because of

---

Barry Naughton is Associate Professor at the Graduate School of International Relations and Pacific Studies at the University of California at San Diego.

the large difference in the intellectual assumptions within which economic debates occur in the different environments. The Chinese debate has unfolded within a profound sense of predicament, with a limited range of options, in which the focus has consistently been on a search for policies that can provide incremental success and room for maneuver. Since at least 1984, an interesting and creative debate has been ongoing in China primarily over the appropriate policies and sequencing of transition within the framework of a gradualist strategy.[1] Almost everyone, in the Chinese context, is a gradualist; there has been little overt support for a more rapid, "big bang" transition. By contrast, debate in the West has generally centered around the question of the big bang transition. Influenced by the dramatic events in Eastern Europe and the former Soviet Union, and by the more direct role that American economists have played in policymaking in those countries, Western debate has usually been concerned with assessing and arguing over the overall speed and thoroughness of the transition process (see World Bank 1996).

Fan writes primarily within the context of the Chinese discussion of transition. But the work of Chinese economists such as Fan—and even more importantly the success of Chinese economic reforms—present profound challenges to the understanding of the transition process which is most current in the West. We need only recall the predominant attitudes toward transition which circulated in the early 1990s. Western analyses of the transition were filled with metaphors that stressed the unavoidable dislocation of transition. Pain was "necessary" and therefore, might as well be experienced up front, and gotten over as soon as possible. A popular metaphor was the idea that it was impossible to leap across a ravine in two steps. It was necessary to implement radical change as rapidly as possible in order to generate maximum forward movement, no matter what the short-term cost. Certainly, no significant Western economist would have advised maintaining the state sector more or less unchanged through a decade of economic transformation.

The paradox of Chinese success is that we can find no such painful early period, and no such eyes-closed leap across the ravine. Instead,

---

[1] I have tried to capture a few key aspects of this debate in chapter five of my book on Chinese economic reform (Naughton 1995: 187–99).

Chinese reform policymaking has been characterized in a telling Chinese phrase as "groping for the stones to cross the river." Each step has been partial and tentative, but each made with eyes wide open, alert to the short-run consequences of each movement. The result has been a cumulative process of institution building, and a gradual acceleration of the pace of economic growth. In his second paragraph, Fan lays out the relationship between this successful incremental process, and the fundamental problem of transition. He says that the fundamental issue is not whether a fully marketized economy based on clear, secure and predominantly private property rights will outperform a hybrid economy with a large state sector, remnants of administrative interference in economic decisionmaking, and ambiguous property rights. Of course it will. The issue is whether a gradualist strategy can be justified in that the delay in moving toward that economic system will be more than offset by the avoidance of a catastrophic drop in output, with the attendant increase in uncertainty and long-lasting reduction in saving and investment. Here Fan argues that such gradualism is in fact justified by this logic.

A Virtuous Cycle

Indeed, Fan goes beyond this, particularly in his section on the "Development of the Nonstate Sector and the Reform of the State Sector," where he produces an interesting list of ways in which the gradual growth of the nonstate sector strengthens the national economy, increases the options in reforming the state sector, and creates new dynamic pressures that both increase the incentive to reform and eventually abolish the state sector, while also increasing the ability to do so. In other words, Fan is arguing that there is a virtuous cycle of reform, in which the difficult early beginnings of gradual reform make it easier to reform down the line. This virtuous cycle is related to one proposed by myself and a collaborator (McMillan and Naughton 1992), but Fan goes beyond our earlier work in several important ways. In particular, as is appropriate in this later era of reform, Fan stresses the fact that the virtuous cycle culminates in a situation in which it becomes much easier to shrink the state sector in absolute terms: job opportunities for reallocation of state employees have multiplied; wealth accumulated in the household sector makes it possible to sell-off small state-owned enterprises (SOEs) on a meaningful scale; enterpreneurship experience and new enterprise forms have developed that make it much easier to convert formerly state-owned firms. Thus, the virtuous cycle induced by reform continues to improve economic prospects for a sustained period during the transition. The idea that gradual reform creates a virtuous circle making further reform easier represents a dramatic reversal of the assumptions and convictions of predominant Western thinking on transition.

Lessons from Chinese Economic Success

It might be possible to abbreviate the lessons learned from Chinese economic success to two simple but powerful principles. The first is the value of entry and competition. The Chinese economy was transformed, as Fan shows, first by the entry and competitive pressure of rural township and village enterprises (TVEs) beginning in 1979 and continuing through the 1980s. Subsequently, foreign-invested firms, predominantly in the 1990s, have brought a second wave of competitive pressures to bear, particularly in high-technology fields and consumer goods sectors in which quality and variety are of central importance. Competition proved to be more crucial than purposeful government restructuring of the state-run economy. Second, the Chinese experience shows the crucial value of civil society. Under the planned socialist economy, civil society withers. Institutions that facilitate voluntary exchange disappear. It is not entrepreneurship that disappears under socialism. Individuals continue to hone their entrepreneurial skills in order to manipulate the irrational bureaucracy; so entrepreneurship lies concealed, waiting for economic opportunities to emerge. But entrepreneurial impulses at first find relatively few opportunities to be manifested in socially productive ways, because of the shortage of institutions that support self-interested cooperation. Only gradually do the marketplaces and fora develop. But as they do develop, economic activity moves to a higher plane.

These two simple principles provide a general reason for optimism about Chinese prospects. China's future in general looks promising, first because China is currently a hyper-competitive society. Competition in product markets is driving down prices, and creates vicious and unrelenting pressures on producers to improve quality and lower costs. Competition for public attention and for political success may also be expected to lead to continued social progress in the future. Second, we can observe a steady accumulation of resources, skills and experience at the "bottom" of society, where it matters the most. Chinese civil society is growing, in economic and non-economic spheres. This growth of capabilities provides grounds for a general optimism.

Is Gradualism a Limited Strategy?

Fan's paper is consistent with this general optimism, but provides a much more specific and rigorous argument about the next stage of gradual reforms. Despite over a decade of success, some observers of Chinese reform have worried that Chinese gradualism might succeed with the early, "easy" parts of economic reform, but later founder on intractable problems relating to the ownership and financial systems. There is an interesting inversion here of the necessary initial pain of the "big bang" strategy and the "easy early" part of the Chinese transition, but the question is nonetheless a valid one: Is gradualism a limited strategy, destined to be superseded by a more traumatic but fundamental economic transformation?

Fan answers this question with both purely economic and political economic explanations. The economic explanations focus on the accumulation of resources outside the state sector. As the diversified economy has become larger and richer, it has gradually achieved the ability to take over the state sector. In a sense, Fan suggests a theory of stages: first the nonstate sector competes with the state sector; subsequently it absorbs the state sector. Today, we are in the midst of a passage from the first to the second stage.

In the political economy part of the paper, Fan focuses on the interests of decisionmakers and provides a sophisticated analysis of government incentives toward reform. This is very much in the tradition of Chinese discussions of transition strategy, which have consistently and explicitly treated the political constraints within which reform must proceed. These constraints have included both the need to generate popular support for reform, and the need to achieve the acquiescence of those privileged with political power and effective control over resources in the old system. Fan argues the gradual decline in the share of total output that was accounted for by SOEs culminated in a fall below 50 percent in the early 1990s. As a direct result, the government became willing to recognize, in

91

1993, the equal legal status of public and private property. He argues further that SOE reform will be launched on an additional, more radical stage when SOE revenues drop to less than 50 percent of budgetary revenues. Fan's general argument about the changing incentives to policymakers as SOE contributions to output and revenues drop is surely correct, and represents an important insight into the way in which the policy process unfolds. One might wonder, though, what is the theoretical justification for a cut off specifically at 50 percent in both cases?

Some Criticisms

A few partial criticisms can be made of Fan's excellent paper:

1. The virtuous cycle presented here operates in only one direction. That is appropriate to the stress of the paper on the growth of the nonstate sector. But we should note that the mutual dependence also works the other way. SOEs provided important markets for TVEs during their crucial formative years. Moreover, SOE output has continued to be dominant in sectors with substantial economies of scale and significant public goods characteristics. These sectors are "harder to reform." Continued growth of SOEs in these areas has guaranteed the supply of crucial infrastructural services and producer goods which might not have been supplied so smoothly if a premature effort had been made to privatize those sectors. We need only ask whether Chinese growth has been substantially slowed in recent years by shortfalls in electric power, highway transport, or communications facilities? In general, despite some bottlenecks, the answer is no. SOEs are providing the telecommunications backbone, and the increased power generation. Governments are building the highways. This may not be the first best optimum path, but it is one that works and in which rapid nonstate development depends on some degree of health in the state sector, at least for a period.

2. Data are presented on the state sector in this picture that permit some additional conclusions beyond those Fan makes explicitly. First, while the financial performance of SOEs is deteriorating and they depend increasingly on extensions of formal and informal credit, they continue to contribute a disproportionate amount of revenue to the government budget. Thus, Fan shows that SOEs

contributed 66 percent of budgetary revenues in 1994, notwithstanding the fact that they represented only 42 percent of industrial output in that year (and the large majority of budgetary revenues come from the industrial sector.) One of the reasons for the weakness of SOEs is that the government continues to extract a disproportionately large share of revenues from them; conversely, the TVE, private, and foreign-invested sectors are extremely lightly taxed. This is appropriate at the beginning of reform. However, as reform deepens, greater efforts to achieve a level playing field must be made.

3. It might seem from the preceding two points that I am making a defense of SOEs and an argument in favor of continued state ownership. Nothing could be further from the truth. It is intellectually important to recognize that a stable state sector contributed positively to the progress of reform in its first decade or so. But the argument for a continuing state role is one based solely on stability, not on efficiency (as Fan points out in his second paragraph). From this standpoint, it is hard to see why SOE divestment cannot proceed more rapidly than it has the past few years.

Fan's assessment of recent progress is perhaps too optimistic. It is important to divest small enterprises, but, to be honest, small SOEs contribute a very small share of total industrial output, and this share has already declined dramatically since reform began. Small SOE output declined from 36 percent of the total in 1978 to only 12 percent in 1991, and further since that time. Meanwhile large and medium SOE output was essentially unchanged, going from 41.5 percent to 40.6 percent. So the admonition to "grasp the big and let the little go" is really just ratifying what has already happened.

Why not go faster, and reap more benefits? Most obviously, there are many sectors that are completely competitive and characterized by large numbers of firms. These sectors include textiles, electronics, and most types of machinery. In these sectors, there is no benefit whatsoever to state ownership. Why not advance a national policy that divestment should take place nationwide in competitive sectors? This would be an enormous help in restructuring troubled sectors like textiles, and would establish much more important principles than simply throwing back the smallest fish.

In a related fashion, I think Fan is a bit too sanguine about the importance of shareholding systems as they operate in China today. In many cases, these are merely systems to facilitate the private appropriation of public assets, or represent gambles on the types of guarantees the government provides to its enterprises. The process could be made much more transparent, much more effective, and much more rapid.

In short, then, Fan has presented an interesting and compelling argument for a gradual approach to past and continuing economic reform. However, arguments for gradualism do not in themselves contain prescriptions for the optimum speed of the gradualist transformation. Just because gradualism is superior, it does not follow that the slower you go, the better it is. Here, it appears that Fan has not given enough attention to the need to do more, faster, while still maintaining the overall benefits of the gradualist approach.

References

Fan, G. (1998) "Development of the Nonstate Sector and Reform of State Enterprises in China." In J.A. Dorn (ed.) *China in the New Millennium: Market Reforms and Social Development*, chap. 5. Washington, D.C.: Cato Institute.

McMillan, J., and Naughton, B. (1992) "How to Reform a Planned Economy: Lessons from China." *Oxford Review of Economic Policy* 8(1) (Spring): 130–43.

Naughton, B. (1995) *Growing Out of the Plan: Chinese Economic Reform, 1978-1993.* New York: Cambridge University Press.

World Bank (1996) *World Development Report 1996.* Washington D.C.: World Bank.

6. A True Market Economy for China

Zhou Dun Ren

As the 21st century approaches, the nations of the world are scrambling to develop or readjust visions of their future for the next millennium. It is little exaggeration to say that economic viability and, if achieved, economic prosperity, will be the bottom line while other aspects like social stability, political development, military security, and cultural identity will be somewhat dependent on the former, and therefore of secondary importance. China is no exception. China's political stance and military behavior will be largely decided by its economic reform and development.

The pointer on the roadmap for China is clearly toward a market economy. The Chinese Communist Party, which gives the marching orders to China's 1.3 billion people, has declared that China is, and will be for a fairly long time, in the "primary stage of socialism." Consequently, policies and supporting theories for moving away from the planned "socialist" economy toward the market economy are justified. They include the transformation of public ownership into a "diversified" form, the drastic reduction of the public sector, and the demise of government intervention in economic affairs. In fact, the words "market economy" have often been on the lips of the Chinese people. That, however, does not mean that there has been no misunderstanding or distortion of the true meaning of "market economy."

Economic Freedom: The Essence of a True Market

Let us go to the very beginning. A market involves the exchange of goods and services in a public way. A true market entails such exchanges on the basis of *economic freedom* that both parties enjoy in the transaction. It simply means that both parties can and do

---

Zhou Dun Ren is Professor and former Deputy Director of the Center for American Studies at Fudan University.

decide whether or not to give away what she or he has in exchange for what the other party offers, only on the economic merits each perceives. If one or both parties think otherwise, the deal is off. In other words, at the moment a transaction is conducted, both parties expect to be better off by voluntary exchange.

Economic freedom is extremely important because it forms the basis for political freedom, although other factors (such as religious freedom) also contribute to the development of political freedom. As Milton Friedman (1962: 8) has pointed out:

> Economic arrangements play a dual role in the promotion of a free society. On the one hand, freedom in economic arrangements is itself a component of freedom broadly understood, so economic freedom is an end in itself. In the second place, economic freedom is also an indispensable means toward the achievement of political freedom.

Trying to separate political freedom from economic freedom in theory or practice is both naive and harmful. To believe that when economic freedom is available political freedom can be withheld is undoubtedly naive. To trumpet for political freedom without ensuring economic freedom is outright harmful. The Chinese process toward a true market economy will definitely promote economic and political freedom in China.

Planning versus the Market

It is relatively easy to accept the true meaning of a market when it is confined to individual transactions and when freedom stops at individuals at the moment of a transaction in the market. This might be the situation of two Robinson Crusoes on an isolated island. But when the focus is moved to a larger dimension, to a national economy, more questions arise. One question that is relevant to China, and other "formerly socialist countries," is the virtue of a "planned economy" as opposed to a free-market economy. A number of positive attributes have been used in defense of state economic planning. But two basic flaws are innate with such planning that no nation can run away from. One has to do with the complexities and dynamism of modern economic life that absolutely defy any scientific or human wisdom. No one could possibly manage the vast array of economic activities, let alone manage them well. One standing joke is that the planners are more often than not working actually on the planning of economic activities that are six months or a year old. The failure of central planning has shown that the heavy tread of government planners is much slower than the nimble feet of the market. Planners who lay claim to power and authority to "guide" the national economy toward achieving specific targets are neither gods nor saints; they are subject to human errors and weaknesses, which political ambitions and special interests have never ceased to exploit. If there were any such godly faultless "scientific" economic planning machine, it would immediately break down in any human and mortal hands.

The planners' job, some say, is to control or prevent the economic crises and the polarization of social wealth that result from the "blind forces" of the market, but one has to realize that there is no perfectly efficient market. The "blind forces" come not from the nature of the market per se, but from the imperfections of the market and market transactions. Each individual transaction may be blind if it stands devoid of connections to other transactions, but with the increasingly powerful information technology and its rapid and wide applications, individual transactions are decreasingly blind. In the information age, a true market has the ability to transfer information rapidly and efficiently. Of course, in a modern society, enterprises often replace individuals in market transactions, but that fact does not change the benefits of a true market. Voluntary exchange at the enterprise level is still mutually beneficial, provided enterprises are privately owned and freedom of contract is enforced.

Difficulties in Understanding a True Market Economy

What constitutes the difficulties in China, and perhaps some other Asian countries and regions, in understanding a true market economy can be traced mainly to two factors. First, the traditional Chinese society has been for a long, long time one that is based on the self-sufficient, small-farmer economy. That is not to say that there were no market exchanges but rather the market was primitive and under-developed. Producers essentially provided produce/products and services for their own immediate use or for the immediate use of the landowners, big and small. Until recently, the incentive to expand markets and take advantage of the division of labor and specialization, as necessitated for market development, has been weak. Most people have not been able to benefit or benefit fully from market transactions. Therefore, the experience of, or exposure to, large scale and consistent voluntary exchange of goods and services is lacking. Even when market transactions do occur, the parties to the exchange often do not have an adequate sense of economic freedom or, sometimes more important, due respect for the economic freedom of the other party. The transacting parties in China, if not frequently, do not know the benefits due them in a voluntary deal and sadly do not honor the obligations such voluntary transactions demand if one party thinks he or she is in a "superior" position. Moreover, such positions come not from the market but from the nonmarket situation that was widely accepted, though morally resented, in the traditional small-farmer economy.

Ironically, some people in China often criticize markets for fostering deception, dishonesty, default, forgery, and price gouging. But they seldom realize that a true market would help to protect them from such malpractices. Deng Xiaoping initiated the economic reform and opened China to the outside world in 1978–79. China has been moving toward a true market economy for only 20 years. Patience is needed. It is going to take time for the basic rules of a free market to develop and mature in China to a point where those who violate the basic rules of the market get duly punished and those who observe the market rules are readily rewarded. I believe that the time is not far away, for the awareness is building up: many Chinese who have visited nations with developed market economies return to China praising the free market. They recognize from personal experience that the market itself is not evil, as erroneously believed or indoctrinated, only a distorted market is.

The second factor that has contributed to a misunderstanding of the free market in China and other Asian cultures is related to Confucian values. One of the most outstanding Confucian doctrines is for *yi* (justice) to overcome *li* (profit or material interest). In other words, the ends should be just (*yi*), which is exactly the common scale of values of the community or a nation. But profit (*li*), the incentive for or the result of a transaction in the market, must be secondary, or even shameful as the occasion dictates. But, a common scale of values and a societal regime to achieve such ends, though highly desirable, do not serve the intended purpose because they curtail individual freedom, which is the essence of a true market economy. This is quite often where the Confucianist East, China in particular, differs from the West.

The East could learn from F.A. Hayek (1976: 110–11) who wrote, "The conception that a common scale of particular values is a good thing which ought, if necessary, to be enforced, is deeply founded in the history of human race." However, it is wrong to believe "that such a common scale of ends is necessary for the integration of the individual activities into an order, and a necessary condition of peace." The market, on the other hand, is means-oriented. In the market order, "men, while following their own interests, whether wholly egoistical or highly altruistic, will further the aims of many others, most of whom they will never know." That is why Hayek considers the market "as an overall order so superior to any deliberate organization."

Political authorities at various levels, with the nation state as the highest, claim that they represent that common scale of values and, with the traditional acceptance of the ends-oriented market, feel a legitimate need to manage both the economy and the government. When economic freedom is separated from the political freedom it entails, as in Singapore and Hong Kong, a duality between economic and political freedom is traditionally and culturally recognized. People from the West either question that duality, because they see the mismanagement and corruption it entails, or marvel at the "economic wonders" and argue that Asian tradition and Confucian culture are conducive to fast economic growth.

Transition to the Free-Market Model

The truth is that, if one examines the evolution of government and the growth and maturing of the market in Asian economies, one can hardly fail to notice that it is the Western model that seems to be winning. Indeed, few nations or regions in the West have in any serious sense been attempting to adopt the Asian model. Economic freedom as well as political freedom born from the emerging market in the East are on the rise.

There is an idea in the West that "anyone who lives within his means suffers from a lack of imagination." That idea contrasts with the Confucian virtue of not living on borrowed means. In China the slogan is popular that "international economic practices are to be followed." International practices, indeed, are mostly Western practices in the developed market economy. This is not to say that the Western model is perfect or that Western economic realities are all pretty. On the contrary, there have existed in the West quite a few things on the negative side. Most unfortunately, the negative things seem easier to copy in the emerging economies where the market remains distorted.

Actually, there are those who claim that a strong and big government is necessary, and who may have a hidden distrust of their own people as players in the market economy. Of course, some of the notions and behaviors of the host of such players do not conform to those of the market economy, and the disciplinary hand of the government seems necessary. Thus, the critics have a point, albeit a weak one. The point is there because the nonmarket-oriented culture and tradition of the East endure and could survive long after their economic basis has shifted. The government has a role to play in the transition process. But the point is also weak because big and strong government often impedes the transition process. Moreover, the point can be an excuse to cover up the economic failures and shocking corruption resulting from the abuse of power and mismanagement of the economy. We must have more trust in the market and trust that the true market practice will change people for the better in their economic decisions.

Conclusion

The pointer on the roadmap of the 21st century is for China to go down the road of a true market economy. Any success of the economic transformation will produce, in its own time, progress in the political and social arena. The more developed China is economically, following the free-market model, the more freedom and democracy will advance. Many of the worries and conflicts that bother us today will be taken care of by the coming generations in their stride toward a more developed and mature market economy in China.

References

Friedman, M. (1962) *Capitalism and Freedom*. Chicago: University of Chicago Press.

Hayek, F.A. (1976) *Law, Legislation, and Liberty*. Vol. 2: *The Mirage of Social Justice*. Chicago: University of Chicago Press.

7. China's Future: Market Socialism or Market Taoism?

James A. Dorn

> Though my heart be left of centre, I have always known that
> the only economic system that works is a market economy,
> in which everything belongs to someone—which means that
> someone is responsible for everything. It is a system in which
> complete independence and plurality of economic entities
> exist within a legal framework, and its workings are guided
> chiefly by the laws of the marketplace. This is the only natural
> economy, the only kind that makes sense, the only one that
> can lead to prosperity, because it is the only one that reflects
> the nature of life itself.
>
> —Václav Havel
> *Summer Meditations*

China's Grand Illusion

China's goal of building a "socialist market economy" is a grand illusion. The market and its supporting institutions, notably private property and the rule of law, cannot be grafted onto socialism. Markets are based on voluntary exchange; socialism destroys the spontaneous nature of markets and substitutes government control for individual responsibility. Market socialism, even with "Chinese characteristics," is an unnatural and artificial system which, like the Yugoslav experiment with workers' management, is destined to fail.

Without widespread private property, economic decisions—especially investment decisions—will continue to be political decisions and be subject to the corrupting influence of government power. The recent chaos in East Asian currency markets attests to the destructive nature of state-led development policy fueled by "crony capitalism."

James A. Dorn is Vice President for Academic Affairs at the Cato Institute and Professor of Economics at Towson University.

Government-run banks in South Korea, for example, based their lending practices more on political factors than on sound economic criteria (Yoon 1998). Preferential loans to Korea's large conglomerates, the *chaebols*, at below-market interest rates may have maintained the cozy relations among business leaders, bankers, and politicians, but they also laid the basis for a boom-and-bust business cycle. Creating Korean-style conglomerates in China would be a costly error. Letting natural market forces weed out inefficient firms would be a step in the right direction.[1]

China's state-owned enterprises (SOEs) and banks do not need partial reform; they need to be divorced from the state and subjected to the full force of market competition. Turning to the half-measure of market socialism will only prolong the costs of transition to a real market system and continue to politicize economic life. What China needs are "free private markets," not regulated socialist markets (Friedman 1990: 5). Privatization of SOEs would create real owners who were responsible for their firms' performance and had an incentive to maximize profits by hiring efficient managers and producing what consumers wanted.

The absence of a hard budget constraint for SOEs means that bankruptcy is a hollow threat for most of China's 305,000 state enterprises. And the absence of that threat means SOEs have little incentive to change their inefficient ways. As a result, 50 percent of China's 118,000 state industrial enterprises reported net losses in 1996 (World Bank 1997: 28).[2]

Although China's leaders have been willing to sell off smaller SOEs, they have not embraced the idea of large-scale privatization, for obvious political reasons. Selling off all SOEs would relieve China's massive headache due to the financial drain on the state budget of having to subsidize SOEs, but it would also jeopardize the authority of the Chinese Communist Party. With socialism being the dominant ideology in China, there remain serious obstacles to fostering the market component of market socialism. Turning SOEs

---

[1]As Nicholas Lardy points out, China "ought to be relying on a much more competitive market to drive out inefficient firms and allow some natural consolidation to take place" (quoted in Restall 1997: A22).

[2]The actual state of SOEs could be much worse. Hugo Restall (1997: A22) reported in the *Wall Street Journal*, "State firms are desperately sick: as many as 70 percent are losing money."

into "public" corporations, with the state retaining a controlling interest and restricting the marketability of shares, may be appealing at first sight, but on closer examination can never replicate real markets. As economist G. Warren Nutter (1968: 144) noted 30 years ago when he examined the theoretical case for market socialism, "Markets without divisible and transferable property rights are a sheer illusion. There can be no competitive behavior, real or simulated, without dispersed power and responsibility." That is why he called the idea of market socialism "a grand illusion."[3]

To "revitalize" SOEs, China has begun to establish large, state-run holding companies, called "state asset operating companies," which are supposed to substitute for real capital markets (Walker 1997: 6). In this setup, the state retains majority ownership, restricts the transferability of "shares," and limits the restructuring process to what is politically acceptable. Thus, politics, not the market, prevails. That approach to SOE reform is akin to the experiment with perestroika in the former Soviet Union: it is a pseudo-reform that tries to dress SOEs in market garb but never really changes the underlying ownership structure from state to private property. Commenting on the Soviet effort to revitalize state enterprises, Alexander Tsypko (1991: 289) wrote,

> It took us five wasted years of perestroika to understand that, essentially, the revitalization of Stalinist socialism is impossible; there is no third way between modern civilization and socialism as it is. The market cannot be combined with . . . public ownership of the means of production. A return to the market is impossible . . . without broad-based privatization.

The same criticism applies to China's experiment with market socialism.

China's state-owned enterprises cannot be revitalized; they have a terminal disease that is eating up China's scarce capital. In 1996, for the first time since 1949, state enterprises as a whole suffered a net loss—"the state received no return for its massive investment in SOEs" (EAAU 1997: 10). SOEs absorb more than 50 percent of

---

[3]Almost 60 years ago, F. A. Hayek ([1940] 1948: 203) observed, "To assume that it is possible to create conditions of full competition without making those who are responsible for the decisions pay for their mistakes seems to be pure illusion."

state investment funds, employ 66 percent of the urban workforce, but produce less than 30 percent of total output (EAAU 1997: 338). China's leaders should have the courage to go beyond the policy of "grasping the big enterprises and giving a free hand to the small ones" (*zhua da fang xiao*). All SOEs should be candidates for privatization.[4] Making large SOEs the "pillars" of the national economy by "corporatizing" them, with the government holding all or most of the stock, is a recipe for disaster. That would be market socialism in spades.[5]

From Market Socialism to Market Taoism

China need not be confined to the ideological cage of market socialism by fear of copying Western traditions of market liberalism. The way of the market is universal. The free-market economy is, as Václav Havel (1992: 62) so elegantly stated in the introductory quote, "the only natural economy, the only kind that makes sense, the only one that can lead to prosperity, because it is the only one that reflects the nature of life itself." Since 1978, market liberalization has substantially increased the standard of living of millions of Chinese, and a recent poll showed that many Chinese now believe that "private property is sacred.[6] Today more than 22 million entrepreneurs in China are members of the National Association of Private Entrepreneurs (Pei 1997: 4).

---

[4]Fan Gang (1997: 7) argues that China's "bottom-up" approach to reforming small SOEs may also work for medium and large SOEs, but it will take a long time. That approach allows market forces to bring about spontaneous privatization and then, once proven successful, to legalize it at higher levels. Fan points out that de facto privatization of small SOEs began three years before formal government approval. The "bottom-up" approach is politically attractive because politicians do not have to precommit to ownership reform, so they can take credit for success without having to bear the risk of failure.

[5]Hugo Restall (1997: A22) writes, "Most of the state-owned enterprises that have been corporatized under the 1993 Company Law are still run as private fiefdoms by management at the expense of the state banks. As long as the state remains in control, it appears, it is impossible to make a credible break from the old days of subsidies and easy credit.... Sooner or later the state will have to face up to the need to relinquish both ownership and control."

[6]Minxin Pei (1998: 76) reports, "In a 1993 poll of 5,455 respondents in six provinces, 78 percent agreed with the statement, 'Private property is sacred and must not be violated'."

The climate is ripe for further market liberalization in China. At the Communist Party's 15th Congress, in September 1997, President Jiang Zemin stood firmly behind Deng Xiaoping's economic reforms and favored turning SOEs into joint-stock companies. And, at the National People's Congress, in March 1998, Premier Li Peng stated, "The incompatibilities of government institutions to the development of a socialist market economy have become increasingly apparent" (quoted in Mufson 1998: A1). China's new premier, economic pragmatist Zhu Rongji, needs to recognize that the only way to eliminate those incompatibilities is by eliminating socialism and moving toward a free society with limited government, the rule of law, and private ownership. The announcement at the NPC that the size of China's civil service will be cut in half and that at least 11 ministries will be abolished or streamlined is an indication that China may be ready to move in the right direction (Kynge 1998, Mufson 1998). Yet, as long as China confines itself to creating a socialist market economy and restricts economic liberties, the future path of China's market economy will remain unclear.

In considering what steps to take next, China's leaders should look to their own ancient culture and rediscover the principle of spontaneous order—the central principle of a true market system.[7] In the *Tao Te Ching* (also known as the *Lao Tzu*), written more than 2,000 years before *The Wealth of Nations*, Lao Tzu instructed the sage (ruler) to adopt the principle of noninterference as the best way to achieve happiness and prosperity:

> Administer the empire by engaging in no activity.
> The more taboos and prohibitions there are in the world,
> The poorer the people will be.
> The more laws and orders are made prominent,
> The more thieves and robbers there will be.
> Therefore, the sage [ruler] says:

---

[7]Nobel laureate economist James M. Buchanan (1979: 81–82) has called "the principle of spontaneous order" the "most important central principle in economics." It is the idea that individuals seeking their own gain in a system of private ownership and free markets bring about mutually beneficial exchanges, and that competitively determined prices coordinate economic decisions without central planning. In fact, central planning cannot lead to the market-determined outcome because no one has sufficient information to know that outcome in advance (see Hayek 1945, Lavoie 1990).

I take no action and the people of themselves are transformed.
I engage in no activity and the people of themselves become
prosperous [*Lao Tzu*, 57; Chan 1963: 166–67].

From a public-choice perspective, the foregoing passage implies
that the more the state intervenes in everyday life, the more rent
seeking and corruption there will be. Alternatively, if people are left
alone to pursue their own happiness, a spontaneous market order
will arise and allow people to create prosperity for themselves and
their country. Like Lao Tzu, China's leaders should realize that
corruption stems not from freedom but from freedom being overly
constrained by government. As Nobel laureate economist Gary
Becker (1996: 75) stated, "Markets grow up spontaneously, they are
not organized by governments, they grow on their own. If individuals are given freedom, they will help to develop markets for products
that one cannot imagine in advance."

Just as the principle of spontaneous order is central to economic
liberalism, the principle of *wu wei* ("nonaction") is fundamental to
Taoism. Rulers rule best when they rule least; that is, when they
take "no unnatural action."[8] When government is limited, it can help
cultivate an environment in which individuals can pursue happiness
and practice virtue (*te*). Thus, Lao Tzu writes, "No action is undertaken, and yet nothing is left undone. An empire is often brought
to order by having no activity" (*Lao Tzu*, 48; Chan 1963: 162).

Like water, the market is resilient and will seek its natural course—
a course that will be smoother, the wider the path the market can
take and the firmer the institutional banks that contain it. The challenge for China is to widen the *free* market and provide the institutional infrastructure necessary to support *private* markets. The solution is to discard market socialism and make the transition to "market Taoism." Or, as Gao Shangquan, vice minister of the State
Commission for Restructuring the Economy, recently stated (in
Chang 1997: 15), the challenge is to throw SOEs "into the sea of the
market economy."

---

[8]Wing-Tsit Chan (1963: 136) notes that the principle of *wu wei* does not mean
" 'inactivity' but rather 'taking no action that is contrary to Nature'. " In essence, "*wu
wei* . . . is the embodiment of suppleness, simplicity, and freedom" (Smith 1991:208).

Breaking the Planning Mentality

The collapse of the Soviet Union and the failure of central planning have ended the debate over whether the plan is superior to the market. As Liu Ji (1997), vice president of the Chinese Academy of Social Sciences, recently remarked, "The only people in China who still cling to the idea of central planning are fossilized, dogmatic Marxists." Yet the planning mentality is hard to break—in both the East and the West. It is very tempting for the "best and the brightest" to imagine that they can improve upon the "invisible hand" of the market. But free markets cannot be planned; they emerge spontaneously as consumers' preferences and technology change, and they require well-defined private property rights and freedom of contract.

The incompatibility of government planning and market forces threatens China's future. The vibrancy of the market-driven nonstate sector, which accounts for more than 70 percent of industrial output value, is propelling the People's Republic into the 21st century, but the ossified state sector—driven by state planners—is acting as a drag on development. The "heavy-industry-oriented development strategy," which is reminiscent of the days of Soviet-style central planning, is still ingrained in the collective consciousness of China's ruling elite (Lin, Cai, and Li 1996: 218). Without free capital markets and widespread private property, investment decisions necessarily become political decisions. Corruption and rent seeking will continue in China as long as economic decisions are government driven instead of market driven. When the government holds interest rates at artificially low levels, politics—not prices—determines who gets scarce capital. People become dependent on government and lose their foresight and freedom. Moreover, one control leads to others, so that once a government departs from free-market principles, it tends to head further down the "road to serfdom" (Hayek 1944; Mises 1980, 1998).

Piecemeal reform creates tensions: the rigidity of the old planning system is pitted against the resiliency of the market. In China, old institutions are giving way to new ones, but not fast enough to eliminate "institutional incompatibility." As Lin, Cai, and Li (1996: 226) point out,

> The overall performance of China's gradual approach to transition is remarkable, but China has paid a price. Because the

reform of the macro-policy environment, especially interest-rate policy, has lagged behind reforms of the micro-management institution and resource allocation mechanism, institutional arrangements in the economic system have become internally inconsistent. As a result of the institutional incompatibility, rent seeking, investment rush, and inflation have become internalized in the transition process. To mitigate those problems, the government often resorts to traditional administrative measures that cause the economy's dynamic growth to come to a halt and retard institutional development.[9]

If China wishes to continue its rapid economic growth into the next century and end corruption, it must strive for institutions that are consistent with free-market principles and the rule of law. That is why Lin, Cai, and Li (1996: 226) argue, "It is essential for the continuous growth of the Chinese economy to establish a transparent legal system that protects property rights so as to encourage innovations, technological progress, and domestic as well as foreign investments in China."

The Soviet system failed because it disregarded reality—namely, the reality that the way of the market, not the plan, is most consistent with human nature and, thus, with individual rights to life, liberty, and property. Soviet-style planning destroyed the institutions of property and contract that underpin the free private market and created a rigid economic system that finally collapsed of its own weight. What Soviet citizens witnessed during perestroika and glasnost was "not the organic revitalization of socialism but the withering away of forcibly imposed economic and political structures" (Tsypko 1991: 290). Today, China is also witnessing the "withering

---

[9]In 1984, China decentralized the allocation of credit by allowing local branches of the central bank to extend credit directly to SOEs. But interest rates were kept artificially low and the banks simply extended new credits, which led to rapid money growth and inflation. Instead of deregulating interest rates, the government reimposed central rationing of credit and directly controlled investment projects. Thus, the "planned system" returned. China's "boom-and-bust cycle" is a result of not going all the way to a market economy and failing to insulate the banking system from political manipulation. Because interest rates are set at below-market levels, nonprice rationing and rent seeking are rampant in the allocation of credit in China. For a discussion of these points, see Lin, Cai, and Li (1996: 219–20).

away" of the state-controlled economy, but its "political structures" still await fundamental reform.

Ultimately, economic and political reform are inseparable. To depoliticize economic life, China needs constitutional change and new thinking (*xin si wei*). Chinese scholar Jixuan Hu (1991: 44) writes, "By setting up a minimum group of constraints and letting human creativity work freely, we can create a better society without having to design it in detail. That is not a new idea, it is the idea of law, the idea of a constitution." To accept that idea, however, means to understand and accept the notion of spontaneous order and the principle of nonintervention (*wu wei*) as the basis for economic, social, and political life.

China's leaders and people can turn to the writings of Lao Tzu for guidance. According to noted Chinese philosopher Wing-Tsit Chan (1963: 137), the *Lao Tzu*

> strongly opposes oppressive government. The philosophy of the *Lao Tzu* is not for the hermit, but for the sage-ruler, who does not desert the world but rules it with noninterference. Taoism is therefore not a philosophy of withdrawal. Man is to follow Nature but in doing so he is not eliminated; instead, his nature is fulfilled.

It is in this sense that Lao Tzu writes,

> When the government is non-discriminative and dull,
> The people are contented and generous.
> When the government is searching and discriminative,
> The people are disappointed and contentious [*Lao Tzu*, 58; Chan 1963: 167].

"Lao Tzu Thought," not "Mao Zedong Thought," is the beacon for China's future as a free and prosperous nation. Deng Xiaoping (1987: 189) implicitly recognized Lao Tzu's way of thinking when he said,

> Our greatest success—and it is one we had by no means anticipated—has been the emergence of a large number of enterprises run by villages and townships. They were like a new force that just came into being spontaneously. . . . If the Central Committee made any contribution in this respect, it was only by laying down the correct policy of invigorating the domestic economy. The fact that this policy has had such

a favorable result shows that we made a good decision. But this result was not anything that I or any of the other comrades had foreseen; it just came out of the blue.[10]

Although China can return to its own vision of freedom by embracing and extending Lao Tzu's thought, the idea of "market Taoism" can be enhanced by a deeper understanding of classical liberal economic thought and a study of free-market institutions and public choice. In breaking the planning mentality, therefore, China can learn both from its own culture and from the West.

The Tao of Adam Smith

In 1776, Adam Smith argued that, if "all systems either of preference or of restraint" were "completely taken away," a "simple system of natural liberty" would evolve "of its own accord." Each individual would then be "left perfectly free to pursue his own interest his own way, and to bring both his industry and capital into competition with those of any other man, or group of men," provided "he does not violate the laws of justice" (Smith [1776] 1937: 651).

In Smith's system of natural liberty, the government would no longer have the obligation of overseeing "the industry of private people, and of directing it towards the employments most suitable to the interest of the society"—an obligation "for the proper performance of which no human wisdom or knowledge could ever be sufficient" (Smith 1937: 651).

Government would not disappear under Smith's market-liberal regime, but it would be narrowly limited to three major functions: (1) "the duty of protecting the society from the violence and invasion of other independent societies"; (2) "the duty of protecting, as far as possible, every member of society from the injustice or oppression of every other member of it"; and (3) "the duty of erecting and maintaining certain public works and certain public institutions" (Smith 1937: 651).

---

[10]Kate Xiao Zhou (1996: 4) describes the demise of China's collective farms and the creation of the household responsibility system (*baochan daohu*), with its township and village enterprises (TVEs), as "a spontaneous, unorganized, leaderless, nonideological, apolitical movement."

110

In the private free-market system advocated by Smith, people get rich by serving others and respecting their property rights. Thus, the system of natural liberty has both a moral foundation and a practical outcome. Private property and free markets make people responsible and responsive. By allowing individuals the freedom to discover their comparative advantage and to trade, market liberalism has produced great wealth wherever it has been tried. There is no better example than Hong Kong.

The chief architect behind the Hong Kong economic miracle was Sir John Cowperthwaite, a Scot who admired the work of Adam Smith and other classical liberals. As Hong Kong's financial secretary from 1961 to 1971, he constantly challenged attempts to increase the power and scope of government in Hong Kong. Like Smith, he believed that free private markets would keep people alert to new opportunities by quickly penalizing mistakes and rewarding success in the use of society's scarce resources. Sir John understood that no system is perfect but that, of all known economic systems, the market price system, with its automatic feedback mechanism, has performed the best:

> In the long run, the aggregate of decisions of individual businessmen, exercising individual judgment in a free economy, even if often mistaken, is less likely to do harm than the centralized decisions of a government, and certainly the harm is likely to be counteracted faster [quoted in Smith 1997: A14].

The idea that people have a natural tendency to make themselves better off if left alone to pursue their own interests, and the notion that a laissez-faire system will be harmonious if government safeguards persons and property, are the foundation of the West's vision of a market-liberal order, but they are also inherent in the ancient Chinese Taoist vision of a self-regulating order—an order we might properly call "market Taoism" (Dorn 1997).

The Taoist system of natural liberty, like Smith's, is both moral and practical: moral because it is based on virtue and practical because it leads to prosperity. The Chinese puzzle is to discard market socialism and institute "market Taoism" by shrinking the size of the state and expanding the size of the market—and, in the process, to give rebirth to China's civil society.

Market Taoism and China's Civil Society

China's transition from central planning to a market-oriented system since 1978 has been bumpy, but China is moving ahead. Market liberalization has opened China to the outside world, increased opportunities in the nonstate sector, generated new ideas, and energized civil society. That China's civil society has benefited from the end of communal farming, the rise of TVEs, the expansion of foreign trade, and the increased competition from nonstate enterprises should be no surprise. The more economic activity occurs outside the state sector, the more freedom individuals have to pursue their own happiness and lead their own lives. The demand for economic freedom cannot long be separated from the demand for other freedoms.

The market and its supporting institutions follow both formal and informal rules. The informal rules of conduct that underlie the free market, however, are entirely different from the obedience-driven rules of behavior under central planning. Zhang Shuguang (1996: 5), an economist at the Unirule Institute in Beijing, one of China's first private think tanks, writes,

> Mandatory economy and market economy belong to entirely different ideologies and different ethics. . . . Planned economy is based upon some idea of ideal society and beautiful imagination, but compulsory implementation has been its only means of realization. In such a system, [the] individual is but a screw in a machine, which is the state, and loses all its originality and creativeness. The basic ethics required in such a system is obedience. In the market system, which is a result of continuous development of equal exchange and division of labor, the fundamental logic is free choice and equal status of individuals. The corresponding ethics in [the] market system is mutual respect, mutual benefit, and mutual credit.

Understanding those differences is the first step in China's long-march to "market Taoism."

Although China has yet to accept the rule of law, a legal system is emerging and property rights are beginning to be respected. Informal codes of business behavior are being adopted to better serve consumers and to improve the efficiency of exchange. The opening of the legal system is important because it paves the way for the transition from "rule by law" to "rule of law." Marcus Brauchli (1995: A1) of the *Wall Street Journal* writes,

> The state's steel-clad monopoly on the legal process, which makes the courts just another arm of government, is corroding. China's economic liberalization . . . has spawned a parallel legal reform that raises the prospect of rule of, not merely by, law.

Princeton University professor Minxin Pei (1994, 1995) argues that the gradual development of China's legal system toward affording greater protection for persons and property, the growing independence and educational levels of members of the National People's Congress, and the recent experiments with self-government at the grassroots level will help transform China into a more open and democratic society. He points to the upward mobility of ordinary people, occasioned by the deepening of market reform, and to the positive impact of China's "open-door" policy on political norms. In his view, public opinion and knowledge of Western liberal traditions, such as the rule of law, "have set implicit limits on the state's use of power" (Pei 1994: 12).

People are beginning to use the court system to contest government actions that affect their newly won economic liberties. According to Pei (1994: 12), "The number of lawsuits filed by citizens against government officials and agencies for infringements of their civil and property rights has risen sharply, and an official report reveals that citizens have won about 20 percent of these cases."

Anyone who has visited China's booming coastal areas and new urban centers, such as Shishi in the province of Fujian, can see firsthand the transformation of economic life that is occurring every day in China and witness the regeneration of civil society."[11] Commenting on China's cultural transformation, Jianying Zha (1995: 202) writes,

> The economic reforms have created new opportunities, new dreams, and to some extent, a new atmosphere and new mindsets. The old control system has weakened in many

[11]For a discussion of China's emerging civil society, see Pei (1997). Kathy Chen (1996) describes the model of development in China's new urban centers, such as Shishi, as "*xiao zhenfu, da shehui*—small government, big society—which advocates less involvement by cash-strapped governments and more by society."

areas, especially in the spheres of economy and lifestyle. There is a growing sense of increased space for personal freedom.

China has a long way to go, but denying China most-favored-nation trading status or imposing sanctions on China with the hope of advancing human rights, as some in the U.S. Congress have threatened to do, would be a costly mistake. It would isolate China and play into the hands of hard liners who are critical of market liberalization, thereby undermining the prospects for further reform. The best way to advance human rights in China is not to close China off from the civilizing influence of trade, but to continue to open China to the outside world (Dorn 1996). That will be a slow process, no doubt, but the progress made since 1978 should not be underestimated.

In the coastal community of Wenzhou, for example, there are now more than 10,000 private enterprises, and life is vastly different and freer than before liberalization. According to Ma Lei (1998: 6):

> The development of the private sector has fundamentally changed the way residents of Wenzhou look at the world. Traditionally, Chinese peasants lived by the motto, "facing the earth with the back toward the sky." They were tied to their land. Where they were born was, almost always, where they would work and where they would die. Their options were limited in the extreme. In comparison, a child born in Wenzhou now has an endless number of choices. He can decide to work the land or work for an industrial firm or even start his own business. Market forces have broadened the horizons of Wenzhou residents and educated them to the ways of the world. They have learned that in a market economy entrepreneurs frequently fail. But they have also learned that risk taking, when combined with foresight and hard work, can produce significant rewards—a fact that many business owners in Wenzhou appreciate.
>
> Most important, the people of Wenzhou realize that on the market all is harmonious—that one earns his living not through coercion or brute force but by serving others. That realization has produced a climate in which private industry and private organizations—including private schools—can thrive.

The Path to China's Future

In the long run, market socialism, like central planning, is bound to fail because it is contrary to human nature. For more than 70

years, various forms of socialism were tried in the Soviet Union—
with no success. Why should "market socialism" succeed in China?
Adding an adjective to socialism—even if it is "market"—will not
cure the institutional inconsistencies in China. As Soviet dissident
Vladimir Bukovsky (1987: 127) wrote in *To Choose Freedom*,

> Those of us who have lived under socialism exhibit the once
> bitten, twice shy syndrome. Perhaps Western socialism is in
> fact different and will produce different results. . . . The truth
> of the matter is that the various ideas that seem fresh and
> innovative to Western specialists have already been tested in
> the USSR. And if some of those experiments were eventually
> repudiated, it was not because socialism has been perverted
> in the USSR, . . . , but because these innovations proved to
> be utterly unfit for real life. A cruel experiment half a century
> long has failed to alter human nature.

The "fatal conceit" inherent in the Soviet vision was to think that
government planners could run an economy like a machine and
achieve long-run prosperity (Hayek 1988). Although China has recognized the error of central planning and has introduced a market
system, that system is still half-baked. The question is: Will China
move all the way to market liberalism or remain mired in market
socialism? Will China jump into the sea of private enterprise or
remain suspended in a trancelike state under the illusion that market
socialism will solve its problems?

In considering that question, China's leaders would do well to
heed the advice of Nien Cheng—who, like many in China, suffered
the grave injustices of the Cultural Revolution. She writes (1990: 334),

> China is faced with the choice between socialism and a mar-
> ket system; a mixed system is doomed to failure. The obsta-
> cles to China's development can be removed only if China
> goes all the way toward a private market system with consti-
> tutional protection for both economic and civil liberties. Chi-
> na's crisis is a crisis of confidence; the people are in a half-
> awakened state of mind. The old regime has lost its legiti-
> macy but a new regime has not emerged to fill the vacuum,
> and there has been no clear commitment to the path of mar-
> kets and freedom of choice.
>
> To regain consciousness and emerge from the semi-con-
> scious state that now envelops China will take time. But

115

reality requires that China recognize the death of communism. Reality also requires that China embark on thorough-
going reform or face the prospect of being left behind in the
wake of the liberal revolution that is now sweeping the globe.

China has been willing to experiment with institutional change
since 1978 and has made great progress in reducing poverty. Future
prosperity, however, will depend on whether China turns away
from the artificial path of market socialism and follows the natural
path of market liberalism. The market-liberal vision is not new to
China; it was inherent in the Taoist doctrine of *wu wei* developed
by Lao Tzu and his disciples. China's leaders need only let the
Chinese people return to their roots to see the wisdom of letting the
spontaneous market process organize economic life, while limiting
government to the protection of life, liberty, and property. In that
effort, Hong Kong can play an important role by spreading the "tao"
of Adam Smith and Sir John Cowperthwaite to all of China—thus
allowing the West and the East to meet in one spirit of "market
Taoism."

References

Becker, G.S. (1996) *Gary Becker in Prague*. Edited by J. Pavlík. Prague: Centre
for Liberal Studies.

Brauchli, M.W. (1995) "China's New Economy Spurs Legal Reforms, Hopes
for Democracy." *Wall Street Journal*, 20 June: A1, A8.

Buchanan, J.M. (1979) "General Implications of Subjectivism in Economics."
In J.M. Buchanan, *What Should Economists Do?* 81–91. Indianapolis: Liberty Press.

Bukovsky, V. (1987) *To Choose Freedom*. Stanford, Calif.: Hoover Institution Press.

Chan, W.-T. (1963) *A Source Book in Chinese Philosophy*. Princeton, N.J.:
Princeton University Press.

Chang, Y.F. (1997) "Temper State-Owned Enterprises in Ocean of Market
Economy." Interview with Gao Shangquan, vice minister of the State
Commission for Restructuring the Economy. *Hong Kong Economic Journal*,
9 May: 15. In FBIS-CHI-97-108: "China: Official on State Enterprise
Reform" (Part 2).

Chen, K. (1996) "Chinese Are Going to Town as Growth of Cities Takes
Off." *Wall Street Journal*, 4 January: A1, A12.

Cheng, N. (1990) "The Roots of China's Crisis." In J.A. Dorn and Wang Xi
(eds.) *Economic Reform in China: Problems and Prospects*, 329–34. Chicago:
University of Chicago Press.

Deng, X.P. (1987) *Fundamental Issues in Present-Day China*. Translated by the Bureau for the Compilation and Translation of Works of Marx, Engels, Lenin, and Stalin under the Central Committee of the Communist Party of China. Beijing: Foreign Languages Press.

Dorn, J.A. (1996) "Trade and Human Rights: The Case of China." *Cato Journal* 16(1): 77–98.

Dorn, J.A. (1997) "The Tao of Adam Smith." *Asian Wall Street Journal*, 18 August: 6.

EAAU (1997) *China Embraces the Market*. Barton, Australia: East Asia Analytical Unit, Department of Foreign Affairs and Trade.

Fan, G. (1997) "The Development of Nonstate Sectors and Reform of State Enterprises in China." Paper presented at the Cato Institute/Fudan University conference, "China as a Global Economic Power," Shanghai, June 15–18.

Friedman, M. (1990) "Using the Market for Social Development." In J.A. Dorn and Wang Xi (eds.) *Economic Reform in China: Problems and Prospects*, 3–15. Chicago: University of Chicago Press.

Havel, V. (1992) *Summer Meditations on Politics, Morality, and Civility in a Time of Transition*. London: Faber and Faber.

Hayek, F.A. ([1940] 1948) "Socialist Calculation III: The Competitive 'Solution'." *Economica* 7 (26), n.s. (May 1940): 125–49. Reprinted in F.A. Hayek, *Individualism and Economic Order*, 181–208. Chicago: University of Chicago Press; Midway reprint, 1948.

Hayek, F.A. (1944) *The Road to Serfdom*. Chicago: University of Chicago Press.

Hayek, F.A. (1945) "The Use of Knowledge in Society." *American Economic Review* 35 (September): 519–30.

Hayek, F.A. (1988) *The Fatal Conceit: The Errors of Socialism*. Vol. 1 of *The Collected Works of F.A. Hayek*. Edited by W.W. Bartley III. Chicago: University of Chicago Press.

Hu, J. (1991) "The Nondesignability of Living Systems: A Lesson from the Failed Experiments in Socialist Countries." *Cato Journal* 11(1): 27–46.

Kynge, J. (1998) "China Plans to Cut Civil Service in Half." *Financial Times*, 7 March: 3.

Lao Tzu (1963) *Tao Te Ching* (or the *Lao Tzu*). In W.-T. Chan, *A Source Book in Chinese Philosophy*. Princeton, N.J.: Princeton University Press.

Lavoie, D. (1990) "Economic Chaos or Spontaneous Order? Implications for Political Economy of the New View of Science." In J.A. Dorn and Wang Xi (eds.) *Economic Reform in China: Problems and Prospects*, 63–85. Chicago: University of Chicago Press.

Lin, J.Y.; Cai, F.; and Li, Z. (1996) "The Lessons of China's Transition to a Market Economy." *Cato Journal* 16(2): 201–31.

Liu, Ji (1997) Remarks at the Cato Institute/Fudan University conference, "China as a Global Economic Power," Shanghai, June 15–18.

Ma, L. (1998) "Private Education Emerges in China." *Cato Policy Report* (March/April): 6.

Mises, L. von (1980) *Planning for Freedom*. 4th ed., enlarged. South Holland, Ill.: Libertarian Press.

Mises, L. von (1998) *Interventionism: An Economic Analysis*. Edited by B.B. Greaves. Irvington-on-Hudson, N.Y.: Foundation for Economic Education.

Mufson, S. (1998) "China's Civil Servants: From Red Tape to Pink Slips." *Washington Post*, 7 March: A1, A16.

Nutter, G.W. (1968) "Markets without Property: A Grand Illusion." In N. Beadles and A. Drewry (ed.) *Money, the Market, and the State*, 137–45. Athens: University of Georgia Press.

Pei, M. (1994) "Economic Reform and Civic Freedom in China." *Economic Reform Today*, No. 4: 10–15.

Pei, M. (1995) "Creeping Democratization in China." *Journal of Democracy* 6(4): 65–79.

Pei, M. (1997) "The Growth of Civil Society in China." Paper presented at the Cato Institute/Fudan University conference, "China as a Global Economic Power," Shanghai, June 15–18.

Pei, M. (1998) "Is China Democratizing?" *Foreign Affairs* (January/February): 68–82.

Restall, H. (1997) "China's Long March to Reform." *Wall Street Journal*, 23 September: A22.

Smith, A. ([1776] 1937) *The Wealth of Nations*. Edited by E. Cannan. New York: The Modern Library (Random House).

Smith, H. (1991) *The World's Religions*. Rev. and updated ed. San Francisco: HarperSanFrancisco.

Smith, N. deWolf (1997) "The Wisdom That Built Hong Kong's Prosperity." *Wall Street Journal*, 1 July: A14.

Tsypko, A. (1991) "Revitalization of Socialism or Restoration of Capitalism?" *Cato Journal* 11(2): 285–92.

Walker, T. (1997) "World Bank Urges China to Privatise." *Financial Times*, 18 July: 6.

World Bank (1997) *China 2020: Development Challenges in the New Century*. Washington, D.C.: World Bank.

Yoon, B.J. (1998) "The Korean Financial Crisis and the IMF Bailout." Working Paper, Department of Economics, State University of New York at Binghamton, February.

Zha, J. (1995) *China Pop*. New York: The New Press.

Zhang, S. (1996) "Foreword: Institutional Change and Case Study." In Zhang Shuguang (ed.) *Case Studies in China's Institutional Change*, Vol. 1. Shanghai: People's Publishing House.

Zhou, K.X. (1996) *How the Farmers Changed China*. Boulder, Colo.: Westview Press.

PART II

LESSONS FOR CHINA FROM HONG KONG

8. Free Trade and the Future of China's Market Economy: Insights from Hong Kong

Yeung Wai Hong

> We are the extreme case of an open economy; we are, as a mathematician would say, at the limit where facts vital elsewhere are negligible, and where facts relatively negligible elsewhere are vital.
>
> —Sir John Cowperthwaite

Hong Kong is a testimony to the efficacy of free trade as a policy for growth. By keeping its door to trade wide open, hence throwing its economy on the mercy of international market forces, Hong Kong has squeezed the last drop of value out of whatever scarce resources it has, for survival and for prosperity.

By deliberately abdicating its power to "plan" (i.e., to control) the economy—a fact that is vital elsewhere—Hong Kong's government has allowed market forces at home and from abroad to dictate the direction that the economy is to take, and to temper it so it will stay competitive.

On the downside, this abstinence has avoided what Sir John Cowperthwaite, the architect of this policy, called the inevitable "errors of universal effect" that bureaucratic planning will entail.[1] On the upside, this abstinence gives individual entrepreneurs the freedom—and responsibility—to try and err by making "small-scale mistakes." Sir John sees these "small-scale mistakes" as "almost a condition of general advance."

Yeung Wai Hong is Editor and Publisher of *Next* magazine.

[1]Sir John Cowperthwaite served as Hong Kong's Financial Secretary from 1961 to 1971. For a summary of his theory of nonintervention, see Nancy deWolf Smith (1997).

121

A Policy of Tough Love

Some see this as economic Darwinism raw and pure, while Sir John's detractors attack it as a policy of colonial neglect. I for one see it as a policy of tough love.

In fact, a casual reading of the records of the debates in Hong Kong's Legislative Council over the last quarter of a century would suggest that Hong Kong bureaucrats, like bureaucrats elsewhere, could have made their lives much easier by simply succumbing to various pressure groups' demands for intervention rather than staying the course of laissez faire. But then Hong Kong would have been the worse for it.

That Hong Kong's government has resisted (though not as success-fully as I would like) such pressure—and temptation—to intervene is a vital, though much neglected, fact in Hong Kong's postwar development. I shall now turn to some of the benefits of a policy of tough love from the perspective of someone who is at the sharp end of the market stick.

A Business without a Fallback Plan

I am in the publishing business, a business that is as competitive as it gets in Hong Kong, where more than 40 daily newspapers and 600 magazines fight over a reading population of a little over 5 million. With competition like this, the first order of survival is to keep costs down.

Publishing, of course, entails much more than cost cutting. It is also an industry that tolerates no disruption in production. A magazine or a newspaper will have to come out come hell or high water. As any economist can tell you, meeting deadline and meeting budget are not always the two most compatible objectives in any business.

To shorten our learning curve on entering this business, we decided from the very beginning to concentrate on the software of our business (i.e., reporting, editorial, graphics, etc.) and to relegate the hardware (i.e., printing, distribution, and so on) to outside contractors.

When we went around looking for printers, I was struck by the fact that one of them had only one printing press, albeit a gigantic commercial web capable of printing 640,000 *Time Magazine*-size pages—on both sides—an hour. I asked the printer what did he have for a fallback plan should something go wrong with the only press that he had?

At the time, each commercial web cost about $5 million. Instead of keeping an expensive web idle merely for backup, the printer told me the Japanese manufacturer of his machine had a team of engineers standing by to fly to Hong Kong at a moment's notice should an emergency occur.

Impressed by the confidence that he had in his Japanese manufacturer, we selected him as one of our three printers. We were not so cavalier as to throw caution to the wind by having only one printer. That was five years ago.

No Planning, No Barrier

I am happy to report that in these five years we suffered no disruption in publication, though the Japanese's rapid deployment capability was tested—and they came through—on several occasions. The fact that international emergency service is literally only a proverbial phone call away speaks volumes of the benefits of Hong Kong being a free port.

If Hong Kong were just another intervention-bent country and not a free port, we would have to erect various barriers to protect those sectors that bureaucrats wanted to promote. Cumbersome customs procedures would then have to be devised—and enforced— in order to give substance to such plans. In a word, we would be very much like Japan, where even over-the-counter antihistamine carried by American tourists can be confiscated by airport customs.

Should that transpire, the Japanese engineers could not have come so readily to our aid even if they were prepared and equipped to render such service. Other than allowing us access to good service, the absence of these hindrances also gives us a cost advantage over our protection-prone competitors by lowering the capital outlay of our printer. In a competitive world, that should work to our benefit as well.

A Happy Dumping Ground

The cost advantage wrought by an open border works in less obvious ways too. For one thing, not having trade barriers means that we become the dumping ground of those countries that use taxpayers' money to subsidize their exports. One of our electricity utilities, for instance, is a happy beneficiary of Britain's export credits. This evidently helps, as Hong Kong's electricity bill is among the lowest in the world.

Similarly, South Korea's policy of encouraging—through implicit or explicit subsidies—its construction companies to seek markets overseas also helps to lower the construction cost of many of our infrastructure projects. Unlike experience elsewhere, most of these are completed ahead of schedule and below budget. Fierce—and unrestricted—competition among foreign as well as local construction and engineering companies is a major factor behind this success.

Lately, the Singapore Government Investment Office has also joined this game by investing in a big way in some of the property development projects that help finance Hong Kong's new airport. As most of you know, the Singapore Government Investment Office is funded by Singapore's central provident fund—that is, by forced savings imposed on the Singaporean people. By bringing these hard-earned savings to Hong Kong, what the Singapore government is in effect doing is to help Hong Kong develop with cheap capital.

Free Port for Intangibles

Hong Kong is of course more than a free port for physical commodities. It is a free port for intangible assets in the form of information, ideas, trade contacts, and, yes, *quanxi*, as well. Though the economic contributions of these intangibles are not as readily measurable as tangible ones, they nonetheless assume an increasing importance as we move away from manufacturing to services.

On the information front, major international publications such as the *Financial Times, Economist, Newsweek, International Herald Tribune, USA Today,* and Japan's *Nihon Keizai Shimbun* are printed and sold just like any other newspapers in Hong Kong. That most British of all news organizations, the BBC, has a local relay station, and is heard in Hong Kong as a local station. In addition, we also have ready access to the electronic media, like satellite TV and, of course, the Internet.

In addition, most of the major news organizations (e.g., Dow Jones, CNN, Reuters, Bloomberg, AP, and AFP) have set up operations in Hong Kong. The presence of this large contingency of media organizations suggests that there is a vast market for information in Hong Kong. This market is largely sustained by the numerous international financial institutions (e.g., banks, brokerages, insurance companies, and investment funds) that have established firm roots in Hong Kong. Unlike most places that have sought to promote the financial sector as a clean, sophisticated, desirable sector, Hong Kong offers no preferential treatment to entice these institutions to come. Rather, these institutions come for the freedom not found elsewhere.

Creating Something Out of Nothing

Hong Kong's story is a story of creating something out of nothing. Outside of the financial sector, tourism is another industry that owes its existence to Hong Kong's adherence to an open border in trade. All told, Hong Kong has only 400 square miles, with no great natural wonders to speak of. Yet nearly 12 million tourists visited Hong Kong in 1996. A few of them no doubt came to look at our concrete canyons, but the majority of them evidently came here to shop.

Had we been protectionist in trade, even if cumbersome customs procedures did not drive these tourists away, they would have few goods to buy once they arrive here. Instead, free trade has turned the whole of Hong Kong into one big emporium stocked with merchandise from every corner of the world. Taking advantage of this large presence of shoppers of every creed, race, and nationality, Japanese manufacturers even use Hong Kong as a proving ground to market test their latest electronic gadgets.

Lest you begin to get the idea that an open border benefits only the Japanese and other foreigners, let me give you an example of how one Hong Kong manufacturer beats the Japanese at their own game.

Zhou Wen Hing is one of Hong Kong's most successful textile manufacturers. He first tasted instant noodles on a business trip to Japan, and saw great potential in this convenience product in Hong Kong, as people here are always on the run. He started local manufacturing in the 1970s and named his instant noodles "Doll." Zhou was so successful that Doll became synonymous with instant noodles.

Smelling opportunities in this market, the leading Japanese instant noodle manufacturer, Nissan, took advantage of our open border to give Zhou some competition by starting up local production. Suprisingly, despite its superior technology and deep pockets, Nissan was no match for Doll. However, Zhou eventually sold out to Nissan, as he moved on to the manufacturing of a herbal cure for cancer.

125

A Sobering Effect

By staying away from industrial planning, Hong Kong's government has cultivated an environment where a businessman can shift from manufacturing textiles to concocting a cure for cancer over a cup of tea. This ease of entry is of course no rose garden. The absence of government-erected entry barriers also means that no businessman can feel entirely secure no matter how successful he is at the moment, as competition can spring up (literally out of the blue) in an equally offhanded manner.

This, so to speak, free-for-all approach to trade must have a sobering effect on any Hong Kong businessman. After all, when anyone and everyone can come to compete on your home turf, would you not constantly be on your toes?

Furthermore, knowing that there is no protective shield to keep your real or imagined competitors out, it is not likely that you will enter an industry unless you know for sure that you command some competitive advantage in this activity. As highlighted by Doll's case, it is not enough that you have this advantage locally; it is imperative that this advantage is world-class.

So there is little wonder that over the years, despite the numerous handicaps, Hong Kong has made its mark as the world's leading manufacturer of clothing, toys, watches, and other products. Against great odds, Hong Kong is also a significant manufacturer of higher-end engineering products such as micro motors and semiconductor machinery. In time, though, nearly all these were relocated to China, but this is a different story altogether.

Hong Kong became a leader in these industries by being a low-cost producer. However, the days of competing on price and price alone are long gone. Increasingly the edge that Hong Kong has over our competitors is not how cheap we can make our products, but how quickly we can deliver them, and how late into the production process can we accommodate specification changes.

For instance, nowadays, after placing an order with a Hong Kong garment manufacturer, a U. S. chain store can start selling shirts in New York in 21 days or less. In the old days, this could take anywhere from three to six months.

What chance does a manufacturer have in meeting this compressed schedule if raw materials, from the cotton or polyester yarn needed for spinning, to specialist dyes for the vibrant colors to appeal to finicky taste, to the button, buckle, zipper, or particular type of string needed to articulate a designer's style all have to go through elaborate customs procedures?

To Compete Is to Be Agile

Yes, in today's international marketplace, to compete is to be agile. To me there is no better measurement of Hong Kong's agility than the economic transformation that took place in the 19 years since China embarked on economic reform.

In 1978, on the eve of China's reform, more than half of Hong Kong's labor force was engaged in manufacturing. Eighteen years on, manufacturing's share of the labor force had dwindled to a mere 14 percent by 1996. Meanwhile, services sector's share nearly doubled from 44 percent to 82 percent.

All along, the economy is operating at full blast with the unemployment rate hovering around 3 percent despite a 50 percent jump in the labor force. Any economy that can pull off such a transformation in a space of less than 20 years—and without any apparent ill effect—is agile indeed.

As Hong Kong's economy becomes more and more service oriented, it becomes increasingly difficult to squeeze one more drop of value out of its primary resource—its people—by increasing their productivity. In such an economy, the ability to change course rapidly is of far greater importance than being able to sustain a rapid rate of growth.

In this I am reminded of the aerial attack strategy pioneered by Colonel John Boyd, the genius behind the legendary F-16 fighter jet. Colonel Boyd's strategy puts maneuverability ahead of firepower and speed. To him the key to victory was not a plane that could climb faster or higher but one that could begin climbing or change course quicker.

Implications for China

An economy is, of course, not a fighter plane. Nonetheless, the F-16's maneuverability does have a market equivalent—namely, the ability to stay close to customers, to react quickly to their changing needs, and to accommodate their demand with the lowest possible cost by keeping inventory lean and the supply route short.

Hong Kong's success offers great hope for China, which is better endowed than Hong Kong. If the Chinese government can keep the same faith that Hong Kong bureaucrats have had in the Chinese people's resourcefulness, and if Chinese bureaucrats can follow the example of Hong Kong's civil servants and abdicate their power to intervene—hence avoiding the inevitable "errors of universal effect"—then there is really no limit as to how far the Chinese economy can go. The chief insight from Hong Kong's success is simple: Open up to trade and let market forces loose.

Reference

Smith, N. deWolf (1997) "The Wisdom That Built Hong Kong's Prosperity." *Wall Street Journal*, 1 July: A14.

9. Hong Kong and Financial Liberalization in China: Past and Future

Joseph Y. W. Pang

The Road to Liberalization

In 1979, a small company was set up in Beijing. The company was called Beijing Air-Catering Company, Limited, and it provided catering services to all outgoing aircraft from the Capitol Airport. It was a very ordinary company with a capital of only US$8 million. However, it was arguably one of the most significant companies in the history of the financial liberalization of modern China. Its significance did not lie in its size or the nature of its business but in the ownership of the company. It was owned jointly by the Civil Aviation Administration of China and a Hong Kong company called China Air-Catering Company, Limited. As such, the formation of this joint venture marked two fundamental changes in terms of ownership in China: private ownership and foreign ownership were allowed for the first time since 1949. With the change in the regulations on ownership, China embarked on the road of financial liberalization and has not looked back.

The joint venture was actually set up under The Law of the People's Republic of China on Sino-Foreign Joint Ventures, which was announced in July 1979. That law was the result of the decision made during the Third Plenary Session of the 11th CPC Central Committee Conference held in 1978, which launched the economic and financial reforms that have continued to this day.

Banking Reform

Following the Third Plenary Session, the banking system was the first to undergo reform. In February, 1979, the Agricultural Bank of

Joseph Y. W. Pang is Executive Director and Deputy Chief Executive of the Bank of East Asia, Limited.

China was made a separate economic entity under the State Council responsible for financing the agricultural system in China. In March the same year, the Bank of China was separated from the People's Bank of China with the mandate to handle foreign exchange. Later in that year, the People's Construction Bank of China became an entity under the State Council independent of the Ministry of Finance. Since then, that bank has been responsible for the financing of infrastructure projects.

With the banking system in China reorganized in 1979, the four foreign banks in Shanghai—the Hongkong and Shanghai Banking Corporation, the Overseas Chinese Banking Corporation, the Chartered Bank, and the Bank of East Asia—all started to resume business after having been dormant for 30 years. This prompted the People's Bank of China to set up a regulatory framework to supervise the banking industry that culminated in the promulgation of the Regulations of the People's Republic of China for the Administration of Foreign and Sino-Foreign Joint-Venture Banks in the Special Economic Zones in 1985. With the regulations in place, more and more foreign banks started to open branches in China, and their presence enabled the local banks—the Bank of China, the People's Construction Bank of China, the Agricultural Bank of China, and the Industrial and Commercial Bank of China—to have contacts with modern banking practices. Trade finance was the first banking practice the Chinese banks modernized. They began to follow the foreign banks in adopting the International Chamber of Commerce Uniform Custom and Practice for Documentary Credits. This very much elevated these banks to a new level in terms of service and made documentary credits opened by them more acceptable by the international banking community. The acceptance of their documentary credits by foreign banks had an important bearing on Sino-foreign trade as the Chinese national corporations were no longer required to pay for imports by making remittances at the time when the orders were placed. As their trading partners could only draw against the documentary credits when the goods were shipped, the use of documentary credits in international trade by national corporations not only facilitated better utilization of foreign exchange, but also reduced trade disputes. Furthermore, the adoption of the International Chamber of Commerce Uniform Customs and Practice also led the Chinese banks to honor documentary credits opened by foreign banks more readily, which helped the export trade tremendously.

Another banking service, the credit card, was introduced into China from Hong Kong in 1979. The card was denominated in Hong Kong dollars and was called the East Asia BankAmericard—a joint venture between the Bank of East Asia and Bank of America. The card was later developed into the VISA Card and, today, all major credit cards are accepted in China. This, of course, has been a great boost to tourism. Chinese banks now also issue their own credit cards.

With these further developments in the banking system in China, the State Council formally declared the People's Bank of China the central bank in the Provisional Regulations on the Administration of Banks of the People's Republic of China, promulgated in 1986.

More and more banks from Hong Kong opened branches in China. By May 1996, there were 25 branches and 49 representative offices in various cities. Of all the syndicated loans for use in China, 90 percent were arranged in Hong Kong. Gradually, a complex banking system emerged in China.

Joint Ventures

The Law on Sino-Foreign Joint Ventures was of special significance in the economic and financial reforms of modern China. It gives a framework of compliance for foreign investors to follow. Manufacturers from Hong Kong all jumped at this opportunity and started moving their operations into China to avoid the high rents and high labor costs in Hong Kong. The influx of manufacturers not only created jobs, but also contributed much to the economic and social development of the coastal cities where most of these factories were situated. By the end of 1996, a total of 283,700 entities with foreign ownership had been approved by the Chinese authorities. Of those, 140,000 have begun operations. The total investment amounts to US$177.2 billion.

The Foreign Exchange Market

The influx of capital has greatly increased China's foreign exchange reserves, and it is estimated that between 25 to 30 percent of the issued Hong Kong dollar notes and coins are being circulated in China. This amounts to HK$30 to HK$40 billion. To make better use of the foreign exchange, the national corporations were first allowed to trade it at special foreign-exchange swapping centers in

October 1980. Another type of foreign-exchange swapping center was established in Shenzhen for foreign companies in November 1988. The two types of swapping centers were later merged in March 1994.

Before 1990, there were basically two rates for all foreign exchange—the market rate and the official rate. The official rate was abolished in that year to reflect the true renminbi value of foreign exchange in China. On April 1, 1994, a national foreign-exchange dealing system was established in Shanghai to facilitate more efficient trading. It also enabled the national corporations to use foreign exchange more effectively.

In 1996, renminbi started to become convertible in terms of current-account items. This was a very important development in the liberalization of monetary policy and was a major step toward full convertibility.

Growth of the Stock Market

Because of the increased economic activities and the expansion of business, the local Chinese corporations faced a shortage of capital. To facilitate the raising of capital from the market by Chinese corporations, the Shanghai Stock Exchange was established on December 19, 1990, and the Shenzhen Stock Exchange on July 3, 1991. Shares of national corporations are traded daily from Monday to Friday. A special category of shares, the B shares, are issued for foreign ownership, mainly by investors from Hong Kong. At times, the daily turnover of the Shanghai Stock Exchange is larger than that of the Hong Kong Stock Exchange.

Apart from raising capital from their own markets, the national corporations also go to Hong Kong for their capital needs. In 1993, six Chinese national corporations were listed on the Hong Kong Stock Exchange, raising HK$6.9 billion. In 1994, nine were listed with HK$9.8 billion raised. In 1995, two were listed raising HK$600 million. In 1996, the number was six and the capital raised was HK$3.2 billion. Two more national corporations have been listed in 1997, with HK$2.243 billion raised. Altogether within a short span of five years, a total of 25 Chinese national corporations have been listed on the Hong Kong Stock Exchange, with a total of HK$22.75 billion raised as capital. The shares of these national corporations appear as H shares on the exchange. The total market capitalization of the national corporations and Chinese companies listed in Hong Kong amounts to HK$200 billion or 6 percent of the market. It is estimated that more national corporations will be listed in 1998 and beyond.

Hong Kong listed companies also invest heavily in China. About 40 percent of them have assets north of the border. The total investment is about HK$500 billion.

The listing of Chinese national corporations on the Hong Kong Stock Exchange requires the submission of accounting records maintained according to internationally accepted accounting principles. This requirement has revolutionized accounting standards in China. Previously, accounting was done more or less on a cash basis, but now it is increasingly being done on an accrual basis, which is a great advancement in terms of commercial practice.

Leasing and Real Estate

Capital expenditure of the national corporations is not only financed by cash but also by more unconventional schemes. Dozens of leasing companies, mostly from Hong Kong, have been set up in China to finance the acquisition of capital goods by these corporations and other Sino-foreign joint-venture companies. In 1996 alone, China bought a total of 40 aircraft, and 16 of them were financed through Hong Kong using complicated leasing schemes.

A substantial portion of the economy of Hong Kong is based on real estate. Because of the scarcity of land in Hong Kong, real estate is always very attractive as an investment opportunity. In order to allow real estate developers to develop real properties for sale to people outside China, mainly from Hong Kong, the Regulations for the Administration of Commodity Properties for the Shenzhen Special Economic Zone were announced by the Guangdong Provincial Government on January 23, 1984. This started China's real estate boom. The regulations were initially only applicable to Shenzhen, but other cities soon followed. In 1987, the Regulations for the Transfer of Land Use Rights for Valuable Considerations for the Shanghai Municipality were released. The Property Mortgage Law for the Guangzhou Municipality was adopted on January 1, 1990. On January 1, 1995, the Regulations for the Administration of Urban Land and Property in the People's Republic of China were promulgated to cover the whole country.

133

With regulations and laws on real estate in place, developers from Hong Kong began to acquire land and to build on it. Hong Kong banks then provided mortgages to purchasers of properties. A real estate market began to take shape.

If one examines these regulations and laws closely, one will discover that there is no freehold of landed property in China, but only land-use rights that are, effectively, the leasehold equivalent in Hong Kong. Mortgage regulations are also, to a large extent, a mirror image of the mortgage law in Hong Kong. So in a sense, the real estate market in China was developed with the help of Hong Kong and also financed by it.

Hong Kong and China: The Balance between Past and Future

Looking back, the prosperity of Hong Kong owes much to the economic development of China. Through mutual cooperation, Hong Kong successfully moved its manufacturing operations into China. It offered capital as well as technical knowhow in exchange for cheap land use and labor costs, which helped to maintain its competitiveness in the international market. The economy of Hong Kong also changed. It changed from manufacturing-based to service-based. Its position as an international finance and trade center was further enhanced.

The capital, technical knowhow, and management skill from Hong Kong, in return, contributed much to the economic development and modernization of China. As an intermediary, Hong Kong provided the contacts for China to reach international markets. As its economy developed further, China saw more and more capital invested and technical knowhow transferred from other countries, which accelerated growth even more.

Presently, China and Hong Kong have become each others' biggest and the most important partners in terms of trading and investment. In 1996, the direct trade between China and Hong Kong amounted to HK$1,050 billion. About 80 percent of the Hong Kong manufacturers have invested in China. Their total investment accounts for 60 percent of all foreign investment in China. Altogether, they employed about 5 million workers.

Looking ahead, we shall see China and Hong Kong continue to interact with each other along the path of economic development. Hong Kong companies will pour more resources into the Motherland because of the business opportunities there. China will develop its economy further and faster because of this influx of resources.

The interaction will become even stronger under the "one country, two systems" concept. The Hong Kong Basic Law, which took effect on July 1, 1997, will let the people of Hong Kong rule themselves and also maintain their way of life for 50 years until 2047.

Hong Kong will be able to keep its identity in international bodies such as the World Bank, the International Monetary Fund, the Asian Development Bank, and the International Chamber of Commerce. The Hong Kong Monetary Authority, which is responsible for the supervision of banks in Hong Kong and manages fiscal reserves, will continue to function independently of the People's Bank of China. The same will apply to the Securities and Futures Commission and the Insurance Authority. The Hong Kong Stock Exchange will continue to make its own rules regarding company listing and stock trading. The Legislature will continue to make laws relating to financial matters.

However, the world is ever changing. While we have total confidence in the "one country, two systems" concept and the determination of our leadership to maintain it, it is difficult, if not impossible, to keep the economic aspects of the two social systems rigidly separate. The two economies will continue to interact and to mingle with each other. The supervision frameworks of the two systems will start to converge. Activities like stock trading, fund transfer, foreign exchange, and money market quotations will amalgamate. All these will have to be completed by 2047. It is an agenda that both China and Hong Kong will try to work out. This must be, I believe, Mr. Deng Xiaoping's wish when he conceptualized the "one country, two systems" solution for Hong Kong.

Talking about wishes, I have one of my own. People often ask me whether I am worried about Shanghai catching up with Hong Kong as a financial center. I always tell them that I am not at all worried because China is big enough for more than one financial center, just like the United States has New York, Chicago, and San Francisco. Besides, if Shanghai catches up with Hong Kong, that means China will no longer be a developing country but a very developed country. I would very much like to see that happen. That is my little secret wish.

Comment

Setting the Foundation for a Modern Financial System in China

Klaus Rohland

I am delighted to offer some comments on Joseph Y. W. Pang's excellent paper, "Hong Kong and Financial Liberalization in China: Past and Future." (Pang 1998). I basically agree with the thrust of his arguments. Indeed, throughout the reform process in China, Hong Kong has served as a point of entry for many ideas that are about to transform China's financial sector. This transfer of ideas has been bolstered by impressive financial flows. Since 1978, 57 percent of foreign direct investment in China was either directly from or funneled through Hong Kong. About 90 percent of the syndicated loans for the mainland were arranged in Hong Kong. By the end of 1996, Hong Kong's banking system owed $39 billion to China, and the corresponding claims on Chinese banks and non-banking entities reached $46 billion. Moreover, the process of financial integration is still unfolding in China. Technological progress, financial innovations, and deregulation have spurred private capital flows across China's borders. Pang mentions the use of Hong Kong dollars as the medium of exchange in parts of southern China in this regard, and large amounts of capital flow are rumored to cross the mainland's border with Hong Kong each day. There is no doubt: Even before reunification the economies of Hong Kong and China were already closely intertwined through trade, investment and, above all, human interaction.

China and Hong Kong have a lot to offer each other. Reunification will make the southern part of the mainland Hong Kong's natural

---

Klaus Rohland is Country Director of the Papua New Guinea and Pacific Islands Country Management Unit at the World Bank.

hinterland. Indeed this process already started years ago. Consider the flow of capital from Hong Kong to Guangdong and Shenzhen and think of the impressive level of investment that took place. Indeed it is fair to say that Hong Kong's integration with its neighboring provinces was a condition for Hong Kong's successful transformation from a manufacturing sweatshop to a sophisticated center for international trade and financial services.

Hong Kong's strength lies above all in its valuable human capital and professional expertise in finance, trade, and public administration—skills that China sorely needs. Again, consider the figures: Hong Kong is home to 405 banks and branch offices of which 335 are foreign. The net daily turnover of its foreign exchange market ranks fifth in the world and the capitalization of its equity market rank's ninth in the world. Hong Kong hosts about 1,300 accounting firms and 3,000 managing consulting firms. Such a high concentration of bankers, accountants, and lawyers could prove to be of some use to China's financial sector reform and development. Over the years, Hong Kong has established a highly responsive lean government and a sound legal system that ensures the free flow of information and transparency of the regulatory framework. These factors have undoubtedly contributed to its success.

Financial Sector Reform

Let me turn to the reform of the financial sector in China. Indeed, as Pang reported, considerable progress has already been made in setting the foundation for a modern financial system. But financial reform is not a choice for policymakers to make. In fact, the markets are making it for them. The choice facing policymakers is how to harness and channel the reform process for the betterment of the economy and the overall soundness of the financial system. These are difficult questions, made more complex by enormous challenges confronting the financial sector. The perilous condition of state finances has placed a growing burden on banks to fund state-directed investments and to extend working capital loans to loss-making state enterprises at government-determined interest rates. The result is a banking system with limited banking skills and a high proportion of nonperforming assets; a central bank with insufficient experience in monetary management, few policy instruments, and inadequate

138

regulatory and supervisory capacity; and a highly volatile capital market.

Further policy reforms and institutional strengthening and modernization of the sector are necessary in order to enhance the efficiency of resource mobilization and allocation. Development of an efficient financial system in China would require an impressive list of actions. At the macro level, it would require: an effective monetary policy that relies on indirect control instruments, further strengthening of the legal and prudential framework for banks and nonbanks, successful transformation into commercial banks of the formerly specialized banks, further reforms of state-owned enterprises (SOEs) in order to deal with delinquent loans and increase their interest sensitivity without which indirect monetary policy cannot be effective, further reforms in the investment regime and public finances in order to provide banks with increased autonomy and for the government to finance its priority investment program as well as some of the public services now supplied by state enterprises, enhanced competition, new financial accounting standards, risk provisioning rules and reduced taxation, and further liberalization of interest rates to provide financial institutions with means to price risk.

At the institutional level, it would require: increased autonomy and accountability of bank managers, new corporate governance and incentive mechanisms, significant reorganization (including reduction of overblown staff), and adoption of new systems and procedures.

Above all, it would require converting human resource into human capital to enable banks to manage commercially their assets and liabilities. At present, neither the regulators nor the financial institutions are capable of identifying and controlling the multiple risks in an increasingly market economy. The existence of strong linkages between the fiscal, banking, and enterprise sectors is a major obstacle, and organizational changes needed to transform the existing institutions with different mindsets, cultures, and traditions into market-based institutions will take time. The pace of commercialization of the formerly specialized banks will to a large extent be influenced by state enterprise reforms, since the financial health of one affects the financial health of the other.

The Credit Plan

The credit plan has been the centerpiece of the system for controlling and allocating credit in China. By setting limits on prices (interest rates) and quantities (credit ceilings on financial institutions), the People's Bank of China (PBC) tried, often unsuccessfully, to accomplish the dual objective of directing credit while maintaining macroeconomic stability. The credit plan remains binding for the state banks, thereby preventing the PBC from using monetary control effectively and efficiently. The authorities are aware of the increasing inconsistency between China's highly decentralized and largely market-driven economy and centrally allocated credit, and have been trying to reduce the scope of the credit plan. They modified the relationship between the PBC and the specialized banks and between the PBC and the government, and are further developing China's financial infrastructure. The new Central Bank Law has improved the institutional framework for monetary policy. Direct central bank lending to the government is now prohibited and, unlike in the past, PBC branches are no longer allowed to extend credit to fund policy loans and local governments. The 1995 credit plan covered the policy banks and the specialized banks, but other financial institutions' lending is now largely controlled through asset/liability management ratios. In addition, lending quotas that used to be fixed by each branch are now fixed by each bank, thereby allowing the formerly specialized banks to experiment with asset/liability management in selected branches.

Monetary Policy

Since the unification of the exchange rate in 1994, the direction, content, and form of monetary policy and its implementation have undergone significant changes. The discontinuation of direct financing of the government, opening of a rediscount facility, centralization of lending at the PBC's Head Office, authority to recall loans extended to banks, and introduction of asset/liability management guidelines for banks have all helped in the increased use of indirect instruments to manage aggregate demand. The government's stated position is to gradually phase out the credit plan, while pressing ahead with the development of indirect instruments. The working capital credit plan is expected to be abolished in 1998 as the large state-owned banks are brought under asset/liability ratio management. The fixed asset credit plan is expected to be phased out by the end of the ninth five-year plan (1996–2000). An integrated interbank market was established in January 1996, allowing for flexibility in short-term money market rates, and the PBC started open market-like operations based on Treasury securities in April 1996. Substantial reduction in the role of the credit plan, setting up a well-designed auction system, and further liberalization of interest rates will permit full-fledged open-market operations. It should be noted that the prevalence of large sectors of the economy operating with no commercial objectives, as evidenced by the large number of loss-making SOEs, limits the effectiveness of indirect monetary policy, which relies on interest-rate elasticity as the main transmission mechanism for monetary policy.

Interest Rates

The term structure of interest rates reflects government priorities on resource allocation across sectors and types of borrowers and incorporates some recognition of a positive, although quite flat, yield curve. However, the rate structure is unduly complex, often obscuring real economic priorities. Margins between lending and deposit rates tend to fluctuate arbitrarily without reflecting an upward-sloping yield curve. On several occasions deposit rates have exceeded lending rates of similar maturity. Low and often negative real interest rates in recent years contributed significantly to the rapid increase in the demand for credit and investment expenditures, encouraging relatively capital-intensive production and complicating the task of aggregate demand management. At the same time, however, the volume of bank deposits has grown enormously, reflecting China's high savings rate, strong public confidence in the banking system, and dearth of alternative financial and real assets for most institutional and household savers. The unusually rapid growth in bank deposits in the last few years also owes something to the reintroduction in 1993 of inflation-indexed deposits for households.

International experience has demonstrated that while interest rates can be deregulated quickly and seemingly easily, it can bring in its wake considerable financial disruption if it is not preceded by adequate institutional and policy preparation and the deployment of skilled and experienced central bank staff. Thus, while deregulated interest rates are an important and desirable objective, they can best be fully attained only in the final stages of the financial reform process after a number of conditions—for example, macroeconomic stability, contestable financial markets, healthy financial institutions and real-sector enterprises, trained bank staff and bank supervisors, and modern accounting and auditing systems—have been put in place. While some of these conditions are unlikely to be met soon in China, the government needs to phase in reforms that reduce the most egregious distortions first and subsequently extend greater freedom to market participants in stages.

The government plans to undertake a phased liberalization of administrative controls on interest rates, establishing initially a regulated interest rate system based on economic conditions. The level of interest rates, especially lending rates, is gradually becoming an important tool for managing aggregate demand. The effectiveness of interest rates should increase as SOEs become increasingly interest-rate sensitive in making their decisions. The government has freed interest rates in the interbank market, and is now adjusting interest rates more frequently to reflect economic conditions. Also, the government has been successful in controlling inflation. By reducing deposit rates by more than lending rates, the authorities are trying to provide banks with higher margins to help them recover costs and build up their capital and reserves. Banks and nonbanks are permitted to vary their lending rates within a prescribed band (from -10 to $+20$ percent) of the base rate. Interest rates at present are positive in real terms.

Reform of the Fiscal Sector and SOEs

Reforms in the financial sector are intricately linked to reforms in the fiscal and SOE sectors. State banks historically have acted as fiscal agents of the government, and these banks, rather than the budget, have financed a large proportion of the investments and working capital needs of state enterprises. Similarly, enterprises, rather than the budget, have been responsible for the provision of a large number of social services—education, health, pension, housing—for their workers. Government's reform measures and the resultant increased competition have had an adverse impact on the financial performance of SOEs. Initially, the SOEs were able to stay in business as a result of government subsidies and new credits from the banking system under a demand-driven and lax credit and monetary policy environment. Concerned with macroeconomic stability and high inflation, the authorities have been gradually reducing subsidies to state enterprises and tightening credit, reflecting both the PBC's policy stance and the banking system's increasingly commercial focus. This has further aggravated the financial position of SOEs and made their structural deficiencies more obvious. Weak SOE performance has led to a further weakening of the banks' portfolios, estimated by the PBC at 20 percent of loan portfolios. If international norms are applied, nonperforming loans may constitute a much higher proportion of total loan portfolios.

The Institutional Infrastructure

The financial sector infrastructure—legal, informational, prudential, and payments and clearance—is weak. Until 1994, financial sector reforms lacked a legal foundation. This gap was filled by the passage in 1995 of a number of important laws, including the Central Bank Law, the Commercial Banking Law, the Negotiable Bills Law, the Insurance Law, and the Guarantee Law. While the Central Bank Law provides the PBC with the powers to regulate and supervise the banking system, the Commercial Banking Law stipulates capital adequacy, legal lending limits and insider trading, asset/liability management, and provides for compensation to financial institutions for losses that may result from loans to special projects at the behest of the government.

The implementation of laws would depend upon how soon the operational guidelines based on detailed rules and regulations are formulated and enforced. The fundamental shift in the role of regulations from compliance with economic directives under the central planning system to setting of prudential norms and their compliance by financial institutions will take time. It also implies the existence of accounting standards and financial reporting, adoption of risk-based loan portfolio classification, and a focus on the overall risk borne by individual banks and nonbanks.

During the last several years, the PBC and the Ministry of Finance have initiated steps toward overhauling the financial and enterprise accounting systems, and prudential banking framework. A modern payment and clearing system has been designed and the pilot phase has been initiated. To date, drafts of about 30 accounting standards have been prepared. The draft basic banking accounting standards include, among others, definition of past due loans and a loan classification system, accrual of interest, and loan loss reserve. Similarly, the PBC has identified deficiencies in the asset quality of banks through reviews of selected branches of specialized and nationwide banks. It has prepared a draft comprehensive examination procedure manual, studied various international models of supervision, organized training courses for its supervisory staff, and reorganized its supervisory functions. Enforcement of regulations, however, would pose a major challenge for the PBC as implementation would require substantial further training of supervisory staff, and development of an off-site surveillance system. The difficulties involved in enforcing prudential control over the various nonbank financial institutions is even more formidable, since supervision of NBFIs is qualitatively different from that of banks. The PBC plans to set up a complete supervisory system for NBFIs in the next five years.

Institutional development of financial institutions is another issue high on the reform agenda. The four specialized banks, with over $1 trillion in total assets, a workforce exceeding 1.6 million, and with almost 150,000 branches and outlets, face important external and internal constraints to commercialization. The external constraints include constraints in the present macroeconomic and policy framework as well as in the broad institutional framework that have a negative impact on the banks in their effort to enhance efficiency. Like other SOEs, these banks have to also shoulder heavy social welfare responsibilities for their staff. The internal constraints are also formidable in view of the specialized banks' past role as fiscal agents of the government. The specialized banks lack the appropriate governance and legal framework, suffer from inadequate financial policies, and weak and fragmented business infrastructure. Accounting standards that do not follow international norms on classified assets and a loan loss provisioning policy that is not based on the banks' actual risk profiles, need to be replaced by modern standards. The issue of shielding the specialized banks from losses on directed credits to SOEs and providing them with an environment to maintain a positive net worth assumes paramount importance in the prevailing monetary and financial conditions in China.

Equally important for banks to operate profitably in a deregulated environment is the existence of human and managerial capital in the banking system. In a market-based competitive system, banks should be able to assess the degree of riskiness of assets, rank them according to the size of risks involved, appraise the creditworthiness of borrowers and the economic and financial viability of projects, and comprehend the significance of changing economic environment domestically and internationally for banks' operations. Such skills are conspicuous by their absence in China, where all decisions about credit allocation and pricing of loans have been centralized until recently in the government. However, the banking system will not remain sound unless there are borrowers with a positive net worth. Reform of SOEs, including the provision of a social safety net, is critical to the full commercialization of the specialized banks. It is only after the specialized banks are placed on strong commercial footing, and the prudential regulatory framework is in place, that further substantial deregulation of the financial sector, including full liberalization of the interest rate policy and increased competition from domestic and foreign banks, can be undertaken.

Some progress has been made over the past years. With the establishment of the policy banks in 1994, the government has given the formerly specialized banks increased autonomy in their lending decisions and they are no longer required to make policy loans at their own risk. The banks now can turn down funding requests for government-approved projects, considered risky or financially nonviable. The Commercial Banking Law has clarified commercial banking principles, and specialized banks are required to draft new corporate charters. Like other banks, the large state banks have also been made responsible for their profits and losses, and under the single legal person concept, lending control has been centralized in the Head Office in order to avoid problems associated with branch lending under pressure from local governments. The banks have been given the liberty to experiment with different systems and processes, for example, closure/merger of unprofitable branches, management by asset/liability ratios, and new incentive systems that link bonus to performance. All specialized banks are following a zero growth employment policy, and giving priority to upgrading the skills of staff and management.

New Policy Banks and Competition

The main objective in establishing the three new policy banks is to gradually shift the burden of financing social and development projects of the government away from specialized banks. The authorities define policy lending as loans for long gestation, low profitability, or high-risk projects considered essential for national economic development that would otherwise not be financed through the commercial banking system. The mandate of policy banks needs to be further clarified, especially their relationship with the rest of the financial system. The government needs to issue detailed regulations on how policy banks will be expected to meet their charters, and how the banks are going to finance their operations, who will bear the burden of any losses against nonpayment of interest or principal, and how those losses are going to be covered by the budget.

Greater competition is a *sine qua non* of financial reform. In order to increase competition in the banking sector, the authorities have decided to diversify ownership of nationwide commercial banks, license nonstate-owned banks, merge and convert the urban credit cooperatives (UCCs) into city united commercial banks, and permit selected foreign banks to conduct local currency business on a pilot basis. The objective for now is to retain the four specialized banks as 100 percent state-owned commercial banks. Two nationwide banks, Hua Xia Bank and Everbright Bank, have already been converted into joint-stock companies and new shareholders now account for between 50 and 80 percent of the equity of the banks.[1] China also licensed its first nonstate-owned bank, Minsheng Bank, which went into operation in early 1996. The provincial capital-level UCCs are being merged and converted into city united commercial banks with new shareholders, including the International Finance Corporation as a potential shareholder in the Shanghai City United Bank. Such mergers and conversions have already taken place in a number of other major cities, and the plan is to have a large number of such banks in the coming 10 to 15 years.

Conclusion

This is a long list of issues that need to be addressed to further advance on the road of financial sector reform. How will reunification with Hong Kong affect this process? Under the guidance of the

[1]While foreign financial institutions are not permitted to take equity positions, the Asian Development Bank has been given special exemption to take a small shareholding in Everbright Bank.

State Council and in accordance with the Basic Law of the Hong Kong Special Administrative Region of the People's Republic of China, the PBC explicitly stated the primary policy of "one country, two currencies, two monetary systems, and two monetary authorities within one sovereign state."

As is the case today, Hong Kong financial institutions that operate in the mainland will continue to be regarded as foreign institutions and mainland financial institutions in Hong Kong will be regulated by the Hong Kong authorities. This seems to indicate that the impact of reunification on the financial sector reform in China will be negligible as, on economic grounds, Hong Kong and mainland China will continue to be different entities. But there is more to it. Surely, the process of unification will strengthen the already existing strong feelings of unity and togetherness between Hong Kong and the mainland. And the process of economic integration based on different systems is already underway. There is a good case for Chinese banks to learn from the experience of their Hong Kong cousins. And if the full set of Hong Kong's experience can be brought to fruit in mainland China, surely the mainland stands to gain.

In the wake of unification, pundits everywhere in the world have pondered the question how this would impact Hong Kong and its economic system. It is time that we focus on the other side of the coin. Let us emphasize the major benefits for the reform process in the economy of the mainland that already have been realized and will continue to be reaped.

Reference

Pang, J.W. (1998) "Hong Kong and Financial Liberalization in China: Past and Future." In J.A. Dorn (ed.) *China in the New Millennium: Market Reforms and Social Development in China*, chap. 9. Washington, D.C.: Cato Institute.

10. Hong Kong as a Model for China
William J. McGurn

The Legacy of Sir John Cowperthwaite

When I was a somewhat younger reporter starting out in Hong Kong, I once rang up Government Information Services for what I thought would be a routine bit of information: Hong Kong's gross domestic product for 1963. My intention was to use the numbers to show how much Hong Kong had grown over the succeeding quarter-century. But a funny thing happened. The GIS chap on the other end of the line apologized that he didn't have the figures. And the reason he didn't have them, he explained, was that the financial secretary at the time, one John James Cowperthwaite, had refused to allow anyone to collect them.

At the time the Cowperthwaite name meant nothing to me, but my curiosity was piqued. After asking around, I found that Cowperthwaite had been financial secretary from 1961 to 1971, and when I looked into his record I discovered that during his tenure industrial wages in Hong Kong doubled, exports grew by an average 13.8 percent each year, and the percentage of households in acute poverty shrunk to 16 percent from more than 50 percent (Rabushka 1979: 18–20). I went back to the *Hong Kong Hansard* and poured through the budget debates in the Legco over which Cowperthwaite presided. Almost 10 years after first having heard his name, I finally met the great man. Over a delightful lunch at the Mandarin Grill I finally put to him directly the question that had long bothered me. "Why on earth," I asked, "did you forbid people to keep figures on Hong Kong's GDP?" Sir John—as he is now called—barely looked up from his plate. "If I had let them keep the figures, they could only

---

William McGurn is a member of the editorial board of the *Wall Street Journal* and former Senior Editor of the *Far Eastern Economic Review*.

misuse them." In that moment I knew that were I ever inclined to become a Boswell, this would be my Dr. Johnson.

Today Sir John's shadow is long gone from the corridors of Hong Kong financial secretariat, but as my fellow Cowperthwaite fan Yeung Wai Hong of *Next* magazine will tell you, Hong Kong—and China—would do well to heed the lessons so easily distilled from his reign. Indeed, such is Yeung's enthusiasm that he has even proposed that the Hong Kong government erect a statue of Sir John outside the entrance to the Legislative Council, so that politicians would have to pass Sir John, at least metaphorically, before going inside to spend the hard-earned dollars of their constituents. For Sir John's own principles were as straightforward as they come: First, that you don't rob Peter to subsidize Paul's preferences; second, that the money the government spends is not its own. It belongs to the people.

In certain quarters—distressingly enough, in the office of Hong Kong's newly appointed chief executive, C.H. Tung—these principles are at times felt to be quaint anachronisms of another century, ill-suited for the complexities of a modern world. In fact, they are more relevant than ever, particularly for a China looking over the horizon to what it hopes will be a prosperous tomorrow. The world knows well about the miracles of Ludwig Erhard in Germany; Park Chung Hee in Korea; or Lee Kuan Yew in Singapore. Indeed, there is even a whole new city, the Suzhou Industrial Park, designed and run in accord with Singapore standards and principles. Yet Sir John remains unknown even to those who most benefitted from his most invisible (and most restrained) of hands. The irony has not gone unnoticed. In Hong Kong following his last visit to China in 1993, Milton Friedman remarked that while he often heard talk in China of the Japanese model, the Korean model, or the Singapore model, he had yet to hear a single Chinese there cite the Hong Kong model. Indeed, in many ways Hong Kong seems to be in the position of the unappreciated second daughter, who is more accomplished than her sister but nonetheless in the background.

Sir John's own anonymity suggests one key reason the Hong Kong model might not have been as attractive to bureaucrats: It removes them from center stage. To accept that as a principle, much less embrace it in practice, demands a special kind of person. Alas, while bureaucratic modesty performs miracles in the economic realm, in the area of public relations this same reticence, more often than not, means the triumph of the more aggressive and interventionist models. Even in retirement, for example, Sir John remains one of the most elusive and self-effacing civil servants I have ever met, and has in fact greeted all attempts by admirers such as Yeung and myself to troll his glories as in exceedingly poor taste. On his annual visits back to the territory, he shuns the spotlight and exudes a marked diffidence about his contributions. "I did very little," he says. "All I did was to try to prevent some of the things that might undo it." That is true enough. But the record of governments all across the globe shows how few in his position who might make the same claim.

The Marriage of British Common Law and Chinese Enterprise

That, of course, has been the entire secret of Hong Kong. From the start, the marriage of the British common law and Chinese enterprise has proved a fruitful union. As Anson Chan, the chief secretary, recently told a meeting of businessmen in Manila, Hong Kong is a place that has prospered on the belief that "business decisions are best left to businessmen, not bureaucrats" (Chan 1997). But do not take Mrs. Chan's word for it. Hong Kong has enchanted even the most revolutionary of spirits. No less than Sun Yat Sen—who was once tossed out of Hong Kong for his politics during his student days—suggested that if he could design a China of the future, it would look like Hong Kong. In a commencement address at the University of Hong Kong in 1923, Dr. Sun came straight to the point. "Where did I get my revolutionary and modern ideas from?" he asked rhetorically.

> I got them in the colony of Hong Kong. I compared Heungs-han with Hong Kong and, although they are only fifty miles apart the difference of the government impressed me very much. Afterwards I saw the outside world and began to wonder how it was that foreigners, the Englishmen, could do so much as they had done for example with the barren rock of Hong Kong within 70 or 80 years, while in 4,000 years China had no place like Hong Kong [in McGurn 1997a: 27–28].

Dr. Sun exhorted the students to "carry this English example of good government to every part of China."

151

Today Hong Kong entrepreneurs are doing just that. In the short time since Deng Xiaoping opened China's door in 1979, the two sides have become each other's largest trading partner. It has been an almost perfect fit. What China offers Hong Kong is a vast source of labour and land, enabling Hong Kong to offload its lower-value-added manufacturing. What Hong Kong offers China is the capital and know-how China needs to modernize. In many ways it is similar to what Mexico and the United States might expect from each other today, though with this compelling difference: China and Hong Kong come from the same culture.

After July 1, 1997, the context of this interaction will change yet again when the Chinese flag is once again raised over Hong Kong soil and the two are once again part of the same country. In the year leading up to that event, the news was dominated by a discussion about the political arrangements that should operate in Hong Kong after the transition. But, there was also a parallel debate, one that did not receive the coverage it deserved. That debate had to do with the kind of economic system that Hong Kong should have in place after 1997. In a speech he made shortly after accepting the nomination as the first chief executive of the post-British Hong Kong, Tung Chee Hwa told the Chinese Chamber of Commerce that the territory might have to rethink its aversion to industrial policy. Shortly before the transition, Tung declared "A non-interference policy would not meet the needs and strengthen the competitiveness" of today's Hong Kong (quoted in Sung 1997: 1). His about-face begs the question: If Hong Kong is itself unsure of its system, by what right should anyone expect China to embrace it?

Applying the Hong Kong Model to China

As it happens I think Tung is wrong. And I think he is wrong in two ways: Empirically, in his mistaken belief that Hong Kong's manufacturers cannot survive without government help, and philosophically, in the idea that the Hong Kong model may have served its purpose in the past but has little relevance in the future. To the contrary, in a world ever more interlinked, where flexibility is at a premium, the Hong Kong model is even more suited to the competitive pressures of the 21st century than the 20th.

The Hong Kong model offers immediate application for China in three broad areas. First, it demonstrates to a China grappling with its own raison d'etre—I think we can all agree that "market socialism with Chinese characteristics" is less an economic philosophy than a political fig leaf—the advantages of an economy with few of the market-distorting policies that now weigh so heavily on pro-business regimes elsewhere in the region. Second, it offers a way to deal with what no less than President Jiang Zemin sees as the great scourge of modern China, corruption, a disease, which he says, "is almost in vogue" in many parts of the country (AFP 1997). And third, it holds out a new social contract between Chinese governments and Chinese peoples, which if embraced, would help spare tomorrow's China of the friction and discord that today plague even the successful tiger economies in the region.

The Benefits of Economic Freedom

Take the first point. As an economy, it is true that Hong Kong enjoys many unique advantages China does not. It has almost no defense expenditures. It is located on the periphery of the world's largest developing economy but at the same time is well-posititioned to tap into Western capital and know-how. And until recently, as a colony it had no real politics to speak of. So the idea that Hong Kong might simply be transposed to China—as Singapore appears to be trying to do in Suzhou—is absurd.

Nonetheless, the broad principles that have proved so successful in Hong Kong are not unique to it; they reflect the larger laws of economics and Hong Kong's relative purity in abiding by them— both the Heritage Foundation and Cato Institute are united in scoring Hong Kong as the freest economy in the world. Surely Hong Kong does provide an important lesson for a China that hopes one day to be as modern and advanced as any Western nation.

The challenges for China remain immense. When Deng Xiaoping began the reforms two decades ago, the obvious strategy was to allow new sectors to bloom rather than trying to discipline the old ones. That approach has worked tolerably well: The de facto privatization of agriculture eliminated the problems of famine, which periodically had plagued China under Mao, and the flowering of a private sector now produces more than two-thirds of China's output. The problem today is the failure to bite the bullet on the country's 118,000 industrial state-owned enterprises. That problem is no secret: Although those enterprises employ two-thirds of China's

170 million urban workforce, they account for less than one-third of industrial output (*The Economist* 1997: 54–55). The money required to maintain those companies, moreover, is constraining the development of China's financial sector. State banks, for example, have argued, with some credibility, that their 30 percent default rate is as much the result of the policy-directed loans they are forced to make as any gaps in their credit analysis (Woo 1997: 34).

Hong Kong's own evolution demonstrates what might be unleashed with simple opportunity. When China opened its door, it could not have come at a more propitious time, for the Hong Kong of the late 1970s was starting to feel the competitive pinch of emerging tigers such as Taiwan and Korea. Although Hong Kong's involvement in the southern coast of China is well known, less appreciated is that Hong Kong capital remains the largest source of foreign investment in most of China's other provinces too. Hong Kong's Census and Statistics Department reports that some 97,300 Hong Kong people are today working in China, representing more than 250,000 Hong Kong ventures, which together, account for almost half of all China's exports. If there is a port or property being developed in China, a utility being built, or a huge joint venture being signed, chances are it involves Hong Kong expertise and Hong Kong capital. Indeed, Hong Kong accounts for almost two-thirds of the foreign capital at work in China—an example not only of China's need but of Hong Kong's maturation as an economy. Of course, this relationship is not all one-way. Nearly 2,000 mainland companies have come to Hong Kong, to the point where China is now the third-largest investor in the colony (Hong Kong Trade Development Council 1997).

Chinese companies in Hong Kong have found it useful to list on the Hong Kong Stock Exchange to gain capital for their projects, as well as to tap into the information Hong Kong has to offer about markets all over the world. It is hard to conceive of a company such as Beijing Enterprises—which was more than 1,276 times oversubscribed for its initial public offering—being able to raise money on such a scale were Hong Kong not there to back it up.

Critics of Hong Kong's growing involvement with China argue that the result has been the "hollowing out" of Hong Kong industry. At least in statistical terms, it has a kind of superficial plausibility. As recently as 1980, Hong Kong manufacturing employed some

870,000 people, but as its economy moved to one that is 84 percent services the share of manufacturing jobs has been cut by more than half, to just under 400,000 today (FEER 1997: 5).

But the "hollowing out" argument is based largely on a statistical slight of hand. True enough, the number of domestic manufacturing "jobs" has been decreasing over the last 15 years. But the "loss" of manufacturing is largely an illusion based on an arbitrary distinction between services and manufacturing. For though most of the Hong Kong economy may today indeed be defined as services, it is services linked to manufacturing.

To put it another way, only the factory is in China, where it takes advantage of cheaper land, labor, and other resources. That is the "back office." The "front office" is Hong Kong, which focuses on design, marketing, prototyping, and logistics. As the authors of *Made by Hong Kong* have put it, "The scale of Hong Kong's manufacturing activities has greatly expanded, even as production within Hong Kong itself has shrunk. 'Made by Hong Kong' has grown, even as 'Made in Hong Kong' has declined" (Berger and Lester 1997: xii).

Does anyone consider Ford or Toyota to have declined once it started manufacturing out of its home base? Of course not. But this process, the result of response to market signals, is hailed as "hollowing out." In another work, *The Hong Kong Advantage*, authors Michael Enright, Edith Scott, and David Dodwell suggest that it is better to look at Hong Kong as the apex of an empire that stretches throughout China and the region. "Hong Kong should not be thought of as a national economy but a metropolitan economy," says Enright. "It ought to be compared to cities like New York and Tokyo and London" (quoted in McGurn 1997b: 37). Even excluding the Hong Kong production in Chinese plants, the value of Hong Kong manufacturing has jumped from $4.1 billion in 1980 to $11.4 billion in 1995 (Enright, Scott, and Dodwell 1997: 19). If the Hong Kong model offers China anything here, it is the value that comes from what the *Made by Hong Kong* authors call "service-enhanced manufactures."

Other countries in the region, most notably Japan, have also moved much of their production offshore. But what may be most valuable to a China trying to come to grips with its own tensions is that Hong Kong's transformation occurred relatively painlessly, almost without having been noticed. To put it another way, in scarcely two

155

decades Hong Kong shed more than half its direct manufacturing jobs, ensured that its manufacturers remained competitive on world markets, and moved well up the value chain—all without ever having had the unemployment rate going over 4.5 percent (and that was a one-time blip). A China now trying to bring its financial sector and state-owned enterprises into the 21st century will be hard-pressed to pull this off as smoothly as an open economy such as Hong Kong has.

A Way to Eliminate Corruption

One reason has to do with corruption. Now, corruption is a hot topic in Asia. When I was at the *Far Eastern Economic Review*, among my tasks each week was to review cartoons from all parts of the region for inclusion on our special "In Other Words" page, and I can tell you that easily one out of every three cartoons we are offered deal with corruption in some form. That is especially true in China. As Jiang argued in a well-publicized speech in January, the idea of "seeking private gain at public expense" (AFP 1997) has become something of an epidemic in China.

But corruption in China is not some national character flaw. It is the byproduct of a system where business and politics are so intertwined. Indeed, upon closer look, all tales of corruption throughout Asia have this in common: some politician selling the influence. Certainly guilty officials need to be held accountable; the Independent Commission Against Corruption has played a key role in reducing corruption in Hong Kong. But the ICAC is only one half of the equation. And it is not even the most important half at that. You cannot prosecute a country into honesty.

You might say, well, Singapore is clean, and it is because they tolerate corruption even less than Hong Kong. True enough, in Singapore the government's intolerance of corruption is not just a matter of rhetoric, and that has helped make it rare. But Singapore's battle against corruption is also helped by the same system that helps keep Hong Kong so clean: a relatively open market. If you want to reduce the favors that politicians can sell, the easiest way to do it is simply to take away the favors politicians might sell. If corruption is less frequent in Hong Kong, it is because Hong Kong has eliminated what we Catholics call the "near occasions of sin." For example, because taxes are low it is not really in the interests of most people to cheat; because the Hong Kong dollar is freely convertible no one need bribe an official to get foreign exchange; and because businesses sink or swim on their own no one need get the Governor's permission to expand or seek a subsidy to do so. Again Milton Friedman's experience in China may be instructive: During his last visit, Friedman noticed that many Chinese politicians listed five or six private companies on their name cards. This blurring of lines between public and private, he said, was an invitation to corruption.

Even in the case of Hong Kong's monopolies there are lessons for China. Hong Kong Telecom, the banking industry, and utilities, for instance, may be protected (almost all Hong Kong protection is in the nontraded sector), but they are at least private. Among Hong Kong's news class there was the easy assumption that 1997 would be merely the substitution of Chinese for British monopolies, but it is in fact much more striking a change than that. For in China those with priviledged markets—such as CAAC—also serve as regulator to their competition. If there is one lesson China might immediately take from Hong Kong, it is that the only way to make a government cleaner is to make it more open.

A New Social Contract

This brings me to my third point: the social contract. Hong Kong is a place that is easy to run so long as it is run benignly. When I first arrived in Hong Kong, what struck me most forcefully, as an American, was the almost complete lack of envy. A British civil servant noted that he used to watch construction workers sweating away at their jobs as they watched the rich kids play away in their pool, all without a trace of the envy that we might expect in the West. But Hong Kong's lack of envy probably owes more to Hong Kong's open system than to any "Asian value," if only because looking around the region today public resentment is taking on a more militant face, now causing strife in places like Korea and Indonesia and threatening to do so in China. Indeed, many Western pundits are already intoning ominously about China's growing income gap and the inevitable social discord that heralds.

If this is true it is certainly bad news for China, because any time you open up an economy you open yourself up to huge income differentials. But Hong Kong has cruised along rather well, and I have to think that it is because of two things: First, the standard of living has been on a steady upward trend; second, people perceive that the opportunity to advance is still there. As Victor Fung, head of Hong Kong's Trade Development Council, told me not long ago, "In Hong Kong when a bus driver sees a man go past in a Rolls Royce, he doesn't resent it. Instead, he thinks to himself, 'someday that might be me—or my son'."

Now skeptics may counter that, until the Asian financial meltdown that began in mid-1997, the standard of living has improved immensely in South Korea too; that the Indonesian economy has sustained an average growth rate of 7 percent for more than a generation; and that in China life is far better than it was than during the Cultural Revolution—and that resentment appears to be growing rather than diminishing. The difference between Hong Kong and those places, however, is that in Hong Kong people not only perceive opportunity but they perceive that it is fair—because it is based on merit and not political connections (*guanxi*). Certainly a Richard Li may have certain opportunities that many of the rest of us do not, but the fact is that in Hong Kong there is still the chance to become another Li Ka-shing on your own merit.

That opportunity stands in marked contrast to places as Indonesia, where wealth depended as much on having been an army buddy of President Suharto's as on any business acumen, or in South Korea, where political access determines everything from credit to expansion. In those places governments have undeniably improved life for their peoples. But opportunities continue to remain rigged, and a middle class is going to resent that more than a desperate class. Affluence brings its own pressures, which explains why a policy that might have been welcomed in 1979, will no longer suffice today.

China too may need to begin to pay attention. With a floating population of 100 million or so, and many of its state enterprises unproductive, the potential for social unrest is bound to escalate. And China has the same problem as Korea and Indonesia—namely, that success is as often dependent on *guanxi* as good skill. If China is to avoid the unrest we now see in places like Korea and Indonesia it might find that Hong Kong's system offers much more than any of the reasonable alternatives, including Singapore's.

Conclusion

So does all this mean that Hong Kong is triumphant? Far from it. The supreme irony mitigating against the Hong Kong model has to do with human nature: It requires far more energy, intelligence, and will not to intervene in an economy than to intervene. Without doubt China has a great deal to learn from Hong Kong, but it appears that Hong Kong may have a lot to learn about itself. Recently, Tung announced that Hong Kong's traditional policy of "noninterference" can no longer "meet the needs and strengthen the competitiveness" of the territory (Sung 1997: 1). It seems to me a fateful turn of events: For if Hong Kong loses faith in its model, how is China supposed to have it?

References

AFP (1997) "Chinese President Horrified by Extent of Corruption." Agence France Presse, 15 May.

Berger, S. and Lester, R.K. (1997) *Made by Hong Kong*. Hong Kong: Oxford University Press.

Chan, A. (1997) Speech by the Chief Secretary, The Honorable Mrs. Anson Chan, CBE, JP, to the 30th International General Meeting of the Pacific Basin Economic Council, Manila, 19 May.

The Economist (1997) "Beijing Rules: China's State-owned Enterprises," 3 May: 54–55.

Enright, M.J.; Scott, E.E.; and Dodwell, D. (1997) *The Hong Kong Advantage*. Hong Kong: Oxford University Press.

FEER (1997) "Capitalist Roader." *Far Eastern Economic Review*, 9 January: 5.

Hong Kong Trade Development Council (1997) *Hong Kong & China Economies*. Hong Kong: HKTDC (April).

McGurn, W. (1997a) *Perfidious Albion: The Abandonment of Hong Kong*. Washington, D.C.: Ethics and Public Policy Center.

McGurn, W. (1997b) "You Can Go Home Again." *Far Eatern Economic Review*, Special Hong Kong Commemorative Issue, June: 36–38.

Rabushska, A. (1979) *Hong Kong: A Study in Economic Freedom*. Chicago: Univeristy of Chicago Graduate School of Business.

Sung, B. (1997) "Laissez-Faire Retreat: SAR to Lift Business Role: Tung." *The Hong Kong Standard*, 28 May: 1.

Woo, W.T. (1997) "What China Must Do." *Far Eastern Economic Review*, 29 May: 34.

11. Hong Kong, Economic Freedom, and Lessons for China

James D. Gwartney

More than a decade ago, Michael Walker, president of the Fraser Institute of Vancouver, British Columbia, and Nobel laureate Milton Friedman organized a series of conferences with the objective of clearly defining and measuring economic freedom. They were able to attract some of the world's leading economists—including Gary Becker, Douglass North, Peter Bauer, and Assar Lindbeck—to participate in the series and provide input for the study. Milton Friedman played an active role throughout and should be properly thought of as the project's godfather. I first attended one of the conferences in 1988 and was attracted by both the challenge and importance of the project.

After writing a number of papers on the topic, I coauthored, with Robert Lawson and Walter Block, *Economic Freedom of the World: 1975–1995*, which was published in 1996 by a network of 11 institutes including the Fraser Institute and the Cato Institute. That publication led to the formalization of the Economic Freedom Network, a group of institutes in 47 different countries seeking to develop the best possible measure of economic freedom. In 1997, the network published an updated edition of *Economic Freedom of the World*, which I coauthored with Lawson.

While this is an ongoing project, considerable progress has been made. As viewed by economists, the central elements of economic freedom are personal choice, freedom of exchange, and protection of private property. We have developed an index that reflects the presence of these factors. Since we want to minimize the significance

James D. Gwartney is Professor of Economics and Policy Sciences at Florida State University.

of "judgment calls" and subjective evaluations, most of the components are objective variables derived from regularly published sources. Our goal is to develop a good measure of economic freedom based on objective components that can be obtained and updated regularly for a large number of countries.

As Table 1 illustrates, our index contains 17 components that are divided into four major areas: money and inflation, government operations, takings, and international trade. The first four components reflect the availability of *sound money*. The second set of components indicates *reliance on markets* rather than the political process to allocate goods and resources. The third set of components indicates the degree to which governments *honor and protect property rights* rather than engage in plunder. Finally, the fourth set of components is indicative of *free trade* policies. In essence, our index indicates the consistency of a nation's policies and institutional arrangements with (a) monetary and price stability, (b) reliance on the market sector rather than the political process, (c) avoidance of plunder and discriminatory taxes, and (d) freedom of international exchange. While these elements are not the sum total, they are important ingredients of economic freedom.

Economic Freedom and Growth

For years, Nobel laureate Douglass C. North has stressed that economic growth is determined by three things: (1) investment in physical and human capital, (2) technological advances, and (3) improvements in the efficiency of institutional arrangements (see, e.g., North 1990). Years ago, I heard Professor North stress these points many times when I was a graduate student at the University of Washington, but I failed to grasp their full significance. In many ways, they seemed too simple to be profound. Obviously, individuals could produce more if they were working with better machinery (physical capital) and if they were better educated and more skilled (human capital). Similarly, improvements in technology, our knowledge about how to transform resources into goods and services, have obviously been a powerful force promoting economic progress throughout history, particularly during the last 250 years.

Improvements in the efficiency of institutional arrangements were more subtle, but their significance if not their source also seemed obvious. As the result of my work on the measurement of economic

TABLE 1
Components of the Index of Economic Freedom

I. *Money and Inflation* (Protection of money as a store of value and medium of exchange.)

(4.7) A. Average annual growth rate of the money supply during the last five years minus the potential growth rate of real GDP.

(5.3) B. Standard deviation of the annual inflation rate during the last five years.

(3.0) C. Freedom of citizens to own a foreign-currency bank account domestically.

(2.7) D. Freedom of citizens to maintain a bank account abroad.

II. *Government Operations and Regulations* (Freedom to decide what is produced and consumed.)

(6.2) A. General government consumption expenditures as a percent of total consumption (private + government).

(6.5) B. The role and presence of government-operated enterprises.

(7.1) C. Price controls—the extent to which businesses are free to set their own prices. (This variable is included in only the 1990 and 1995 indexes.)

(6.7) D. Freedom of private businesses and cooperatives to compete in markets. (This variable is included only in the 1995 index.)

(4.7) E. Equality of citizens under the law and access of citizens to a nondiscriminatory judiciary. (This variable is included only in the 1995 index.)

(3.4) F. Freedom from government regulations and policies that cause negative real interest rates.

III. *Takings and Discriminatory Taxation* (Freedom to keep what you earn.)

(10.9) A. Transfers and subsidies as a percent of GDP.

(12.7) B. Top marginal tax rate (and income threshold at which it applies).

(3.6) C. The use of conscripts to obtain military personnel.

continued

TABLE 1
COMPONENTS OF THE INDEX OF ECONOMIC FREEDOM, *continued*

IV. *Restraints on International Exchange* (Freedom of exchange with foreigners.)

(6.7) A. Taxes on international trade as a percent of exports plus imports.

(6.2) B. Difference between the official exchange rate and the black market rate.

(3.7) C. Actual size of trade sector compared to the expected size.

(5.9) D. Restrictions on the freedom of citizens to engage in capital transactions with foreigners.

NOTE: The numbers in parentheses indicate the weight attached to each component when the summary rating is derived.
SOURCE: Gwartney and Lawson (1997: 4).

freedom, I am now convinced that what North referred to as improvements in institutional arrangements and movement toward economic freedom are one and the same. Legal, monetary, and political arrangements consistent with economic freedom provide the key to the mystery of economic progress.

Of course, the linkage between economic freedom and prosperity is not a new idea. It goes back at least to Adam Smith's "invisible hand" and the recognition of the gains from specialization and trade. The market process highlights the linkage. In a competitive market economy, individuals have a strong incentive to develop their talents and provide resources that are highly valued by others because provision of such resources will lead to higher income levels. Similarly, businesses have a strong incentive to discover and provide goods and services that consumers value highly *relative to their cost* because provision of such goods will generate economic profit. At the most basic level, economic profit is nothing more than a reward that accrues to entrepreneurs who discover and produce goods and services that are more valuable to consumers than the resources required by their production. On the other hand, losses are a penalty imposed on entrepreneurs who reduce the value of resources. Entrepreneurs also have an incentive to discover and achieve the least-cost method of production because, other things constant, lower costs will mean higher profits. Thus, while they are motivated by pursuit of profit, markets provide owners with a strong incentive to develop their resources and instill entrepreneurs with a strong incentive to produce efficiently and undertake activities that increase the value of resources.

As Friedrich Hayek (1945) has illustrated so clearly, the information concerning what goods and services are valued most, relative to their costs, and how these items can be produced at the lowest possible costs is unavailable to any central authority. It can only be attained through the market process directing the actions of resource suppliers, consumers, and entrepreneurs. Furthermore, in a dynamic world the best combination of goods to produce and least-cost methods of production are constantly changing. The discovery of new products and superior production processes often renders prior products and methods obsolete. This "creative destruction," as Joseph Schumpeter (1962) referred to it, is an important dynamic source of technological advancement and the discovery of better ways of doing things.

All of this suggests that there is good reason to expect that economic freedom will promote prosperity and growth. But does the real world really work this way? Without a good measure of economic freedom, we are unable to investigate directly the importance of economic freedom as a source of growth and prosperity. Our index helps to fill that vacuum.

Economic Freedom and Growth of Hong Kong

We were able to derive an index of economic freedom for 115 countries in 1995 and ratings for approximately 100 countries for the years 1975, 1980, 1985, and 1990. Countries were rated on a scale of 0 to 10 for each of the 17 components in our index. The highest component rating—a 10—was generally assigned to only about 10 percent of the countries included in our study. Figure 1 presents the 1995 summary rating for each of the 115 countries. By a wide margin, our index indicates that the economy of Hong Kong was the freest in the world not only in 1995, but also during each of the prior rating years. Hong Kong earned a rating of 8 or above for just about every component in our index. Its 9.3 summary rating in 1995 was a full point above that of Singapore, the next highest rated economy. New Zealand, the United States, and surprisingly, Mauritius round out the top five. Switzerland, the United Kingdom, Thailand, and

FIGURE 1
SUMMARY RATINGS AND RANKINGS, 1995

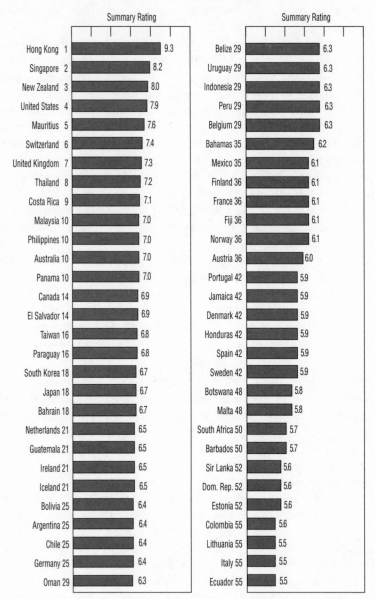

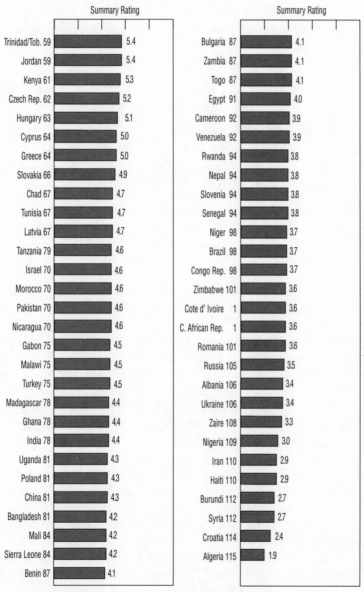

Summary Rating	
Trinidad/Tob. 59	5.4
Jordan 59	5.4
Kenya 61	5.3
Czech Rep. 62	5.2
Hungary 63	5.1
Cyprus 64	5.0
Greece 64	5.0
Slovakia 66	4.9
Chad 67	4.7
Tunisia 67	4.7
Latvia 67	4.7
Tanzania 79	4.6
Israel 70	4.6
Morocco 70	4.6
Pakistan 70	4.6
Nicaragua 70	4.6
Gabon 75	4.5
Malawi 75	4.5
Turkey 75	4.5
Madagascar 78	4.4
Ghana 78	4.4
India 78	4.4
Uganda 81	4.3
Poland 81	4.3
China 81	4.3
Bangladesh 81	4.2
Mali 84	4.2
Sierra Leone 84	4.2
Benin 87	4.1

Summary Rating	
Bulgaria 87	4.1
Zambia 87	4.1
Togo 87	4.1
Egypt 91	4.0
Cameroon 92	3.9
Venezuela 92	3.9
Rwanda 94	3.8
Nepal 94	3.8
Slovenia 94	3.8
Senegal 94	3.8
Niger 98	3.7
Brazil 98	3.7
Congo Rep. 98	3.7
Zimbabwe 101	3.6
Cote d' Ivoire 1	3.6
C. African Rep. 1	3.6
Romania 101	3.6
Russia 105	3.5
Albania 106	3.4
Ukraine 106	3.4
Zaire 108	3.3
Nigeria 109	3.0
Iran 110	2.9
Haiti 110	2.9
Burundi 112	2.7
Syria 112	2.7
Croatia 114	2.4
Algeria 115	1.9

SOURCE: Gwartney and Lawson (1997: 27).

167

FIGURE 2

PER CAPITA GDP AND GROWTH OF REAL INCOME BY QUINTILE RATINGS OF ECONOMIC FREEDOM

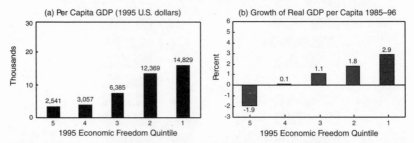

NOTE: The summary ratings of the five quintiles were top quintile = 6.5 and above; second highest quintile = 5.9 to 6.4; third highest = 4.7 to 5.8; fourth highest = 3.9 to 4.6; lowest quintile = 3.8 and lower. The per capita GDP data are updates of the *Penn World Tables* data of Robert Summers and Alan Heston (1994) which were derived by the purchasing power parity method.

SOURCE: Gwartney and Lawson (1997: 34).

Costa Rica occupy spots six through nine. Four countries—Malaysia, the Philippines, Australia, and Panama—are tied for the 10th place ranking.

In order to illustrate the relationship between economic freedom and income, we arrayed the summary ratings for our 115 countries from the highest to the lowest and divided them into quintiles— five groups of 23 (one group had 24 and another 22 as the result of ties). Then the average per capita GDP in 1996 and annual rate of growth during 1985–1996 were derived for each of the quintile groups. These figures are presented in Figure 2. For the top quintile of "most free" economies, the average per capita GDP was $14,829. The figure for the next quintile was $12,369 and it declined for each quintile down to $2,541 for the countries comprising the "least free" quintile. Clearly, there was a strong positive relationship between per capita GDP and economic freedom as measured by our index.

The growth of real GDP between 1985 and 1996 (or the most recent year available) is also presented by quintile. The top quintile registered per capita growth of 2.9 percent. The figure for the second quintile fell to 1.8 percent, and it continued to decline by approximately 1 percent as one moved down each quintile. For the "least free" quintile (countries in this group had summary ratings of 3.8 or less), per capita GDP fell at an annual rate of 1.9 percent during 1985–96.

Thus, both per capita GDP and its growth rate are positively linked with economic freedom. This relationship is not an artifact of the construction of the index. The components of the index were all indicators of institutional structure and economic policy. None of them were "proxies" for level of income or development. If economic freedom did not exert a positive impact on growth and eventually the level of income achieved, there would be no reason why the income and growth figures would be positively correlated with the index rating. They could just as well have been negatively correlated. Or there could have been no relationship at all. This positive correlation suggests that countries that follow policies more consistent with economic freedom reap a payoff in the form of more rapid economic growth that leads to higher living standards.

Using the ratings for the earlier years, we were also able to identify countries that substantially liberalized their economies during the last two decades. Economic theory indicates that economic freedom will enhance the gains from trade, specialization, and entrepreneurship. Thus, one would expect countries that achieve large *increases* in economic freedom to also achieve impressive growth rates. Correspondingly, one would expect that movement away from economic freedom would lead to sluggish growth and perhaps declines in income. In order to investigate the relationship between changes in economic freedom and growth, the 95 countries that we were able to rate throughout the 1975–95 period were arrayed by the *change* in their summary rating between 1975 and 1995. Then, we derived the average growth rate of per capita GDP according to the *change* in economic freedom between 1975 and 1995. As Figure 3 illustrates, there was a strong positive relationship between *change* in economic freedom and growth of per capita GDP. When economic freedom increased by two units or more between 1975 and 1995, growth of per capita GDP averaged more than 2 percent during the 1985–96 period. In contrast, countries experiencing reductions in economic freedom experienced declines in per capita GDP.

Lessons for China

These findings, along with the economic record of Hong Kong during the last several decades, provide important lessons for China

169

FIGURE 3

CHANGE IN ECONOMIC FREEDOM AND GROWTH OF PER CAPITA GDP

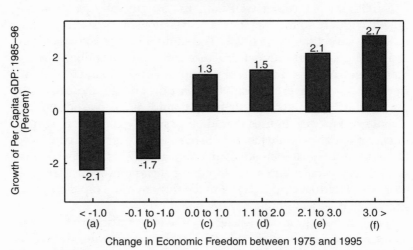

Change in Economic Freedom between 1975 and 1995

NOTES: (a) The countries in this group were Haiti, Honduras, Iran, Nicaragua, and Venezuela. All five had a negative growth rate of per capita GDP during 1985–96 period.

(b) The countries in this group were Algeria, Bahamas, Bahrain, Cameroon, Congo, Cote d'Ivoire, Mali, Niger, Nigeria, Rwanda, Senegal, Sierra Leone, Syria, and Zaire. The per capita GDP declined in 11 of these 14 countries during the 1985–96 period.

(c) The countries in this group were Bangladesh, Belgium, Benin, Brazil, Canada, Chad, Cyprus, Germany, Guatemala, Hong Kong, Jordan, Malawi, Morocco, Nepal, Netherlands, Oman, Panama, Switzerland, Togo, and Uruguay. GDP declined in 4 of these 20 countries during the 1985–96 period.

(d) The countries in this group were Australia, Austria, Barbados, Bolivia, Columbia, Denmark, Ecuador, Egypt, Fiji, France, Gabon, Ghana, Greece, India, Indonesia, Italy, Japan, Kenya, Malaysia, Mexico, Pakistan, Paraguay, Singapore, South Africa, Spain, Sri Lanka, Tanzania, Taiwan, Tunisia, Turkey, the United States, and Zambia. The per capita GDP declined in 6 of the 32 countries.

(e) The countries in this group were Botswana, Costa Rica, Dominican Republic, El Salvador, Finland, Israel, Ireland, Jamaica, Norway, Peru, Philippines, Russia, South Korea, Sweden, Thailand, Trinidad/Tobago, and the United Kingdom. Per capita real GDP fell in only 2 (Russia and Trinidad/Tobago) of these 17 countries between 1985 and 1996.

(f) The countries in this group were Argentina, Chile, Iceland, Mauritius, New Zealand, Portugal, and Uganda. All seven of these countries achieved increases in per capita real GDP between 1985 and 1996.

SOURCES: Gwartney and Lawson (1997), and World Bank (1997).

170

and other less-developed countries. Economic freedom—that is, sound money, reliance on markets, secure property rights, and an open economy—provides the ingredients for growth and prosperity. If countries want to get the most out of their resources, they need to move toward economic freedom. The experience of China itself reinforces this view. While China's summary rating is still low (its 4.3 rating in 1995 placed it 81st among our 115 countries), its rating has persistently increased since 1980. No doubt this economic liberalization has contributed to China's impressive growth record during this period.

Visiting Hong Kong today, it is easy to overlook the magnitude of this Chinese economic miracle. In 1960, Hong Kong was a relatively poor country. According to the Summers and Heston (1994) *Penn World Tables* estimates derived by the purchasing power parity method, the 1960 per capita GDP of Hong Kong was approximately the same as that of Peru, South Africa, and Greece. By way of comparison, Argentina's per capita GDP was twice that of Hong Kong. The per capita GDP of Venezuela was three times that of Hong Kong in 1960, and that of the United States was more than four times the figure for Hong Kong. What a difference 36 years of rapid sustained growth can make. Today, the Summers and Heston data indicate that Hong Kong, along with the United States, has the highest per capita GDP in the world.

Adjusted for inflation, China's current per capita income is actually slightly higher than that of Hong Kong in 1960. In today's environment of innovation; rapid capital movements, transportation, and communications; and emulation of successful ideas, the growth potential of low-income countries is greater than at any time in history. To realize that potential, however, countries must adopt institutions and follow policies consistent with economic freedom. If China follows the course of Hong Kong down this path, it too will achieve an "economic miracle."

References

Gwartney, J.; Lawson, R.; and Block, W. (1996) *Economic Freedom of the World: 1975–1995*. Vancouver, B.C.: Fraser Institute.

Gwartney, J., and Lawson, R. (1997) *Economic Freedom of the World: 1997 Annual Report*. Vancouver, B.C.: Fraser Institute.

Hayek, F.A. (1945) "The Use of Knowledge in Society." *American Economic Review* 35 (4) (September): 519–30.

North, D.C. (1990) *Institutions, Institutional Change, and Economic Performance.* Cambridge, Mass.: Cambridge University Press.

Schumpeter, J.A. (1962) *Capitalism, Socialism, and Democracy.* New York: Harper and Row.

Summers, R., and Heston, A. (1994) *Penn World Tables.* Cambridge, Mass.: National Bureau of Economic Research.

World Bank (1997) *World Development Indicators: 1997, CD-ROM.* Washington, D.C.: World Bank.

PART III

CHINA'S PLACE IN THE GLOBAL TRADING ORDER

12. The WTO and China's Objectives as a World Trading Power

Wen Hai

The completion of the GATT Uruguay Round negotiation, the establishment of the World Trade Organization (WTO), together with the end of the Cold War and the economic transition in former planned economies signal that a new international economic order is emerging. This new international economic order is characterized by trade liberalization and multilateral economic cooperation. In this order, the WTO is to be the "Economic United Nations," charged with implementing the GATT Uruguay Round agreements, settling trade disputes, and promoting global free trade.

The validity and stability of the new international economic order largely depend on the effectiveness of the WTO. To be a truly universal system, the WTO should incorporate all the leading economic powers, especially China and Russia, into the global system and bring them on the bandwagon of trade liberalization. Currently, China is still in the process of economic reform. For this reason, some aspects of the Chinese economic system and trade policies have not yet met WTO standards. At the same time, however, China has become an increasingly important country in the world economy. It is one of the largest and fastest-growing economies of the world in the past two decades. China is too big to be changed and too important to be ignored. "Keeping China outside the WTO, which no longer prevents it from playing a major role in real global trade, has become more costly for the multilateral trading system" (MITI 1996). Clearly, how to admit China as a member and to ensure it plays a constructive role in the new international order is a challenge for the WTO.

Wen Hai is a Visiting Fellow at the China Center for Economic Research at Peking University and Assistant Professor of Economics at Fort Lewis College.

What are China's objectives, efforts, and problems in its accession to the WTO? What are the main obstacles for China's WTO membership? What will be the costs and benefits for the global economy from keeping China outside of the multilateral trading system? This paper discusses these issues.

An Emerging World Trading Power

In discussing China's WTO accession, it is important to understand China's place in the global trading order. Through almost 20 years of economic reforms and openness, China has clearly become a major participant in the world economy.

Before it adopted an open-door policy in the late 1970s, China was almost completely isolated from the world. By the end of the Cultural Revolution and before the economic reforms, China exported only $6.9 billion worth of merchandise in 1978, less than 1 percent of total world exports. In spite of its large geographic size, rich natural resources, and large population it was the 34th largest exporting country in the world.

China has quickly become an important trading power. Its foreign trade has increased almost 15 percent annually in the past 20 years. In less than two decades, the total value of China's merchandise exports has expanded more than 20-fold. In 1996, China exported a total of $151 billion and imported a total of $139 billion worth of goods. China's total share of world merchandise trade reached 2.7 percent in 1996, and China became the ninth-largest exporting country in the world (fifth-largest if we count the European Union as one group). If Hong Kong is included as part of China (excluding trade between the mainland and Hong Kong), then China is the fourth-largest trading power in the world.

China is a dominant exporter of labor-intensive products. In 1995, China exported more than 20 percent of the world's labor-intensive manufactured products. China is the major exporter of textiles, toys, cotton, clothing, and shoes. It has an increasing share of world exports for radios, clocks, televisions, machinery, motorcycles, auto parts, and other manufactured goods.

In the international capital market, China has become the second-largest recipient (after the United States) of foreign investment. Before reforms started in 1978, China rarely had any foreign direct investment. This situation did not change much in the early 1980s.

Total foreign investment from 1979 to 1982 was less than $12.5 billion, an average of about $3 billion per year. In the early 1990s, after Deng Xiaoping visited southern China, China launched a new round of reforms and adopted more open foreign-investment policies. High expected returns and tax exemptions attracted a record double-digit level of capital inflows in 1992. The trend has continued as economic reforms have deepened. In 1996, China attracted commitments of $81.6 billion in investment from foreign countries, with an actual inflow of $54.8 billion. From 1979 to 1996, China's total foreign investment was $283.4 billion, with most of that investment (71 percent) occurring after 1991.

China's Objectives as a Member of the GATT/WTO

As China becomes a leading trading power, it has an increasing incentive to join the WTO. A general objective for China is to further integrate its economy into the world trading system. "China's economic relations with the world are simply too large and too pervasive to manage effectively through a maze of arbitrary, shifting, and unstable bilateral deals," stated Renato Ruggiero, secretary general of the WTO, at a speech at Peking University in April 1997. China needs a stable and freer world market for export growth, especially for its labor-intensive products. It also needs high-tech imports for its industrialization and modernization. As a reforming economy, China wants a policy that facilitates interaction with other countries in order to establish an efficient market system. Thus, China desires to join the WTO and to play a constructive role in the new world economic order.

In particular, China wants to join the WTO in order to (1) obtain permanent most-favored-nation (MFN) trading status, (2) participate in a multilateral framework for dispute settlement, and (3) play an active role in writing rules for the future world trading order.

Obtain a Permanent Nondiscrimination Status in the World Trade Order

Since China is not a member of the WTO, it does not automatically have MFN status with other trading partners. It needs to negotiate trade agreements with each individual country. So far, China has signed bilateral MFN agreements with more than 110 countries. However, some of those agreements are not stable. The annual review and debate of China MFN status in the United States has damaged Sino-U.S. economic relations since 1989. By joining the WTO China wants to ensure stable and nondiscriminatory trade relations with all countries.

Participate in a Multilateral Framework for Dispute Settlement

Currently China's economic relations with other countries are based on bilateral agreements. As a nonmember of the WTO, the settlement of trade disputes between China and its trade partners largely depends on bilateral negotiations, many of which are settled by domestic legislation. In recent years, there have been more than 200 "dumping" charges against China. When negotiations fail, unilateral trade sanctions and retaliation are often used as solutions. As China integrates into the world economy and becomes a major trading power, an effective multilateral dispute settlement framework is needed for business security, fairness, and confidence.

Play an Active Role in Writing Rules for the Future

The GATT has completed its most recent round of trade negotiations, but the WTO is continuing in the effort to increase free trade. The WTO will resume negotiations on agriculture, services, and other sectors in two years. The continuing negotiations in the WTO are establishing rules for the future. As an emerging and large world trading power, China does not want to stand on the sideline while others write the rules of the game.

It is clear that there are benefits and adjustment costs for each country in the process of trade liberalization and globalization. Each country tries to maximize its future gains and reduce its adjustment costs in the new order to be established by the multilateral negotiations. China's interests were not fully represented in past GATT negotiations, which makes China's GATT/WTO accession very difficult. China cannot afford to be left outside again during future rounds of negotiations.

China's Accession to the GATT/WTO and Trade Relations

China's effort to return to the world trade regime began in the late 1970s when China started its economic reforms and adopted an open-door policy. After more than 30 years of isolation and a centrally planned economy, both China and the GATT contracting countries needed time to understand each other before China's re-entry into the GATT. China was granted observer status in the GATT and sent its first delegate to the 38th meeting of the contracting GATT parties in 1989. On July 11, 1986, China formally requested resumption of its seat in the GATT.

A Working Party was established on March 4, 1987, to start the process of China's re-entry into the GATT. The main tasks of the Working Party were to examine and evaluate China's trading regime, define areas and timetables for negotiation and adjustment, and prepare a report for the GATT Council. The Working Party had seven productive meetings in the period through April 1989, but was suspended after the Tiananmen Square incident and not reconvened until 1992.

In 1992, which was a very important year in the history of China's efforts to re-enter the GATT, the Working Party held three meetings and completed the general hearing and assessment of China's trading system. Negotiations on the commitment and conditions for entry into the GATT also started in 1992. More significantly, China speeded up its reform in the direction of a market economy.

Following the conclusion of the Uruguay Round, China launched a major campaign to join the GATT. China wanted to become a founding member of the new WTO. Along with nationwide propaganda to promote the internationalization of the economy and disseminate knowledge on the GATT, China made a series of reforms in line with the GATT rules.

China's reforms in its external sector include:

1. *Decentralization of foreign trade.* Prior to the reform, the Ministry of Foreign Trade conducted and controlled all trade. Since 1988, foreign trade has been decentralized to local authorities and foreign trade corporations (FTCs). In 1980, the central government controlled about 98 percent of total trade. By 1991, only 11 percent of foreign trade was still controlled by the Ministry of Foreign Trade and Economic Cooperation (Garnaut and Huang 1995, Zhang 1993). In the past two WTO working meetings, China indicated that it will release control on all trading rights after it becomes a member.

2. *Reduction of tariff and nontariff barriers.* Since January 1992, China has reduced tariffs several times and brought the average rate down from 47.2 percent to 21.5 percent in 1997. China has also

179

substantially reduced the number of goods subject to quotas and licensing. By 1994, China had eliminated quotas and import licenses for 283 products. In May of 1994, China abolished another 195 quotas. Currently, China has only 28 products (15 electronic goods and 13 others) that are still subject to import quotas and licenses, 8 (mainly agricultural products) that are subject to nonquota licenses, and 103 that are subject to import registration.

3. *Elimination of export subsidies.* In 1991, the Chinese government abolished all explicit export subsidies. From then on the FTCs had the responsibility for their own losses.

4. *Increases in transparency.* China issued a Foreign Trade Law on July 1, 1994, to make regulations more transparent. It also started to change the method of allocating licenses from bureaucratic application procedure to open competition.

5. *Foreign exchange reforms.* Reforms in foreign exchanges market converted the RMB official exchange rate to the market rate and abolished the dual exchange rate system on January 1, 1994.

Regardless of China's effort and enthusiasm, the bilateral and multilateral negotiations were not very successful. China was still not able to return to the GATT and join the WTO after decades. The U.S. attitude toward China is firm: "China must follow the rule of the WTO if it wants to join the international trade body," remarked chief U.S. negotiator Charlene Barshefsky (quoted in Chong 1995). The United States insisted that China must meet all the WTO's rules for accession.

On November 10, 1995, Barshefsky provided a "road map" for China's accession. China's response was that this was a "positive initiative" but that it demanded too much (O'Ouinn 1996). China argued that the United States was obstructing China's accession to the WTO for political reasons. China's economic system is much closer to the WTO requirements than the United States portrays, but the gaps between the two negotiating positions remain wide.

In February and in May of 1997, China and the WTO had another two rounds of negotiations. In both of these talks, both parties made compromises so that the negotiation made some progress. China showed some flexibility on foreign trading rights, and the US indicated a willingness to compromise on the time requirements in the adjustment period.

Currently, China is working with the United States and other major members for accession to the WTO, but it is not clear when and how China will be able to join the world's most important trade organization.

Barriers for China to Enter the WTO

China has formally requested to renew its membership in the GATT and to join the WTO for more than 10 years. The deadline proposed initially for China's re-entry to the GATT was the end of 1989, but China is still outside the world trading system. Perhaps it is the most complex and difficult accession process in the history of the GATT. Why is it so difficult for China to join the WTO even though China is already the world's ninth-largest trading country? According to Nicholas Lardy (1994), China, in some respects, is one of the more open economies in Asia: "Its economy is more open than that of other East Asian economies at comparable stages of economic development and in certain respects is even more open than they are now." What, then, are the main barriers or obstacles for China's accession to the world trading system?

There are many differences between China's position and the demands made by the United States. The main differences are: (1) China wants a gradual system adjustment, the United States wants a rapid change; (2) The United States and other developed countries want to have special safeguard options to protect their economies against future import surges from China, but China does not accept this; and (3) China wants to maintain protective measures for its "infant industries" as a developing country but the United States does not agree to grant the full range of protective measures to China as it does to other developing countries.

Gradual versus Rapid Adjustment

In the area of *tariff reduction,* China has reduced its average tariff rate from 47.2 percent to 21.5 percent in less than six years, but its rate is still high compared to other developing countries in the WTO. China has indicated a willingness to cut its average tariff rate to 15 percent in three years for industrial products and six years for agricultural products, but the United States wants a 7 percent tariff rate as a precondition to accession to the WTO, and the European Union wants an 8 percent rate.

181

With regard to the *trading license system*, China has offered to phase out the current trading license system in five years, but the United States is pushing for two to three years. In addition, the OECD countries have requested that China open up its distribution sector within a few years, but China does not want to do so until 2020.

Finally, with regard to *discriminatory industrial and investment policies*, China's current policies discriminate against foreign investors. Foreign companies are restricted in certain sectors. The United States, the European Union, and Japan want China to change these policies upon accession, but China needs a much longer time to achieve these reforms.

Safeguards versus MFN

As a condition of accepting China into the WTO, the European Union wants to have the right to impose "safeguard" tariffs or quotas on China's exports. China objects to this as a violation of the MFN principle. As a precondition, the safeguard option will undermine the objective of China's WTO accession. China will be easily discriminated against even as a member of the WTO.

Developing- versus Developed-Country Status

China insists on developing-country status in accession to the GATT/WTO, but the United States wants China to enter the system as a developed country. As a developing country, China can take a longer time to liberalize international trade and have more time to protect its "infant" industries. By the World Bank's definition, China is a developing country, but the United States argues that China is an "export powerhouse" (Chong 1995). The United States claims that China is so big and so significant in the world market that China cannot be treated as a regular developing country. In short, the United States wants China to liberalize trade and foreign investment *before* it becomes a member of the WTO.

An Evaluation

Is the United States asking for too much, or are these requests minimal requirements for a new WTO member? If we look at the history of the GATT, it is not difficult to find that China has experienced a more complex process and faced higher entry barriers than many other countries.

The United States and other OECD countries often claim that China is still not a market economy. However, a full market economy is not a necessary condition for accession into the GATT/WTO. When Poland joined the GATT in 1967, it was a centrally planned economy. Poland undertook no tariff reductions, but pledged to increase imports from Western market economies by 7 percent per year. The only condition on Romania's entry was that it should increase imports from market economies at least as fast as total imports during its then-current five-year plan. When Hungary entered the GATT in 1973, its tariff rate was 32 percent, and it promised to reduce it to 21 percent. Compared to these countries, China is a far more open and decentralized market economy in terms of importing goods and attracting investment from developed countries. China's imports from the world market grew at almost a 17 percent annual rate. Its average tariff rate is already down to 21.5 percent. More importantly, China has been carrying out a market-oriented reform for 20 years. China has even officially announced that it has given up central planning in favor of a market economy. The achievement and trend of market-oriented reforms are so clear and so fundamental in China as to be unquestionable.

According to Chinese negotiators, the current WTO demands are much greater than they were in the late 1980s when China's economy was much less open and free. As Lardy (1994) has pointed out, "It is time to recognize that the United States has already demanded and received more from China in terms of economic reforms than was demanded of other comparatively developed countries when they entered the GATT."

Regarding the developing- versus developed-country argument, it is true that China is a large exporting country, but it should not be penalized for its good performance. The GATT's definition of a "developing country" (or less-developed country) is based on standards of living, not on export performance. Therefore, the United States interpretation of China's case is not justified.

It is clear that China has experienced a much more complicated entry process into the GATT/WTO than many other countries. Now, the question is, why do the United States and other WTO member countries push so hard and demand so much? There are both economic and political reasons. Economically, China is growing too fast and becoming too important; politically, China is too independent and is still led by a Communist Party.

183

From an economic point of view, the recent growth in China's economy and the rapid increase in exports have made developed countries rather nervous about the future challenge from China. One popular concern in the United States is: Will China become another Japan? The United States has had a huge trade deficit with Japan for many years. If China becomes another Japan, the potential for an even larger trade deficit is realistic. The United States wants to learn a lesson from the past and access the Chinese market before this concern becomes a reality.

A World Bank study shows that, under the Uruguay Round trade liberalization, China's exports to the United States, the European Union, and Japan would increase by 40 percent (World Bank 1993). Many WTO member countries believe that China will receive large benefits by joining the WTO. This belief gives a strong incentive to the United States and other countries to use this opportunity to demand more from China.

Politically, the United States and Western countries want to ensure that China's market-oriented economic reforms continue. They do not want Chinese state-owned enterprises to benefit from China's WTO membership. After the collapse of the former Soviet Union, China has become the number-one target to be watched by the United States. Clearly, the United States and other OECD countries are attempting to use this opportunity to maximize their access to the Chinese market and to shape the Chinese trade position in the new world economic order.

China's Concerns and Choices

Can the United States successfully reach its goals? Will China make compromises in the WTO membership negotiations? The answer is rather pessimistic.

So far, the Chinese government is reluctant to accept demands from the United States and the other major GATT/WTO contracting countries. China is even willing to postpone its entry to the WTO. It is not difficult to see the economic and political reasons behind China's action.

Slow Reform in State-Owned Enterprises

China's main reason for rejecting the market accession conditions requested by the United States is to prevent domestic industries

TABLE 1
CHINA'S INDUSTRIAL SECTORS LIKELY TO BE AFFECTED BY
ACCESSION TO THE WTO

Sector	1994 Output Value (billions of RMB)	Share (%)	Employees (millions)	Share (%)
Chemical Materials and Products	380.3	7	4.50	7
Medical and Pharmaceutical Products	87.5	2	0.97	1
Smelting and Pressing	536.8	10	4.47	7
Metal Products	170.8	3	1.96	3
Transportation Equipment	318.6	6	3.45	5
Electronic Equipment and Machinery	232.7	5	2.33	4
Electronic and Telecom	199.99	4	1.63	2
Total	1,926.6	38	19.31	29

SOURCE: *China Statistical Yearbook* (1995).

from failing. As a developing country and a former planned economy, China has a large number of inefficient industrial sectors. To avoid rapid social and political change and possible turmoil, China has adopted a gradual approach in its economic reforms. The Chinese government understands the cost of slow reform in its state-owned enterprises (SOEs), but social stability is the first priority for the current political regime.

Table 1 shows the current situation in affected import-competing sectors. These sectors do not have a comparative advantage or competitive advantage in international competition. Research indicates that one-third of Chinese industries will face international competition once China enters the GATT/WTO. These sectors account for almost 40 percent of China's total industrial output value and about 30 percent of industrial employment. Furthermore, most of the firms in these sectors are SOEs with a very low level of efficiency. The competition from domestic non-SOEs, including township and village enterprises (TVEs) and joint ventures, has already caused many SOEs to suffer losses. The Chinese government is hesitant to subject SOEs to more competition for fear of high unemployment and social unrest.

On the other hand, China's export sectors have already been decentralized. Most enterprises in the export sector are not state owned. Their activities are more profit-driven and market oriented. In the past decades, despite difficulties in accessing foreign markets as a non-GATT member, China's exports have grown at an average of 18.7 percent, 11 percent higher than the world export growth rate, from 1978 to 1994. Without being a member of the WTO, China's export share in world trade has increased from less than 1 percent in 1978 to more than 4 percent in 1994. Many of China's labor-intensive products are already major exports in the world. By joining the WTO, China's exports will find it easier to enter foreign markets, but the situation may not improve that much in the short run.

Who in China supports the accession and who opposes it? It is very clear that the majority of high-tech or capital-intensive sectors will face more competition and bear most of the adjustment costs. These sectors are mainly owned or controlled by the state. In the current situation, the state-owned import-competing groups have more political and economic influence in the central government than do the supporters of the export sector. If China follows the "road map" provided by the United States and other developed countries, the market gain from accession to the WTO will be very marginal, while the internal adjustment costs will be very large. Therefore, at the current stage of reform, it is unlikely that the Chinese government will fully commit to trade liberalization and open markets.

Rising Nationalist Sentiment

Since the 1989 Tiananman incident and the fall of the Soviet bloc, the political relationship between the United States and China has deteriorated. (President Clinton's recent visit, however, may have reversed or slowed this deterioration.) The U.S. resolution to oppose China's Olympic bid, the Clinton administration's invitation to Taiwan President Lee Tung Hui to visit the United States, the American news media's constant China bashing, and the presence of U.S. naval ships in the Taiwan Strait during the missile crisis prior to Taiwan's first democratic election have had very negative effects in China and have increased nationalist sentiment among the Chinese people and policymakers. It has become very popular to support the government in "saying no" to America and other Western countries.

Also, China is in a period of economic as well as political transition, and it is very difficult for the current Chinese leaders and WTO negotiators to accept all of the requests from the United States. Any compromise to someone who is not friendly to China will be seen as weak leadership. The rising of nationalist sentiment makes it far more difficult for the Chinese government to be flexible on WTO accession.

Prospects for China's Accession to the WTO

The process of negotiation over China's accession to the WTO is an international "game." Both sides want to maximize gains through the process. For the United States and the Western countries, it is an opportunity to access the Chinese market and formalize the future direction of China's economic development. For China, it is an important step in gaining international recognition and integrating itself into the world economy.

No one will disagree that bringing China into the WTO will benefit both China and the WTO member countries.[1] The problem is how to accurately estimate the benefits and costs, and then to design a creative solution. Currently, the United States, Europe, and Japan may overestimate the net gain to China or underestimate the benefits they may have if they can bring China into the WTO earlier. On the other hand, China may underestimate the long-run gains of its integration into the world economy. It is unlikely that China will accept the conditions proposed by the United States for both economic and political reasons.[2]

[1]There have been numerous studies on the economic impact of China's accession to the WTO (e.g., Drysdale and Elek 1992; Lardy 1994; Garnaut and Huang 1995a, 1995b; Zhang and Warr 1995; Drysdale 1997; and many papers in China). Many of these studies show that China's accession to the WTO will not only benefit the Chinese economy, but also benefit most developed countries and the world economy.

[2]Speaking at the 30th General Meeting of the PBEC on June 20, 1997, Vice Premier Li Lanqing said, "China is ready to join WTO. However, China, being a developing country, adheres to the principle that rights and obligations should be in balance,

China will not be admitted to the WTO in the near future unless the United States changes its global political and economic policy. Considering the domestic situation, China is not ready yet for full commitment to the WTO principles. China will continue to reform its economic system and trade policies for its sake, but it may take more time than Western countries wish. It is now up to the WTO to make the choice of adopting China as a special case or postponing China's accession to the WTO.

Meanwhile, as an alternative, China will play an active role in APEC. The "unilateral" and "voluntary" principles will make China more comfortable about deciding its own pace of reform and trade liberalization. "Peer pressure" from APEC countries will provide a positive external role in pushing China's economic reform and trade liberalization, which, in turn, will pave a road for China's accession to the WTO.

References

China Statistical Yearbook (1995) Compiled by the State Statistical Bureau, People's Republic of China. Beijing: China Statistical Publishing House.

Chong, F. (1995) "APEC, WTO, 301: The United States Team Forging Access to Regional Markets." Asia Today 13 (10) (October).

Drysdale, P., and Elek, A. (1992) "China and the International Trading System." Pacific Economic Papers, No. 214 (December). Australia-Japan Policy Centre, Australian National University.

Drysdale, P. (1997) "The Implications of China's Membership in the WTO for Industrial Transformation." Paper presented at the Conference on Chinese Industrial Upgrade: Institutional Transformation and International Cooperation, CASS, Beijing, 17–18 January.

Garnaut, R., and Huang, Y. (1995a) "China's Trade Reform and Transition: Opportunities and Challenges for OECD Countries." A report prepared for the OECD Trade Directorate, Department of Economics. RSPAS4 ANU, February.

Garnaut, R., and Huang, Y. (1995b) "China and the Future International Trading System." Pacific Economic Papers, No. 250. Australian-Japan Policy Centre, Australian National University.

Lardy, N.R. (1994) China in the World Economy. Washington, D.C.: Institute for International Economics.

Li, L. (1997) Speech at the 30th General Meeting of the PBEC, 20 June.

---

and cannot commit itself to what exceeds its capacity and ability. Without China, the World Trade Organization can not fully exert its influence."

MITI (1996) "China's Accession to the WTO." In the *1996 Report on the WTO Consistency of Trade Policies by Major Trading Partners*. Tokyo: Ministry of International Trade and Industry, Subcommittee on Unfair Trade Policies and Measures of the Industrial Structure Council. (This report was officially released on 29 March 1996.)

O'Ouinn, R.P. (1996) "How to Bring China and Taiwan into the World Trade Organization." Asian Studies Center Backgrounder, No. 140. Washington, D.C.: Heritage Foundation.

Ruggiero, R. (1997) "The WTO and China." Speech at Peking University, 21 April. Excerpted in the CCER Newsletter, No. 2, China Center for Economic Research, Peking University.

World Bank (1993) *China-Foreign Trade Reform: Meeting the Challenge of the 1990s*. Washington, D.C.: World Bank.

Zhang, X. (1993) "Reforming a Centrally Planned Trade System: The Chinese Experience." Economic Division Working Paper, East Asia, 93/6. Research School of Pacific and Asian Studies, Australian National University.

Zhang, X., and Warr, P.G. (1995) "China's Re-entry into the GATT: A General Equilibrium Analysis of Tariff Reduction." *Pacific Economic Papers*, No. 250. Australian-Japan Policy Centre, Australian National University.

Comment

China and a Liberal Trading Order

William A. Niskanen

As Wen Hai (1998) has summarized so effectively, the government of China has dramatically liberalized its policies affecting international trade. And China first petitioned for re-entry into GATT in 1986. China receives most of the benefits of GATT membership through its network of bilateral MFN agreements, but the government understandably seeks the additional benefits of permanent MFN status, dispute resolution by the WTO, and the opportunity to participate in negotiations on new or broader multilateral trade rules. Even without GATT membership, China has become one of the world's largest international traders and the single largest exporter of labor-intensive products.

The Principle of Nondiscrimination

The distinctive principle of a liberal trading order is nondiscrimination—that is, equal treatment under the rules to which all parties have agreed. Chinese officials make this point when they assert that China faces higher barriers to GATT membership than did other countries at a comparable stage of development. U.S. and European trade officials make this same point when they claim that China has not yet met the common standards for GATT membership.

On this basis, the Chinese have the better part of this argument. China now has lower barriers to imports than other centrally planned economies that were admitted to GATT many years ago. The European Union wants a system of "safeguard" limits on imports from China—a demand, to my knowledge, that has never been applied to any other country. China wants to enter GATT as a "developing"

William A. Niskanen is Chairman of the Cato Institute and a former member of the Council of Economic Advisers under President Reagan.

country, based on its still low average personal income. U.S. officials insist that China enter as a developed country, because it is already an "export powerhouse."

Two Concerns Not Resolved by the Nondiscrimination Principle

The continued stalemate on the admission of China to the GATT, however, reflects two major concerns that will not be resolved by appeals to the nondiscrimination principle. China wants a slow phase-down of its remaining import barriers, primarily to allow a more gradual adjustment of the many state firms to foreign competition; all that seems left of communism in China is a concern to protect the special privileges of those employed by these state firms. On the other hand, the U.S. and European position is based more on the magnitude of China's current and potential future trade; no other country with an economy this large has been admitted to GATT on a developing country basis. The stalemate continues because China will not dismantle its many inefficient state firms quickly, and the West seems prepared to tolerate China's large exports only if its import barriers are reduced quickly to developed country levels.

Conclusion

There seems little prospect of ending this stalemate soon. Under these conditions, a tit-for-tat strategy, a reciprocal pattern of small steps, seems the best way to resolve this stalemate. Such a process now seems to be underway. Following the visit to China by President Clinton in 1998, Congress renewed China's MFN status, now fortunately redefined as "normal trade relations," without any substantial controversy. And the government of China directed the People's Liberation Army to divest its many firms. A continuation of such reciprocal steps now seems the best way to achieve the shared objective: a full integration of China into the world trading system.

Reference

Wen, H. (1998) "The WTO and China's Objective as a World Trading Power." In J.A. Dorn (ed.) *China in the New Millennium: Market Reforms and Social Development*, chap. 12. Washington, D.C.: Cato Institute.

13. China's Telecommunications Sector and the WTO: Can China Conform to the Telecom Regulatory Principles?

Milton Mueller

China's strategy of economic development is encapsulated by the term "socialist market economy."[1] This means using market forces to improve the efficiency of production while retaining a managed, predominantly state-owned economy and authoritarian control over political activity. China's leaders want to achieve "an economic system that integrates the basic system of socialism with the market economy in an organic way whereby, under macro-regulation and control by the state, the market mechanism plays a fundamental role in the disposition of resources and [the state achieves] a high degree of balance between efficiency and fairness" (Chang 1994: 24). That economy, as Ramon Myers (1994: 2) has observed, needs to be "firmly connected to a political and legal system managed by the Chinese Communist Party."[2]

Many pro-China Western analysts do not take the concept of socialist market economy seriously. They see it as a semantic fig leaf for reforms that are intended to move China toward Western-style liberal capitalism. All they can see in China's reforms is China becoming "more like us." Human rights and other political issues, they

---

Milton Mueller is an Associate Professor at the School of Information Studies at Syracuse University.

[1]"The purpose of restructuring China's economic system is to establish a socialist market economy" (Jiang 1992).

[2]Myers elaborates: "[The political and legal system,] although not allowing opposition parties, will gradually allow voters to elect delegates to representative bodies that will discuss and ratify laws. Moreover, only those ideas that do not degrade, endanger, or replace Marxism and its related thought will be allowed to compete in education and the ideological market-place."

think, will take care of themselves as China develops. This belief in the inevitability of convergence has been aptly dubbed "reverse Marxism," in that it posits a deterministic link between market-oriented "forces of production" and a particular kind of social, political, and legal order.

Let us leave the issue of "reverse Marxism" aside for now. In the long run, there may indeed be a contradiction between China's exposure to market forces, the viability of large state enterprises, and political authoritarianism (although Singapore provides a sobering counter-example). In the short and medium terms, however, refusing to accept and understand the concept of socialist market economy is a big, and dangerous, mistake. Whatever one thinks about the long-term viability of the concept, China's leaders really do believe in it. It remains the touchstone of the Communist Party-led reform process and defines its procedures and constraints. While there are factions in China who do want the reform process to converge with the West, they are not in power; and besides, there are also minority elements in China who want to return to central planning or even Maoism. China is not Eastern Europe. Its mainstream ruling elites want to reform socialism and strengthen the Communist Party, not abandon them. To ignore or dismiss the socialist market economy is to fundamentally misread the intentions of China's rulers. And to misunderstand their intentions and policies is dangerous, because it is bound to lead to continual conflicts and disappointments when their actions fail to conform to the West's misguided expectations.

Reform and the Telecommunications Sector

The tension between competitive markets and China's reform socialism is nowhere clearer than in the telecommunications and information sectors. China's telecommunications sector is dominated by a traditional post, telephone, and telegraph monopoly and insulated from foreign competition in services and operation. China's leadership is corporatizing this monopoly and gradually introducing market forces into a variety of telecommunication markets. But it has no immediate plans to privatize its national service provider. China definitely wants to embrace the economic development potential of information technology and the global trading system, but it also wants to retain the traditional levers of control over national industrial policy and political and social communication associated with the monopoly structure of the past.

An open door and free market in telecommunications and information services would attract more investment, improve efficiency, and stimulate development. But it would also undercut the central government's ability to build up national enterprises in that sector. An information and networking industry with too much diversity, free trade, and commercial competition would erode the government's powers of surveillance and censorship, and work against its desire for a more geographically balanced distribution of wealth. China cannot, therefore, simply follow global trends toward a private, liberalized telecommunications order. It must carefully manage the introduction of market forces and balance development goals with its need for control and national protection. This tension is an inescapable byproduct of China's commitment to the model of the socialist market economy.

China's telecommunications sector is dominated by the Ministry of Posts and Telecommunications (MPT).[3] The MPT is a fascinating case study, so far successful, of the socialist market economy in operation. Unlike many large state enterprises, the MPT and its associated business enterprises have been strengthened by the post-1978 reforms rather than weakened. The industrialization process has created tremendous demand for telecommunication services and equipment. Although the MPT, like most monopolies, has not been able to meet all of that demand, it has achieved impressive and even historic rates of growth. Since 1992, in fact, the number of telephone main lines in China has doubled every two years. The MPT has also constructed a fairly comprehensive fiber optic, long distance trunk infrastructure connecting the capital cities in each province.

How did it achieve these impressive rates of growth? By administrative, managerial, and accounting reforms enacted within the framework of a state-owned enterprise system. It began with some decentralization of decisionmaking and profit, via the contractual responsibility system. The CRS was supplemented by a new nationwide accounting system in 1985 (Xu 1996). Further structural reforms, separating postal and telecommunication operations from

---

[3] Most of the information and points contained in this section are discussed in more detail in Mueller and Tan (1996).

each other and from governmental oversight functions, were implemented in 1988–91. The MPT is undoubtedly more efficient, more wealthy, more corporatized, and more technologically up-to-date than it was 10 years ago. However, it is important to remember the following facts as well:

- It is not privatized and its ministers and other government officials have made it clear that they have no immediate plans to privatize any parts of it.
- In an age of vertical disintegration of telecommunication services, the MPT's operational entities are still completely integrated, from terminal equipment manufacture, sales, and leasing to local service, long distance service, international service, mobile, paging, Internet access, and other value-added services.
- Although government functions such as regulation and policy-making are departmentally separated from business operations within the MPT, they are still part of the same ministry; that is, there is still no clear legal or institutional separation between the public and private sector.

Recently (in 1993 and 1994), China formally authorized domestic competition with MPT entities in certain telecommunication markets. Most of this competition is in new wireless and value-added service markets such as paging, telephone information services, and cellular telephony. The wireless competitors got their start through an informal and unplanned commercialization of radio spectrum resources by enterprises controlled by municipalities, other ministries, or the People's Liberation Army. Another important pro-competitive initiative took place when the Ministry of Electronics, Ministry of Railways, and Ministry of Power joined forces to form a nationwide telecommunications enterprise known as *Lian Tong*, or China Unicom. Unicom was sanctioned as a national competitor in 1994. So far, however, its activities are confined to mobile telephone and paging services in a few cities. Unicom is important because it is authorized to compete with the MPT in almost all markets except for international service. Nevertheless, in any given telecommunication service market, the MPT holds a dominant share. And in fact, true to the model of the socialist market economy, the controlled introduction of market forces has improved the efficiency of the existing telephone monopoly. At the same time, regulations and restrictions on foreign investment have kept new competitors from growing to a size that might threaten the MPT's control of the basic infrastructure.

WTO: Disruptive Change or Next Step in Gradual Reform?

China's accession to the World Trade Organization is one of the most important economic policy issues in the world. China's relationship to WTO is an important test for all parties involved: A test of China's willingness to take reform and opening to new levels; of the WTO's ability to be truly global and universal in scope; of the meaningfulness and consistency of the WTO's rules (making too much of an exception for China will undermine the world trading system).

China is prepared to make important concessions in traditional merchandise trade in order to gain entry to WTO. According to a recent study, the tariff reductions proposed by China would result in $21.9 billion a year in additional income by 2005 for China, and $17 billion a year for Hong Kong. But as is often the case, China and the Western world are not quite on the same wavelength. Western countries such as the United States are interested in *services* trade, where it may have an advantage, as well as commodities trade, where China has a cost-advantage. In the advanced economies, services make up over 70 percent of GDP, whereas in China the percentage is only around 30 percent. The advanced economies, especially the United States, are particularly interested in freer trade in telecommunication and information services.

The WTO Agreement on Basic Telecommunications

The rest of the world is moving rather quickly toward a regime of free trade in telecommunication services. On 15 February 1997, the General Agreement on Trade in Services of the World Trade Organization concluded its negotiations on basic telecommunication services. The governments of 69 countries, including the United States, European Union, Japan, India, Pakistan, Korea, and Malaysia, comprising more than 90 percent of global telecommunication revenues, made commitments to open up their respective telecommunication markets beginning January 1998. Commitments involved three basic areas: (1) market access, (2) foreign investment, and

(3) acceptance of certain regulatory principles intended to make market openings meaningful. The governments of 53 nations made commitments to open up market access to international services: 56 governments promised to permit foreign ownership or control of telecommunications to varying degrees, and 65 governments committed themselves to observe the regulatory principles contained in the WTO reference paper.

China's telecommunications regime is miles apart from the WTO agreement. China does allow the establishment of wholly foreign-owned enterprises and equity or contractual joint ventures in manufacturing of communication equipment. But in all types of telecommunication services, China strictly prohibits foreign investors to operate, or take part in operations, whether they are provided as part of the public communications network or as specialized, dedicated communication networks. China's restrictions on foreign involvement in telecom services are among the tightest in the world.

Furthermore, there are indications that China is simply not prepared to offer any additional opening in the telecommunications sector. At a November 1996 meeting in Manila, members of the Asia Pacific Economic Cooperation organization prepared detailed "individual action plans" on trade and investment liberalization. With regard to merchandise tariffs and nontariff barriers, China prepared specific, substantive proposals for short-term (1997–2000), mid-term (2001–2010), and long-term (2010 on) change. In services such as banking and insurance, China also set out specific plans for gradual liberalization over the next 20 years.

China's APEC proposals for telecommunication services, on the other hand, are notable for their lack of substance and the absence of any long-term agenda. All China offered in telecommunications was this: "Short-term (1997–2000): Work out a program for compliance with the international rules for trade in value-added network services." The language suggests that trade in telecom services will be confined to "value-added network services," which comprises only about 10 percent of services markets, and leaves the domestic operator in total control of the infrastructure. The action plan contains no long-term plans for further opening.

Institutional Change and the Regulatory Principles

The most jarring disparity between the WTO agreement and China concerns the reference paper on regulatory principles. This is where the conflict between the Western world's liberal-capitalist legal/ regulatory order and the socialist market economy comes into full view.

The WTO agreement on basic telecom services was based on 20 years of experience with the liberalization of telecommunication markets around the world. The negotiators recognized that incumbent telephone monopolies enjoy certain structural advantages that can nullify or minimize competition, even when markets are legally open. In addition to opening markets, therefore, the negotiators sought to define certain aspects of the regulatory environment in the signatory countries that would be required to make competition effective. In particular, the WTO agreement defined six basic regulatory principles. An enumeration and brief explanation of each follows:

1. *Competition safeguards.* The principles call for "appropriate measures" to be maintained to prevent anti-competitive practices by a dominant supplier. Anti-competitive practices includes cross-subsidization, exploiting information obtained from competitors, and not making available to competing suppliers on a timely basis technical information about essential facilities and other commercial information required to provide services.
2. *Interconnection.* Because of the network externality, competing telecom networks often need access to existing networks to exchange traffic and allow intercommunication among users of the different systems. The WTO regulatory principles call for ensuring interconnection with a major supplier "at any technically feasible point in the network." Interconnection must be provided on nondiscriminatory terms, in a timely fashion, at cost-oriented rates, with sufficient unbundling so that competitors need not pay for network components or facilities it does not require. Moreover, the procedures for interconnection must be publicly available and transparent. And to settle disputes about interconnection there must be recourse to an independent regulator with the power to resolve disputes in a reasonable period of time.
3. *Universal service.* Members of the agreement have the right to establish universal service obligations, but they must be administered in a transparent, nondiscriminatory, and competitively neutral manner, and not be so burdensome as to constitute a barrier to competition.

4. *Licensing criteria.* Where licenses to operate a service are required, the country must make publicly available all licensing criteria and the time period required to reach a decision about an application for a license. Signatories are also committed to make the terms and conditions of individual licenses publicly available.

5. *Independent regulators.* Regulatory bodies should be "separate from, and not accountable to," any supplier of services. Decisions and procedures of the regulator should be impartial.

6. *Resource allocation.* Procedures for the allocation of resources such as telephone numbers and radio frequencies should be "carried out in an objective, timely, transparent, and nondiscriminatory manner."

How does China stack up against the WTO-proposed regulatory principles? The following subsections go through each principle individually to see whether China conforms or not.

Competitive Safeguards

China passed an Anti-Unfair Competition Law in September 1993. The law prohibits price-fixing, prevents predatory pricing, and protects trade marks and patents. Enforcement responsibilities, however, are vaguely assigned to "authorities above the county level." There is no specialized agency to monitor, interpret, or enforce the provisions of the law. It is difficult to find any evidence that the law has ever been applied. Effectively, then, China does not have any substantive or predictable procedures in place to prevent anticompetitive behavior by the dominant operators associated with the MPT. In support of this conclusion, there is already evidence of anticompetitive cross-subsidization. Confronted with new competition in cellular markets from Unicom, one MPT subsidiary reduced cellular prices drastically while increasing the price of international telephone calls. (International calls are a protected monopoly.) Furthermore, the MPT's accounts and technical information regarding the network are not transparent to an independent regulator or to its domestic competitors. It is difficult to imagine the MPT making this information available to foreigners. Currently, the MPT will not even provide foreigners a copy of its statistical yearbook.

Interconnection

Physical interconnection of the MPT-administered public telephone network and the alternate networks administered by Unicom does exist. However, Unicom spokespersons have expressed a great deal of dissatisfaction with the timeliness with which interconnection facilities are offered and the limited scope of interconnection. There is still no firm agreement as to the commercial arrangements (i.e., the price charged and level of unbundling). The MPT has not defined a transparent template for interconnection arrangements. China has set up a "Leading Group on Economic Informatization," and this group serves as a rudimentary hearing and dispute resolution body in matters of telecom policy. But this leading group is basically a committee that contains representatives of all ministries interested in telecommunications and "informatization," not a full-time, professional, independent regulator with a formal, timely decisionmaking process. Because it represents the main stakeholders within China, it is difficult to imagine foreign competitors obtaining a fair hearing from the Leading Group.

Universal Service

In telecommunications as in other sectors, China's leadership is concerned about geographic disparities in its development. It thus attaches importance to the concept of "universal service." Indeed, the MPT's revenue accounting system is structured to cross-subsidize high-cost areas in a manner similar to the predivestiture separations and settlements system of the Bell system. This kind of universal service subsidy, which is embedded internally into the monopoly provider's accounting, does not conform to the WTO regulatory principles. It is not transparent, explicit, or competitively neutral. At the same time, however, China does not impose any specific universal service contribution upon competing service providers. So in this area, China neither complies nor fails to comply—it is off the map. It is likely that if enough competition developed to threaten the MPT's internal cross-subsidies, then this issue would have more salience.

Licensing Criteria

MPT Directive 675 has defined licensing criteria for the open value-added services (see Mueller and Tan 1996: 77). China partially conforms to this principle. The licensing directive contains some explicit criteria to be used, and technically (at least to service providers within China) the criteria are "publicly available," although foreigners attempting to get a copy of them will not have an easy time. China's licensing regime notoriously does give the government considerable discretion, however. Various businesses, from McDonald's to Jimmy Lai's Giordano clothing stores, have discovered that licenses can be revoked or withdrawn in an arbitrary fashion.

Independent Regulators

In this area China fails to conform to the WTO standards. The MPT and its provincial branches are the primary regulators and policymakers for the telecommunications sector; the same entities are the dominant service providers in the sector. Although the MPT and its Provincial Telecommunication Administrations (PTAs) have separated the functions of policy/regulation and enterprise operation into different departments, there is still a close financial and administrative connection between government and operator. China's existing domestic competitors already complain loudly that the MPT is both player and referee, and that they cannot expect impartial treatment from it. That is one reason why the Leading Group on Informatization was set up. But the Leading Group is simply a more representative body of supplier interests, not an independent regulator.

Resource Allocation

Allocation of radio frequencies within the PRC was, until recently, rather disorganized but conducive to domestic competition. Control was fragmented among local, provincial, and national authorities. This made it possible for entrepreneurial organizations to obtain licenses and start new telecom businesses. New regulations issued in May 1994 recentralized spectrum allocation in the hands of a State Radio Regulatory Commission dominated by the MPT. This made the procedures for obtaining spectrum more explicit and orderly. But it also gives the MPT, one of the major players in paging, cellular, and satellite service markets, direct control over who gets what resources. Numbering also appears to be totally in the hands of the MPT.

Conclusion

In telecommunication services trade, compliance with the WTO agreement will require a level of institutional development that China currently has not attained. A close connection between government ministries and business enterprises is true not only of the MPT, but also of its domestic competitors. China lacks the legal and regulatory framework required to implement interconnection agreements and prevent anti-competitive behavior. China's main telecoms infrastructure provider, the MPT and its provincial PTAs, are too close to the government to freely and impartially provide information about their systems to competitors, especially if the competitors are foreign-owned or managed. All this says nothing about the political barriers to freer trade in information and communication services. China's Communist Party and state apparatus both maintain a strong interest in monitoring and controlling information flows. Their recent enactment of Internet regulations and restrictions on foreign news reporting show that they are willing and able to exploit the monopolistic status of state enterprises to maintain this control.

All this leads to the 64 billion dollar question: Will integration with the global market economy through the WTO force China to break with the socialist market economy model? If it joins the WTO, can China maintain its current balance of state ownership and management, market forces, and political control?

References

Chang, M. (1994) "The Chinese Communists Start to Cultivate a New Foreign Policy Toward the Major Powers and Set Forth Three States for Press Forward with a Market System." *The Mirror*, October: 24–27.

Jiang, Z. (1992) Speech at the Communist Party of China's 14th Congress (October).

Mueller, M., and Tan, Z. (1996) *China in the Information Age: Telecommunications and the Dilemmas of Reform.* The Washington Papers, No. 169. Washington, D.C.: Center for Strategic and International Studies with Praeger.

Myers, R. (1994) "The Socialist Market Economy in the People's Republic of China: Fact or Fiction?" The George Ernest Morrison Lecture in Ethnology. Pamphlet. Canberra: Australian National University.

Xu, Y. (1996) "Competition Without Privatization: the Chinese Path." Paper delivered at the 11th Biennial Conference of the International Telecommunications Society, Seville, Spain, 18 June.

14. Liberalizing China's Foreign Exchange Regime

Y. C. Richard Wong and M. L. Sonia Wong

This chapter examines the way in which China has transformed itself from a highly centralized foreign exchange regime toward a more open regime with current account convertibility. The focus is on the endogenous aspect of the liberalization process. We describe the way in which the open-door policy and other reforms in China have expanded the foreign exchange rate's role in the Chinese economy and have compelled the government to remove regulatory barriers on foreign exchange transactions. We also describe the way in which reform in the foreign exchange regime fueled itself and created pressures for further reforms, especially in banking. Consistent with China's approach to economic reform, relaxation of exchange controls has proceeded incrementally, experimentally, and pragmatically–in order to minimize the number of conflicts with vested interests.

Historical Background

Before China's economy opened up, all foreign trade in the country was conducted strictly according to mandatory plans. These consisted of import and export plans upon which the central planning authority decided. In determining these plans, the authority sought to achieve a balance in foreign exchange requirements. The heavy reliance on mandatory plans implied that the foreign exchange rate had very little influence on the level and the pattern of foreign trade. Rather, it was essentially an accounting device used in the formulation of foreign trade plans. In China's pre-reform period,

Y. C. Richard Wong is Professor of Economics at the University of Hong Kong and Director of the Hong Kong Centre for Economic Research. M. L. Sonia Wong is a doctoral candidate in economics at the University of Hong Kong.

the exchange rate played no direct role as a price signal in either foreign trade or in the allocation of resources in China.

The role of the exchange rate began to change in 1978, after China decentralized foreign trade authority to localities and enterprises. When foreign trade corporations (FTCs) were given a certain degree of freedom to conduct foreign trade, the exchange rate began to act as a signal to motivate importing and exporting decisions. Because the domestic currency was overvalued, FTCs had little incentive to expand exports. To counteract the disincentive effects of exports due to exchange rate overvaluation, China began to modify its foreign exchange policy shortly after the decentralization of foreign trade took place. The modifications that occurred were as follows:

First, the official exchange rates were steadily devalued so as to compensate for the rising costs of exports. Second, the foreign exchange retention scheme, whereby exporting enterprises and local governments were allowed to retain a certain portion of their foreign exchange earnings to finance their own imports, was introduced. Third, foreign exchange swap markets, which allowed exporters to convert their retained foreign exchange earnings at more favorable exchange rates, were established in 1988. Although the retention scheme and the swap markets were designed to provide incentives to exporters, they also helped to increase the convertibility of China's domestic currency.

From 1988 to 1993, China had a two-tier foreign exchange system (see Will 1990). It consisted of (1) the administrative allocation system through foreign exchange plans, and (2) the buying and selling of the retained foreign exchange earnings through swap markets. As compared with the highly centralized foreign exchange allocation system of the pre-reform period, the two-tier foreign exchange system allowed markets to play a role in the allocation of foreign exchange. It was reasonably effective at stimulating the growth of exports and at improving the efficiency of China's foreign trade. The system, however, had problems. It introduced distortions in price signals, which could in turn exert a pervasive influence on the allocation of resources as the Chinese economy became increasingly open and price responsive.

On January 1, 1994, China unified its official and swap market exchange rates and established a unified interbank foreign exchange market. The 1994 reform was a major step toward current account

TABLE 1
CHINA'S FOREIGN TRADE, INVESTMENT, AND EXCHANGE RESERVES,
1983–96
(BILLIONS OF DOLLARS)

Year	Exports	Imports	Foreign Direct Investment (Actual)	Foreign Exchange Reserves	Exports as a Percentage of China's GDP
1983	$22.23	$21.39	$0.64	$8.901	7.59
1984	26.14	27.41	1.26	8.220	8.48
1985	27.35	42.25	1.66	2.664	8.96
1986	30.94	42.90	1.88	2.072	10.47
1987	39.44	43.22	2.31	2.923	12.31
1988	47.52	55.28	3.19	3.372	11.85
1989	52.54	59.14	3.39	5.550	11.70
1990	62.09	53.35	3.49	11.093	16.03
1991	71.84	63.79	4.37	21.712	17.69
1992	84.94	80.59	11.01	19.443	17.59
1993	91.74	103.96	27.52	21.109	15.32
1994	121.04	115.69	33.77	51.620	23.18
1995	148.77	132.08	37.52	73.596	21.52
1996	151.17	138.95	42.35	105.029	18.53

SOURCES: Data for 1989–95 were obtained from the *Statistical Yearbook of China*. Data for 1996 came from China's most recent economic statistics and from *China Economic News*.

convertibility. Afterwards, exports, tourism, and foreign direct investment grew briskly, at rates of 31.9 percent, 56.4 percent, and 22.7 percent, respectively, in 1994 (see Table 1). Foreign exchange reserves increased by 114.5 percent in 1994, and by 42.6 percent in 1995. At the end of 1996, China's foreign reserves had reached $105 billion, and China was able to meet the IMF requirements for current account convertibility on December 1, 1996, without causing a major fluctuation in the foreign exchange market.

From Plans to a Two-Tier System

When foreign trade was decentralized in 1978, China recognized that the practice of requiring FTCs to surrender all their foreign exchange earnings to the government at an overvalued exchange rate would depress the returns received from exports and, hence, reduce FTCs' export incentives. Starting in 1978 China modified the foreign exchange management so as to promote exports. Measures adopted included the devaluation of the renminbi, the introduction of the foreign exchange retention scheme, and the establishment of foreign exchange swap markets. These measures not only helped to promote exports, they also created a more liberalized two-tier foreign exchange system and paved the way for current account convertibility.

Devaluation

Before the decentralization of foreign trade took place, the effect of the exchange rate on exports and imports was not the main issue at stake for exchange rate determination in China, because trade flows were determined largely by plans. The exchange rate was set with an eye toward its influence on a few nontrade items such as remittances from overseas Chinese and earnings from tourism. As a result, the exchange rate was fixed mainly on the basis of the relative prices of a basket of consumer goods in China and in other major cities in the world. Because many consumer goods in China were underpriced, this led to a substantial overvaluation of the renminbi (Wang 1991, Lardy 1992).

To alleviate the disincentive effects of the overvaluation on exports, the government began steadily devaluing the renminbi after 1980. The first round of devaluation began on January 1, 1981, with the introduction of an internal settlement rate of 2.8 yuan per U.S. dollar in trade transactions.[1] The internal settlement was determined on the basis of the average cost of generating one U.S. dollar of foreign exchange earnings plus a 10 percent margin (Wang 1991: 67). That devaluation marked a turning point for China's foreign exchange rate policy. From 1981 to 1993 exchange rates in China were determined largely on the basis of the costs of generating foreign exchange earnings (Lardy 1992). In line with the rising average costs of generating foreign exchange earnings, the exchange rates were being adjusted downward gradually so as to make exports

---

[1]When the dual exchange rate system was created, China began to devalue the official exchange rate, which was 1.55 yuan per U.S. dollar in January 1981. By the end of 1984, the official exchange rate had reached 2.8 yuan per U.S. dollar, and the internal settlement rate had been abolished.

TABLE 2
MAJOR DEVALUATION EPISODES IN CHINA, 1980–93

Time	Jan. 1, 1981	Jan. 1– Oct. 10, 1985	Jul. 5, 1986	Dec. 16, 1989	Nov. 17, 1990	Apr. 17– Dec. 30, 1993
Official Exchange Rate (Yuan/$)	1.55	2.8–3.2	3.7	4.7	5.2	5.2–5.8
Internal Settlement Rate (Yuan/$)	2.8	–	–	–	–	–
Devaluation (%)	44.7	12.5	13.5	21.3	9.6	10.3

NOTE: Devaluation is from the official exchange rate to the internal settlement rate. The internal settlement rate was abolished at the end of 1984.

profitable. The major devaluations before the unification of exchange rates in 1994 are shown in Table 2.

From 1981 to 1993, there were six devaluations in China. The amount of devaluation ranged from 9.6 percent to 44.9 percent. The devaluations that took place in 1981, 1986, 1989, and 1990 were major ones in which the exchange rate was adjusted in one shot. The devaluations that took place in 1985 and 1993 were minor ones in which the exchange rate was continuously adjusted downward by small amounts.

The changes to China's exchange rate before 1994 had an important feature. Although the exchange rate was set to make exports profitable, the official exchange rates were usually lower than were the costs of generating foreign exchange earnings, as is revealed in Table 3. This suggests that devaluation in this period was employed to passively compensate for the rising costs of exports rather than to actively promote exports. As devaluation implied a gain for exporters and a loss for importers, it was politically easier for the government to introduce it when the average costs of generating foreign exchange earnings had already exceeded the official exchange rate.

The fact that the official exchange rate moved in accordance with the average costs of generating foreign exchange earnings also implied that devaluation in this period might have been driven by the domestic price reform, the enterprise reform, and the exchange

TABLE 3
AVERAGE COSTS OF GENERATING FOREIGN EXCHANGE EARNINGS
AND THE OFFICIAL EXCHANGE RATES, 1979–96

Year	Average Costs of Generating Exchange Earnings (Yuan/$)	Official Exchange Rate (Yuan/$)
1979	2.40	1.56
1980	2.31	1.50
1981	2.48	2.80
1982	2.67	2.80
1983	3.03	2.80
1984	2.79	2.80
1985	3.20	2.94
1986	3.50	3.45
1987	4.20	3.72
1988	4.15	3.72
1989	5.06	3.77
1990	5.87	4.78
1991	5.50	5.32
1992	5.58	5.51
1993	–	5.81
1994	–	8.61
1995	8.40	8.35
1996	–	8.31

SOURCES: For average costs of generating foreign exchange earnings, data for 1979–88 and 1990 were obtained from Zhang (1993: 86); data for 1989 were obtained from Sung (1994: 126); and data for 1991–92 came from Lin (1992: 224). Data for 1995 came from Xiao (1996). Official exchange rates were obtained from the *Statistical Yearbook of China*.

rate policy itself. Before the introduction of the price reform and the enterprise reform, the government had relatively good control over export costs, because domestic enterprises had to deliver fixed quantities of domestic goods to FTCs at fixed prices according to plans. As price reform and enterprise reform in China continued, domestic enterprises could set the prices and the quantities of goods that they supplied to FTCs. The relative shortage of goods in the domestic market meant that FTCs had to compete for the exportables and bid up the costs of exports. The government was forced to devalue the currency. The devaluation itself fueled further rises in prices and once again exerted pressure on the exchange rate.

Foreign Exchange Retention

Except for a very few years during which the internal settlement rate was used, the average costs of generating foreign exchange earnings in China have generally been higher than the official exchange rate. Why did exporting enterprises have an incentive to export when the costs of generating foreign exchange earnings were higher than the official exchange rates? In China, the differential between the average cost of generating foreign exchange earnings and the official exchange rate does not reflect the true profitability of FTCs, because of the foreign exchange retention system. The foreign exchange retention scheme was introduced in 1978 to enhance exporting enterprises' incentives to export.[2] After exporting enterprises had sold all their foreign exchange earnings to the government at the official rate, the government allowed exporting enterprises and local governments to repurchase a certain amount of foreign exchange. If they wanted to use the retained foreign exchange, they could use renminbi to buy it back from the government according to the prevailing exchange rate, as long as the use of the foreign exchange fell within the confines of regulation. As the official exchange rates were overvalued, the right to buy back foreign exchange at the official rates further devalued the domestic currency. Foreign trade corporations thus had an incentive to expand their exports until the average costs of generating foreign exchange earnings were higher than the official exchange rates (Zhang 1993).

The permitted rates of foreign exchange retention in China have changed considerably since 1978. In 1979 the retention rate for exports handled by ministerial trading enterprises was 20 percent of earnings above the level of exports achieved in 1978. The retention rate for exports of local governments was 40 percent of earnings above the 1978 level.[3] In 1982 the government-fixed retention rates for each region were equal to the share of total export revenues

[2]In 1979 the government approved the expansion of the system to the nontrade sector.

[3]There were also separate retention rates applying to certain new types of trade. For example, the retention rate for fees from processing and assembly of foreign components was 30 percent of all earnings.

retained in the previous year. The provincial rates ranged from as low as 3 percent to as high as 25 percent. In 1985 the government raised the retention rate to a minimum of 25 percent for all regions.[4] In addition to the basic retention rate, all provinces could also retain 70 percent of the above-plan foreign exchange earnings. In 1987 the government granted a preferential retention rate of 70 percent for foreign trade enterprises in light industry, arts and crafts, and garments. In 1988 the contract responsibility system was implemented in the foreign trade system. Under the new system, the amount of foreign exchange earnings submitted to the central government was fixed by contract and, above that, foreign exchange earnings would be shared by the local and central governments at a ratio of eight to two. According to the estimate of the World Bank (1994), the effective retention rate from 1987 to 1990 was about 44 percent of all foreign exchange earnings. In 1991 the government increased the retention rate further when export subsidies were abolished. For most commodities, 80 percent of total foreign exchange earnings could be retained. The government, however, reserved the right to purchase at the swap rate 30 percent of foreign exchange earned from commodity exports.

Although the foreign exchange scheme was designed to provide incentives to exporters, it broke the monopoly the government had during the pre-reform regime on the access to and the use of foreign exchange. Now the government had to share foreign exchange earnings with exporters. Although there were various restrictions on the use of retained exchange, the holders of foreign exchange quotas usually had a considerable degree of discretion when it came to the use of foreign exchange earnings, especially after 1988.[5] The continuous increase in the permitted retention rates represented a continuous diminution of the government's monopoly power over the access to and the use of foreign exchange. The Chinese transition to currency convertibility was gradual. It started in 1979 with the introduction of the foreign exchange retention scheme.

[4]The rate for Guangdong and Fuijian was raised to 30 percent, and the rates for Inner Mongolia, Xianjiang, Guangxi, Yunnan, Guizhou, and Qinghai were raised to 50 percent.

[5]In 1985, after a sharp fall in foreign exchange reserves, the government imposed very restrictive controls on the use of retained foreign exchange and froze a large share of the retained earnings. The controls were removed in 1988.

Foreign exchange reform in many developing countries has failed due to opposition from vested interests. China was fortunate in that the volume of imports in the pre-reform period was low, and hence vested interest in the old regime was not great. The rapid and continuous expansion of exports allowed the central government to maintain its desired volume of imports when the permitted foreign exchange retention rates were raised for enterprises and local governments. In 1993 the permitted retention rate had reached 80 percent, but exports also increased to \$91.74 billion. The government meanwhile could still obtain more than \$18 billion to finance its imports, an amount nearly double its volume of imports in 1978.

Foreign Exchange Swapping

Shortly after the foreign exchange retention system was introduced, exporting enterprises and local governments received permission to sell foreign exchange quotas to units that sought access to foreign exchange to purchase imports. The possibility of swapping foreign exchange further enhanced export incentives, because it gave holders of foreign exchange quotas another opportunity to capture the value of retained earnings. In addition to purchasing imports, they could convert retained earnings at rates that were more favorable than were the official rates.[6] Similar to the foreign exchange retention system, foreign exchange swapping, in effect, permitted further devaluation of the domestic currency. The exchange rates in swap centers and the transaction volumes from 1980 to 1993 are shown in Table 4.

The first foreign exchange swapping service was established by the Guangdong Branch of the Bank of China in 1980, and it was soon extended to 12 major cities (Wang 1991). The price of early transactions was 3.08 yuan per U.S. dollar (Wang 1991). As the swapping price was only 10 percent more than the internal settlement rate and the rate of foreign exchange retention was not high in the early 1980s, the transaction volume in the early years was modest. Nevertheless, the early transactions represented a breakthrough in China's foreign exchange allocation system. They marked

---

[6] As noted by Lardy (1992), some exporters failed to utilize all their retained foreign exchange because they were unable to obtain licenses for the imports they desired.

TABLE 4
SWAP MARKET PRICES AND TRANSACTION VOLUME, 1980–93

Year	Swapping Rate (Yuan/$)	Transaction Volume (Billions of Dollars)
1980	3.08	–
1981	3.08	–
1982	3.08	–
1983	3.08	–
1984	3.08	–
1985	3.08	–
1986	4.20	1.89
1987	5.41	4.20
1988	6.31	6.26
1989	6.43	8.57
1990	5.81	13.2
1991	5.85	20.4
1992	6.58	25.0
1993	8.65	–

SOURCES: For swap rates, data for 1980–86 were obtained from Wang (1991: 81–2); data for 1987–92 come from the World Bank (1994: 35). The transaction volumes were obtained from Lin (1993: 195, 224). The 1993 figures come from the *Almanac of China's Finance and Banking*.

the beginning of an era in which the price mechanism would be used to allocate foreign exchange in China.

The first foreign exchange swap market opened in 1985 in Shenzhen. Markets then opened in Shanghai and Beijing in 1986, and in Tianjing in 1987. From 1985 to 1987, the foreign exchange swap markets provided swapping services to joint ventures only. Domestic enterprises were not allowed to participate. The annual transaction volume in foreign exchange swap markets in this period was low, at $1.89 billion in 1986 and $4.2 billion in 1987 (Lin 1993: 195).

In 1987, domestic enterprises in light industry, arts and crafts, and garments were allowed to sell their retained foreign exchange in the foreign exchange swap markets. In April 1988, all domestic enterprises were allowed to sell their retained earnings in foreign exchange swap markets. The relaxation of exchange controls gave further impetus to the expansion of the number of swap markets as well as to the transaction volume. It also provided additional incentives to exporters. By the end of December 1992, there were more than 100 swap markets, and the transaction volume had reached $25 billion (World Bank 1994).

The foreign exchange swap markets were not entirely free markets. Initially, the government attempted to control swap rates by imposing ceiling rates. In February 1986, a price cap of 4.2 yuan per U.S. dollar was imposed (Wang 1991: 82). In 1988–89, there was a price cap of 5.7 yuan per U.S. dollar (Lin 1993: 224). Since 1989, swap market prices have been liberalized gradually. To achieve this gradual liberalization, the government has pegged the prices by intervening in swap markets rather than by setting prices directly.[7]

Secondly, the government imposed controls on the sources and the use of foreign exchange. In the late 1980s, sellers had to provide documents to show that foreign exchange had been acquired legally. In most cases, buyers had to obtain import licenses (or other relevant documents) from the Ministry of Foreign Economic Relation and Trade (MOFERT) and administrative approval for their transactions from the State Administration of Exchange Control (SAEC). Beginning in December 1991, when all domestic residents were allowed to sell their foreign exchange in the swap markets without being required to show proof of their sources of foreign exchange income, selling foreign exchange at the swap markets was virtually unrestricted. In contrast, buying foreign exchange from the swap markets was still subject to the administrative approval of MOFERT and SAEC. SAEC's authorization was based on a priority list that reflected the industrial policy of the state.[8]

Finally, transactions across swap markets were restricted. There were significant differentials in exchange rates across markets in different parts of the country. Exchange rates in the eastern and western regions were generally higher than the average rates, and the southern region's swap rates were usually the lowest in the country (Huang and Wong 1995). The market segmentation implied that there were barriers to direct arbitrage between markets.

---

[7]In February 1993, the government again imposed a price cap of 8 yuan per U.S. dollar on swap centers in an attempt to stem the year-long fall in the yuan. That price ceiling was removed in May 1993.

[8]For details of the priority list, see World Bank (1994).

Although transactions in the swap markets were subject to various restrictions, the establishment of the swap markets was a major step toward current account convertibility. With the increase in transaction volume in the swap markets, the price mechanism began to play a more and more important role in the allocation of foreign exchange in China.

From a Two-Tier System toward Current Account Convertibility

In 1994, China moved to unify the exchange rates and establish a unified inter-bank foreign exchange market. The demise of the two-tier foreign exchange system was caused, in part, by its own success. The system had helped China to expand its foreign trade and foreign investment. China's increased openness, however, strengthened the link between the external sector and the internal sector. It increased the distorting effects of the multiple exchange rates (the official rate, the swap market rates, and the black market rates) on the allocation of resources in China. There were increasing pressures on the government to correct the exchange rate. On the other hand, expansion in exports and foreign investments also resulted in substantial foreign exchange reserves, which made the strict exchange controls less of a policy imperative.

On January 1, 1994, China unified the two-tier exchange rates at the prevailing swap rate of 8.7 yuan per U.S. dollar. Foreign exchange swap markets were replaced by a national interbank foreign exchange market with its headquarters in Shanghai.[9] The foreign exchange retention scheme and the foreign exchange plans were abolished, and a foreign exchange selling and buying system was introduced. All foreign exchange income derived from all sources by all Chinese enterprises and institutions had to be sold to designated banks. In exchange for the compulsory selling of foreign exchange, enterprises were granted more freedom to buy back foreign exchange from banks. For general imports, enterprises could buy foreign exchange at authorized banks by presenting import contracts and payment notices issued by financial institutions abroad. For imports under quota, license, and registration management, enterprises could buy foreign exchange by presenting the corresponding

---

[9] From January 1994 to July 1996, foreign-funded enterprises continued to buy and sell foreign exchange through the swap markets.

contracts and other "valid certificates" issued by MOFERT. Although the purchase of foreign exchange was still restricted, the 1994 reform was a major step toward the convertibility of the renminbi for current account transactions.

The new exchange rate system introduced in 1994 is a managed floating system. At the beginning of each trading day, the People's Bank of China (PBOC) publishes the renminbi exchange rate, based mainly on the dealing rates at the foreign exchange market on the previous day. The designated foreign exchange banks quote their own rates within a floating range set by the PBOC. The establishment of the national interbank foreign exchange market has improved the efficiency of foreign exchange allocation, since foreign exchange is traded at a unified rate in a unified national market.

As part of the 1994 reform, foreign-funded enterprises were allowed to continue to keep their foreign exchange in designated accounts instead of selling it to an authorized bank, as domestic enterprises were required to do. They were, however, denied access to the interbank market. They continued to buy and sell foreign exchange through swap markets, generally under case-by-case review and with the approval of the SAEC. Starting in the first half of 1996, foreign-funded enterprises in certain trial areas are permitted to buy and sell foreign exchange from authorized domestic banks without the SAEC's approval for most current account transactions. Their access to the interbank exchange market was extended nationwide beginning on July 1, 1996. They are allowed to maintain a foreign exchange settlement bank account within preapproved limits. Also following a trial period, foreign bank branches in China are allowed to provide foreign exchange settlement and exchange business for foreign-funded enterprises. On November 27, 1996, Dai Xianglong, governor of the PBOC, announced that China would meet the IMF requirements for current account convertibility beginning on December 1, 1996.

China's move from a two-tier system toward current account convertibility has been gradual. The 1994 reform was an incremental change rather than an abrupt plunge into an entirely new foreign exchange regime. Most of the practices in the new system had already existed before the introduction of the reform. Starting on December 1, 1991, Chinese residents and permanent foreign residents were already allowed to sell and buy foreign exchange from swap markets. In March 1993, residents and travelers were allowed to carry a maximum of 6,000 yuan in and out of China. In June 1993, a pilot scheme launched in Guangzhou allowed foreign travelers to change foreign exchange directly into renminbi. At the end of 1993, swap market rates already covered 80 percent of China's current account transactions (World Bank 1994). What the unification of exchange rates achieved was essentially an expansion in the coverage of the swap market rates to all international payments and capital flows.

In 1996, after the interbank foreign exchange market had been operating quite smoothly for almost three years, foreign-funded enterprises were permitted to join in as well. On the other hand, restrictions prevailing before the reform on the convertibility of renminbi were retained. Buyers of foreign exchange still had to present a "valid certificate" to authorized banks. Foreign-funded enterprises still had to comply with their foreign exchange balancing requirement by means of an annual foreign exchange review and foreign registration procedures.

Perhaps the most fundamental change to take place after 1993 was the abolition of the swap markets and the establishment of a unified interbank foreign exchange market for domestic enterprises. Under the new system, exchange rate stability and current account balance have to be maintained through monetary policies of the PBOC and administrative controls of MOFERT rather than through foreign exchange controls on the current account transactions. Consequently, exchange rate determination is no longer simply a trade or current account issue. Broader economic concerns relating to macroeconomic stability and monetary and fiscal policy were brought into the picture, as were different political and economic constituencies. Exchange rate determination had an effect beyond imports and exports, but with wide sectors of the economy through the inter-linkages of various markets and bureaucracies. These changes make it increasingly urgent for China to speed up banking reform and to develop a set of market-based policy instruments. They also make it increasingly important for China to speed up enterprise reform. It will be difficult for the central bank to stabilize the exchange rate as long as authorized domestic banks have not been completely commercialized, interest rates are not market determined, and enterprises have not yet been subject to hard budget constraints.

The establishment of the unified foreign exchange market in an increasingly open and market-oriented economy also means that the exchange rate policy of the PBOC has direct implications for the macroeconomic stability of the economy. In 1994, there was a surge in the foreign exchange supply due to the rapid expansion of exports and foreign direct investment (see Table 1). In order to maintain a stable foreign exchange rate, the PBOC bought a large amount of foreign exchange on the foreign exchange market. The intervention of the PBOC increased the money supply and was one of the important factors behind the high rate of domestic inflation, which reached about 25 percent at that time.

Such interrelations between the internal and external sectors of the Chinese economy imply that exchange rates in China cannot be set with an eye simply toward promoting exports. In fact, following the 1994 reform, exchange rates in China could no longer be determined on the basis of the costs of generating foreign exchange earnings. From 1994 to 1996, the general price level in China rose more than 40 percent, and there was a substantial increase in the costs of generating foreign exchange earnings. The renminbi, however, appreciated slightly due to an increase in the supply of foreign exchange, as was evidenced by the rising foreign exchange reserves. The currency appreciation and rising export costs reduced the profitability of exports. Exports grew at a rate of only 1.5 percent in 1996. Despite the strong voice from the exporting sector to devalue the renminbi so as to promote exports, the PBOC maintained a stable renminbi due to its concern over controlling domestic inflation. The strengthened link between the internal and external sectors of the Chinese economy has expanded the constituents of the exchange rate policy beyond the foreign trade sector. China now has less latitude in which to employ foreign exchange policy to promote exports.

Foreign Exchange Reform and Export Performance, 1981–96

When China began implementing the open-door policy, it had inherited from the old regime a foreign exchange control system that was extremely unfavorable for export expansion. From very early on, the government began to adjust exchange rates and to relax foreign exchange controls so as to increase export incentives. The liberalization measures created a two-tier foreign exchange system that played an important role in stimulating and sustaining export growth. In 1994, China unified the exchange rates and established a unified interbank foreign exchange. The reform shifted the focus of the foreign exchange policy from promoting exports to maintaining macroeconomic stability. The effects of foreign exchange reform on export performance from 1981 to 1996 are shown in Figure 1.

Figure 1 shows that export growth from 1981 to 1993 was quite closely related to the differential between effective exchange rates and the average costs of generating foreign exchange earnings (ACOGFEE), expressed as the percentage of the ACOGFEE (see Table 5). As we have argued, the differential between the official exchange rates and the average costs of generating foreign exchange earnings is not a good indicator of the profitability for exports. The effective exchange rate faced by exporters in China is the weighted average of the official and swap market rates, with the weights being determined by the foreign exchange retention ratio. Figure 1 suggests that devaluation, the foreign exchange retention scheme, and the swap markets were effective in raising the profitability of exports. The exporting enterprises in China were responsive to these reform measures, and hence foreign exchange reform was one of the important causes of China's export growth. It should be noted that from 1988 to 1993, when the swap markets were in operation, export growth was less closely related to the differential between the effective exchange rates and the average costs of generating foreign exchange earnings. The major reason for this was that the swap markets had provided exporters with the opportunity to hoard retained foreign exchange quotas for speculative purposes. With the abolition of the swap markets and the introduction of the foreign exchange buying and selling system in 1994, the export performance is once again corresponding closely to the differential between the effective exchange rate and the average costs of generating foreign exchange earnings. China, however, has less freedom to use exchange rate policy to promote exports.

Conclusion

A central economic planning system is essentially a set of complex and intertwined regulations imposed by central planners to straitjacket market forces. The objective of central planners is to achieve a pattern of resource allocation that is different from the pattern

FIGURE 1

FOREIGN EXCHANGE REFORM AND EXPORT PERFORMANCE IN CHINA, 1981–96

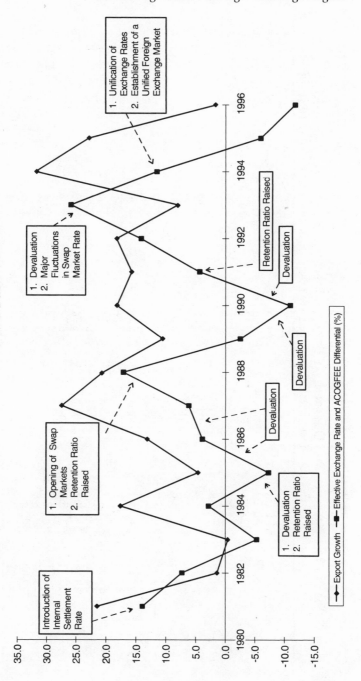

TABLE 5
EXPORT PERFORMANCE AND DIFFERENTIAL BETWEEN EFFECTIVE FOREIGN EXCHANGE RATES AND AVERAGE COSTS OF GENERATING FOREIGN EXCHANGE EARNINGS IN CHINA, 1981–96

Year	Export Growth (%)	Official Exchange Rates (Yuan/$)	Swap Market Rates (Yuan/$)	Effective Exchange Rates (Yuan/$)	Average Costs of Generating Foreign Exchange Earnings (ACOGFEE)	Differential between Foreign Exchange Rates and ACOGFEE (% of ACOGFEE)
1981	21.47	2.80	3.08	2.83	2.48	14.11
1982	1.41	2.80	3.08	2.87	2.67	7.49
1983	−0.40	2.80	3.08	2.87	3.03	−5.28
1984	17.59	2.80	3.08	2.87	2.79	2.87
1985	4.63	2.94	3.08	2.97	3.20	−7.19
1986	13.13	3.45	4.20	3.64	3.50	4.00
1987	27.47	3.72	5.41	4.46	4.20	6.19
1988	20.49	3.72	6.31	4.86	4.15	17.11
1989	10.56	3.77	6.43	4.94	5.06	−2.37
1990	18.18	4.78	5.81	5.23	5.87	−10.90
1991	15.70	5.32	5.85	5.74	5.50	4.36
1992	18.23	5.51	6.58	6.37	5.58	14.15
1993	8.01	5.32	8.65	7.77	6.32	22.96
1994	31.94	8.62	—	8.62	7.73	11.51
1995	22.90	8.35	—	8.35	8.87	−5.86
1996	1.51	8.31	—	8.31	9.41	−11.69

NOTE: The effective exchange rates are calculated as a weighted average of the official rates and the swap rates. For 1981, the retention rate is 9 percent (Lardy 1992). The retention rates for 1982–86, 1987–90, and 1991–93 are obtained from the World Bank (1994). They are 25 percent, 44 percent, and 80 percent, respectively. The average costs of generating foreign exchange earnings for 1993–96 are estimated by inflating the average cost of generating foreign exchange earnings in 1992 by the retail price index.

dictated by the market forces. Removing regulatory barriers in a centrally planned economy is path-dependent (see McKinnon 1991). Removing certain regulations in a particular sector releases the market forces and affects the functioning of other regulations in that sector. Pressures are created for the removal of some of the remaining regulations in that sector. Further liberalization of a sector releases market forces, which affect the functioning of other sectors. Removing regulatory barriers in different sectors then becomes interrelated. The removal of regulations in one sector creates pressures to remove regulations in other sectors. The removal of regulations in other sectors provides a new impetus to remove the remaining regulations in the original sector. It is possible for a liberalization process in a particular sector to trigger a gradual liberalization process that eventually transforms the very nature of the original economic system.

China's reform of its foreign exchange regime during the past two decades has been a gradual, evolutionary process. China's transition toward current account convertibility was not governed by a grand blueprint designed to construct a well-functioning foreign exchange market. The coherence that emerged was certainly not envisaged by the Chinese reformers when the internal settlement rate and the foreign exchange retention scheme were introduced. At the outset of the reform, relaxation of foreign exchange controls was driven by the decentralization of foreign trade. It expanded the role that the exchange rate played in the Chinese economy and compelled the government to remove the regulatory barriers to foreign exchange transactions. The relaxation of exchange controls stimulated foreign trade and strengthened the link between the external and internal sectors of the economy. Pressure arose to implement further reforms of the foreign exchange regime. With the establishment of a unified interbank foreign exchange market in 1994, there was an urgent need for China to speed up the banking and enterprise reform.

After the 1996 reform, current account convertibility in China remained restricted. The restrictions can be justified by the fact that the foreign exchange reform took place prior to reforms in other sectors of the economy. The immediate removal of all controls in an environment in which state-owned enterprises were still not subject to hard budget constraints and in which the banking sector had not been completely commercialized could have caused massive devaluation and created severe macroeconomic instability. Restrictions have to be phased out eventually so as to improve the efficiency of the interbank foreign exchange market. At this point, China's basic challenge is that of speeding up its banking and enterprise reform so as to coordinate its further reform in the foreign exchange regime.

References

Huang, G., and Wong, Y.P. (1995) "Unification of China's Foreign Exchange Rates." Working Paper Series, No. 64. Hong Kong: Department of Economics and Finance, City Polytechnic of Hong Kong.

Lin, J. (1992) *Practices of Foreign Trade and Foreign Exchange Rate*. Shangdong: Shangdong People's Publishing House (in Chinese).

Lardy, N.R. (1992) *Foreign Trade and Economic Reform in China, 1978–1990*. Cambridge: Cambridge University Press.

McKinnon, R.I. (1991) *The Order of Economic Liberalization: Financial Control in the Transition to a Market Economy*. Baltimore: Johns Hopkins University Press.

Sung, Y.W. (1994) "An Appraisal of China's Foreign Trade Policy, 1950–1992." In T.N. Srinivasan (ed.) *Agriculture and Trade in China and India*. San Francisco: International Center For Economic Growth.

Wang, H.Q. (1991) *Theories and Practices of China's Foreign Exchange Rate Management*. Shanghai: Shanghai People's Publishing House (in Chinese).

Will, M. (1990) "Two-tier Pricing in China's Foreign Exchange Market." China Working Paper No. 90/4. Canberra: Research School of Pacific Studies, Australian National University.

World Bank (1994) *China Foreign Trade Reform*. Washington D. C.: World Bank.

Xiao, G. (1996) "One Country, Two Currencies: How Did China Come Close to and then Miss Full Convertibility of Renminbi?" Paper presented at the Pacific Rim Allied Economic Organizations 2nd Biennial Conference, Economies in Transition, Hong Kong, 10-15 January.

Zhang, X.G. (1993) "China's Trade Patterns and International Comparative Advantage." Ph.D. Dissertation. Canberra: Australian National University.

15. Trade and the Troubled U.S.-China Relationship

Ted Galen Carpenter

Relations between the United States and the People's Republic of China (PRC) have become increasingly testy in recent years, with disputes over a variety of issues, including human rights, trade, and the status of Taiwan. Indeed, there is a growing sense that a hostile relationship, perhaps even armed conflict, between the two countries is probable over the long term.[1] One reflection of that attitude on the Chinese side is the proliferation of books and articles exhibiting a tone of strident, even belligerent, nationalism.[2] Its counterpart on the U.S. side is the mounting sentiment in Congress and elsewhere for a more hard-line policy toward Beijing. In its extreme form that sentiment favors the adoption of a full-blown containment policy, treating China as the Soviet Union was treated during the Cold War.[3]

There are few, if any, tasks facing Washington and Beijing that are more important than preserving a productive and peaceful long-term relationship. Success in that endeavor will provide enormous

---

Ted Galen Carpenter is Vice President for Defense and Foreign Policy Studies at the Cato Institute.

[1]Manifestations of that attitude can be found in House (1995); Bernstein and Munro (1997); Huntington (1996: 168–74, 218–38); Weinberger and Schweizer (1996: 3–98); and, from a British perspective, Hawksley and Holberton (1997).

The principal roots of the gradual estrangement between the United States and the PRC include the bloody Tiananmen Square incident and, perhaps even more important, the decline of the anti-Soviet rationale—the dominant strategic factor that had sustained the relationship during the 1970s and 1980s (see Harding 1992: 173–89, 216–46).

[2]Examples include Song, Zhang, and Qiao (1996), and Chen et al. (1996). For a discussion of that phenomenon and its implications, see Zhang (1996).

[3]Examples include Krauthammer (1995: 72), Center for Security Policy (1997), and Tierney (1997). For critical assessments of the mounting campaign for a containment policy, see Holloway (1997: 14–16), Erlanger (1997), and McDougall (1997).

benefits to both societies and enhance the prospects for peace and stability throughout the Pacific Basin. Failure will damage both societies and create the risk of a catastrophic military collision.

It would be an especially tragic mistake for the United States to embrace a containment policy. Such an approach could produce a self-fulfilling prophecy, as a cornered China lashed out against its superpower tormentor, thereby becoming the "aggressor" that the containment policy was designed to prevent.

The challenge for the United States is to craft an effective policy toward the PRC that will avoid either provoking needless confrontations or allowing a strategic environment to develop in which Beijing can threaten important American interests. The challenge for China is to fully assume its place among the global great powers in a manner that contributes to the overall peace and stability of Asia and the Pacific.

Trade Issues

U.S. policymakers need to understand that no country, even one as powerful as the United States, can dictate to other major powers. Washington's relations with China in recent years, however, seem to consist of a lengthy series of demands with little realistic hope that Beijing will respond positively to any of them. Perhaps the least constructive aspect of the relationship has been the annual controversy about whether the United States should extend China's most favored nation trade status for another year. Beijing's critics in Congress and elsewhere use the recertification requirement to mount campaigns to condition extension on improvements in the PRC's human rights record, reductions in the $50 billion bilateral trade deficit, greater protection for the intellectual property rights of American firms, and a host of other issues.

The annual spectacle does little except cause needless friction in U.S.-Chinese relations. The temptation to link trade and human rights is understandable, since Beijing's intolerance of political and religious dissidents troubles anyone who values individual freedom. Such repression is all too common in the world, however, and the United States cannot allow moral outrage to govern its trade relations with foreign countries. America would have to sever commercial ties to numerous nations if it applied moral considerations on a consistent basis. How could we justify the purchase of oil from Saudi

Arabia, for example? Moreover, the freedom to buy or sell products and services without arbitrary government interference is itself an important human right—for Americans as well as Chinese.

Conditioning MFN status on a reduction in the trade deficit is even less justified. The obsession with eradicating deficits with such countries as China and Japan is one of the more unfortunate features of Washington's trade policy.[4] The notion that trade deficits injure the American economy while surpluses strengthen it is unsupported by either contemporary or historical evidence (Kober 1995: 5–7). Indeed, the United States ran sizable trade surpluses during much of the Great Depression in the 1930s, and the last surplus occurred in 1975, a recession year. The bilateral trade deficit should be a nonissue in U.S.-China relations.

Concerns about Beijing's response to the pervasive piracy of American intellectual property in China are more substantive. Yet it would still be a mistake to condition MFN status on a resolution of that problem. Instead, U.S. officials should redouble their diplomatic efforts to pressure the Chinese government to take action against such theft. Some progress has been made in the past two years, and both governments can build on that record.

Those Americans who believe that restricting or severing trade relations will coerce the Chinese government into being more cooperative and democratic advocate precisely the wrong policy. Sanctions would primarily injure the sectors of China's economy that are the most dynamic and have the most extensive connections to the outside world. Those sectors are dominated by younger, cosmopolitan Chinese who favor accelerated political as well as economic reforms. We should want to strengthen such forces for change in China, not weaken them by disrupting trade relations.

There is an outside chance that economic engagement might produce a worst-case scenario—a powerful Chinese economy exploited by an authoritarian government with an aggressively expansionist agenda. It is more likely, however, that economic liberalization will be followed by political liberalization, as we have seen in South Korea and other East Asian (as well as Latin American) countries.

---

[4]Examples of that obsession include Greider (1997) and Mastel and Szamosszegi (1997).

Maintaining, indeed increasing, our economic relations with China maximizes the probability of that benign outcome.[5]

Washington should end the annual squabbling by granting China unconditional and indefinite MFN status—which should be renamed "normal trade relations" to better reflect what MFN actually gives any nation with that designation. To the extent that the United States wants to address such issues as the treatment of political dissidents and the protection of intellectual property rights, those matters should be handled through diplomatic channels. Americans acting in the private sector are, of course, well within their rights to mount informational campaigns and consumer boycotts to get the Beijing regime to alter its behavior. A "personal" (i.e., unofficial) presidential endorsement of such efforts in response to an especially egregious action by Chinese officials would also send a powerful message to the PRC that such conduct endangered their country's lucrative position in the American market.

Trade frictions seem to be getting worse, not better. Indeed, China's desire to join the World Trade Organization (WTO) is in danger of becoming a casualty of deteriorating Sino-American relations—exacerbated most recently by allegations that the PRC government tried to influence the outcome of the 1996 U.S. elections by channeling funds to President Clinton's campaign (Melloan 1997). Even before the latest round of political tensions, negotiations about the terms of China's entry into the WTO had encountered a number of difficulties. The PRC seeks entry as a developing country, a status that would give it a lengthy period of time to phase out many protectionist trade barriers and anticompetitive regulations and exempt the PRC from a few WTO standards entirely. The United States and the other industrialized powers understandably oppose that attempt, arguing that although China may have some of the characteristics of a developing country, the sheer size of its economy makes it a major factor in global economic affairs. Consequently, they contend that China should join the WTO on, for the most part, the terms accepted by developed states.

This is an issue on which compromise should be possible. Indeed, there has been modest movement by Beijing to accommodate the wishes of the current WTO members. China has reduced its average

[5]For a more detailed discussion of these themes, see Hadar (1996).

import tariff in recent years from 36 percent to 23 percent, and in November 1996, President Jiang Zemin pledged to cut the average tariff to 15 percent by the year 2000. More recently, China agreed to change its trading rules so companies can import and export on their own terms instead of having to operate through state trading organizations. Some nettlesome problems remain, to be sure. PRC authorities are reluctant to open China to agricultural imports, and there is still an Byzantine assortment of taxes, subsidies, regulations, and other annoying trade barriers (Lardy 1996, Walker 1997, Abruzzese 1997).

Nevertheless, it would seem to be in the best interest of the United States and the other major economic powers to have China inside the WTO and subject to the open-market policies the organization requires of its members. A China that continues to operate outside that system of international norms will certainly not be a more congenial trading partner. It would, of course, be better for all concerned if the PRC joined the WTO on the terms expected of developed states. But China will primarily hurt its own economy if it seeks to prolong foolish barriers to commerce, and the principal victims will be the Chinese people, not foreign economic actors. On the issue of WTO entry, the United States and the other capitalist powers should suggest, not insist, that China accelerate its economic liberalization.

Security Issues

One cannot ignore that there are growing tensions in the security as well as the economic relationship. Allegations that the PRC had exported military technology to Iran, Syria, and other anti-American countries has led to protests from U.S. officials and calls in Congress for sanctions. Similarly, various incidents in East Asia have strained Sino-American ties. Those incidents have included the PRC's military exercises in the Taiwan Strait in early 1996 and the subsequent dispatch of two U.S. aircraft carriers to waters near Taiwan; confrontations between the PRC and other claimants to the Spratly Islands in the South China Sea; and heated exchanges between the PRC and Japan over eight islands—known as the Diaoyu Islands in China and the Senkaku Islands in Japan (Mufson 1996a, 1996b). Even as Washington should seek to defuse the confrontations over trade,

229

U.S. officials need to express concern about other aspects of the Sino-American relationship, especially security issues. For if tensions rise in the security arena, the economic relationship will be in severe jeopardy.

In late 1996 and early 1997, the Chinese government pursued initiatives to improve relations with several adjacent countries, including India, Russia, and Vietnam. One agreement outlined troop reductions along China's borders with Russia, Kyrgystan, Tajikistan, and Kazakstan, and was hailed by President Jiang as "a model of security differing from the Cold War mentality" (Hoffman 1997). Such actions lend credence to the view that the PRC harbors no expansionist ambitions and is serious about playing a peaceful and constructive role in international affairs.

The PRC can help allay remaining American concerns by matching its conciliatory initiatives toward its major land neighbors with similar moves in the western Pacific. A proposal from Beijing to submit the various island disputes to international arbitration would provide compelling evidence of China's peaceful intentions. A statement renouncing the use of force to resolve the Taiwan issue—unless the Taiwanese authorities issue a declaration of independence—would defuse that dangerous situation and offer even stronger evidence that worries about possible aggressive behavior by the PRC in East Asia are misplaced.

Relinquishing America's Role as East Asia's Hegemon

Just as the PRC needs to adopt a more restrained and conciliatory policy toward other states in East Asia, the United States needs to make major changes in its policy. Since the end of World War II, the United States has sought to protect and advance its interests throughout East Asia by assuming the role of regional hegemon. Preserving that position has now become something bordering on an obsession.

America's most important interest in East Asia is that no single power dominate the region. A regional hegemon might have the power not only to exclude American trade and investment but also to tap the area's vast population and technological resources and thereby pose a serious security threat to the United States. Consequently, Washington's goal should be to foster the emergence of multiple centers of power in East Asia. The United States should play the role of balancer of last resort in the event that a country disrupted the regional balance of power and achieved a "breakout" that threatened vital American security interests.

It is imperative to distinguish that approach from a U.S.-led containment policy directed against China. Some hard-liners in the United States favor an "upgraded" military alliance with Japan for that purpose. That would be a risky and provocative strategy. Such an alliance would provide tangible evidence to those individuals in the PRC who contend that Washington is intent on adopting a confrontational policy toward China (Lippman 1995).[6]

The United States should reduce, not intensify, its security ties with Japan. Specifically, Washington should announce a phased withdrawal of all U.S. forces from Japan (and South Korea as well) and replace the alliance with a more limited and informal security relationship (see Carpenter 1995: 23–26). An ongoing strategic dialogue combined with periodic joint military exercises would be the appropriate level of cooperation. America could still have a potent power-projection capability with a reduced military presence based in Guam and other U.S. territories in the central and west-central Pacific.

At the same time, the United States should seek opportunities to work with China when the security interests of the two countries overlap. The situation on the Korean peninsula would seem to be an occasion for such cooperation. Both the PRC and the United States have an interest in keeping North Korea's nuclear program on hold and reducing the danger of a second Korean war. More broadly, both countries ought to coordinate their responses to the growing probability that the North Korean regime will unravel in the not too distant future and that political reunification will likely take place on South Korea's terms—much as West Germany absorbed an economically destitute and politically discredited East Germany. Unlike the situation in 1950, when the PRC refused to accept the prospect of a united, pro-Western Korea on its borders, there is no

[6]Chalmers Johnson (1996: 7–8) rightly notes that even the Pentagon's 1995 East Asia security strategy report (the so-called Nye Report) and the April 1996 Clinton-Hashimoto summit created apprehension in China about a U.S.-Japanese effort to contain the PRC. I am less inclined than is Johnson, however, to believe that the Chinese interpretation of those events is valid. Indeed, the changes in the alliance arising from the summit agreements are largely cosmetic (see Carpenter 1996).

need this time for a U.S.-Chinese clash over that issue. Washington can assuage any lingering Chinese apprehension about a united Korea by promising that all U.S. military forces would be withdrawn from the peninsula.

Relinquishing America's hegemonic role in East Asia would materially reduce the likelihood of a military collision between the United States and China. It would even reduce the number of occasions in which contentious issues between the two countries were likely to arise, thereby maximizing the chances of a cordial bilateral relationship. Eliminating some of those sources of friction would clear the path for continued economic and cultural engagement, a strategy that is most likely to promote the evolution of a more tolerant and democratic China.

Managing a wide-ranging relationship between two great powers is never an easy task, and accommodating the ambitions of a rising great power has proven especially difficult.[7] During the coming decades, U.S. and Chinese interests and policy preferences will sometimes be in accord; on other occasions they will differ, perhaps sharply. It is imperative that both governments seek to maximize the opportunities for cooperation and to contain, if not resolve, areas of disagreement. The U.S.-Chinese relationship is too important, both economically and strategically, to let it drift into acrimony and conflict. Keeping that relationship on course will require realism, prudence, and patience on the part of policymakers in both countries.

References

Abruzzese, L. (1997) "China, Politics and the WTO." *Journal of Commerce,* 25 April: 7A.

Bernstein, R., and Munro, R. (1997) *The Coming Conflict with China.* New York: Simon and Schuster.

Carpenter, T. (1995) "Paternalism and Dependence: The U.S.-Japanese Security Relationship." Cato Institute Policy Analysis no. 244, 1 November: 23–6.

Carpenter, T. (1996) "Smoke and Mirrors: The Clinton-Hashimoto Summit." Cato Institute Foreign Policy Briefing no. 41, 16 May.

---

[7]Discussions of such problems in the context of China's reemergence as a great power include Dibb (1995), Christensen (1996: 37–52), and Shambaugh (1996: 180–209).

Center for Security Policy (1997) "Deng's Demise Is an Opportunity to Take Stock, Change Course on One-Sided U.S. Policy of 'Engagement' with China." Decision Brief no. 97 D31, 22 February.

Chen, F. et al. (1996) *Trials of Strength between China and the United States.* Beijing: Zhongguo Renshi Chubanshe.

Christensen, T. (1996) "Chinese Realpolitik." *Foreign Affairs* 75(5) (September/October): 37–52.

Dibb, P. (1995) "Towards a New Balance of Power in Asia." Adelphi Paper no. 295, May.

Erlanger, S. (1997) "Searching for an Enemy and Finding China." *New York Times,* 6 April: E4.

Greenberger, R.S. (1997) "Favored-Nation Status for China Loses Its Certainty." *Wall Street Journal,* 15 April: A20.

Greider, W. (1997) "The Real China Threat." *New York Times,* 5 March: A27.

Hadar, L. (1996) "The Sweet-and-Sour Sino-American Relationship." Cato Institute Policy Analysis no. 248, 23 January.

Harding, H. (1992) *A Fragile Relationship: The United States and China since 1972.* Washington, D.C.: Brookings Institution.

Hawksley, H., and Holberton, S. (1997) *Dragonstrike: The Millennium War.* London: Sidgwick and Jackson.

Hoffman, D. (1997) "Border Pact Signed by Asian Powers." *Washington Post,* 25 April: A31.

Holloway, N. (1997) "Making an Enemy." *Far Eastern Economic Review,* 20 March: 14–6.

House, K. (1995) "Drifting Toward Disaster in Asia." *Wall Street Journal,* 26 July: A12.

Huntington, S. (1996) *The Clash of Civilizations and the Remaking of World Order.* New York: Simon and Schuster.

Johnson, C. (1996) "American Economic and Security Interests in Japan." Paper presented to the second meeting of the Study Group on American Interests in Asia: Economic and Security Priorities, sponsored by the Economic Strategy Institute, Washington, D.C., 14 November.

Kober, S. (1995) "The Fallacy of Economic Security." Cato Institute Policy Analysis no. 219, 24 January: 5–7.

Krauthammer, C. (1995) "Why We Must Contain China." *Time,* 31 July: 72.

Lardy, N. (1996) "China and the WTO." Brookings Policy Brief no. 10, November.

Lippman, T. (1995) "U.S. Sees Engagement in Current Policy, But China Feels Containment." *Washington Post,* 9 July: A23.

Mastel, G., and Szamosszegi, A. (1997) "China's Growing Trade Surplus: Why It Matters." *Washington Quarterly* 20(2) (Spring): 201–12.

McDougall, W. (1997) "Foreign Monsters, False Alarms." *New York Times,* 15 April: A33.

Melloan, G. (1997) " Of Gore, Asian Values, China, and the WTO." *Wall Street Journal,* 24 March: A19.

Mufson, S. (1996a) "Chinese Warnings Heighten Tension Over Island Dispute with Japan." *Washington Post*, 25 September: A26.

Mufson, S. (1996b) "Premier of China Joins Fray." *Washington Post*, 1 October: A15.

Shambaugh, D. (1996) "Containment or Engagement of China? Calculating Beijing's Responses." *International Security* 21(2) (Fall): 180–209.

Song, Q.; Zhang, Z.; and Qiao, B. (1996) *The China That Can Say No*. Beijing: Zhonghua Gongshang Lianhe Chubanshe.

Tierney, J. Jr. (1997) "Containing China's Aggression." *Journal of Commerce*, 13 March: 6A.

Walker, T. (1997) "China More Flexible on WTO Entry." *Financial Times*, 22 April: 8.

Weinberger, C., and Schweizer, P. (1996) *The Next War*. Washington, D.C.: Regnery.

Yang, J., and Harris, J. (1997) "Shorter Trade Leash for Beijing Could Protect Hong Kong, Gingrich Says." *Washington Post*, 1 May: A20.

Zhang, M. (1996) "The Shifting Chinese Public Image of the United States." National Defense University, Institute for National Strategic Studies, Strategic Forum no. 89, November.

PART IV

SOCIAL DEVELOPMENT IN CHINA

16. Civil Society versus Political Society: China at a Crossroads

Edward H. Crane

Ways to Order Society

There are two fundamental ways to order society: Voluntarily, through the private interaction of individuals, associations, religious organizations, businesses, and so on—which we can term civil society—or coercively, through state mandates—which we can term political society.

That we require a certain element of political society seems evident enough. We need protection against crime at home and threats from abroad. But what should also be evident is that a free society, if that is indeed what one desires, should have an expansive civil society or voluntary sector. In fact, I would say that it is axiomatic that the primary goal of public policy should be to enhance the ability of individuals to control their own lives, develop their own values and goals, and realize their fullest potential.

None of which should be interpreted as a call for atomistic individualism. It is absurd to suggest, as both Hegel and Marx did, that individuals, left to their own devices, will choose not to interact with one another cooperatively in social, commercial, and myriad other ways. Human interchange and association will be high on virtually everyone's list of values and priorities. The only question is, will that association be coerced or will it be voluntary?

In civil society, as we define it, you make the choices about your life. In political society, someone else makes those choices. Do you choose the career path that you desire, or does someone else assign that career to you? Do you choose the literature you read, or are your choices limited by someone in authority? Do you spend the

---

Edward H. Crane is President of the Cato Institute.

money you earn or does someone else spend it for you? The opportunities for political society to intervene in our lives are as great as the infinite choices a free individual faces in civil society.

That is why it is encouraging to learn that the growth of voluntary organizations in China over the past several years has been significant, laying the groundwork for the solid growth of true civil society in China. As my colleague Tom Palmer points out, however, it is important that commercial enterprises be viewed a part of the voluntary sector, as part of civil society.

Spontaneous Order: Hayek and Lao Tzu

The 20th century, of course, has been a long and bloody experiment in political society. The great nations of the world have, to one degree or another, all experimented with what the great Nobel laureate economist and social philosopher F.A. Hayek (1988) called the "fatal conceit" of believing that one or a few very smart people could order societal affairs in ways that were somehow going to yield results superior to those that would spring from the spontaneous order of a free society—that is, the order that results from the voluntary interaction of millions of individuals in civil society.

Hayek himself described the enormous economic benefits that resulted from the unplanned, spontaneous order of the marketplace. But his thinking about economics and civil society, while in many ways original, reflected the insights of the great thinkers throughout history who have understood the dangers of giving political power to a few to rule a multitude.

Perhaps none of those thinkers was as great as the Chinese philosopher Lao Tzu, whose writings are as fresh today as they were some 26 centuries ago, and provide a solid intellectual basis for civil society. He wrote in the *Tao Te Ching*, 57, "Therefore the Master says: I let go of the law, and people become honest. I let go of economics, and people become prosperous. I let go of religion, and people become serene. I let go of all desire for the common good, and the good becomes common as grass."[1]

Lao Tzu was speaking great wisdom. He was talking about the superiority of civil society over political society. Jim Dorn's suggestion that China follow the path of "market Taoism" is a good one.

---

[1]All passages from the *Tao Te Ching* are from Stephen Mitchell's (1988) translation.

More recently, just two and one-half centuries ago, the first American president, George Washington, expressed similar sentiments when he wrote, "Government is not reason; it is not eloquence. It is force. Like fire, it is a dangerous servant and a fearsome master." Government is not reason or eloquence, it is force. In civil society people interact with one another through reason and persuasion—eloquence in Washington's words—whereas in political society force, or coercion, is the basis of action.

And because it is in the nature of man to be free, Lao Tzu described how much better off society is—not just economically, but spiritually—when politics plays as small a role as possible in societal affairs.

The Market as a Discovery Process

We know from empirical evidence that civil society is preferable to political society in economics by the many failed experiments in central economic planning in this century and by the many success stories of the free market. From Hong Kong to the United States to Chile and New Zealand, where government restraints on economic activity are removed, the economy and the people prosper. Indeed, in the United States the computer industry is both the least regulated and the most dynamic sector of the economy. The beneficial results of freeing the economy are increasingly evident in Shanghai, as well.

But it is not just empirical observation that leads us to appreciate the importance of getting politicians and bureaucrats out of economic decisionmaking. The great economists of the 20th century—Ludwig von Mises, F.A. Hayek, Milton Friedman, George Stigler, and others—have shown that the market is not a machine, but more like an organism. It does not have rigid input and output relationships, but instead involves a constant discovery process. What is more, the entrepreneurial spirit that drives an economy is based on knowledge that is not centralized, but widely dispersed. Not only is it widely dispersed, but most of it isn't even articulated. It is tacit, local knowledge that is the essence of any economy. Only freedom can allow that knowledge to be coordinated in a manner that will yield dynamic economic growth. The essence of such a free economy is competition *and* cooperation. The tremendous complexity of a highly integrated free-market economy is the greatest example of human cooperation the world has ever known, contrary to what its critics may claim.

239

To give you just one example of how the market is a discovery process and not something that can be efficiently directed by politicians and bureaucrats, consider the trucking industry in the early 1970s in the United States. It was a heavily regulated, cartelized industry with few companies that served regulated routes at regulated rates. At long last the politicians decided to deregulate the industry on the basis of the obvious fact that more competitors would enter the trucking business and rates would therefore go down.

As it turned out, that is exactly what happened. Rates went down and the economy saved money. But what the politicians and experts did not predict was that by far the greater savings to the economy were to come not from lower rates but rather from the radical downsizing of inventories that the now flexible route and pricing system allowed for—savings on the order of tens of billions of dollars a year.

Government regulation proscribes certain entrepreneurial activities and thereby short-circuits the discovery process of the free market. The opportunity costs to the world economy, which means to the people of the world, imposed by governments from France to China to the United States that continue to follow Hayek's fatal conceit of regulation, are in the trillions of dollars every year, year in and year out. Future generations will look back at the 20th century's efforts at political control of the economy and shake their heads in bewilderment.

Political Freedom and Civil Society

But civil society is much more than economics. Political society does not just stifle economic growth, it ultimately denies the sense of human fulfillment that can only come from having lived our lives in freedom—making our own decisions, pursuing our own values— so that in the end our life's achievements, whether raising a family, inventing a new computer chip, or helping those in need, are something we can take pride in for having been *our* achievements, not merely activities others have imposed on us.

Thus, political freedom—the freedom to make decisions about one's life not just in the economic sphere, but regarding all of life's choices—is of paramount importance if we are to have true civil society. When the Cato Institute first came to Shanghai in the Fall of 1988, Milton Friedman received an exceptionally warm reception from our Chinese friends who attended that conference. It was at a time of strong political liberalization in China, which I trust will return with even more energy and commitment in the years ahead.

In his great 1962 book, *Capitalism and Freedom*, Milton Friedman wrote about the relationship between economic freedom and political freedom, the two prerequisites for civil society. After discussing the nature of the free market, Friedman (1962: 15) writes:

> The fundamental threat to freedom is power to coerce, be it in the hands of a monarch, a dictator, an oligarchy, or a momentary majority. The preservation of freedom requires the elimination of such concentration of power to the fullest possible extent and the dispersal and distribution of whatever power cannot be eliminated—a system of checks and balances. By removing the organization of economic activity from the control of political authority, the market eliminates this source of coercive power. *It enables economic strength to be a check to political power rather than a reinforcement* [emphasis added].

Of course, I believe Friedman was right, that economic liberalization has very positive implications for political liberalization. But we should not forget that throughout the world the political class— those who believe in and benefit from a strong political society— while sometimes recognizing the obvious benefits of a free-market economy, nevertheless persist in trying to control all other aspects of civil society. They can't seem to learn the wisdom of Lao Tzu, who said, "True mastery can be gained by letting things go their own way. It can't be gained by interfering" (*Tao Te Ching*, 48).

In the United States, the Cato Institute spends much of its time and resources fighting those politicians and bureaucrats who are constantly trying to undermine civil society, trying to sever the tendrils of community by replacing private, voluntary initiatives in education, charity, and health care, to name a few, with government-run bureaucratic enterprises. We have a Constitution in the United States that says individuals have rights to do those things without interference from government and that, indeed, government itself has no right to interfere, as Lao Tzu would say. Without a constitution and the rule of law, government will continue to sever the tendrils of community. As Thomas Jefferson wrote, "The natural progress of things is for government to gain ground and for liberty to yield."

A Constitution of Liberty

China's struggle, in part, is to *create* what Hayek (1960) called "a constitution of liberty." The fact that China has allowed the publication of Hayek's *The Constitution of Liberty*, which is already in its second printing (see *Far Eastern Economic Review* 1998: 82), is a positive sign. Our task in the United States, however, is once again to enforce the constitution of liberty we created over 200 years ago.

The patronizing attitude of many U.S. politicians—such as Vice President Al Gore, who was quoted (in Sobieraj 1997) as saying, government should be "more like grandparents in the sense that grandparents perform a nurturing role"—is anathema to the American heritage of limited government, of a government with no powers not delegated to it by the people in the first place. The people have a right to live free in civil society. The government's role, at least in the United States, is not to "nurture" but to protect our rights to life, liberty, and property and to otherwise leave us alone.

The Individual versus the State

China and the United States have much to learn from each other, and I would never presume to fully understand the nature of China's complex and rich culture. But I would suggest that it is not in the interest of the Chinese people to create what Reuters described as "a powerful new ideological watchdog body," called "the Central Leading Committee for Construction of Spiritual Civilization," for the purpose of reviving "communist doctrines of civic responsibility and self-sacrifice." Such a body poses a real threat to the growing infrastructure of civil society in China today.

Governments of all stripes, left, right, and center, have through the centuries employed the concept of "self-sacrifice," of subjugating the dignity of the individual to the alleged greater good of society, as a means of enhancing the power of the political class over civil society. One of the most articulate critics of that idea was the Russian-born American author Ayn Rand. She wrote of such a system:

> It is a moral system which holds that man has no right to exist for his own sake, that service to others is the sole justification of his existence, and that self-sacrifice is his highest moral duty, value and virtue. This is the moral base of collectivism, of all dictatorships. In order to seek freedom and capitalism, men need a ... rational code of ethics—a

242

morality which holds that man is not a sacrificial animal, that he has the right to exist for his own sake, neither sacrificing himself to others, nor others to himself [in Toffler (1964) 1997: 167].

Those who advocate state control over the lives of individuals are not just morally wrong, they are on the wrong side of history. As world trade develops, as the peoples of the globe get to know one another, to appreciate the traditions of other cultures, to form communities through the Internet and other means that transcend mere political boundaries, they will develop a growing distrust of and disinterest in the pronouncements of the political class.

Conclusion

Political control of the economy today is not only a bad idea, but increasingly infeasible. Control over how people communicate with each other around the globe—efforts at censorship—are increasingly futile. And that is good news.

Those who cling to a past of political society would do well to consider once again the words of Lao Tzu: "When taxes are too high, people go hungry. When the government is too intrusive, people lose their spirit. Act for the people's benefit. Trust them; leave them alone" (*Tao Te Ching*, 75). Perhaps we should call that the wisdom of "market Taoism."

References

Far Eastern Economic Review (1998) "Hayek's Children." *FEER*, 14 May: 82.

Friedman, M. (1962) *Capitalism and Freedom.* Chicago: University of Chicago Press.

Hayek, F.A. (1960) *The Constitution of Liberty.* Chicago: University of Chicago Press.

Hayek, F.A. (1988) *The Fatal Conceit: The Errors of Socialism. The Collected Works of F.A. Hayek,* Vol. 1. Edited by W.W. Bartley III. Chicago: University of Chicago Press.

Mitchell, S., trans. (1988) *Tao Te Ching* (by Lao Tzu). New York: Harper Collins.

Sobieraj, S. (1997) "Gore Attacks Extreme Individualism." *Washington Post,* 12 June.

Toffler, A. ([1964] 1997) "The *Playboy* Interview with Ayn Rand." In D. Boaz (ed.) *The Libertarian Reader,* 161–68. New York: The Free Press.

17. The Growth of Civil Society in China
Minxin Pei

The breathtaking changes unleashed by China's economic reforms since 1979 have not only transformed its economy but reshaped and redefined state-society relations. As the state continues to withdraw its influence in economic and social activities, Chinese society has gradually gained more space previously claimed and controlled by the state under the pre-reform regime. Predictably, the question whether market-oriented reforms in China have fostered a stronger civil society has inspired a spate of scholarly works on the emergence of a "civil society" in China. Chinese and Western scholars have studied the emergence of various cultural, social, and business associations in post-Mao China and speculated on the impact of that development on the future of Chinese politics (Ding 1994; White 1993; Ma 1994; Unger 1996; Wang, Zhe, and Sun 1993; He 1993; Pearson 1994; Brook and Frolic 1997; White, Howell, and Shang 1996). Two main arguments have emerged from this growing body of literature on civil society in China. One group of scholars—Unger (1996), White (1993), and Pearson (1994)—view the emergence of associations in China in the last two decades from a state-corporatist perspective. They argue that such associations do not form the cells of civil society as defined in the Tocquevillian sense because Chinese associations are mostly officially sponsored, given little autonomy, and used by the government as instruments of policy implementation and social control.

The second group of scholars provides a more complex assessment of civic groups in China. Based on their in-depth fieldwork in Xiaoshan in Zhejiang province and in Nanhai in Guangdong province in the early 1990s, Wang, Zhe, and Sun (1993) and Sun (1994) contend that the close relationship between civic groups and the government

Minxin Pei is Assistant Professor of Politics at Princeton University.

is a product of China's closed political system, underdeveloped market economy, and lack of private financial resources. While recognizing the dualist (official-private) nature of most Chinese associations and the high degree of official penetration of these civic groups, they also find that the new civic associations have begun to develop their own identities and programs. Disputing the state-corporatist argument, Sun and others provide evidence suggesting that new Chinese civic associations voluntarily seek official sponsorship in order to overcome many practical obstacles.[1] They view this relationship not as one of state domination, but as a complex mutually beneficial arrangement by which new civic groups gain initial space and resources under difficult political and economic conditions through some forms of official sponsorship. In exchange, these groups give up a measure of operational autonomy and even cooperate with the government on certain public policy issues. However, these authors imply that such an arrangement may be temporary and tactical in nature. Although political and economic constraints currently force these groups to maintain close ties to government agencies and officials, these groups have the potential gradually to gain genuine autonomy once these constraints are lifted with greater political and economic liberalization and more access to private funding.

While the literature cited above has rightly identified the rise of civil society in China—even in its most embryonic form—as an important theoretical and empirical question and laid the foundations for further investigation, it suffers from a serious weakness: this literature has focused only on a few case studies and failed to provide more complete information about the growth of civil society in China.

This paper attempts to provide and analyze the national data on the growth of associations in the early 1990s to understand the various patterns underlying such growth. Moreover, it focuses on the data on registered civic organizations from two provinces, Jiangsu and Shanghai, to understand the various organizational characteristics of these groups.

---

[1]The Chinese law on civic associations (1989) stipulates that each civic group must seek a "relevant government agency" as its main sponsor. Most civic groups need government support for funding and office space. They typically place local officials on their boards to enhance their prestige and access to resources.

The Growth of Civil Society under Reform

Studies of the growth of associations in China show that few associations were active during the Cultural Revolution (1966–76) and that only associations fully sponsored by the state existed.[2] Analysis of national and provincial data also indicates that, while the number of associations in China prior to 1978 was quite small, the growth of these associations has been rapid since economic reform began. In Jiangsu province, of the 587 registered provincial associations as of October 1992, only 65 (11 percent) were founded before 1978, 254 (43 percent) were founded between 1978 and 1985, and 268 (46 percent) were founded between 1986 and 1992 (Fan 1996: 694–735). In Shanghai, there were only 628 social associations in 1981; by 1988, the city had 4,299 associations (Ma and Liu 1993: 5). Data for other provinces reflect a similar pattern (Fan 1996).

Table 1 contains official data on the growth of associations in China in the 1990s. Because there was no legal requirement for associations to register with the government prior to the issuance of the State Council's Regulations on the Registration of Civic Organizations in 1989, the central government did not have accurate data on the growth of associations in the 1980s.[3] After the implementation of the State Council's 1989 regulations, all associations in China were required to reregister with the Ministry of Civil Affairs after obtaining approval from "relevant government authorities."[4] This reregistration requirement was responsible for the big surge of applications in 1991 and 1992; therefore, the huge increase of associations in these two years was the result of a regulatory change, and did not reflect real growth of these groups in China. After the

[2]A fully state-sponsored association receives all its funding from the government's budget; its officers are appointed by the government as cadres; it is treated essentially as part of the government. Such organizations include the writers' unions, film-makers' associations, and sports associations. See Wang, Zhe, and Sun (1993: 77).

[3]In the 1980s, associations could receive approval for registration from a variety of authorities. A Shanghai survey of associations in 1985 found that 24 percent were approved by local organizations of the Communist Party, 52 percent received approval from other associations, and 6 percent did not have approval from any authorities (Ma and Liu 1993: 12).

[4]Article 9 of the regulations stipulates that every association must first obtain approval from a government agency or department with jurisdiction over the activities and programs the association will be carrying out. The association may register with local offices of the Ministry of Civil Affairs only after first obtaining this approval.

TABLE 1
GROWTH OF CIVIC ORGANIZATIONS IN CHINA, 1991–95

	Total	Provincial	Prefecture	County
Number of Civic Organizations Applying for Registration				
1991	118,691	11,396	33,726	73,569
1992	62,891	4,833	16,706	41,115
1993	29,773	2,528	9,835	17,368
1994	18,826	2,025	6,107	10,682
Number of Civic Organizations Approved to Register				
1991	89,969	6,787	26,831	56,351
1992	54,852	4,842	14,440	35,132
1993	25,958	2,627	8,628	14,680
1994	15,235	1,556	5,382	8,285
1995	12,823	1,365	4,432	7,024

NOTE: All civic organizations were required to be registered between late 1990 and early 1992 following the promulgation of the State Council's Regulations on the Registration of Civic Organizations in 1989 ("Shehui Tuanti Dengji Guanli Tiaoli"). The numbers of applicants and approved associations were unusually large for 1991 and 1992 mainly because most preexisting associations registered with the government in compliance with the new regulations.

SOURCE: *Law Yearbook of China* (various years).

completion of the reregistration process in 1992, the rate of growth of associations plunged. In 1993, associations experienced a net increase of 8.4 percent; in 1994, the net increase was 3.9 percent; in 1995, it was 3.7 percent (Table 2).

The data in the bottom half of Table 1 show that most applications for registration were approved, although the rate of approval varied from year to year. In 1991, the rate of approval was 76 percent, the lowest in the four-year period for which data were available.[5] That rate rose to 87 percent in 1992 and 1993, and fell to 81 percent in 1994. In all likelihood, the 1994 and 1995 data on associations may more accurately reflect current trends. This means that the average net growth of associations may be about 4 percent a year, with 80 percent of applications approved by the government. The total

---

[5]The relatively low rate in 1991 was probably the result of a large number of applications received for that year to meet the reregistration requirement.

TABLE 2
NET GROWTH OF REGISTERED CIVIC ORGANIZATIONS IN CHINA,
1991–95

	Total	Provincial	Prefecture	County
Number of Registered Civic Organizations at Year-End				
1991	115,738	9,518	36,306	69,914
1992	154,502	13,652	45,791	93,789
1993	167,506	16,314	53,085	97,725
1994	174,060	17,792	56,555	99,605
1995	180,538	19,001	59,309	102,215
Net Growth of Registered Civic Organizations (percentage)				
1991	–	–	–	–
1992	33.4	43.4	26.1	34.1
1993	8.4	19.5	15.9	4.2
1994	4.0	9.0	6.5	2.0
1995	3.7	6.8	4.9	2.6

SOURCE: *Law Yearbook of China* (various years).

number of associations in China at the end of 1995 reached 180,538, with provincial-level associations accounting for 10 percent, prefecture associations for 33 percent, and county associations for 57 percent.

A notable feature of the growth of associations in the 1980s and early 1990s is that an overwhelming majority of them were semi-official and private (compared with the dominance of fully official associations prior to 1978).[6] Another characteristic is the formation of more specialized associations representing the new economic and social forces created by China's economic reform and modernization. The following is a list of some of those groups:

- Associations of Private Entrepreneurs, with a national association founded in 1986 that had a membership of 22.5 million at the end of 1994;

[6]Wang, Zhe, and Sun reported in their study of one county that there were only four associations in Xiaoshan before 1978, all of them official ones. In 1979–83, 18 associations were formed; of these, one was official and 17 were semi-official. In 1984–1990, 77 were formed; of these, one was official, 52 were semi-official, and 24 were private (Wang, Zhe, and Sun 1993: 77).

249

- Associations of Village and Township Enterprises, with a national association founded in 1991 to represent China's growing rural industries;
- Association for the Study of the Private Sector, an academic organization founded in 1993;
- Chinese Association of Body-Builders (1992);
- Chinese Athletic Association for the Mentally Retarded (1985);
- Chinese Mayors' Association (1988), with 2,500 members;
- Chinese Association for Prevention and Treatment of Substance Abuse, a volunteer group formed in 1991;
- Chinese Association of Hoteliers, formed in 1993 to represent the country's fast-growing hotel industry;
- Associations of Lawyers; and
- Associations of Consumers.

Under Chinese law, a civic organization may dissolve and de-register itself; the government can also suspend and revoke the registration of civic organizations that are found to have engaged in fraud or for-profit activities, violated their charters, or participated in "activities against the interest of the state."[7] Government statistics report the number of associations deregistered (*zhuxiao*) each year. As an indicator of the "mortality rate" of civic organizations in China, these figures may reflect two trends: (a) whether the government closely monitors the activities of civic organizations and penalizes violators by cancelling their registrations, and (b) whether Chinese civic organizations are becoming more durable and less likely to fold.

Table 3 shows that the mortality rate of civic organizations has been falling since 1991 (with the exception of 1993). De-registered civic organizations accounted for only 3.4 percent of the total number of civic organizations in China in 1995. This implies that the probability of a forced shutdown by the government is declining and that Chinese civic organizations are gaining organizational durability. The mortality rate of civic organizations also varies across different levels of jurisdiction. The lower half of Table 3 shows that provincial civic organizations have the lowest mortality rate and county civic organizations have the highest rate. This evidence reflects the positive relationship between the amount of organizational capital

[7]Article 25 of the State Council's 1989 regulations on civic organizations.

TABLE 3
THE MORTALITY RATE OF CHINESE CIVIC ORGANIZATIONS

	Total	Provincial	Prefecture	County
	Number of Civic Organizations Deregistered			
1991	9,974	543	2,982	6,449
1992	7,654	463	880	6,311
1993	11,331	110	1,950	9,255
1994	8,298	78	2,006	6,213
1995	6,472	156	1,675	4,641
	Rate of Mortality of Civic Organizations (percentage)			
1991	8.6	5.7	8.2	9.2
1992	5.0	3.4	1.9	6.7
1993	6.8	0.6	3.6	9.5
1994	4.7	0.4	3.5	6.2
1995	3.4	0.8	2.8	4.5

NOTE: The mortality rate is the number of registered social associations divided by the number of deregistered social groups each year.

SOURCE: *Law Yearbook of China* (various years).

invested in a civic organization and its durability. Provincial civic organizations require much greater start-up organizational capital. As a result, once established, these organizations are less likely to fold. County civic organizations have less start-up organizational capital and are more likely to cease activities.

There are significant regional variations in the density of civic organizations across China. Table 4 provides a rough estimate of the relative amount of social capital possessed by individual provinces in China. In addition to looking at the absolute number of civic organizations in each province, I construct a proxy for each province's social capital in relative terms. This is the differential between a province's share of civic organizations and its share of population. A province with a positive differential may mean that it possesses an above-average amount of social capital. A province with a negative differential may mean that it has a below-average amount of social capital. The data in Table 4 confirm the positive relationship between higher levels of economic development and the level of social capital—although the direction of the causation remains undetermined.

TABLE 4
REGISTERED CIVIC ORGANIZATIONS IN PROVINCES, 1994

Province	Number	Share[a]	Differential[b]	Wealth Rank[c]
Zhejiang	10,913	6.3	2.7	6
Fujian	8,982	5.2	2.6	8
Shandong	17,044	9.8	2.6	10
Jiangsu	14,055	8.0	2.2	7
Sichuan	19,014	10.9	1.6	24
Shanghai	3,109	1.8	0.7	1
Tianjin	2,669	1.5	0.7	3
Jilin	4,807	2.8	0.7	13
Liaoning	6,838	3.9	0.5	4
Beijing	2,250	1.3	0.4	2
Qinghai	1,312	0.8	0.4	17
Ningxia	1,008	0.6	0.2	21
Xingjiang	2,461	1.4	0	12
Tibet	170	0.1	−0.1	28
Inner Mongolia	3,027	1.7	−0.2	16
Hubei	7,851	4.5	−0.2	15
Gansu	3,229	1.8	−0.2	29
Hainan	678	0.4	−0.2	9
Heilongjiang	4,755	2.7	−0.3	11
Yunnan	4,864	2.8	−0.4	25
Shaanxi	4,403	2.5	−0.4	27
Guangdong	8,679	5.0	−0.6	5
Shanxi	3,097	1.8	−0.7	18
Jiangxi	4,673	2.7	−0.7	22
Hebei	7,724	4.4	−0.9	14
Guangxi	4,621	2.7	−1.0	19
Guizhou	3,090	1.8	−1.1	30
Hunan	7,194	4.1	−1.2	20
Anhui	4,872	2.8	−2.2	23
Henan	6,671	3.8	−3.7	26
Total	174,060			

[a]May not add up to 100 because of rounding.
[b]Differential = share of social groups − share of national population; a positive differential means above-average share of social groups; population data for all provinces are obtained from *Zhongguo Tongji Nianjian* (1995: 60).
[c]Based on per capita GDP in 1994.
SOURCE: *Law Yearbook of China* (1995: 1083).

On the one hand, a higher level of economic development can be expected to be the underlying cause of the growth of civic organizations in a region. On the other hand, greater social capital may contribute to higher economic growth and, hence, more wealth (Putnam 1993). In the Chinese case, more developed coastal and industrialized provinces (with the exception of Guangdong) have more civic organizations than less developed inland and agrarian provinces (with the exception of Sichuan).

Understanding Chinese Civic Organizations

As there are no detailed national data on the types of civic organizations, I provide a close analysis of the data from Jiangsu and Shanghai to seek a deeper understanding of the composition and other organizational characteristics of civic groups in contemporary China. The data on provincial-level civic organizations in Jiangsu and on civic organizations formed in six Shanghai districts and counties in the post-Mao era may yield valuable information about the growth, size, and missions of these organizations that available national data do not contain.

Provincial Civic Organizations in Jiangsu

At the end of 1992, Jiangsu had 587 registered provincial civic organizations, 522 of which (89 percent) were formed after 1978. Analysis of the time of their founding, presented in Table 5, shows that there were two waves of the formation of civic organizations in Jiangsu. The first mini-wave began in 1979 and ended in 1981. The second wave spanned the six-year period of 1984–89. During the mini-wave of 1979–81, 95 civic associations were founded. The relative relaxation following the end of the Cultural Revolution was a principal factor in the growth of civic organizations in this period. However, lingering fear of the political risks of organizing semi-official or private associations had a powerful impact on the types of civic organizations that first emerged in this period. Our analysis of the data for this period indicates that most associations formed in 1979–81 were generally considered low-risk organizations with at least semi-official sponsorship. Of the 95 associations, 40 were scientific or academic associations, 28 were cultural and educational associations, and 14 were sports associations. It should be noted here that, in terms of their share of the total number of associations

TABLE 5
THE GROWTH OF CIVIC ORGANIZATIONS IN
JIANGSU PROVINCE, 1978–92

Year	Number of Civic Organizations Founded
1978	8
1979	20
1980	38
1981	37
1982	19
1983	15
1984	61
1985	56
1986	45
1987	55
1988	64
1989	64
1990	11
1991	15
1992	14
Total	522

SOURCE: *Zhongguo Shehui Tuanti Dacidian* (1995).

formed in 1979–81, these three types of associations were "over-represented" because their share for 1979–81 was higher than their share in the general population of civic organizations at the beginning of the 1990s. At the same time, few new types of associations such as industry associations, business groups, professional societies, and managerial associations were formed in this period. Only eight industry and business associations, and two professional and managerial groups were established. This evidence shows that at the beginning of the 1980s, Chinese civic organizations were much less diverse and more concentrated in politically safe categories. However, this situation changed as the result of the second wave of civic revival in 1984–89. As the economic reform accelerated in the mid-1980s (with the formal launching of the reform in urban areas in 1984) and as the political atmosphere grew more tolerant (prior to the Tiananmen Square incident and the issuance of the

TABLE 6
PROVINCIAL CIVIC ORGANIZATIONS IN JIANGSU, BY INDIVIDUAL
CATEGORIES, 1992

Category	Number	Percent
Science, technology, and academic	181	30
Industry and business	152	26
Cultural and educational	127	21
Professional and managerial	53	9
Sports	31	5
Friendship	21	4
Health	11	2
Religious	10	2
Political	5	1
Public affairs	3	–
Charitable	1	–
Total	595	100

SOURCE: *Zhongguo Shehui Tuanti Dacidian* (1995).

restrictive State Council's regulations on civic organizations in 1989), the growth of civic organizations was explosive. Moreover, this period also saw the emergence of new and more diverse civic organizations that represented the newer social and economic forces in Chinese society. The most notable was the emergence of two new types of associations: (1) specialized industry and business groups and (2) professional and managerial groups.

As shown in Table 6, specialized industry and business groups, which were nonexistent before reform and accounted for a small share of civic organizations in Jiangsu in the early 1980s, became the second-largest type of civic organization by the early 1990s. The rise of this form of organization was primarily due to the decline of the system of vertical state planning and its replacement by market-oriented horizontal linkages among producers in the same industries. The rapid rise of professional and managerial groups (including associations of private entrepreneurs, private firms, and township and village enterprises) also characterized the growth of civic organizations during the second wave. Nonexistent before 1979, these associations grew quickly in the 1980s and accounted for 9 percent of all civic organizations in Jiangsu by 1992.

However, the rapid growth of civic organizations in Jiangsu—as well as across China—came to an abrupt end in 1990, mainly as the result of the tightening of political control after the 1989 Tiananmen incident. In particular, the regulations on civic organizations issued by the State Council in October 1989 and implemented in 1990 definitely impeded the growth of these organizations by setting two requirements: approval by a government agency and registration with the Ministry of Civil Affairs. While the registration requirement was in line with similar practices in most other countries, the stipulation that civic organizations must first obtain approval from a government agency having jurisdiction over their proposed activities imposed an undue burden on civic organizations and discouraged many potential groups from going through this bureaucratic process.

Analysis of the data from Jiangsu also shows an uneven pattern of growth and distribution of civic organizations. Of the 595 provincial associations (as of 1992), four types of associations (scientific and academic associations, industry and business groups, cultural and educational associations, and professional and managerial associations) accounted for 86 percent of all associations. Other types of associations were underdeveloped, especially charitable and public affairs associations.[8] Jiangsu had only one charitable organization (the semi-official Red Cross), and no provincial charitable groups or private foundations. The lack of charitable groups may be directly related to the lack of the needed financial resources. The small number of public affairs associations (the consumers' association being one of the three) was probably due to the significant risks of organizing public "cause groups" in a closed political system.

County and District Civic Groups in Shanghai

The data on provincial associations in Jiangsu do not adequately reflect the organizational characteristics of civic organizations at the grassroots level. In this section, I analyze the data on three urban

---

[8]The political associations allowed in China are those that were established explicitly to promote the official ideology and policies. The small number of religious groups at the provincial level should not be a surprise because of the small number of religions being practiced in China. Nearly all the religions practiced in Jiangsu were represented by the 10 associations.

TABLE 7
CIVIC ORGANIZATIONS IN SIX SHANGHAI DISTRICTS AND COUNTIES, BY INDIVIDUAL CATEGORIES, 1992

	3 Urban Districts	3 Suburban Counties	Total
Science, technology, and academic	76	109	185
Cultural and educational	41	21	62
Sports	34	23	57
Industry and business	31	24	55
Professional and managerial	21	13	34
Friendship	20	11	31
Health	9	7	16
Religious	5	7	12
Public affairs	5	3	8
Charitable	4	2	6
Political	3	0	3
Total	249	220	469

SOURCE: Ma and Liu (1993).

districts and three suburban (agrarian) counties in Shanghai.[9] This analysis of civic organizations at the grassroots level is intended to yield new information on the size, activities, and membership of civic organizations that play a more direct role in Chinese society. The selection of three urban districts and three suburban counties is also meant to help us understand the differences between urban civic organizations and their rural counterparts.

In the analysis, I focus on nonacademic and nonscientific associations. Since most academic and scientific associations are mostly semi-official, a focus on nonacademic and nonscientific associations should lead to a more accurate understanding of the growth of genuinely private civic organizations in post-Mao China. As shown in Table 7, there were altogether 469 civic associations in these six jurisdictions in 1992, with 185 (nearly 40 percent) of them academic and scientific associations. The composition of civic organizations in these six districts and counties in Shanghai both resembles and

[9]The three urban districts are Huangpu, Luwang, and Jingan; the three suburban counties are Qingpu, Chuansha (now part of Pudong New District), and Jiading.

differs from that of provincial associations in Jiangsu. In both cases, scientific and academic associations accounted for a very large share (30 percent in Jiangsu and 40 percent in the six Shanghai jurisdictions); the top five groups in both cases were identical. However, a careful look at the Shanghai data shows that civic organizations at the grassroots level tend to be more diverse and, after excluding the mostly semi-official academic and scientific associations, much less concentrated in a small number of categories than at the provincial level (in Jiangsu, 86 percent of all provincial associations was concentrated in four categories). Several under-represented groups at the provincial level—such as religious, public affairs, and charitable associations—had a greater presence at the grassroots level. Moreover, given the fact that private associations accounted for a large share of these nonacademic associations, civic activities at the grassroots level in China are clearly more autonomous, vibrant, and diverse than at the higher level of administrative jurisdictions.

The data in Table 7 provide an interesting comparison of social capital between urban and rural areas. If we exclude the mostly semi-official academic and scientific associations, it becomes clear that there is more social capital (formed mostly through private efforts in this case) in urban than in rural areas. The three Shanghai urban districts had more sports clubs, industry and business associations, professional and managerial organizations, and friendship associations (the difference ranging from 30 to 100 percent). This important difference stems chiefly from the differences in levels of economic development and the complexities of the economic and social organizations and activities between urban and rural areas. The evidence from Shanghai may explain why, for China as a whole, more economically developed areas tend to have more civic organizations.

In analyzing the data from Jiangsu in a preceding section, we have noted two waves of civic revival in China in the post-Mao era. We find that the formation of semi-official scientific and academic organizations was the driving force of the first mini-wave (1979–81) and the formation of private and more specialized groups propelled the second wave (1984–89). The growth of civic organizations in the six Shanghai jurisdictions (Table 8) reconfirms this finding. In the Shanghai case, 199 of 289 civic organizations (nonacademic associations) were formed between 1985 and 1989. A close look at the civic

TABLE 8
THE GROWTH OF CIVIC ORGANIZATIONS IN
SIX SHANGHAI DISTRICTS AND COUNTIES,
1978–92*

Year	Number of Civic Groups Founded
pre-1978	15
1978	2
1979	2
1980	6
1981	7
1982	7
1983	12
1984	22
1985	24
1986	24
1987	44
1988	45
1989	40
1990	4
1991	16
1992	19
Total	289

*Excluding science, technology, and academic associations.
SOURCE: Ma and Liu (1993).

organizations formed in this period reveals that most of them were private and specialized groups—suggesting that the second wave greatly contributed to the diversity and autonomy of China's civic organizations.

Although official sponsorship was not explicitly identified in the data on the six Shanghai jurisdictions, the nature of the organizations that were formed suggests that official sponsorship was unlikely. For example, the following groups would most likely fall outside official sponsorship: (1) hobby groups such as the Huangpu Associations of Bird-Lovers (1984), the Huangpu Association of Bridge Players (1987), the Huangpu Association of Carrier Pigeons (1984), the Jingan Associations of Fans of Foreign Languages (1986), the Luwan Association of Dance Enthusiasts (1987); (2) self-help groups such as the Huangpu Association for the Disabled (1991) and the Jingan Club of Recovering Cancer Patients (1992); (3) groups catering to individuals the state may not have a strong incentive to support or control such as the Huangpu Association of Retired Teachers (1984) and the Jingan Association of Retired Intellectuals (1987); and (4) new professional groups such as the Jingan Association of Hair Dressers and Beauticians, the Jingan Association of Gourmet Chefs, and the Luwan Association of Consultants.

Chinese civic organizations have two types of membership: group membership and individual membership. A business firm, a school, or a research institution may join a civic organization as a group member. Most industry and business associations have group members, as is the case in Western countries. In order to ascertain the size of the truly voluntary, private civic organizations, I examine the data on membership from the six Shanghai jurisdictions covered in our study (Table 9).

The Red Cross and the associations of private entrepreneurs are excluded from this analysis because the Red Cross is a semi-officially sponsored organization and membership in the associations of private entrepreneurs is often compulsory. Of the three categories of civic organizations (group membership only, group membership and individual membership, and individual membership only) included in Table 9, I focus on those civic groups with only individual members because these groups more closely resemble typical Western civic groups.

The data on membership in Table 9 show that half of Shanghai's civic organizations have only individual members, 22 percent have only group members, and 28 percent have both group and individual members. There are slightly more civic organizations with only group members in urban areas than in rural areas because urban areas have more commercial, cultural, and educational entities. Urban areas also have slightly more individual-member only civic organizations because urban residents are generally more wealthy than rural residents and can form civic groups without financial support from commercial or government-affiliated entities (groups).

Most civic organizations in Shanghai are relatively small. Table 9 shows that the average size of membership of the 123 groups examined here is 386. A few groups have very large memberships, such

TABLE 9
TYPE AND SIZE OF MEMBERSHIP OF CIVIC ORGANIZATIONS IN SIX
SHANGHAI JURISDICTIONS, 1992*

	3 Urban Districts	3 Suburban Counties	Total
1. Type of membership			
Group members only	35	18	53
Both group and individual members	34	36	70
Individual members only	77	46	123
Subtotal	146	100	246
2. Total number of members of organizations with only individual members	39,299	8,225	47,524
3. Average size of membership per organization	510	179	386

*Excluded from the individual membership only category are the Red Cross, the associations of private entrepreneurs, and two very large religious organizations in Qingpu County. Only the organizations disclosing their membership information are included here.
SOURCE: Ma and Liu (1993).

as associations of retired teachers (averaging 2,400 for each of the three urban districts) and the sports associations of senior citizens (6,725 in Jingan and 2,900 in Luwan). Most groups are relatively small. Of the 123 groups in this sample, only 15 (12 percent) had more than 500 members each, 56 (46 percent) had fewer than 100 members each. There is a dramatic contrast between urban and rural civic organizations in the size of their individual membership. On average, urban civic organizations have many more members per group—about three times more—than rural civic organizations. The comparison between Shanghai's urban and rural jurisdictions further confirms that there is more social capital in urban than in rural areas: rural areas have fewer civic organizations and rural civic organizations have fewer members.

Promises and Challenges

The analysis and evidence presented in the preceding sections suggest that, despite its relatively small size and the severe political and economic constraints placed on its growth, civil society has expanded at a rapid pace in China since economic reform began in 1979. Such expansion was particularly notable during the two waves in the early and late 1980s. Although the restrictions reimposed on civic organizations in October 1989 had a severe negative effect on the growth of civic organizations in the 1990s, a nascent civil society is beginning to emerge in China.

This development has profound implications for the evolution of China's economy, society, and political system. With the rise of increasingly autonomous civic organizations, ordinary Chinese are beginning to reclaim the public space that used to be monopolized by the state. Such organizations will play an important integrative function in maintaining and strengthening social cohesion when Chinese society itself is undergoing two fundamental changes— modernization and transition to a market economy. The growth of these organizations will further reduce the state's role in controlling social activities and providing social services. In the not-too-distant future, civic organizations will gradually assume more direct political roles and become advocates of certain causes, such as environmental protection, public education, and public health. The organizational maturity gained by Chinese civic organizations will likely make them important actors in China's gradual movement toward a more pluralist and open political system. Admittedly, Chinese civic organizations will face many political and economic obstacles in the future. But a heartening sign that they will continue to grow is that the underlying factors responsible for their rapid growth in the 1980s continue to be present in China in the 1990s.

Five key factors and their persistence can be discerned:

1. The revolutionary transition to a market economy. If anything, China's march to a full-fledged market economy is likely to accelerate in the late 1990s in the post-Deng era. Despite the enormous difficulties facing the state-owned enterprises and the agricultural sector, China's economic institutions and structures have been transformed in the last two decades and will further reduce the state's role in the economy and encourage the growth of the private sector.

2. The decline and decay of the institutional components of the pre-reform system that stifled private initiatives and prevented the accumulation of social capital. Especially noteworthy is the decline of the *danwei* (work-unit) system that severely restricted social and physical mobility of Chinese citizens. The decline of the *danwei* system was caused by two forces. First, as the state began to claim a lesser share of national wealth after reform, it had fewer resources to maintain the *danwei* system. Second, with the rise of market forces, especially in the housing, health care, and labor markets, *danwei* no longer had the same degree of control over its employees (although it remains a very important institution in today's China).

3. The evolution of the Chinese political system. The post-Mao era saw a gradual and voluntary withdrawal by the state from many areas of social control. The state no longer exercised total control of its citizens' private activities. As a result, more firm boundaries between the state and society began to emerge in the last two decades. Take, for example, the amount of leisure time available to Chinese citizens. Since this factor is crucial in the accumulation of social capital, less leisure time (or leisure time devoted to activities not directly contributing to the accumulation of social capital) has a negative impact on the growth and health of civic organizations. In pre-reform China, as one scholar noted, the state had a near-total claim on a citizen's leisure time (by limiting its amount, form, and content). But since reform, the time for leisure expanded dramatically (from 2 hours 21 minutes per day in 1980 to 4 hours and 48 minutes in 1991) and citizens reclaimed their control of their leisure time completely (Wang 1995: 113). The rapid growth of leisure time available to Chinese citizens was an important factor in the unprecedented growth of civic organizations in China in the last decade.

4. Rapid modernization, economic growth, and rising affluence. The accumulation of social capital, to a large extent, depends on the accumulation of wealth. There is a clear positive correlation between the level of economic wealth and the growth of civic organizations in China. An underlying factor of the rise of a nascent civil society in China in the last two decades was undoubtedly the high rates of economic growth and fast-paced modernization. Growing affluence in China provides more resources to its citizens to pursue private interests and engage in civic activities than would have been possible without such resources. Modernization has made Chinese society

263

more complex, diverse, and led to the rise of new economic organizations and professions. A clear trend in the formation of civic organizations in the late 1980s and early 1990s was that these organizations represent the new economic and social forces that are fast emerging in China.

5. Integration with the international community. The growth of Chinese civil society has received considerable support from the international civil society. Private Western foundations, universities, and civic groups have, in the last two decades, established regular channels of exchange with China's emerging civic organizations and contributed expertise and financial support to their development. American foundations, for example, annually provide millions of dollars in grants to fund their programs in China, most of which support activities of Chinese civic organizations and academic institutions (Kamura 1995).

However, the growth of civil society in China also faces severe limitations. Two obstacles stand out. First, there are considerable political obstacles to the rise of an autonomous civil society. The current regulation on the civic organizations is too restrictive and has evidently slowed down the growth of civic groups for the last six years. The government continues to fear and distrust such organizations, treating them as potential sources of political dissent and challenge. A fundamental change of the government's attitude to civic organizations is required before the next take-off of these groups can occur. In the short-term, the removal of the restrictions imposed on civic organizations by the 1989 regulation should be a priority. In the long-term, official and semi-official sponsorship of civic groups must cease so that civil society can achieve its genuine autonomy.[10]

Second, Chinese civic groups lack material resources to sustain themselves. Despite the record economic growth in the last two decades, China remains a developing country with no well-endowed private foundations that can finance the growth of civic groups. In

[10]Although there is no official figure on the percentage of official, semi-official, private associations, a field study of one county in the early 1990s showed that 69 percent of the civic groups were semi-official, 24 percent were private, and 6 percent were official (Wang, Zhe, and Sun 1993: 77).

my study, I found no private national foundations and few provincial or local foundations. This is in sharp contrast with the United States, where 7,500 private foundations, with about $180 billion in assets, provided $10 billion in grants in 1993–94 (Foundation Center 1996: vii). A vibrant civil society can hardly be created or sustained with scarce financial resources. Indeed, the lack of sufficient financial resources controlled by private foundations is a primary cause of the underdevelopment of civic groups and the heavy dependency on the state by existing civic groups in China. Chinese civic groups turned to the government mainly to seek its financial support. A study of the funding of civic organizations in Shanghai shows that, in 1985, 17 percent of the civic organizations surveyed received all their funding from the government, 40 percent received subsidies from the government or from state-owned enterprises, and only 43 percent were fully self-funded (Ma and Liu 1993: 12). In the long-term, continual rapid economic growth and accumulation of private wealth will provide a conducive macro-environment for the creation of private foundations. In the short-term, the government must further encourage the establishment of such foundations through more liberal policies and favorable tax treatment.

As an independent sector between the state and the market, civil society has long been recognized as a unique force in constraining and remedying the excesses of both the state and the market (Wuthnow 1991). Therefore, whether such a sector can develop and gain its strength and maturity has immense significance for China's future as one of the world's great nations. Although various historical factors have severely retarded the growth of civil society in China, its recent rapid development is a sign that, perhaps at long last, there are powerful underlying forces driving this development. If this trend is real and irreversible, there are grounds to believe that China's future greatness will not only be defined by its economic power and modern political institutions; it will be defined by the vitality of its civil society.

References

Brook, T., and Frolic, M., eds. (1997) *Civil Society in China*. Armonk, N.Y: M.E. Sharpe.

Ding, X. (1994) "Institutional Amphibiousness and the Transition from Communism: The Case of China." *British Journal of Political Science* 24: 293–318.

Fan, B., ed. (1996) *Zhongguo Shehui Tuanti Dacidian* (*Directory of Associations in China*). Beijing: Jingguan Jiaoyu Chubanshe.
Foundation Center (1996) *The Foundation Directory: 1996 Edition*. New York: The Foundation Center.
He, B. (1993) "Dual Roles of Semi-Civil Society in Chinese Democratization." *Australian Journal of Political Science* 29(1): 154–71.
Kamura, H. (1995) "The Role of U.S. Foundations in Asia Pacific." In T. Yamamoto (ed.) *Emerging Civil Society in the Asia Pacific Community*, 687–727. Singapore: Institute of Southeast Asian Studies.
Law Yearbook of China (various years) Beijing: Press of Law Yearbook of China.
Ma, S. (1994) "The Chinese Discourse on Civil Society." *China Quarterly* No. 137 (March): 180–93.
Ma, Y., and Liu, H., eds. (1993) *Shanghai Shehui Tuanti Gailan* (*Handbook of Social Associations in Shanghai*). Shanghai: Shanghai Renmin Chubanshe.
Pearson, M. (1994) "The Janus Face of Business Associations in China: Socialist Corporatism in Foreign Enterprises." *Australian Journal of Chinese Affairs* No. 31 (January): 25–46.
Putnam, R. (1993) *Making Democracy Work: Civic Traditions in Modern Italy.* Princeton, N.J.: Princeton University Press.
Sun, B. (1994) "Xiangzhen Shetuan yu Zhongguo Jiceng Shehui." (*Township Associations and the Chinese Society at the Grassroots*). *Chinese Social Sciences Quarterly (HK)* No. 9 (Autumn): 25–36.
Unger, J. (1996) " 'Bridges': Private Business, the Chinese Government and the Rise of New Associations." *China Quarterly* No. 147 (September): 795–819.
Wang, J.; Zhe, X.; and Sun, B. (1993) *Zhongguo Shehui Zhongjian Ceng: Gaige yu Zhongguode Shetuan Zuzhi (The Intermediary Level of Chinese Society: Reform and China's Public Associations)*. Beijing: Zhongguo Fazhan Chubanshe.
Wang, S. (1995) "Siren Shijian yu Zhengzhi" ("Private Free Time and Politics"). *Chinese Social Sciences Quarterly (HK)* No. 11 (Summer): 108–25.
White, G. (1993) "Prospects for civil society in China: A Case Study of Xiaoshan City." *Australian Journal of Chinese Affairs* No. 29 (January): 63–87.
White, G.; Howell, J.; and Shang, X. (1996) *In Search of Civil Society: Market Reform and Social Change in Contemporary China*. Oxford: Clarendon Press.
Wuthnow, R., ed. (1991) *Between States and Markets: The Voluntary Sector in Comparative Perspective*. Princeton, N.J.: Princeton University Press.
Zhongguo Shehui Tuanti Dacidian (Comprehensive Guide to China's Civic Organizations) (1995) Beijing: Zhongguo Shehui Tuanti Dacidian.
Zhongguo Tongji Nianjian (Statistical Yearbook of China) (various years) Beijing: Zhongguo Tongji.

Comment

Civil Society and Business Enterprise in China

Tom G. Palmer

Measuring Social Capital

Professor Minxin Pei (1998) has admirably advanced our knowledge of the development of civil society in China. His definition of the "relative amount of social capital" as "the differential between a province's share of civic organizations and its share of population" and his attempt to measure that differential are quite suggestive and interesting. I should like to add, however, that the metric may diminish in value as civil society becomes more established in China. A province in which associations merely multiply, with little organizational mortality, might show a greater relative amount of social capital, as Pei has defined it, yet merely be evidence of an ossification of institutions and a lack of social dynamism. Research done some years ago on rates of business dissolution, for example, indicated that high bankruptcy rates may be a good sign of economic vitality, because they are a sign of a willingness to experiment with new products and firms (Palmer 1984). David Birch of MIT's program on Neighborhood and Regional Change, for example, noted in his study of business failures in America that "the more dynamic the local economy (e.g., Houston) the greater the risk-taking and the greater the proportion of firms that fail.... The reality is that our most successful areas are those with the highest rates of innovation and failure, not the lowest" (Birch 1981: 7).

Pei does acknowlege that we must be careful in making judgements about the direction of causation between "higher levels of

---

Tom G. Palmer is Director of the Cato University and a doctoral candidate at Herford College, Oxford University.

economic development and the level of social capital." He asks whether greater wealth leads to a greater demand for complex forms of voluntary cooperation—or social capital—or whether greater social capital leads to more economic development and wealth formation. Establishing the causal arrow may be harder than even Pei acknowledges, however, for reasons that I will develop at greater length shortly: the exclusion of business enterprises from civil society in Pei's definition of civil society. Pei has distinguished business enterprises from other forms of voluntary interaction and excluded the former from civil society. We can still ask, however, whether one kind of cooperation might influence another. The mutual trust and resulting opportunities for cooperation and coordination made possible by interactions of one kind tend to spill over into other kinds of interaction; the direction of causation need not be uniquely one way or the other, but may be mutually reinforcing.[1]

As I know relatively little about recent Chinese politics or history, I will focus my comments on a comparison with the trans-Atlantic experience. By comparing the development of civil society in Europe and North America, we may come to understand a little better the conditions for a healthy civil society in China.

I have two principal comments to make; in the process of making them a number of lesser points will emerge.

Defining Civil Society

First, I would encourage Pei and others who are studying civil society to reconsider the currently trendy approach to the topic, according to which civil society is, to quote Pei, "an independent sector between the state and the market." This approach is, I am convinced, quite unsatisfactory for understanding civil society. It leads to insoluble problems such as the one discussed above—whether economic development (wealth creation through business enterprises) supports the nonprofit sector (which Pei defines as civil society), or whether the non-profit sector supports economic development.

But there are other problems with the definition of civil society offered by Pei. For one thing, the term is used to mean exactly the

---

[1]The issue of trust and cooperation is well explored in Klein (1997). Trust is treated as a kind of capital by Harisalo and Miettinen (1997).

negation of what it meant only a relatively short time ago. When G. W. F. Hegel, for example, used the term, it was as a description of the society of self-interested persons. In *The Philosophy of Right*, Hegel (1977) notes that "individuals in their capacity as burghers in this state are private persons whose end is their own interest" (p. 125) and characterizes civil society as "the battleground where everyone's individual private interest meets everyone else's" (p. 189). The interests of civil society were for Hegel always and only partial and selfish, whereas the state's interest was, he mistakenly believed, universal. Karl Marx (1987: 146) identified civil society with the institutions definitive of the market when he argued, "Private property . . . forms the basis of civil society. It leads man to see in other men not the realization but the limitation of his own freedom." Marx referred to "egoistic man, man as he is in civil society, namely an individual withdrawn behind his private interests and whims and separated from the community." Both Hegel and Marx saw civil society as essentially co-extensive with the legal relations and institutions that structure markets and identified the motivations of persons in civil society almost exclusively with egoism or self-interest.

This narrow approach to civil society has simply been turned on its head in recent years, with civil society identified only with the nonprofit sector, to the exclusion of business enterprises altogether. Both of these approaches are too narrow and depart from the traditional understanding of civil society, which encompassed both for-profit and nonprofit associations that were organized on the basis of voluntary consent among free and equal individuals.

Antony Black (1984: 32) articulated the basic values of civil society as follows:

> Briefly, the values of civil society comprise, first, personal security in the sense of freedom from the arbitrary passions of others, and freedom from domination in general. This involves freedom (or security) of the person from violence, and of private property from arbitrary seizure. But these, it would appear, can only be maintained if legal process is credibly and successfully enforced as an alternative to physical force, in settlement of disagreements, and in redressing wrongs committed by violence. This leads to the notion of legal rights (whether or not so called), both in the sense of the right to sue in court on equal terms with anyone else—

legal equality—and in the sense of claims, for example to property, recognized and upheld by the law.

Conditions of Civil Society

Immanuel Kant identified as a condition of civil society the equal subjection of all to a known law—and therefore the equal freedom of all to the enjoyment of what is properly theirs. In *The Metaphysics of Morals*, Kant (1985: 65) argued,

> With respect to an external and contingent possession, a unilateral Will cannot serve as a coercive law for everyone, since that would be a violation of freedom in accordance with universal laws. Therefore, only a Will binding everyone else—that is, a collective, universal (common), and powerful Will—is the kind of Will that can provide the guarantee required. The condition of being subject to general external (that is, public) legislation that is backed by power is the civil society. Accordingly, a thing can be externally yours or mine only in a civil society.

Kant identified general and equally applicable laws as central to civil society, and in this he was building on the longer tradition that Antony Black has described. The security of person and property in a system of compossible rights—that is, a system in which the mutual exercise of Subjective Right is the condition for the realization of Objective Right—is a precondition for civil society. What is disputable in Kant's view is whether having one and only one enforcement agency is necessary to maintain a system of compossible rights, but Kant is surely right that a system of compossible rights is a necessary condition for civil society.

With the decline and fall into disrepute of socialism in the 1980s, thinkers behind the Iron Curtain began to call for a return to civil society.[2] If Marx had opposed it, it only seemed reasonable that there had to be something good about it. And especially in Poland the growth of institutions independent of the state, including trade unions, church associations, business and entrepreneurial associations (notably in Gdansk and Krakow), and self-help groups, hastened the fall of the communist state. In the West, however, intellectuals who still maintained socialist inclinations and hostility to free

[2]For a discussion focusing on the contributions of the "Czechoslovak School," which arose as criticism of Marxism-Leninism, see Rau (1991).

enterprise insisted that civil society be so construed as *not* to include business enterprises. Civil society could not be construed as identical with the state, but socialist-leaning intellectuals have done their best to ensure that the idea not be construed to include for-profit firms or forms of association.[3] This left theorists in the position of defining civil society simply in terms of what it is not. It is not the state and it is not profit-seeking business enterprises.

This approach harbors a serious conceptual confusion. One is on treacherous ground when one defines something, not in terms of what it is, but exclusively in terms of what it is not, as Plato showed in his dialogues.

The distinction between force and voluntary cooperation is more useful, as well as one which is far more in accord with the tradition of thinking about civil society. It has the considerable virtue of actually distinguishing parts of the world in a logically coherent way. What distinguishes the cooperation that characterizes civil society from more intimate forms of cooperation is its extent. Civil society encompasses not only intimate social groupings of persons, such as hunter/gatherer bands, or natural associations, such as the family, but also complete strangers, to whom civil treatment is extended as a matter of course. Civil society is based on abstract rules that allow persons wholly unknown to one another to cooperate.

Ernest Gellner (1994) has identified the condition for such cooperation among people who may have no intimate connections as "modularity." Not atomistic man, but modular man lives in civil society. Although he also uses the notion of atomization, Gellner introduced the most useful concept of modularity as a corrective to it. As he notes (p. 97),

> There are firms which produce, advertise and market modular furniture. The point about such furniture is that it comes

[3]One commentator, determined to find fault with capitalism, dismissed the American experience with civil society as follows: "The United States, which, in contrast to both Eastern and Western Europe, always lacked a coherent concept of the state, has traditionally been presented as a model of civil society. Yet in the closing decades of the twentieth century the adequacy of this model is increasingly being questioned" (Seligman 1992: 9). Apparently, a constitutional republic legally grounded on a written constitution specifying enumerated powers lacks a coherent concept of the state. What is notable is the attempt by Seligman, also found in many other treatments of the topic, to recast the idea of civil society so as to comport better with the very socialism with which civil society was being contrasted in the socialist countries.

> in bits which are agglutinative: you can buy one bit which
> will function on its own, but when your needs, income or
> space available augment, you can buy another bit. It will fit
> in with the one acquired previously, and the whole thing
> will still have a coherence, aesthetically and technically. You
> can combine and recombine the bits at will. . . . What genuine
> Civil Society really requires is not modular furniture, but
> modular man.

Gellner's point is that in civil society one can form attachments
of one's own choosing; one can recombine them in new ways; and
one can withdraw from them without thereby withdrawing from
or becoming an enemy to the entire social order, as one would in a
little hunter/gatherer band or a perhaps a primitive society, at least,
as organicists conceive them. In his work on the modern corporation,
Otto von Gierke (1990: 208) made a similar point:

> The modern tendency towards precise definition of aims
> comes to predominate over the earlier undefined universal-
> ity. The prescription of the aims is connected with the defin-
> ing of that portion of the personality which the fellowship
> demands its members should sacrifice. No modern associa-
> tion of fellows encompasses the totality of a human being,
> even in economic terms; the aspect of their economic person-
> ality which forms part of the association is strictly defined.

Commerce and Civil Society

We should see for-profit enterprises, whether individual proprie-
torships, partnerships, cooperatives, joint-stock firms, or other forms,
as part of civil society. They allow cooperation among individuals
lacking intimate connections and rest on the same fundamental legal
principles as nonprofit institutions. And like churches, self-help associations, and neighborhood associations, they are schools for virtue,
as Adam Smith (1982: 538–39) noted:

> Whenever commerce is introduced into any country, probity
> and punctuality always accompany it. These virtues in a
> rude and barbarous country are almost unknown. Of all the
> nations in Europe, the Dutch, the most commercial, are the
> most faithfull to their word. The English are more so than
> the Scotch, but much inferior to the Dutch, and in the remote
> parts of this country they [are] far less so than in the commer-
> cial parts of it. This is not at all to be imputed to a national

character, as some pretend. There is no natural reason why an Englishman or a Scotchman should not be as punctual in performing agreements as a Dutchman. It is far more reduceable to self interest, that general principle which regulates the actions of every man, and which leads men to act in a certain manner from views of advantage, and is as deeply planted in an Englishman as a Dutchman. A dealer is afraid of losing his character, and is scrupulous in observing every engagement. When a person makes perhaps 20 contracts in a day, he cannot gain so much by endeavouring to impose on his neighbors, as the very appearance of a cheat would make him lose. Where people seldom deal with one another, we find that they are somewhat disposed to cheat, because they can gain more by a smart trick than they can lose by the injury which it does their character.

I suspect that this is what a Shichuan migrant meant when she told Kate Xiao Zhou in 1995 that "she was learning in *shehui daixue* (society university)" (in Zhou 1998).

Pei seems to incline in the direction of including business firms as part of civil society when he includes "specialized industry and business groups" among civic organizations and notes that "the rise of this group was primarily due to the decline of the system of vertical state-planning and its replacement by market-oriented horizontal linkages among producers in the same industries."[4] Inclusion of newly founded private enterprises in his indices of civil society would have offered a more accurate picture of the growth of civil society in China.

It is interesting that Pei notes that "an underlying factor of the rise of a nascent civil society in China in the last two decades was undoubtedly the high rates of economic growth and fast-paced modernization." This may reflect a different experience from that of transatlantic civil society, in which the causal relationship was not

---

[4]On the significance of horizontal, rather than vertical, arrangements among economic enterprises for social and economic development, see Goodell (1985). Goodell traces the development of horizontal relationships of contract and cooperation, rather than of vertical relations of command and coercion, through the history of a number of societies and demonstrates its importance to economic development. Contrary to Marxist analyses that posit a material base and an ideological or institutional superstructure, Goodell shows how the institutions of law and production are co-determining.

so unequivocal. The growth of associations, such as communes, trade and merchant guilds, religious orders, merchant leagues, and the like is commonly seen as the foundation for the growth of productivity and wealth. Being based on contractual relationships, rather than natural ones, such as kinship, these associations provided the foundation for the creation of social capital in the form of trust relationships. Such relationships are essential to economic development through the market.[5]

Eliminating Obstacles to the Growth of Civil Society

My second principal comment is to endorse Pei's call to eliminate "political obstacles to the rise of an autonomous civil society" and his insistence that "in the long term, official and semi-official sponsorship of civic groups must cease so that civil society can achieve its genuine autonomy." But one must remember that such official sponsorship was also a part of the history of transatlantic civil society, as well, and required a struggle for the institutions of civil society to break free of the state. For example, a very important part of the Western heritage of constitutional government is the existence of municipal government. The formation of independent cities, which were not simply creatures of central power but were freely formed by citizens, is a defining feature of Western European and North American experience. But often the citizens forming them sought royal or imperial charters as protection against other powers. As the legal historian Harold Berman (1983: 362) writes,

> The new European cities and towns of the eleventh and twelfth centuries were also legal associations, in the sense that each was held together by a common urban legal consciousness and by distinctive urban legal institutions. In fact, it was by a legal act, usually the granting of a charter, that most of the European cities and towns came into being; they did not simply emerge but were *founded*. Moreover, the charter would almost invariably establish the basic "liberties"

[5]See Rosenberg and Birdzell (1986), especially the section on "Economic Association without Kinship" (pp. 123–26). ("The inescapable fact is that the merchant class evolved a moral system suited to life in highly organized enterprises. In no other way could the enterprises that went beyond family and organized such ventures as colonization, foreign trade, and canal building (and, later, railway building) have found the institutional loyalties essential to carrying out their economic functions— and find them they plainly did" [p. 126]). See also Goodell (1980).

274

of citizens, usually including substantial rights of self-government.

Once the charter has been granted and the members of the association have developed a sense of autonomy, it is easier to assert the rights of the association against the powerful persons or institutions from whom the charter was originally sought. A similar history can be told of the business enterprise, which broke free from chartering requirements and achieved independence from the state. The historians Nathan Rosenberg and L. E. Birdzell (1986: 195) distinguished between state-chartered corporations and the modern joint-stock company:

> Neither chartered trading companies nor franchised corporations were the direct ancestors of the modern business corporation. That distinction belongs to the joint-stock company, a form of business association developed by English merchants from the seventeenth century on. It differed from the corporation in that it lacked a royal charter, and it differed from the partnership in that financial interests in the enterprise, represented by stock certificates, were freely transferable.[6]

It should in no way detract from my admiration for Professor Pei's achievement in measuring the growth of civil society to note that it would have been even greater had he adhered to the traditional understanding of civil society and included in it profit-seeking business enterprises.

References

Berman, H. (1983) *Law and Revolution: The Formation of the Western Legal Tradition.* Cambridge, Mass.: Harvard University Press.

Birch, D.L. (1981) "Who Creates Jobs?" *The Public Interest*, No. 65 (Fall): 3–14.

---

[6]Rosenberg and Birdzell go on to describe the history of the liberalization of corporation laws, much along the lines that Professor Pei proposes for China. It bears noting, however, that there remains a residual conflict over the nature of the corporation, with some (Ralph Nader, for example) insisting that the corporation is purely a creature of the state and can be made to serve the ends of the state, and others who insist that the corporation is a creature of contract, autonomous and independent of the state. For a review of the literature and a criticism of the view that corporations are creatures of the state, see Hessen (1979).

Black, A. (1984) *Guilds and Civil Society in European Thought from the Twelfth Century to the Present.* Ithaca, N.Y: Cornell University Press.

Gellner, E. (1994) *Conditions of Liberty: Civil Society and Its Rivals.* New York: Penguin Books.

von Gierke, O. ([1868] 1990) *Community in Historical Perspective.* Edited by A. Black. Cambridge: Cambridge University Press.

Goodell, G. (1980) "From Status to Contract: The Significance of Agrarian Relations of Production in the West, Japan, and in 'Asiatic' Persia." *European Journal of Sociology* 21: 285–325.

Goodell, G. (1985) "The Importance of Political Participation for Sustained Capitalist Development. *European Journal of Sociology* 26: 93–127.

Harisalo, R., and Miettinen, E. (1997) *Trust Capital: The Third Force of Entrepreneurship.* Tampere, Finland: Tampere University Press.

Hegel, G.W.F. (1977) *The Philosophy of Right.* Trans. by T. M. Knox. Oxford: Oxford University Press.

Hessen, R. (1979). *In Defense of the Corporation.* Stanford, Calif.: Hoover Institution Press.

Kant, I. (1985) *The Metaphysical Elements of Justice.* Trans. by J. Ladd. New York: Macmillan.

Klein, D.B., ed. (1997) *Reputation: Studies in the Voluntary Elicitation of Good Conduct.* Ann Arbor: University of Michigan Press.

Marx, K. (1987) "On the Jewish Question." In J. Waldron (ed.) *Nonsense Upon Stilts: Burke, Bentham and Marx on the Rights of Man.* London: Methuen & Co.

Palmer, T.G. (1984) "Industrial Policy, Business Failures, and Economic Evolution." *Policy Report* 6(3) (March): 1,3–4.

Pei, M. (1998) "The Growth of Civil Society in China." In J.A. Dorn (ed.) *China in the New Millennium: Market Reforms and Social Development*, chap. 17. Washington, D.C.: Cato Institute.

Rau, Z. (1991) "Human Nature, Social Engineering and the Reemergence of Civil Society." In Z. Rau (ed.) *The Reemergence of Civil Society in Eastern Europe and the Soviet Union, 25–50.* Boulder, Colo.: Westview Press.

Rosenberg, N., and Birdzell Jr., L.E. (1986) *How the West Grew Rich: The Economic Transformation of the Industrial World.* New York: Basic Books.

Seligman, A.B. (1992) *The Idea of Civil Society.* Princeton, N.J.: Princeton University Press.

Smith, A. (1982) *Lectures on Jurisprudence.* Glasgow ed. Indianapolis: Liberty Classics.

Zhou, K.X. (1998) "Market Development and the Rural Women's Revolution in Contemporary China." In J.A. Dorn (ed.) *China in the New Millennium: Market Reforms and Social Development*, chap. 18. Washington, D.C.: Cato Institute.

18. Market Development and the Rural Women's Revolution in Contemporary China

Kate Xiao Zhou

The relation between market development and social development in China should be obvious. Anyone can see how the development of markets in China facilitates rapid social change. First of all, markets speed up the process of urbanization, as more and more Chinese farmers move into nonagricultural occupations. Second, market development is also directly responsible for the revival of Chinese culture and civil society, which was suppressed for many years. As a result, the monolithic state communist culture has changed, replaced by a diversity of locally based and autonomous cultures. For example, local community identities, religious groups, private charity organizations, and ethnic-specific traits are flourishing all over China. Anywhere you go, especially beyond the city limits, you can see local festivals and temple fairs existing in all major *jishi* (farmers' markets). As in the agora of ancient Greece, the market is a stage for the culture. No markets, no development in China.

My main hypothesis is that social developments in China came mainly as a result of unintended consequences of the market development. I will use the rural women's revolution as an example to test my hypothesis.

Globalization of the world market economy influences every nation and people everywhere. With notable exceptions (for example, Blumberg et al. 1995; House-Midamba and Ekechi 1995), most studies on women and market development stress the negative

Kate Xiao Zhou is Assistant Professor of Political Science at the University of Hawaii at Manoa. She thanks Marion J. Levy Jr., Mark Selden, Feng Yuan, and Thomas David Burns for their comments and support during the writing of this paper.

impact of markets on the lives of women. Some argue that development of markets has hurt women's interest and undermined their power (for example, Boserup 1970; Tinker and Bramsen 1976). Other feminist critics (such as Fernandez-Kelly 1983, Fuentes and Ehrenreich 1983, Milkman and Townsley 1994) focus on the new forms of exploitation that economic development in general and capitalist development in particular have created. Economic development is allegedly accompanied by the exploitation of women's sexuality and physical and mental health (Commonwealth Secretariat 1990). For instance, women tend to dominate in "dirty work" and in "dirty working conditions" (see Fuentes and Ehrenreich 1983). Furthermore, women are disadvantaged with respect to the resources that facilitate economic activities because they have lower levels of education and thus earn much less than men. Finally, scholars also argue that the process of modernization and development creates the distinction between public and private, forcing women into private spheres (Tilly and Scott 1978).

Market development in China has produced some contrary findings. This paper examines the social status of rural women by looking at the role of rural women in China's market transition (1978–present) as well as the market's impact on rural women's lives. The paper argues that the post-*baochan daohu*[1] farmers' economic movement (markets, rural industrialization, and migration) is the primary cause of the changing position of rural women—that is, 80 percent of all Chinese women (see Zhou 1996).[2]

Background of the Women's Revolution

Before discussing the new women's revolution, I shall discuss the social basis from which changes took place. For this analysis, that basis is the social structure of socialist collective farming. Before Mao initiated China's socialist revolution, rural women's lives were largely confined to the family context. The ideal image of women was *sancong side* (three dependencies and four virtues). *Sancong* means that a woman depended on her father as a child, on her

---

[1]*Bouchan daohu* refers to the practice of turning over agricultural production to the individual household.

[2]Rural women may be defined as women born of rural parents and reared initially in rural areas.

husband as a married woman, on her son as a widow. *Side (fude, fuyan, furong, and fugong)* required a woman to be virtuous in morality, mannerly in both speech and appearance, and good at women's work (cooking and sewing).[3]

In spite of this, rural markets historically permitted female villagers to earn needed cash from peddling, trading, laboring, and selling household sideline products. So vital were market activities even to poor tillers that the market disruption and social disorder caused by war, political chores, and foreign intervention ruined many villagers (Friedman et al. 1991). Chinese women were present in many local markets throughout China. The reality of prerevolutionary women's lives contradicted the ideal image.

After the establishment of People's Republic of China (PRC), one of Mao's intended goals was to eradicate the oppression of women. The state tried to use political means to bring sexual equality by introducing laws and propaganda. The 1950 marriage law banned prostitution and concubinage. The government also expanded the education of many rural women, although not enough was done to eliminate female illiteracy. More importantly, improved medical technology reduced the infant mortality rate. Government policy also encouraged rural women's economic participation in agricultural production.

But the state's anti-market policies also frustrated the desires and aspirations of rural women. Starting in 1952–53, socialist policies curbed markets and exploited the rural people for urban industrialization and for the support of a rapidly growing bureaucracy. The banning of markets enabled the state to secure a monopoly on grain and cotton at imposed low prices. As a result, every pound of grain the rural people sold to the state represented an economic loss, while the state sold goods to farmers at high prices (the "scissors" price). During a period of 30 years, the exploitative scissors price policies enabled the government to take more than 600 billion yuan from farmers (Meng 1993: 147).

Moreover, the imposed collective commune system ended the household economy and transformed village traditions in ways that actually harmed women. Women often received three or four workpoints per day fewer than men, or else were assigned tasks worth

---

[3]For a discussion of the family social structure prior to Communist China, see Levy (1948).

fewer workpoints. The sexual division of labor under the collective system remained rigid, with rural cadres making almost all decisions for members of the collective. To make sure that rural people did not escape from their agricultural slavery, the government imposed the *hukou* system (in which one's grain rationing is tied to one's residence). Thus, 80 percent of Chinese rural people were tied to the land. The destruction of markets and the household economy and the exploitation led to miserably low levels of consumption. Deprived of commercial and sideline income, rural people saw their income decline. Although everyone suffered from this miserable fate, women often suffered more than men. (Custom gave lower priority to women's nutritional needs than those of men.) Although the party state sometimes preached equality across gender and generation, it in fact ignored women's problems (Johnson 1983). On the collective farm, women everywhere were ranked as lower-paid workers. They were regarded as "weaker bodies."[4]

In short, the anti-rural economic policies of the People's Republic, Mao's own cultural limits, and Mao's male constituency closed social mobility for almost all rural women (Wolf 1985, Stacey 1983). The changes affected the source of farming decisions directly and decisively. Above all, Mao's socialist revolution changed the social context into which family patterns fit. Despite the government's ideological protestations and explicit laws about equality of women, the closed nature of Communist China's social structure provided little potential for rural women to achieve independence. China was a women's paradise just as it was a workers' paradise, in name only. Although communist ideology made sexual equality an ideal pattern, the actual power patterns for rural women were quite diminished.

The New Rural Women's Revolution

Baochan Daohu Movement

The systematic change from commune to *baochan daohu* in the late 1970s and early 1980s was the mechanism for the transformation of

[4]Chinese working women in the city gained a certain degree of independence in marriage and work. Urban women who worked in the factories and other nonfarm related work usually were able to live in nuclear families and preferred to do so. Recently urban feminists within China have criticized the state patriarchy and some

occupation and market activities for most rural people, rural women in particular. The *baochan daohu* system changed the principles and the organization of family to produce for markets.[5] The rural population became predominantly, if not totally, money-oriented. Generally speaking, under the new incentive system of *baochan daohu*, women's participation in economic activities increased rapidly compared with their lives under the commune system.

That is why rural women actively participated in dismantling the commune system in the late 1970s and the early 1980s. Women helped to bring about *baochan daohu* in two important ways. First, rural women in the 1970s turned to household sidelines to avoid the low pay and long hours of collective work (Wolf 1985). Some were able to do so by asking for sick leave; others pretended to work and saved their energy for their family chores. They were behind their husbands or fathers in pushing for family farming, as part of the movement toward *baochan daohu*. Second, women helped to spread the practice of *baochan daohu*. Rural women used marriage to show their preferences by marrying farmers who adopted *baochan daohu*. Women also helped the spread of *baochan daohu* by *zou qinqi* (visiting relatives), carrying information between their village of origin (their parents) and their village of procreation (their husbands). The knowledge of *baochan daohu* occurring elsewhere was crucial for farmers to have the guts to seek *baochan daohu* for their own families.

Most rural women preferred the family economy because they preferred to deal with husbands or fathers rather than deal with local cadres, who are nearly all male but are not family. The family economy is patriarchal, but it was a double patriarchy under the collectives. What was left of family control was patriarchal, and all other local power was patriarchal, despite the ideal patterns of Mao.

Economically, women also gained a certain degree of control after *baochan daohu*. First of all, the sexual division of labor in production was less rigid under the family economy although a sharply differentiated division of labor remained in terms of housekeeping and childbearing. But with most work carried out within the household context, women's

---

even accuse the government of being the source of constraints on women's emancipation.

[5] For a negative evaluation of *bouchan daohu*'s impact on women, see Davin (1988) and Bossen (1992).

TABLE 1
DIVISION OF MAJOR DECISIONS IN THE CHINESE RURAL HOUSEHOLD
(BY PERCENTAGE)

Decisions	Husband	Wife	Joint
Buying animals	29	4	57
Buying tools	27	4	60
Building a house	17	2	76
Buying durable goods	18	13	67
Sending money gifts	14	10	73
When to send the children to school	10	6	82
Whether to continue the children's education	9	6	82
Children's mate selection	4	9	67
Preparing for a son's wedding	5	7	74
Preparing for a daughter's wedding	5	8	73
Accounting and management	10	7	81
Birth decision	2	7	83

SOURCE: Institute of Population Studies (1994).

traditional role as mothers became easier and often was more appreciated. Women had more flexibility working both in the fields and at home. It is common knowledge that women worked harder than men in the countryside. More importantly, women together with men have the power of making decisions about labor allocation for family members.

Wives Take Part in Decisionmaking

Baochan daohu made the family responsible, once again, for major economic decisions. Wives began to share in making many of those decisions—even major family economic decisions—although they still have not achieved equality, as indicated by Table 1. The survey suggests that rural women shared most major decisions with their husbands. In children's education, mothers and fathers shared almost equal decisionmaking power. In children's mate selection, wedding preparations, accounting and management, and birth decision, women have more power than men. This finding is supported by another survey done in Zao Yang county in Hubei province. While husbands and wives shared most of the major decisions in production, consumption, and marketing, sometimes women have more decision power than men (Zaoyang Women's Federation 1995). This has never occurred in Chinese history.

In many cases, women's increasing power within the family during the period from 1978 to the early 1980s was directly linked to their economic contribution to the family. Rural women became an important source of family income through raising chickens, ducks, pigs, eggs, and other sidelines. While men and women worked together in the fields to satisfy the grain quota, women worked alone on these sideline items that were the first to bring in cash after markets formed. One survey in Zaoyang county, Hubei, showed that in most households, wives had the same income as their husbands. In fact, the better off the households, the more equal the income contribution between the sexes. Among the households with annual income below 2,500 yuan, husbands made more than wives in 37 percent of households, while among the median income households (2,500–5,000 yuan), women made more than men in 31 percent of households. Still, among the high-income households (5,000 yuan and above) women and men had the same income in 32 percent of households (Zaoyang Women's Federation 1995: 44).

There are of course problems within the family contract system. For example, young women who are married to men from other villages must give up the land they have contracted for in the villages where they have been living, but are unlikely to be able to replace it with a new plot in the new village. Although there is still no way for women to enjoy complete equality with men, they have come a long way. Never in Chinese history have so many women's income surpassed that of men in farmer households.

Rural Women and Markets

The development of markets not only changed family relations and marital decisions but also directly changed the position of women in rural China. Rural women have always played an important role in local markets in China. Those roles were vastly increased by the explosive market growth that followed *baochan daohu* in the early 1980s. Throughout the 1980s, they occupied such a conspicuous place in *jishi* (farmers' markets) of all sorts that many markets in China were called *nuren jie* (the Street of Women). There were often more women than men managing local and intermediate *jishi*. Life as a merchant became a significant alternative for rural women as a result of the proliferation of markets. Ten years after the introduction of *baochan daohu*, the contribution of rural women began to influence everyone's life in China because between 80 to 90 percent of meat, eggs, and fowl were produced and marketed by rural women (Liu and Gu 1990: 6).

Rural men tended to take responsibility for transporting goods to markets. Selling did not require a lot of strength and was thus regarded as more suitable for women. But more importantly, women were thought to be especially good at human relationships such as selling and dealing. It was regarded unmanly to argue or bargain over prices. This new form of sexual division of labor is itself sexual stereotyping, but it is sexual stereotyping that allows broader and more varied economic roles for women. In an era of trucks, carting goods to market may not be a matter of brute strength beyond the strength of women. A greater obstacle may have been the fear of women out on roads alone. But the presence of rural markets did provide many rural women with new ways of life that were not possible under the collectives.

In Imperial China and under collective farming, only men were barbers. In fact, it was considered bad luck for a woman to touch a man's head. Since barbers went from door to door to provide their service, no women were allowed or willing to become barbers because a proper woman's place was at home. Now, it is fashionable for a man to have a haircut by a female barber. Increasingly, rural women constitute the main body of barbers and beauticians.

For thousands of years, fishing was a male occupation and women were not allowed to fish. With the exception of knitting, any fishing tool touched by women was considered bad luck. But after the family economy system was in place, more and more women have participated in fishing. For example, in three counties in Jiangsu, although men outnumbered women four to one in terms of making a fish contract, men and women shared almost equally in terms of fish production (Fang et al. 1995). Moreover, women have become indispensable in the fishing industry—they are responsible for fishing food process production and for fishing tool and machine production.

Similarly, in pre-Communist China and under the collectives, there were no women butchers in the countryside. Slaughtering

TABLE 2
HOW WELL DO YOU GRASP THE FOLLOWING KNOWLEDGE
COMPARED WITH YOUR HUSBAND?
(PERCENTAGE)

Item	Better than Husband	Same as Husband	Worse than Husband	No Knowledge
Plowing	4.4	14	53	23
Fertilizing	6.2	82	12	0
Pest control	11	64	25	0
Family husbandry	69	31	0.6	0
Fruit growing	18	51	32	0
Farm machinery	6	27	17	49
Harvesting	29	67	4	0
Marketing/Selling	22	68	10	0
Purchase of seeds	21	53	18	0
Family craft	55	31	8	0

SOURCE: Zaoyang Women's Federation (1995: 53).

pigs was an important male ritual in many villages in China. The cooperation of several men during the process showed a strong male bonding. Women were not even allowed to cut meat for sale at the market. But now it is common to see female butchers at markets both in the city and in the countryside.

For thousands of years, women were not allowed to engage in plowing fields. Now women have begun to break the tradition and to accomplish the impossible. In a survey in Zaoyang county, Hubei, women increasingly overcame sexual discrimination, even in the field of technology (Zaoyang Women's Federation 1995: 53). Table 2 shows that although a relatively restrictive sexual division of labor in terms of farm machine operation and cultivation still exists, in all other fields women more or less share technological know-how with men. This is the case even though women have a very low level of education.

Some rural women with little capital grasped the inefficiency of the planned system, which lacked basic services. Many rural women opened restaurants, repair shops, and retail stores. For example, in Guanzhong district of Shaanxi province, among female commercial producers, 42 percent initiated business by themselves (Liu 1995).

For example, Zhang Junmin from Yijin village of Xianghe county, Hebei province, learned the skill of chicken farming while working as a temporary worker in a chicken farm. She set up her own chicken farm in 1988 and became a rich chicken farmer. Moreover, 103 women in her village followed her example and set up their own chicken farms. As a result, chicken farming became the most important source of income for the village of 330 households (Gu 1995: 84). Mao, a woman with little education, set up a Mao restaurant, claiming that she could cook the dishes Mao loved since she is from Mao's hometown, Shaoshang.

Increased economic roles for women—that is, increased roles for women in the allocation of goods and services—cannot exist without changes in the political roles of women. If they have a broader range of economic roles, they will weaken patriarchy. As women gain economic power, they will come to realize that they can be successful on their own.

Once the markets became increasingly important for the lives of millions upon millions of rural households, women's lives were in turn affected by the new forces. First of all, the commercial revolution in the countryside started with a change in the consumption patterns of rural people, especially household consumption, in the 1980s. The 1991 survey suggests that in 80 percent of rural households, husbands and wives shared important family consumption decisions, a higher percentage than urban households. The saying "use money to buy time and to buy convenience" (*na quan mai shijian, nan quan mai fang bian*) gained acceptance. Women preferred to live in brick houses.

Second, the development of markets also brought about an increase in the standard of living. As people got richer, they could afford new luxuries such as soap, toothbrushes, and toothpaste, which had not existed in the 1970s for the majority of rural people. For example, most Chinese women before 1980 used ashes and dirty rags when they had their menstrual periods. Such unsanitary methods caused some women to have problems. But now most rural women use paper sanitary tissues and some even have begun to use sanitary napkins. Since women still are in charge of washing, the access to soap has been very helpful. In some better-off areas, washing machines and rice cookers are available.

The new pattern of consumption also liberated women from endless work, especially sewing and shoe making. For thousands of years, women were required to make shoes and clothes for their family members. Shoe making was a very time-consuming activity. It would take an average woman four or five evenings to finish the soles for one pair of shoes and two evenings to finish the upper part of a shoe. So it would take an average woman one week to finish one pair of shoes. How many evenings would it take for a woman to make shoes and clothes for a family of six? Weaving, sewing, and shoe making occupied too much of a woman's time. In less than five years after 1979, most rural women stopped making shoes, socks, and clothes on their own. Women and their family members preferred women to concentrate on making goods to be sold at the market and then buy shoes and clothes. For many women, such convenience itself was a liberation.

Rural Women and Industrial Transformation in China

Just as the plight of women's health is linked to economic opportunity, so is women's economic opportunity dependent on market growth. Under the collective arrangement, almost all rural women were denied opportunities for nonagricultural work. The few chances for upward mobility (joining the army or the Communist Party) in the countryside were almost completely reserved for men, although a few token rural women were regularly presented as show cases. As more and more farmers entered into nonagricultural work, more and more rural women chose nonagricultural work. By 1992, of 130 million farmers who took nonagricultural jobs, about 31 percent were rural women (Ren 1995: 29).

Rural women played an important role in the rural industrial take-off. According to the official statistics, by 1993, 50 million female workers worked in rural industry, making up 42 percent of the entire rural industrial labor force (Chinese Women's Federation 1993: 23). The economic participation of rural women in rural industry not only helped the transformation of Chinese industrial structure but also increased women's autonomy. Such economic activity reduced their dependence on their husbands. What is more, some rural women even became private industrialists themselves. For example, Zhang Huanyun, from rural Hubei, set up a straw craft factory and became one of the richest people in her village. There are thousands of examples like this in many rural areas across China. In Zaoyang county of Hubei province (a middle level development area), there are 18,600 private enterprises set up by women (Zaoyang Women's Federation 1995: 46).

The industrial setting also altered some traditions. Traditionally, economic cooperation took place mostly among the male kinship network. The rise of markets and rural factories has increased the interaction between married women's natal family networks and their husband's networks. The goal to make profits has overcome the traditional barriers. Thus, people cooperate with whoever brings them benefits. With poor legal enforcement in terms of contracts, many people tend to trust someone they have known. Thus the importance of female relatives was magnified. For example, in rural Shanghai, one fourth of the families have some sort of economic cooperation through female relatives (Lei, Yang, and Cai 1994: 153). For poor provinces like Huban and Sichuan, this sort of cooperation is more prevalent.

The transformation from agriculture to industry also gives rise to the culture of individual performance. This new culture has been beneficial to rural women because a merit-based versus birth related reward system began to take root in Chinese society. In rural factories where the piece rate system is the norm, women workers often out perform men. For example, in the early 1990s, in Nanyang village of Yutao county, Zhejiang province, the average women worker's monthly wage was 120–140 yuan, which was about 10 to 20 yuan higher than an average male worker (Meng 1993: 152).

Compared with most agricultural settings in China, factory work often and increasingly does not require much physical strength. The performance of each individual becomes more important. What is more, workers in the factories are often paid more than the farmers. Most rural women have a strong preference to opt for industrial jobs. Thus, they have exhibited more patience and enthusiasm than men workers. For most of those working women, the most important thing is to secure industrial employment. They need savings to prepare themselves to find other alternatives in case they are fired. Thus they work hard and save more for their own future rather than sending money home. In many developed regions where export production has soared, there are more opportunities for women to get jobs. A recent survey of 149 factories in Guangdong suggests that 78 percent of workers agreed with the statement that "it is easier for women to get jobs than for men" (Rural Economy Research Center 1995: 2).

288

The autonomy and independence of women workers in factories enabled many rural women to be economically and physically independent of their male family members. Such economic independence increases their self-confidence and gives them a sense of pride in their labor. It also gives them whatever increases in power go along with the control of money. Patriarchy is extremely vulnerable to the control of money by women (see Zhou 1996).

One social survey done in rural Shanghai suggests that the rapid development of rural industry increased rural women's sense of self-worth. Only 26 percent of rural women (15 percent of young women) still believed that "men are born superior to women" (Lei, Yang, and Cai 1994: 160).

The independence of women can be expressed as women's four new selfs: *zizun* (self-respect), *zixing* (self-confidence), *zili* (self-reliance), *ziqiang* (self-improvement). Such independence has also altered the family relations at home. For example, the frequency of wife beating declined, especially among households with a factory working wife.

Moreover, the attitude toward marriage also changed. For many years, the economic condition of one's family was the most important criterion for most rural women and their families in choosing a marital partner. For example, a survey of women in 122 rural factories, conducted by the Women's Federation in Jiangsu, suggests that the most important considerations in selecting a spouse are that he be (1) a hard worker, ethical, and career-minded (32 percent); (2) respectful of older people and honest (22 percent); (3) intelligent and skilled (22 percent); and (4) rich and from a good family (2 percent) (Meng 1993: 152). Before 1978, the hardship of rural life meant that both men and women placed family economic conditions and family social networks (which played an important role for family subsistence) as the prime considerations, while personal ability ranked third and personal character fourth. An individual's personal ability and personal characteristics were ranked one and two for rural women in villages, while family economic conditions and social networks were ranked the third and fourth (Wang 1991). Considering the centrality of the family in Chinese society, this shift from family priority to individual priority is a revolution indeed.

An increase in independent work in the factories has enabled rural women to place personal quality above family backgrounds. Since their own work is often merit-based, it is natural for them to choose someone based on merit.

The development of the nonstate industrial sector has also provided rural women with new opportunities and has given rise to the concept of "women-initiated divorce." For thousands of years, Chinese women accepted their marital arrangement as their fate, as expressed by a popular saying: "If one marries a rooster, she will stick to the rooster; if she marries a dog, she will remain the wife of the dog." There was in effect no such a thing as divorce. Although the 1950 Family Laws provided the legal right for both women and men to divorce, the economic structure of collectivization and the threat of poverty made it impossible for most rural people to actualize that right.

As women, especially young women, began to participate in the industrial work force and in market activities, more attention came to be paid to the quality of the marriage. In one survey done in rural Shanghai, only 7 percent of young women believed that they should stick to their married spouse whatever their husband's personal qualities (Lei, Yang, and Cai 1994: 163). According to the 1991 national rural survey, about 50 percent of rural women disagreed that "a woman should be loyal to only one man in her life" (Meng 1993: 303). The quality of marriage and divorce are the by-products of the market and industrial development. In short, nonstate rural industrial development has increased merit-based social value and women have benefited from this value transformation.

Women and the Labor Markets

Throughout the 1980s, rural migrants who filled the Chinese landscape destroyed the social immobility imposed on them by the collective system. Rural women were an important part of that flux. In fact, rural women are very resolute and interested in overcoming obstacles by their own efforts—even more so than some men. For example, given the persistence of the *hokou* system, many rural male migrants expressed the desire to go back to villages if things did not work out. But few rural female migrants expressed that desire because most of them preferred the life away from villages. Such determined or die-hard female migrants moved from one place to the next looking for work and business opportunity. Thus, rural women contributed to the rise of free labor markets in China.

Migration and relatively free labor markets have brought direct benefits to rural women. One such benefit is an increase in women's autonomy. Many migrants have gained knowledge and valuable experience and wider occupational opportunities. They have to depend upon themselves to develop new social relations while sustaining old ties. As one Shichuan migrant told me in 1995, she was learning in *shehui daixue* (society university).

It is in this sense that most rural migrants are in fact entrepreneurs who try to improve their lot by venturing into the unknown. One recent survey of female migrant workers in Guangdong suggests that as many as 38 percent of female migrant workers would try to set up their own firms if they were forced to go back to their villages (Rural Economy Research Center 1995). This source of entrepreneurship is an important factor in long-term economic development in general and for women's independence in particular.

Migrant Women Increase Their Power in the Family

Married female migrants also gained power within their families. Women's participation in nonagricultural and nonvillage settings affects their position in the family. Facing the hostile new social environment, husbands and wives are often partners in their search for economic opportunities. Both men and women go where opportunities lead. Working couples tend to form nuclear families which, because of lack of in-law control, give young married women more responsibility and power than their counterparts in the extended or stem families. According to one estimate, 68 percent of Chinese rural families follow the nuclear pattern, whereas before 1949 the extended family was the ideal but not the real pattern of Chinese society (Zeng, Li, and Liang 1992).

Migrant families as well as families of working wives are undergoing structural change not only in demography but also in values. For example, wives no longer solely depend on their husbands for social mobility. Those that are able to improve the economic life of their family will become the focus of the family regardless of gender. My interviews of market women in Guangdong, Wuhan, and Shenzhen in 1994, 1995, and 1996 suggest that many migrant women are the main provider for their families.

The rapid increase of geographical mobility makes it hard for migrants to retain their kinship network. Their relations with village kin become less important in life, though they make the best use of old kinship ties to pursue new opportunities. As a result, migrant husbands have less reinforcement from their kinship network in villages and hence have less control over women (see Zhou 1996). Moreover, since it is difficult for the state to impose family planning on migrants, most migrants prefer to have two or three children.

Enlarging Social Networks

Although rural migrants have made the best use of social networks (village and kin network), they also enlarged the social networks. New *guanxi* (connections) eclipsed the kinship network in importance. Many migrants travel long distances. Many of them can not even write to their kin, forcing them to make it on their own or depend on their small nuclear families. Other migrants have replaced kin as the main external force in family life.

Women from poor areas migrate to rich areas to find husbands and resettle. According to one survey in the rich area of Zhejiang, more than 100,000 women from other provinces had married Zhejiang farmers. The main motivation for the migration of those rural women was to "find a rich husband" and "live a better life" (Wang 1994). This pattern of marriage was suppressed under the collectives. The growth of markets, rural industrialization, and migration (both rural-rural and rural-urban) allowed more diversified marriage alliances.

Although migration was always a way out for women in poor areas, the new marriage migration is radically different from the old way both in numbers and in quality. For example, many contemporary women themselves initiate migration marriages, while in the old times, parents and relatives found partners for them or sold them to men in better areas. Although traffic in women persists in some poor regions, most migrant marriages have been initiated by the women themselves.[6]

One of the amazing developments in rural China is the rise of cross-provincial women marriage networks. Under these circumstances *gunxueqiu* (snowballing) marriage networks took shape. Some women go where they think opportunities are and literally

---

[6]About 0.6 percent of marriages in Zhejiang involved trafficking in women (Meng 1993: 284).

292

ask door to door about the eligibility of bachelors in villages. When a woman migrates to a rich rural area and settles with a family, she writes or sends home information about life in the new land. She may ask her sisters, cousins, or other friends to join her. In many cases, she helps those female relatives and friends look for marriage partners. When those friends come, they inform others. The information circle enlarges whenever a new migrant marriage takes place. Women from one county tend to settle down in one rich area. A typical example of marriage arrangements among migrants is that of Zhou Xianhua, from rural Hunan. Beginning in 1980, Zhou was on the road, falling in love three times before she was finally married to a migrant worker in Yuanjiang, Hunan. She met all three men through her migrant friends.

In this *gunxueqiu* marriage network arrangement, women themselves are the major players. Sometimes one brave woman would bring 10 to 20 old acquaintances to the developed area. Those migrant wives are not just parasites. They are good workers and carry with them their local skills in production and knitting, providing important income for the family.

The transformation from family dependence to individual independence has enlarged the network circles and allowed rural migrants to interact with people who are not kin. Moreover, the old kinship networks have new functions, like job hunting information gathering and capital formation.

New Marriage Patterns

With the rise of migration and with strong emphasis on wage earnings, women migrants began to have more control in the formation of their marriages. Arranged marriages have decreased, and the trend continues. According to a 1988 social survey done in rural Shanghai, Beijing, and Sichuan, only 3 percent of newly married young women entered marriage without being consulted in the decision (Lei, Yang, and Cai 1994: 164). According to a 1990 survey by the *Journal of China's Women*, 74 percent of new marriages in China are not arranged marriages (Wang 1992: 24–25). Indeed, 80 percent of marriages are formed through "introductions," in which only the persons involved have the final say. Introductions come more from friends and coworkers than from kin in the village and *meipo* (professional go-betweens). Dating has become a norm for many rural young people. Totally autonomous marriage reached 13 percent, while old fashioned parental arranged marriages constitute only 7 percent (Dai 1992).

In short, rural women have gained considerable mobility. Although marriage is still important for women's social mobility, it is no longer the most important one. In fact, access to markets and entrepreneurship have increasingly become the most important indicators for women's upward mobility. First beginning in the Republic of China and late Imperial China, sons could threaten to move away if fathers were too strict and severe (Levy 1948). Now more and more women can run away from villages and still survive. Some of them are doing very well. As a result, those who treat women harshly realize that women do not have to grin and bear it—and above all they do not have to stay put.

Conclusion

In conclusion, rural women have actively participated in the development of markets, the rise of rural industry, and migration. Those developments have helped transform China's social structure and have dramatically improved rural women's lives by providing new opportunities while increasing rural women's economic power and giving them chips to bargain for family status. According to the latest study done by the Rural Development Institute, there are only 250 million pure agricultural workers in rural China while the rest have either moved off land, work in industry, or are looking for jobs (*Far Eastern Economic Review* 1997: 26). As more people make their living outside agriculture, women find more opportunity outside villages, outside the reach of traditional patriarchal control. In most agricultural societies, men make decisions unilaterally according to rigid, traditional sex roles, as witnessed by recent rural men's violence against working women in Afghanistan. When women are economically independent of men, patriarchy is weakened, even without the development of an explicit ideology.

Of course, China is so huge that there are many regional differences in the degree of these changes. And not every woman is able to leave farming. A recent social survey from China suggests that farm women occupy between 60 to 70 percent of the agricultural labor force.[7] In a cross-provincial study, Barbara Entwisle et al. (1995) found that "working-age women are more than twice as likely as men to work exclusively in agriculture (including agricultural sidelines)." In Imperial China and under the collectives, the gender pattern in Chinese villages had been either *nan geng nü zhi* (men farm and women weave) or *nannü gong geng* (men and women farm together). Now two new patterns—*nan gong nü geng* (men work outside and women farm) and *nannü gong gong* (both men and women work outside) have begun to take root in rural China. The new sexual division of labor is totally different from the old *nan geng nü zhi* because, in many cases, women are in total control of family farming.

The contemporary rural women's revolution in China has several implications for the study of women and development. First, the development of markets is a very important means for reducing the absolute degree of sexual discrimination and of sexual division of labor. More and more women enter into occupations previously occupied only by men. As I have argued elsewhere, when money making becomes a more important factor in family and other social relations, the preoccupation with patriarchy weakens.

Second, the Chinese experience contradicts or at least complicates the feminist interpretation of the connection between the development of markets and the evolution of gender relations. Many feminists believe that the rise of industrial capitalism led to the division between the female household and the male economy. According to this view, women's work underwent a process of social redefinition; as wages increasingly came to define an individual's social worth, housework was devalued by virtue of being unpaid (Tilly and Scott 1978). The Chinese case suggests that this process is much more complicated, involving class as well as gender differences. While some upper- and middle-class women are able to stay home and become housewives, the majority of Chinese women have gained employment outside their homes and even outside their villages (Beaver, Hou, and Wang 1985). So for the majority of Chinese women, the development of markets and the development of industry have provided them with more opportunities outside the home

---

[7]*Zhongguo Funü (China's Women)*, No. 390 (1991: 8); No. 392 (1991: 13); and No. 402 (1992: 2).

and thus have empowered them. Markets and industrialization in China have provided a necessary but not sufficient basis for changing women's position in Chinese society.

Third, there is a myth among many feminists in the West that the exploitation of poor women in an agrarian society was in some ways less harsh than in an industrial society. In the Chinese case, the degree of gender inequality has lessened as the result of rural industrialization and the growth of markets. The fact that so many rural women jumped onto the wagon of capitalist development in China indicates that they preferred it to their limited alternatives.

Finally, the contemporary rural women's revolution in China has no organization, no leader, and no ideology. That is why people do not regard this as a revolution, although it has affected millions of rural women's lives. But the social context created in the last decade by the Chinese farmers' spontaneous, unorganized, leaderless, non-ideological, and apolitical movement has, quite unintentionally, done more to dilute China's age-old patriarchal patterns than has the political leadership of the PRC in more than four decades.

References

Beaver, P.; Hou, L.; and Wang, X. (1985) "Rural Chinese Women: Two Faces of Economic Reform." *Modern China* 21(20): 205–32.

Blumberg, R.L.; Rokowski, C.A.; Tinker, I.; and Monteon, M. (1995) *Engendering Wealth and Well-Being: Empowering for Global Change.* Boulder, Colo.: Westview Press.

Boserup, E. (1970) *Women's Role in Economic Development.* New York: St. Martin's Press.

Bossen, L. (1992) "Chinese Rural Women: What Keeps Them Down on the Farm?" In C.K. Gilmartin et al. (eds.) *Engendering China: Women, Culture, and the State.* Cambridge, Mass.: Harvard University Press.

Chinese Women's Federation (1993) Rural Work Division (Quanguo Funian Nongcun Chu) "Zhongguo Nongcun de 1.8 Yi" (Chinese Rural 180 Million). *Zhongguo Funü (Chinese Women)* (11): 23.

Commonwealth Secretariat (1990) *Engendering Adjustment for the 1990s: Report of a Commonwealth Expert Group on Women and Structural Adjustment.* London: Commonwealth Secretariat.

Dai, K. (1992) "Zhongguo Shisishengshi Nongcun Funü Jiben Zhuangkuang Jiqi Shenghuo Jianxi" (Position of Rural Women in Fourteen Provinces and Cities of China). *Shehuixue Yanjiu (Sociological Studies)* 4 (July): 104–9.

Davin, D. (1988) "The Implications of Contract Agriculture for the Employment and Status of Chinese Peasant Women." In S. Feuchtang (ed.) *Transforming China's Economy in the Eighties: The Rural Sector, Welfare and Employment.* Boulder, Colo.: Westview Press.

Entwisle, B.; Henderson, G.E.; Short, S.; Bouma, J.; and Fengying, Z. (1995) "Gender and Family Businesses in Rural China." *American Sociological Review* 60(1) (February): 36–57.

Fang, Y.X., et al. (1995) "Zhongguo Funü Zai Yuye Zhong de Diwei yu Zuoyong" (Chinese Women's Status and Role). In J. Sha (ed.) *Dangdai Zhongguo Funü Diwei (Women's Status in Contemporary China).* Beijing: Beijing University Press.

Far Eastern Economic Review (1997) "China in Transition," 3 April: 26.

Fernandez-Kelly, M.P. (1983) *For We Are Sold, I and My People: Women and Industry in Mexico's Frontier.* Albany: State University of New York Press.

Friedman, E., et al. (1991) *Chinese Village, Socialist State.* New Haven, Conn.: Yale University Press.

Fuentes, A., and Ehrenreich, B. (1983) "Women in the Global Factory." *Multinational Monitor.* New York: Institute for New Communications.

Gu, L.Y. (1995) "Nongcun nü Zhuanyehu Xianxiang Cutan" (Preliminary Study of the Phenomenon of Women Specialized Families in the Country-side). In *The Development and Strategy of Contemporary Women:* 78–88. Edited by *Rural Women Knowing All Magazine* and Women Research Center of Tianjing Normal University. Beijing: Zhongguo Funü Chubanshe (Chi-nese Women's Press).

House-Midamba, B., and Ekechi, F.K. (1995) *African Market Women and Economic Power: The Role of Women in African Economic Development.* West-port, Conn.: Greenwood Press.

Institute of Population Studies (1994). *Dangdai Zhongguo Funü Diwei Chouy-ang Diaocha Ziliao (Sampling Survey Data of Women's Status in Contemporary China).* Beijing: Wanguo Xueshu Chubanshe.

Johnson, K. (1983) *Women, the Family and Peasant Revolution in China.* Chicago: University of Chicago Press.

Lei, J.; Yang, S.; and Cai, W. (1994) *Gaige Yilai Zhongguo Nongcun Hunyan Jiating de Xingbianhua (The Change of the Marriage and the Family in the Chinese Countryside Since the Reform of the Economic System).* Beijing: Beijing University Press.

Levy, M.J., Jr. (1948) *The Family Revolution in Modern China.* New York: Atheneum.

Liu, P.H., and Gu, B.C. (1990) "Shenhua Gaige Dui Funü Jiuye de Xin Tiaozhan" (New Occupational Challenges for Women in the Deepening Reform). *Renke Dongtai (Population Information)* (6).

Liu, X. (1995) "Nongcun Funü Feinong Jiuye di Xing Cunxiang" (New Trend of Nonagricultural Employment for Rural Women). In J. Sha (ed.) *Dangdai Zhongguo Funü Diwei (Women's Status in Contemporary China).* Beijing: Beijing University Press.

Meng, X.F. (1993) "Nongcun Laodongli Zhuanyi Zhong di Zhongguo Non-gcun Funü" (Chinese Rural Women in Rural Laborer Transformation). *Shehui Kexue Zhanxian (Social Sciences Frontier)*, No. 4: 147–54.

Milkman, R., and Townsley, E. (1994) "Gender and the Economy." In J. Neil and R.S. Swedberg (eds.) *The Handbook of Economic Sociology*, 600–19. Princeton, N.J.: Princeton University Press.

Ren, Q.Y. (1995) "Zhongguo Nongcun Nangong Nü Geng de Xingcheng ji Yingxian"(The Formation and Influence of the Pattern Men as Workers and Women as Farmers). In *The Development and Strategy of Contemporary Women*, 27–34. Edited by *Rural Women Knowing All Magazine* and Women Research Center of Tianjing Normal University. Beijing: Zhongguo Funü Chubanshe (Chinese Women's Press).

Rural Economy Research Center (1995) "Zhongguo Nongcun Laodongli Liudong yu Renkou Qianyi Yanjiu Zhongshu" (Summary of the Studies on China's Rural Labor Mobility and Population Migration). Beijing: Nongcun Jingji Yanjiu Zhongxin (Rurual Economy Research Center).

Stacey, J. (1983) *Patriarchy and Socialist Revolution in China*. Berkeley: University of California Press.

Tilly, L.A., and Scott, J. (1978) *Women, Work and Family*. New York: Holt, Rinehart and Winston.

Tinker, I., and Bramsen, M.B. (1976) *Women and World Development*. Washington, D.C.: Overseas Development Council.

Wang, H. (1991) *Dangdai Zhongguo Cunluo Jiazhu Wenhua (Contemporary Chinese Village Culture)*. Shanghai: Renmin Chubanshe (People's Press).

Wang, J. (1992) "Shuju Xianshi Zhongguo Funü Shehui Diwei" (Data Reveals Social Status of Chinese Women). *Zhongguo Funü (Chinese Women)* 1: 24–25.

Wang, J. (1994) "New Characteristics of Marriages between Zhejiang Farmers and Women from Outside the Province." *Social Sciences in China* (Summer): 59–64.

Wolf, M. (1985) *Revolution Postponed: Women in Contemporary China*. Stanford, Calif: Stanford University Press.

Zaoyang Women's Federation (1995) "Investigation Report on Rural Women's Participation in Economic Activities in Zaoyang City." In *The Development and Strategy of Contemporary China*, 42–57. Edited by *Rural Women Knowing All Magazine* and Women Research Center of Tianjing Normal University. Beijing: Zhongguo Funü Chubanshe (Chinese Women's Press).

Zeng, Y.; Li, W.; and Liang, Z. (1992) "Zhongguo Jiating Jiegou de Xianzhuang, Quyu Chayi ji Baindong Qushi" (Contemporary Chinese Family Structures, Regional Differences and Perspectives). *Zhongguo Renkou Kexue (Chinese Population Science)* 2.

Zhou, K.X. (1996) *How the Farmers Changed China: Power of the People*. Boulder, Colo.: Westview Press.

19. Getting Over Equality

P. J. O'Rourke

The Foundation of Collectivism

The idea of collectivism goes beyond Chinese socialism; it is a premise of almost all political systems in the world. The foundation of collectivism is simple: There should be no important economic differences among people. No one should be too rich. No one should be too poor. We should "close the wealth gap."

This is a very powerful idea. This is a very common idea. This is a very bad idea.

"Gaps"—differences—are innate to mankind. Do we want to close the "beauty gap" and make every woman look like Margaret Thatcher? Do we want to close the "talent gap" and field a World Cup football team with the athletic ability of, for instance, me?

In a world without gaps we'd all be the same. We'd all be the same sex. Who'd get pregnant? We'd all know the same things. What would we talk about? We'd all have the same work. Some job that would be. We'd all get the same vacation. Five point seven billion people playing a game of beach volleyball—2.85 billion to a side. The idea of a world where all people are alike—in wealth or in anything else—is a fantasy for the stupid.

The Fallacy of Collectivism

But proposing to close the "wealth gap" is worse than silly. It entails a lie. The notion of economic equality is based on an ancient and ugly falsehood central to bad economic thinking: There's a fixed amount of wealth. Wealth is zero-sum. If I have too many cups of tea, you have to lick the teapot. But wealth is based on productivity.

P. J. O'Rourke is Foreign Affairs Correspondent for *Rolling Stone* and Mencken Research Fellow at the Cato Institute. This chapter is drawn from his latest book, *Eat the Rich*.

Productivity is expandable. Otherwise there wouldn't be any economic thinking, good or bad, or any tea or tea pots either.

Since the beginning of the industrial revolution human productivity has proven to be fabulously expandable. The economist Angus Maddison has been studying economic growth since the 1950s. In 1995, under the auspices of the Organization for Economic Cooperation and Development, he published a book, *Monitoring the World Economy 1820–1992*. The earth had fewer natural resources and no more farmland in 1992 than it had in 1820 and in that period the earth's population multiplied by five. But, in 1990 U.S. dollars, the value of everything produced in the world grew from $695 billion in 1820 to almost $28 trillion in 1992 and the amount of that production per person went from $651 to $5,145.

A collectivist can hear these figures and claim they are just averages, claim they don't show who actually got that money. The collectivist can recite the old saying: "The rich get richer and the poor get poorer." But there is no statistical evidence of this. The United Nations Population Division's *World Population Prospects: 1996 Revision* contains past and present statistics on infant mortality and life expectancy at birth. And these figures don't present the same averaging problems as per capita world product. No matter how rich the elite of a country is, its members aren't going to live to be 250 and distort the averages. And if the few rich babies in a country live and the mass of poor babies in a country die, that country will not have a "normal" infant mortality rate but a very bad one. Infant mortality and life expectancy are reasonable indicators of general well-being in a society.

Besides giving figures for individual countries, the UN consolidates averages into three groups: "More Developed Regions," "Less Developed Regions," and "Least Developed Regions." The last meaning countries that are damn poor—Laos, Madagascar, Chad. In the early 1950s the richer countries in the world had an average of 58 deaths per 1,000 live births. They now have an average of 11. Over the same period the poorest countries went from 194 deaths per 1,000 to 109. The "gap" was 136 dead babies 40 years ago and the "gap" is 98 dead babies now. This is still too many dead babies, of course, but the difference isn't increasing. The rich are getting richer but the poor aren't becoming worse off. They're becoming parents.

The same trend is seen in life expectancy. In the early 1950s, people in rich countries had a life expectancy of 66.5 years. Now they live 74.2 years. In the poorest countries, average lifespans have increased from 35.5 years to 49.7 years. The difference in life expectancy between the world's rich and poor has decreased by 6.5 years. The rich are getting richer. The poor are getting richer. And we're all getting older.

So, if wealth is not theft, if the thing that makes you rich doesn't make me poor, why don't collectivists concentrate on the question, "How do we make everyone wealthy?" or better, "How have we been managing to do this so brilliantly since 1820?" Why, instead, do collectivists concentrate on the question, "How do we redistribute wealth?" And it is especially the collectivists in the nonsocialist West who do this. Bill Clinton is more concerned with redistribution than anyone in the Chinese government.

The Immorality of Collectivism

Such collectivism is, I think, not only silly and untruthful but immoral. The Ten Commandments in the Old Testament of the Bible are very clear about this. Now the Bible might seem to be a strange place to do economic research—particularly for a person who is not very religious. However, I have been thinking—from a political economy point of view—about the Tenth Commandment. The first nine commandments concern theological principles and social law: thou shalt not commit adultery, steal, kill, etc. All religions have such rules. But then there's the Tenth Commandment: "Thou shalt not covet they neighbor's house, thou shalt not covet thy neighbor's wife, nor his manservant, nor his maidservant, nor his ox, nor his ass, nor anything that is thy neighbor's."

Here are God's basic rules about how the Tribes of Israel should live, a very brief list of sacred obligations and solemn moral precepts, and right at the end of it is, "Don't envy your friend's cattle."

What is that doing in there? Why would God, with just 10 things to tell Moses, choose, as one of them, jealousy about the things the man next door has? And yet think about how important to the wellbeing of a community this commandment is. If you want a donkey, if you want a meal, if you want an employee, don't complain about what other people have, go get your own. The Tenth Commandment sends a message to collectivists, to people who believe wealth is

301

best obtained by redistribution. And the message is clear and concise: Go to hell.

Should We Fear the Rich or the Government?

Collectivism is silly, deceitful, a sin. It's also cowardly. We fear the power others have over us. And wealth is power. So we fear the rich.

But how rational is this fear? Take a midnight stroll through a rich neighborhood then take a midnight stroll through the U.S. capital. Yes, you can get in a lot of trouble in Monte Carlo. You can lose at roulette. But you're more likely to get robbed in the slums of Washington.

Not that we should begrudge the crimes of those poor people. They're just practicing a little "free-lance collectivism." They're doing what the U.S. government does, in their own small way. Because the real alternative to the power of the rich is not the power of the poor but plain, simple power. If we don't want the world's wealth to be controlled by people with money, then the alternative is to have the world's wealth controlled by people with guns. Governments have plenty of guns.

The theory of government collectivism is quite good. The robber puts down his pistol, picks up the ballot box and steals from rich people instead of from you. But the reality is different. Witness the track record of collectivism in this century: the Holocaust, Stalin's purges, and the suffering caused by the "Great Leap Forward" and the "Cultural Revolution."

We should quit thinking about the "wealth gap" and start thinking about wealth. Wealth is good. Everybody knows that about his own wealth. If you got rich it would be a great thing. You'd improve your life. You'd improve your family's life. You'd purchase education, travel, knowledge about the world. You'd invest in wise and worthwhile things. You'd give money to noble causes. You'd help your friends and neighbors. Your life would be better if you got rich. The lives of the people around you would be better if you got rich. Your wealth is good. So why isn't everybody else's wealth good, too?

Wealth is good when many people have it. It's good when few people have it. This is because money is a tool, nothing more. You can't eat money or drink money or wear money. And wealth—an accumulation of money—is a lot of tools.

Tools can be used to do harm. You can hit somebody over the head with a shovel. But tools are still good. When a carpenter has a lot of tools we don't say to him, "You have too many tools. You should give some of your saws and hammers and nails and screws to the man who's cooking omelets. We don't try to close the "tool gap."

Wealth brings great benefits to the world. Rich people are heroes. They don't usually mean to be, but that's their moral problem, not ours. Most of the world now admits free enterprise works. Economic liberty makes people rich. But in our residual collectivism and our infatuation with equality, we keep trying to get rid of rich people.

There's a joke President Reagan told about the way collectivists treat rich people: A traveling salesman stays overnight with a farm family. When the family gathers to eat there's a pig seated at the table. And the pig has three medals hanging around his neck and a wooden leg. The salesman says, "Um, I see a pig is having dinner with you."

"Yes," says the farmer. "That's because he's a very special pig. You see those medals around his neck? Well, the first medal is from when our youngest son fell in the pond, and he was drowning, and that pig swam out and saved his life. The second medal, that's from when the barn caught fire and our little daughter was trapped in there and the pig ran inside, carried her out and saved her life. And the third medal, that's from when our oldest boy was cornered in the stock yard by a mean bull, and that pig ran under the fence and bit the bull on the tail and saved the boy's life."

"Yes," says the salesman, "I can see why you let that pig sit right at the table and have dinner with you. And I can see why you awarded him the medals. But how did he get the wooden leg?"

"Well," says the farmer, "a pig like that—you don't eat him all at once."

References

Maddison, A. (1995) *Monitoring the World Economy 1820–1992*. Paris: OECD.
United Nations (1996) UN Population Division, *World Population Prospects: 1996 Revision*. NewYork: United Nations.

20. Empowering People: What China Can Learn from Chile

José Piñera

The pay-as-you-go pension system that has reigned supreme in this century has a fundamental flaw, one rooted in a false conception of how human beings behave: it destroys, at the individual level, the essential link between effort and reward—in other words, between personal responsibilities and personal rights. Whenever that happens on a massive scale and for a long period of time, the end result is disaster.

Two exogenous factors aggravate the results of that flaw: (1) the global demographic trend toward decreasing fertility rates; and, (2) medical advances that are lengthening life. As a result, fewer workers are supporting more retirees. Since the raising of both the retirement age and payroll taxes has an upper limit, sooner or later the system has to reduce the promised benefits, a telltale sign of a bankrupt system.

Whether this reduction of benefits is done through inflation, as in most developing countries, or through legislation, the final result for the retired worker is the same: anguish in old age created, paradoxically, by the inherent insecurity of the "social security" system.

In 1980, the government of Chile decided to take the bull by the horns. A government-run pension system was replaced with a revolutionary innovation: a privately administered, mandatory system of Pension Savings Accounts.

After 17 years of operation, the results speak for themselves. Pensions in the new private system already are 50 to 100 percent

---

José Piñera is President of the International Center for Pension Reform and Co-Chairman of the Cato Project on Social Security Privatization. As Minister of Labor and Social Security from 1978 to 1980, he was responsible for the privatization of the Chilean pension system.

higher—depending on whether they are old-age, disability, or survivor pensions—than they were in the pay-as-you-go system. The resources administered by the private pension funds amount to $33 billion, or around 44 percent of GNP. By improving the functioning of both the capital and the labor markets, pension privatization has been one of the key reforms that has pushed the growth rate of the economy upwards from the historical 3.5 percent a year to 7.0 percent on average during the last 12 years. It is also a fact that the Chilean savings rate has increased to 26 percent of GNP and the unemployment rate has decreased to 5.5 percent since this reform was undertaken.

More important, still, pensions have ceased to be a government issue, thus depoliticizing a huge sector of the economy and giving individuals more control over their own lives. The structural flaw has been eliminated and the future of pensions depends on individual behavior and market developments.

The success of the Chilean private pension system has led seven other South American countries to follow suit. Peru was first, in 1993, followed by Argentina and Colombia in 1994. The new system is already working. In 1995 Uruguay went in the same direction, although with a very partial reform. And in 1996, Mexico, Bolivia, and El Salvador approved legislation creating a system of Pension Savings Accounts. In 1998 more than 20 million workers in Latin America have a funded, individually owned and privately operated retirement plan.

The Chilean experience is being studied by several countries around the world. Officials from the People's Republic of China have come to Chile to study the private pension system. One of the results is this particularly interesting feud reported three years ago by *The Economist (1995: 16)*:

> There is usually more acrimony than comedy in the long-running row between Britain and China over the future of Hong Kong. Yet a smile may have flickered across the face of Chris Patten, Hong Kong's governor, even as China scuppered his plans to introduce a [pay-as-you-go] pension scheme in the colony. Zhou Nan, Communist China's main representative in Hong Kong, harrumphed that Mr. Patten, a British conservative, was trying to bring "costly Euro-socialist" ideas to Hong Kong.

It is possible that before entering the new millennium, several other countries, including all those in the Americas, will have privatized their pension system. This would mean a massive redistribution of power from the state to individuals, thus enhancing personal freedom, promoting faster economic growth, and alleviating poverty, especially in old age.

The Chilean PSA System

Under Chile's Pension Savings Account (PSA) system, what determines a worker's pension level is the amount of money he accumulates during his working years. Neither the worker nor the employer pays a social security tax to the state. Nor does the worker collect a government-funded pension. Instead, during his working life, he automatically has 10 percent of his wages deposited by his employer each month in his own, individual PSA. (This percentage applies only to the first $25,000 of annual income.) A worker may contribute an additional 10 percent of his wages each month, which is also deductible from taxable income, as a form of voluntary savings if he wants to retire early or obtain a higher pension.

A worker chooses one of the private Pension Fund Administration companies (Administradoras de Fondos de Pensiones, AFPs) to manage his PSA. These companies can engage in no other activities and are subject to government regulation intended to guarantee a diversified and low-risk portfolio and to prevent theft or fraud. A separate government entity, a highly technical AFP Superintendency, provides oversight. Of course, there is free entry to the AFP industry.

Each AFP operates the equivalent of a mutual fund that invests in stocks and bonds. Investment decisions are made by the AFP. Government regulation sets only maximum percentage limits both for specific types of instruments and for the overall mix of the portfolio; and the spirit of the reform is that those regulations should be reduced constantly with the passage of time and as the AFP companies gain experience. There is no obligation whatsoever to invest in government or any other type of bonds. Legally, the AFP company and the mutual fund that it administers are two separate entities. Thus, should an AFP go under, the assets of the mutual fund—that is, the workers' investments—are not affected.

Workers are free to change from one AFP company to another. For this reason there is competition among the companies to provide a higher return on investment, better customer service, or a lower commission. Each worker is given a PSA passbook and every three months receives a regular statement informing him how much money has been accumulated in his retirement account and how well his investment fund has performed. The account bears the worker's name, is his property, and will be used to pay his pension (with a provision for survivors' benefits).

As noted above, worker contributions are deductible for income tax purposes. The return on the PSA is tax free. Upon retirement, when funds are withdrawn, taxes are paid according to the income tax bracket at that moment.

The Chilean PSA system includes both private and public sector employees. The only ones excluded are members of the police and armed forces, whose pension systems, as in other countries, are built into their pay and working conditions system. (In my opinion—but not theirs yet—they would also be better off with a PSA.) All other employed workers must have a PSA. Self-employed workers may enter the system, if they wish, thus creating an incentive for informal workers to join the formal economy.

A worker who has contributed for at least 20 years but whose pension fund, upon reaching retirement age, is below the legally defined "minimum pension" receives a government subsidy to attain that minimum. What should be stressed here is that no one is defined as "poor" a priori. Only after his working life has ended (and his PSA has been depleted), does a poor pensioner receive a government subsidy. (Those without 20 years of contributions can apply for a welfare-type pension at a much lower level.)

The PSA system also includes insurance against premature death and disability. Each AFP provides this service to its clients by taking out group life and disability coverage from private life insurance companies. This coverage is paid for by an additional worker contribution. (The cost of this insurance has gone down dramatically: it began around 3 percent and it is now less than 1 percent of salary.)

The mandatory minimum savings level of 10 percent was calculated on the assumption of a 4 percent average net yield during a 40–year working life, so that the typical worker would have sufficient money in his PSA to fund a pension equal to 70 percent of his final salary.

The so-called legal retirement age is 65 for men and 60 for women. Those retirement ages—the traditional ages in the Chilean pay-as-you-go system—were not discussed in the privatization reform because they are not a structural characteristic of the new system. But the meaning of "retirement" in the PSA system is different than in the traditional one. First, workers can continue working after retirement. If they do, they receive the pension their accumulated capital makes possible and they are not required to contribute any longer to a pension plan. Second, workers with sufficient savings in their accounts to fund a "reasonable pension" (50 percent of the average salary of the previous 10 years, as long as it is higher than the "minimum pension") may choose to take early retirement whenever they want.

Workers must continue making a 10 percent contribution to their PSAs until they reach the 65–60 threshold, unless they have chosen early retirement—that is, to retire their money, as a monthly pension, which is not the same as retirement from the workforce. In addition, however, workers must reach those threshold ages to be eligible for the government subsidy that guarantees a minimum pension.

But in no way is there an obligation to cease working, at any age, nor is there an obligation to continue working or saving for pension purposes once you have assured yourself a "reasonable pension" as described above. As should be expected, individual preferences about old age differ as much as any other preferences. Some people want to work forever; others cannot wait to cease working and to indulge in their true vocations or hobbies, like writing or fishing. The old, pay-as-you-go system did not permit the satisfaction of such preferences, except through collective pressure to have, for example, an early retirement age for powerful political constituencies. It was a one-size-fits-all scheme that exacted a price in human happiness.

The PSA system, on the other hand, allows for individual preferences to be translated into individual decisions that will produce the desired outcome. In the branch offices of many AFPs there are user-friendly computer terminals that permit the worker to calculate the expected value of his future pension, based on the money in his account, and the year in which he wishes to retire. Alternatively, the worker can specify the pension amount he hopes to receive and ask the computer how much he must deposit each month if he wants to retire at a given age. Once he gets the answer, he simply asks his employer to withdraw that new percentage from his salary. Of course, he can adjust that figure as time goes on, depending on the actual yield of his pension fund. The bottom line is that a worker can determine his desired pension and retirement age in the same way one can order a tailor-made suit.

Upon retiring, a worker may choose from two general payout options. In one case, a retiree may use the capital in his PSA to purchase an annuity from any private life insurance company. The annuity guarantees a constant monthly income for life, indexed to inflation (there are indexed bonds available in the Chilean capital market so that companies can invest accordingly), plus survivors' benefits for the worker's dependents. Alternatively, a retiree may leave his funds in the PSA and make programmed withdrawals, subject to limits based on the life expectancy of the retiree and his dependents. In the latter case, if he dies, the remaining funds in his account form a part of his estate. In both cases, he can withdraw as a lump-sum the capital in excess of that needed to obtain an annuity or programmed withdrawal equal to 70 percent of his last wages.

The PSA system solves the typical problem of pay-as-you-go systems with respect to labor demographics: in an aging population the number of workers per retiree decreases. Under the PSA system, the working population does not pay for the retired population. Thus, in contrast with the pay-as-you-go system, the potential for intergenerational conflict and eventual bankruptcy is avoided. The problem that many countries face—unfunded pension liabilities—does not exist under the PSA system.

In contrast to company-based private pension systems that generally impose costs on workers who leave before a given number of years and that sometimes result in bankruptcy of the workers' pension funds—thus depriving workers of both their jobs and their pension rights—the PSA system is completely independent of the company employing the worker. Since the PSA is tied to the worker, not the company, the account is fully portable. Given that the pension funds must be invested in tradeable securities, the PSA has a daily value and therefore is easy to transfer from one AFP to another. The problem of "job lock" is entirely avoided. By not impinging on labor mobility, both inside a country and internationally, the PSA system helps create labor market flexibility and neither subsidizes nor penalizes immigrants.

A PSA system is also much more efficient in promoting a flexible labor market. In fact, people are increasingly deciding to work only a few hours a day or to interrupt their working lives—especially women and young people. In pay-as-you-go systems, those flexible working styles create the problem of filling the gaps in contributions. Not so in a PSA scheme where stop-and-go contributions are no problem whatsoever.

The Transition

One challenge is to define the permanent PSA system. Another, in countries that already have a pay-as-you-go system, is to manage the transition to a PSA system. The transition has to take into account the particular characteristics of each country, and especially the constraints posed by the budget situation.

In Chile we set three basic rules for the transition:

1. The government guaranteed those already receiving a pension that their pensions would be unaffected by the reform. This rule was important because the social security authority would obviously cease to receive the contributions from the workers who moved to the new system and therefore it would be unable to continue paying pensioners with its own resources. Moreover, it would be unfair to the elderly to change their benefits or expectations at this point in their lives.

2. Every worker already contributing to the pay-as-you-go system was given the choice of staying in that system or moving to the new PSA system. Those who left the old system were given a "recognition bond." (This zero coupon bond was indexed and carried a 4 percent real interest rate.) The government pays the bond only when the worker reaches the legal retirement age. The bonds are traded in secondary markets, so as to allow them to be used for early retirement. This bond reflected the rights the worker had already acquired in the pay-as-you-go system. Thus, a worker who had made pension contributions for years did not have to start at zero when he entered the new system.

3. All new entrants to the labor force were required to enter the PSA system. The door was closed to the pay-as-you-go system

because it was unsustainable. This requirement assured the complete end of the old system once the last worker who remained in it reaches retirement age (from then on, and during a limited period of time, the government has only to pay pensions to retirees of the old system). This rule is important because the most effective way to reduce the size of the government in our lives is to end programs completely, not simply scale them back so that a new government might revive them at a later date.

After several months of national debate on the proposed reforms, and a communication and education effort to explain the reform to the people, the pension reform law was approved on November 4, 1980. The political economy of this process can be found in my book about this reform (Piñera 1991).

To give equal access to creating AFPs to all those who might be interested, the law established a six-month period during which no AFP could begin operations (not even advertising). Thus, the AFP industry is unique in that it had a clear day of conception (November 4, 1980) and a clear date of birth (May 1, 1981).

In Chile, as in most countries, May 1 is Labor Day. The choice of that date was not a coincidence. Symbols are important, and that date of birth allows workers to celebrate May 1 not as a day of class struggle but as the day when they were freed to choose their own pension system and thus freed from "the chains" of the state-run social security system.

We also ended the illusion that both the employer and the worker contribute to social security, a device that allows political manipulation of those rates. From an economic standpoint, workers bear the full burden of the payroll tax because all the contributions are ultimately paid from the worker's marginal productivity, since employers take into account all labor costs—whether termed salary or social security contributions—in making their hiring and pay decisions. By renaming the employer's contribution, the system makes it evident that all contributions are made by the worker. Together with the creation of the new AFP system, all gross wages were redefined to include the employer's contribution to the old pension system. The worker's contribution was deducted from the increased gross wage, thus not reducing the take home pay of the worker. Of course, the final wage level is determined by the interplay of market forces.

The financing of the transition is a complex technical issue and each country must address this problem according to its own circumstances. But I would like to emphasize that it can be done both in emerging economies and in mature, developed countries.[1]

It should be emphasized that the transition does not entail economic costs but only cash flows considerations arising from the fact that an unfunded liability is being recognized. The transitions financial requirements should be viewed as the initial "investments" required to obtain later the benefits of what is a very profitable "project" (both for the economy and for the budget).

Chile used five methods to finance the transition to a PSA system:

1. Since the contribution needed in a capitalization system to finance adequate pension levels is generally lower than the current payroll taxes, a fraction of the difference between them was used as a temporary transition payroll tax without reducing net wages or increasing the cost of labor to the employer (the gradual elimination of that tax was considered in the original law and, in fact, that happened, so that today it does not exist).

2. Using debt, the transition cost was shared by future generations. In Chile roughly 40 percent of the cost has been financed issuing government bonds at market rates of interest. These bonds have been bought mainly by the AFPs as part of their investment portfolios and that "bridge debt" should be completely redeemed when the pensioners of the old system are no longer with us.

3. The need to finance the transition was a powerful incentive to reduce wasteful government spending. For years, the budget director has been able to use this argument to kill unjustified new spending or to reduce wasteful government programs, thereby making a crucial contribution to the increase in the national savings rate.

4. The increased economic growth that the PSA system promoted substantially increased tax revenues. Only 15 years after the pension reform, Chile was already running fiscal budget surpluses of around 2–3 percent of GNP.

5. In a theoretical state's balance sheet (where each government should show its assets and liabilities), state pension obligations may

---

[1]For a concrete proposal to substitute gradually the pay-as-you-go system of Spain for a fully funded, privately managed, individual capitalization system, see Piñera (1996).

be offset to some extent by the value of state-owned enterprises and other types of assets. Privatizations in Chile were not only one way to contribute, although marginally, to finance the transition, but had several additional benefits such as increasing efficiency, spreading ownership, and depoliticizing the economy.

The implicit pay-as-you-go debt of the Chilean system at the time of the reform has been estimated at around 80 percent of GDP by a well-known World Bank study (1994) that concluded, "Chile shows that a country with a reasonably competitive banking system, a well-functioning debt market, and a fair degree of macroeconomic stability can finance large transition deficits without large interest rate repercussions" (p. 268).

The Results

The PSAs have already accumulated an investment fund of $33 billion. This long-term investment capital has not only helped fund economic growth but has spurred the development of efficient financial markets and institutions.

The decision to create the PSA system first, and then privatize the large state-owned companies, resulted in a "virtuous sequence." The pension funds participated actively buying shares of the companies being privatized. This gave workers the possibility of benefiting handsomely from the enormous increase in productivity of the privatized companies by allowing them, through higher stock prices that increased the yield of their PSAs, to capture a large share of the wealth created by the privatization process.

There are around 12 AFP companies (and there could be as many as the market would accomodate). Some belong to insurance or banking conglomerates. Others are worker-owned or tied to labor unions or specific industry or trade associations. Some include the participation of international financial companies, such as AIG, Aetna, Citicorp, and Banco Santander. Several of the larger AFP companies are themselves publicly traded on the Chilean stock exchange, and one of them recently issued ADRs on Wall Street (helped by the recent A − credit rating of Chilean sovereign bonds).

One of the key results of the new system has been to increase the productivity of capital and thus the rate of economic growth in the Chilean economy. The PSA system has made the capital market more efficient and fueled its enormous growth over the last several years. The vast resources administered by the AFPs have encouraged the creation of new kinds of financial instruments while enhancing others already in existence, but not fully developed. Another of Chile's pension reform contributions to the sound operation and transparency of the capital market has been the creation of a domestic risk-rating industry and the improvement of corporate governance. (The AFPs appoint outside directors in the companies in which they own shares, thus shattering complacency at board meetings.)

Since the system began to operate in 1981, the average real return on investment has been 11 percent per year (almost three times higher than the anticipated yield of 4 percent). Of course, the annual yield has shown the oscillations that are intrinsic to the free market—ranging from minus 3 percent to plus 30 percent in real terms—but the important yield is the average one over the long term.

Pensions under the new system have been significantly higher than under the old, state-administered system, which required a total payroll tax of around 25 percent. According to a recent study by Sergio Baeza (1995), the average AFP retiree is receiving a pension equal to 78 percent of his mean annual income over the previous 10 years of his working life. As mentioned, upon retirement workers may withdraw in a lump sum their "excess savings" (above the 70 percent of salary threshold). If that money were included in calculating the value of the pension, the total value would come close to 84 percent of working income. Recipients of disability pensions also receive, on average, 70 percent of their working income.

The new pension system, therefore, has made a significant contribution to the reduction of poverty by increasing the size and certainty of old-age, survivors, and disability pensions, and by the indirect but very powerful effect of promoting economic growth and employment.

The new system also has eliminated the unfairness of the old system. According to conventional wisdom, pay-as-you-go pension schemes redistribute income from the rich to the poor. However, several studies have shown that once certain income-specific characteristics of workers and of the operation of the political system are taken into account, public schemes generally redistribute income to the most powerful, generally not the poorest, groups of workers.

Conclusion
It is not surprising that the PSA system in Chile has proven so popular and has helped promote social and economic stability.

Workers appreciate the fairness of the system and they have obtained through their pension accounts a direct and visible stake in the economy. Since the private pension funds own a sizable fraction of the stocks of the biggest companies of Chile, workers are actually investors in the country's fortunes.

When the PSA was inaugurated, workers were given the choice of entering the new system or remaining in the old one. Half a million Chilean workers (one fourth of the eligible workforce at that time) chose the new system by joining in the first month of operation alone. Today, 95 percent of Chilean workers are in the new system.

As the state pension system disappears, politicians will no longer decide whether pension checks need to be increased and in what amount or for which groups. Thus, pensions are no longer a key source of political conflict and election-time demagoguery as they once were. A person's retirement income will depend on his own work and on the success of the economy, not on the government or on the pressures brought by special interest groups.

For Chileans, pension savings accounts now represent real and visible property rights—they are the primary sources of security for retirement. In fact, already the typical Chilean worker's main asset is not his used car or even his small house (probably still mortgaged), but the capital in his PSA.

Finally, the private pension system has had a very important political and cultural consequence. The overwhelming majority of Chilean workers who chose to move into the new system decided to abandon the state system even though some of the national trade-union and political leaders advised against it. Workers care deeply about matters close to their lives, such as pensions, education, and health, and make their decisions thinking about their families and not according to political fashions.

Indeed, the new pension system gives Chileans a personal stake in the economy. A typical Chilean worker is not indifferent to the behavior of the stock market or interest rates. Intuitively he knows that a bad minister of finance can reduce the value of his pension rights. When workers feel that they own a part of the country, not through party bosses or a Politburo, they are much more attached to the free market and a free society.

The ultimate lesson for China and other emerging economies is that the only reforms that are really successful are those that trust the individual, and the wonders that individuals can do when they are free.

References

Baeza, S. (1995) *Quince Años Después: Una Mirada al Sistema Privado de Pensiones*. Santiago: Centro de Estudios Públicos.

The Economist (1995) "Is Welfare unAsian?" 11 February: 16–17.

Piñera, J. (1991) *El Cascabel al Gato*. Santiago: Editorial Zig Zag.

Piñera, J. (1996) *A Proposal for the Reform of the Pension System in Spain*. Madrid: Circulo de Empresarios (with the assistance of Alejandro Weinstein).

World Bank (1994) *Averting the Old Age Crisis*. New York: Oxford University Press.

21. Using Market Mechanisms to Provide Retirement Security and Health Care in China

Michael Tanner

The rapid aging of China's population, accelerated by the nation's one-child policy, will soon put a severe strain on its ability to provide retirement security. Only through the use of market mechanisms can China ensure that it will be able to provide for future retirees.

China has one of the world's fastest aging populations. By 2030, nearly 22 percent of China's population will be over the age of 60. Indeed, as Figure 1 shows, China will experience large percentage increases in its elderly population (the largest percentage increase will be among those age 80 and older), while actually experiencing a percentage decrease among the young. The result will be a rapidly decreasing ratio of workers to retirees. Currently, there are approximately six workers for every retired person. By 2030, there will be only 2.3 (Gao and Chi 1996: 61).

At the same time, China has begun a massive transformation of its traditional system of providing retirement security. For much of the rural population, government-provided retirement benefits have been rudimentary, often little more than emergency relief. Urban workers relied on pensions from state-owned enterprises (SOEs), financed by government budget grants (Li and Xu 1995). But employment at SOEs is no longer the centerpiece of the Chinese economy. At the same time, declining tax revenue and the increasing cost of an aging population has made it difficult for the government to continue financing its pension obligations. As a result, China will soon be facing important decisions about the future of its retirement system.

Michael Tanner is Director of Health and Welfare Studies at the Cato Institute.

FIGURE 1

CHINA: AGE-SPECIFIC POPULATION CHANGE, 1990 to 2000

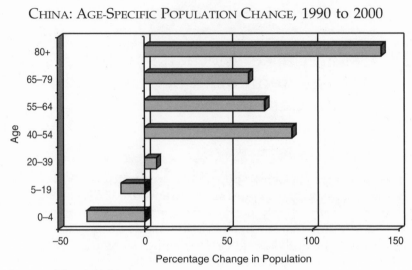

SOURCE: Silva (1996).

Options for Providing Retirement Security

Despite variations from country to country, it can be said that there are three general models for a national system of retirement pensions: the United States and Europe, Chile, and Singapore.

The United States, Europe, and Japan rely on pay-as-you-go (PAYGO) systems of public retirement pensions. In a PAYGO system today's benefits to the old are paid by today's taxes from the young, relying primarily on a payroll tax. Tomorrow's benefits to today's young are to be paid by tomorrow's taxes from tomorrow's young. A PAYGO structure, therefore, is an intergenerational transfer from younger workers to older retirees.

To be successful, a PAYGO system requires a high ratio of workers to retirees. However, as Figure 2 shows, that ratio is shrinking in nearly every country. In the United States there were 15 workers to every retiree as recently as 1950. Today, there are only 3.3. By 2025, there will be only two. In Japan and Europe, the problem is even worse.

To one degree or another, every PAYGO system is facing financial problems as the system's structure is overtaken by demographics.

FIGURE 2

RATIO OF RETIREMENT-AGE TO WORKING-AGE POPULATION

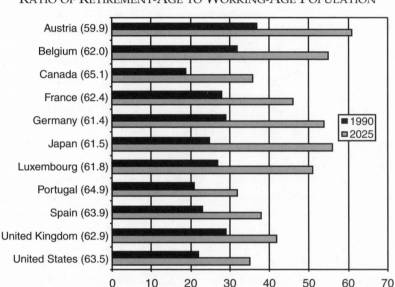

NOTE: Ratios represent the number of persons at or above the average retirement age per 100 persons between the age of 20 and the average retirement age in 1984. Each national average retirement age is in parentheses after the country name.

SOURCE: Ferrara and Tanner (1998: 130).

In the United States, Social Security may be running a deficit as early as 2013.

Both Chile and Singapore have rejected PAYGO in favor of a mandatory savings system based on defined contributions, individual accounts, and private investment. However, there are important differences in approach between the two models.

Chile was the first nation in the Western Hemisphere to adopt a social security system, in 1926. It was a PAYGO scheme that ran into demographic problems. In the late 1970s its benefit payments were greater than its taxes, and it had no funded reserves. Based upon the anticipated decline in its benefit-support ratio, the problems were only going to get worse. Chile decided to fundamentally restructure its system and not merely reform the flawed PAYGO scheme.

The new system is one of forced savings. It requires workers to contribute 10 percent of their wages to their own account at a pension fund company (Administradoras de Fondos de Pensiones, AFPs) that invests the wages in securities such as stocks and bonds. Contributions and investment returns are not taxed, but withdrawals are. Upon retirement, participants have the option of purchasing a life-long annuity, withdrawing a monthly benefit from their AFP account, or purchasing an annuity that is effective at a future specified date. Participants also have the right to contribute an additional 10 percent of after-tax wages to their accounts which compounds tax-free.

The AFPs are single-purpose companies that are licensed and regulated by the government. Among other obligations, they are required to invest the contributions, distribute the benefits, offer insurance, conduct participant record keeping, and keep a certain level of reserves. Much like the mutual fund industry, the workers' assets are separate from the AFP's assets. If an AFP were to go out of business, workers' assets would be transferred to another AFP. Individuals have the right to choose and change their AFP.

The success of Chile's public pension privatization can be measured in many ways. Whereas in the late 1970s there were virtually no savings, now the cumulative assets managed by AFPs are about $30 billion or roughly 43 percent of GDP (Palau 1996: 3). During the past decade Chile's real GDP growth has averaged over 7 percent, more than double that of the United States. Most important, since the privatized system became fully operational on May 1, 1981, the average rate of return on investment has been 12.8 percent per year. As a result, the typical retiree is receiving a benefit equal to nearly 78 percent of his average annual income over the last 10 years of his working life, almost double the replacement value under the old PAYGO system (Baeza 1995: 166).

Chile's reforms are seen as such a huge economic and political success that countries throughout Latin America, including Argentina, Bolivia, Columbia, El Salvador, Mexico, Peru, and Uruguay, are beginning to implement similar changes. In Europe, Britain has allowed some people to opt out of its upper tier of benefits, and Italy has begun to privatize some aspects of its social security system. Several former Soviet bloc countries, including Hungary and Poland, are also beginning to privatize their systems.

Beginning in 1955, Singapore introduced a compulsory savings program that now covers about three out of four Singapore workers.[1] Both employers and employees contribute to the government-run Central Provident Fund (CPF), which maintains accounts for each worker. Employees have a property right to the funds accumulating in their accounts, are able to withdraw funds for the purchase of a home or to buy life insurance or home mortgage insurance, and may borrow money from their account to pay for the college education of a family member. Funds may be withdrawn at retirement, in the event of permanent disability, or if the individual emigrates from Singapore.

Unlike Chile, there is a single fund whose investment policy is controlled by the government. Until 1986, the government directed all the fund's investment. However, recently the government has increasingly allowed individuals to control more and more of their own investment decisions. Currently, individual's are allowed to direct the investment of a portion of their accumulated balance (approximately 80 percent of funds in excess of S$35,400) in certain government approved stocks, government bonds, and annuities.

The funds not directed by individuals must be invested in Singapore government bonds. However, because the Singaporean government is running a budget surplus, the funds used to purchase those bonds are not used to finance government expenditures (as is the case in the United States, for example) but are invested through the Singapore Government Investment Corporation. No information on the investment portfolio is made public (it is, in fact, a state secret), but it is believed that most funds are invested abroad. The Singaporean government provides a return on the bonds based on the rates provided by the nation's major banks, with a guaranteed minimum of 2.5 percent (Butler, Asher, and Borden 1996: 44). Similar systems have been implemented in many countries of Southeast Asia and the Pacific (Sri Lanka, Fiji, Nepal, among others), Africa (Kenya, The Gambia, Tanzania), and the Caribbean (Dominica, Grenada, St. Lucia). The success of these systems has been mixed.

---

[1]Malaysia was actually the first nation to institute a mandatory savings program with a Central Provident Fund in 1951. India and Indonesia also established such systems, albeit with limited coverage, in the early 1950s. However, the system has largely come to be identified with Singapore.

FIGURE 3

AVERAGE ANNUAL INVESTMENT RETURNS FOR SELECTED PROVIDENT FUNDS, 1980s

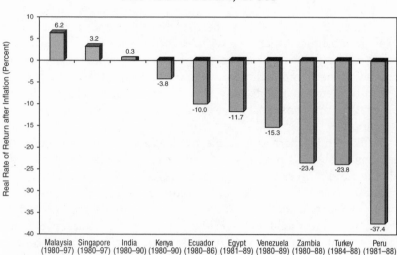

SOURCE: Ferrara and Tanner (1998: 149).

Because provident funds are compulsory monopolies, with government control of investment, the system's success has depended on the success of the government's investment policy. Some countries such as Malaysia and Singapore have pursued conservative investment strategies, heavily focused on their own government debt, which have produced stable—but low—rates of return. In many other countries, however, the government has been tempted to politicize its investment policy, using invested funds to shore up unprofitable state enterprises or make other unproductive investments. For example, during the 1980s, Peru, Turkey, Zambia, Venezuela, Egypt, Ecuador, and Kenya all failed to earn a positive real rate of return on the monies invested in their provident funds (see Figure 3).

The Best Choice for China

China has correctly rejected a PAYGO system as the sole basis of retirement security.[2] Despite China's robust rate of economic growth,

[2]Interestingly, when China rejected Hong Kong Governor Chris Patten's attempt to implement a PAYGO system, China's Hong Kong representative Zhou Nan dis-

demographic realities will eventually make a PAYGO system unsustainable. Indeed, given the declining ratio of workers to retirees, maintaining a PAYGO system could eventually require payroll taxes as high as 44 percent (Wu 1997).

In 1996, the Third Plenary Session of the 14th Central Committee of the Communist Party of China called for a system "integrating social pooling with personal accounts" for urban workers. The introduction of that program has given China a solid foundation to build on. Urban workers, in both state enterprises and private companies, including the self-employed, contribute a portion of their wages to a personal pension account. Their employer also contributes to the individual account as well as to a pooled social insurance system.[3] China should move beyond this modest program and implement a nationwide system of individual accounts based on the Chilean model.

First, workers should be allowed a larger range of investment options for funds in their individual accounts. Currently, accounts are paid a uniform rate of interest determined by the People's Bank of China (Gao and Chi 1996: 66). However, evidence from other countries suggests that workers could earn a far higher rate of return if they were able to take full advantage of the wide range of investment alternatives available in a competitive environment. As shown by Figure 4, returns from privately managed pensions have exceeded those of even the best government managed systems.

The World Bank (1996) points out that all the prerequisites for running a privately managed system of fully funded individual accounts are present in China—indeed, more so than in most countries at a similar stage of development. Although capital markets in China are relatively young and hampered by a lack of well-defined private property rights, there are many opportunities for sound financial investment—including nascent stock and bond markets. Moreover, with the return of Hong Kong to Chinese control, new opportunities for investment will become available in that stable

---

missed it as a "costly Euro-Socialist" proposal, clearly differentiating such welfare-statism from the Chinese goal of a "socialist market economy" (*The Economist* 1995: 16–17).

[3]The mandated savings rate for individual accounts and the rate of employer contributions to both the individual accounts and social insurance pools vary from province to province, as do administrative rules.

FIGURE 4

AVERAGE ANNUAL INVESTMENT RETURNS FOR PRIVATELY INVESTED FUNDS

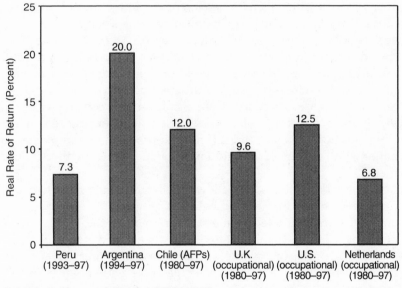

SOURCE: Ferrara and Tanner (1998: 150).

and lucrative capital market. In addition, there are many foreign institutions that would be willing to jump into the Chinese investment management market if given the opportunity.

Second, the business contribution to pension pools should be phased out, with that contribution being redirected to the worker's individual account. Pension pools are designed to provide benefits for current retirees and near retirees, ensure a minimum level of retirement security for all workers, and spread pension costs between firms with large numbers of retirees or older work forces and firms with few retirees or younger work forces. However, all those functions could be better performed through other mechanisms. Moreover, continuation of social insurance pooling will lead to serious problems in the future.

The pension pools are essentially a PAYGO system. As the number of pensioners increases in future years, while the relative number of workers declines, the required benefit payments will easily overwhelm the system's ability to finance them. The first signs of this future crisis can be seen in the funding problems experienced by pension pools in four provinces in 1991 (Xin 1994).

Finally, China should begin to extend the system of individual accounts beyond urban workers to rural and underdeveloped areas. However, rather than making such a system compulsory, it would be preferable to use incentives to promote voluntary participation.

Health Care

The same reforms used to develop a secure retirement system can be adapted to help China develop an effective market-based health care system.

China is already rapidly developing a health insurance market. However in doing so, China must be careful to differentiate between routine, low-cost care and catastrophic, unforeseeable expenses. The latter are properly the subject of insurance, which at its core is a method for spreading risk. The former should be paid by the individual consumer. When insurance begins to cover routine, low-cost health care expenses, where there is little risk to spread, it simply becomes an administratively costly mechanism for prepaying the cost of health care.

Moreover, whenever the cost of health care is paid by someone other than the individual consuming the health care goods or services, there will be a strong tendency to overconsume, leading to upward pressure on health care costs.

Therefore, China should combine insurance for catastrophic health events with a mechanism to enable individuals to save in order to pay for their own routine, low-cost health expenses. Singapore provides an excellent model for such a system. In 1984, Singapore began to require that a certain portion of CPF contributions be put into "medical savings accounts" to provide funds for hospitalization. These accounts operate as part of the country's Central Provident Fund system that also provides retirement benefits. Currently, 6 percent of an employee's salary is put in a medical savings account until the account balance reaches approximately $8,522. As long as that balance is maintained, additional contributions are automatically placed in the individual's ordinary pension account (Choon and Low 1997: 59).

327

Funds in medical savings accounts can be withdrawn to pay for routine, low-cost health expenses. At the same time, nearly all Singaporeans have private health insurance (with a large deductible) to provide protection against catastrophic illness.

Singapore's system has been remarkably successful in holding down health care costs. Not only have Singapore's health care costs been rising at a rate below that of most other countries, but, measured as a proportion of total private consumption, health care expenditures have actually declined since 1986. At the same time, the Singapore government spending on health care has also declined, both as a percentage of the country's total social service budget and as a percentage of total government spending (Choon and Low 1997: 60–61).

Experimentation with such a system has already begun. In Jiujang and Zhenjiang provinces, workers pay for health care first out of individual accounts (financed through individual and employer contributions), turning to state and employer-funded insurance only as a secondary method of payment. Early results from this experiment indicate that it has restrained medical costs and improved medical service (Wu 1997).

It should be relatively easy to integrate such medical savings accounts with the retirement security accounts discussed above.

Side Benefits: Public Participation and Economic Growth

While the primary purpose of developing a market-based system for retirement and health care security is to provide for the security and protection of individual workers within the context of a financially sustainable system, there are important side benefits that can be realized from such a system.

China is committed to an economy that combines private and public ownership. However, as Deng Xiaoping pointed out, public ownership does not necessarily mean state ownership. In fact, Deng endorsed a shareholding system as a means to provide public ownership (Wu 1996: 157).

A system of individually owned, privately invested retirement and health accounts would accelerate the move to a shareholder-based economy. Since every worker would have an individual pension account, every worker would have the opportunity to own stocks. Even the poorest worker would become a shareholder.

As minister of labor, José Piñera was the architect of Chile's successful privatization of social security. He explains the change that privatization brought to the Chilean workers:

> The new pension system gives Chileans a personal stake in the economy. A typical Chilean worker is not indifferent to the stock market or interest rates. When workers feel that they own a part of the country ... they are much more attached to the free market and a free society [Piñera 1996: 17].

A Chilean-style pension system would also assist China in the privatization of SOEs, as it did in Chile. Piñera (1996: 12) notes that by creating a system of pension accounts first, and then privatizing SOEs, Chile established a "virtuous sequence," allowing workers to use the funds in their accounts to purchase shares in the newly privatized companies. This not only reduced political opposition to privatization but allowed workers to capture a large portion of the wealth created through the privatization process.

The World Bank has also suggested that Chilean-style private pension funds would help China develop its capital markets and would facilitate privatization efforts (World Bank 1994: 2).

Finally, it should be noted that a public pension system based on individual accounts and private investment can lead to increased economic growth. Chile's system has been credited with being a major reason behind that country's prolonged economic growth. Harvard economist Martin Feldstein (1997) estimates that the privatization of the U.S. Social Security system would permanently add 5 percent to U.S. GDP, a present value of at least $10 trillion.

Conclusion

The aging of the Chinese population, combined with the restructuring of the Chinese economy, provides a unique opportunity for China to develop market-based systems for providing old-age and health protections. Indeed, given the rapid aging of China's population, its shrinking workforce, and the gradual privatization of state enterprises, only market forces can provide for China's future health care and retirement needs.

Moreover, a health and retirement system based on individual accounts and private investment can promote full participation by workers in China's economic system. Finally, such a system can increase economic growth and assist economic restructuring.

329

References

Baeza, S. (1995) *Quince Anos Despues: Una Mirada al Sistema Privado de Pensiones*. Santiago, Chile: Center for Public Studies.

Butler, E.; Asher, M.; and Borden, K. (1996) *Singapore v. Chile: Competing Models for Welfare Reform*. London: Adam Smith Institute.

Choon, A.T., and Low, L. (1997) "Health Care Provisions in Singapore." In T.T. Meng and L.S. Beng (eds.) *Affordable Health Care: Issues and Prospects*. Singapore: Prentice-Hall.

The Economist (1995) "Is Welfare UnAsian?" February: 16–17.

Gao, S., and Chi, F. (1996) *China's Social Security System*. Beijing: Foreign Language Press.

Feldstein, M. (1997) "Privatizing Social Security: The $10 Trillion Opportunity." Social Security Privatization Paper No. 7. Washington, D.C.: Cato Institute.

Ferrara, P., and Tanner, M. (1998) *A New Deal for Social Security*. Washington, D.C.: Cato Institute.

Li, L., and Xu, D. (1995) "How to Reform China's Old-Age Insurance System: What We Can Learn From the US Experience." Paper presented to a conference on Economic Reform in China, Toronto, September.

Palau, A. (1996) "Chile: Results and Lessons After 15 Years of Reform." Paper presented to a conference on The Pension Fund Revolution in Latin America, Miami, 9 September.

Piñera, J. (1996) "Empowering Workers: The Privatization of Social Security in Chile." Cato's Letters No. 11, Cato Institute, Washington, D.C.

Silva, J. (1996) "World Economic Outlook." Zurich Kemper Investments, 28 August.

World Bank (1994) *Averting the Old Age Crisis: Policies to Protect the Old and Promote Growth*. New York: Oxford University Press.

World Bank (1996) "China Pension System Reform." World Bank Resident Mission in China and Mongolia. Washington, D.C.: World Bank.

Wu, J. (1996) *On Deng Xiaoping Thought*. Beijing: Foreign Language Press.

Wu, J. (1997) "China's Social Security System." Paper presented at the Cato Institute/Fudan University conference on China as a Global Economic Power: Market Reforms in the New Millennium, Shanghai, 15 June.

Xin, R. (1994) "Current State of China's Urban Old-Age Insurance Pooling Schemes." *Economic Research Materials* 2.

PART V

INSTITUTIONAL CHOICE AND CHINA'S DEVELOPMENT

22. A Constitution of Liberty for China

Roger Pilon

Over the past 20 years, China has become increasingly free and prosperous, even if those gains are selective and still relatively modest by world standards. Under the current Chinese Constitution, however, that progress is anything but secure. Rooted in socialist ideas and institutions that are dying—no less in China than in the rest of the world—the Constitution sanctions power that can fairly be described as arbitrary. If China is to preserve and expand upon its recent achievements, therefore, it will need a constitution that institutionalizes, not simply tolerates, the forces that have led to improvements there.

Fortunately, debate about such issues is alive in China today (Chen 1998: A11). This volume and the conference that brought it about are evidence, as is a more recent conference, held in February 1998 at China's Unirule Institute, where a new translation of F.A. Hayek's 1960 classic, *The Constitution of Liberty*, was the focus of discussion. That book has become an instant bestseller in China, reports the *Far Eastern Economic Review*, and is already in its second printing after the first 20,000 copies sold out immediately (*FEER* 1998: 82; *AWSJ* 1998). The importance of such developments cannot be overstated, for the constitutional principles Hayek defends—like the principles to be discussed and defended here, which are drawn from the American Constitution—are very different than the principles one finds in the Chinese Constitution.

To illustrate those differences, their importance, and their bearing on the future of China, it will be useful first to take a brief but critical look at the Chinese Constitution, especially at how it is ill-suited to ensure that the gains of the past 20 years will not be lost. By way of contrast, the principles of the American Constitution will then be

Roger Pilon holds the B. Kenneth Simon Chair in Constitutional Studies and is Director of the Center for Constitutional Studies at the Cato Institute.

drawn out, especially as they may have application beyond the American context. It will then remain to apply those principles, very generally, to the Chinese context.

The conclusion reached is quite simple, but no less important for that. The modest steps China has taken toward privatization and local democracy, which have produced the recent progress, need to be expanded and institutionalized in a constitution that not only separates power functionally and divides it between central and more local institutions but, of even greater importance, limits it in scope and purpose. Present arrangements—whereby all human affairs are subject, in principle, to state control—are unjust, inefficient, and fraught with the perils of self-dealing and corruption. Democracy is often urged as the natural corrective to each of those problems, but it is only one aspect of what needs to be done—and the less important aspect. In fact, democracy itself, especially under conditions of ubiquitous government, is hardly free from the perils of self-dealing and corruption—directly, by majorities, and indirectly, by special interests manipulating the majoritarian process.

To check such tendencies at the outset, therefore, the objects of government concern, even democratic government, need to be constitutionally limited. That was the fundamental insight that led to the American Constitution. The American Founders instituted not simply constitutional government but limited government—government limited primarily to securing individual liberty.

The Chinese Constitution

China's present Constitution, its fourth since the People's Republic of China was established in 1949, was adopted in 1982, amended in 1988, and amended again in 1993. Reflecting Marxism-Leninism and Mao Zedong Thought, as its Preamble says, the Constitution makes it clear from the start that the PRC "is a socialist state under the people's democratic leadership," that "the socialist system is the basic system" of the PRC, and that "disruption of the socialist state by any organization or individual is prohibited" (Article 1). Although a very limited sanction of market-like arrangements has found its way recently into the Constitution—and especially into the underlying Civil Law, adopted in 1986, and Economic Contract Law, adopted in 1993—the provisions authorizing those arrangements are highly qualified. As a matter of "law," therefore, they can be compromised easily—a feature common to all socialist constitutions.

To an American, two things, especially, stand out about the Chinese Constitution: (a) it is programmatic; and (b) there are no genuine provisions for popular ratification. The programmatic character of the Constitution is made clear from the start: after recounting briefly "the protracted and arduous struggles" of the Chinese people, "led by the Communist Party of China with Chairman Mao Zedong as its leader," the Preamble states that "the basic task before the nation is the concentration of efforts of socialist modernization construction in accordance with the theory of building socialism with Chinese characteristics." Thus, the document is written with a specific agenda in mind—"building socialism"—which gives it less the feel of a constitution than of articles of incorporation for, say, "China, Inc.," a body constituted for a specific, yet all-encompassing end. Given that character, the second feature looms especially large. For if the nation is organized along vast programmatic lines, one wants to know how it is that citizens join or consent to so far-reaching a program. Unfortunately, the Constitution gives little indication of that and thus raises fundamental questions about legitimacy. According to what principles are individuals bound to "the protracted and arduous struggle"?

A Program for Unlimited Government

The programmatic character of the present Constitution can be seen throughout the document. In the name of building socialism— the ultimate end of government—the related ends and means are essentially unlimited—reaching economic, cultural, social, and even personal affairs. To put it uncharitably, yet accurately, this is a constitution for totalitarian government, even if the actual exercise of power in recent years has fallen short of that in many respects.

To appreciate the point, one need simply reflect upon a few of the more salient articles in the document. As noted above, the Preamble summarizes the history of the Chinese people, focusing on the establishment of "the dictatorship of the proletariat" after 1949, then lays down the socialist agenda for the future. Article 1, as also noted above, states plainly that the PRC "is a socialist state." Article 2 indicates the breadth of both the ends and the means of that state: "all power" in the PRC belongs not to people, in their individual capacities, but to "the people," which they exercise through "the National People's Congress and the local people's congresses at various levels," managing "economic, cultural, and social affairs." That covers just about everything. In fact, it covers not only all economic affairs, as one would expect in a system based upon "socialist public ownership of the means of production" (Article 6), but education (Article 19), health and sports (Article 21), art, culture, and the media (Article 22), training and expanding the ranks of intellectuals (Article 23), morals and ethics (Article 24)—even family planning (Article 25). There is really nothing that is not, in principle, a proper subject of state concern.

It is true, of course, that the Constitution contains a section entitled "The Fundamental Rights and Duties of Citizens" (Chapter Two), which has led many in the West, including in the U.S. State Department, to believe that the human rights problem in China stems from the Chinese government's failure to follow its own law (Nathan 1997; U.S. Dept. of State 1998). But a careful reading of that section will show that the "law" provides virtually no protection for individual rights, notwithstanding its use of the language of rights. To be sure, all citizens of the PRC "are equal before the law" and are "entitled to the rights . . . prescribed by the Constitution and the law" (Article 33), including "freedom of speech, of the press, of assembly, of association, of procession and of demonstration" (Article 35), "freedom of religious belief" (Article 36), "freedom of the person" (Article 37), "freedom and privacy of correspondence" (Article 40), and other such rights. But in addition to qualifications that are included in several of the articles that stipulate rights, Article 51 sets out a general defeasance clause: "Citizens of the People's Republic of China, in exercising their freedoms and rights, may not infringe upon the interests of the state, of society, or of the collective." Given that those "interests" are boundless in principle, and vague besides, any claims that individuals might have *against* the state can always be trumped *as a matter of constitutional law*.

It should hardly surprise that the Constitution elevates the interests of the state above the rights of the citizen. After all, the whole point of the Constitution is to order affairs—including the affairs of individual citizens—toward the goal of building socialism. Given that all-encompassing end, it stands to reason that individuals should not be permitted to act in ways that might compromise the

336

end. In fact, when they do, their acts are branded as "counter-revolutionary" and subject to suppression (Article 28).

Under a programmatic constitution of the kind that China has, then, there are only two basic kinds of people—those who are "with the program" and those who are against it. The point is stated very nicely in a recent publication describing the Chinese constitutional and political system, issued by the authoritative China News: "The people's democratic dictatorship has two sides: democracy is practiced within the ranks of the people; dictatorship is exercised over the enemies of the people" (China News 1997).

Yet even the "democracy" that is practiced "within the ranks of the people" is a programmatic undertaking, not a clash of opposing ideas and aims. Indeed, the state organs in the PRC, Article 3 tells us, apply the principle of "democratic centralism," which amounts to a kind of top-down management of economic, cultural, and social affairs. Even "the division of functions and powers between the central and state organs," which one might think would have been designed to pit power against power, is "guided"—"by the principle of giving full scope to the initiative and enthusiasm of the local authorities *under the unified leadership of the central authorities*" (Article 3, emphasis added). Far from a check on power, the "division" of functions and powers is a kind of division of labor, aimed at implementing the program efficiently.

The ultimate source of "guidance," of course, is the Communist Party of China, although the party is nowhere mentioned in the Constitution, except in the Preamble. In that respect, the Chinese Constitution is more subtle than the final Soviet Constitution, the so-called Brezhnev Constitution, which stated in Article 6 that the Communist Party of the Soviet Union is "the leading and guiding force of Soviet society and the nucleus of its political system, . . . directing the great constructive work of the Soviet people" (Ramundo 1978: 73; Pilon 1986: 2). Less subtle than the Chinese Constitution is the above-mentioned China News piece: discussing the relationship between the CPC and the eight other "democratic" parties in China—not to be confused with "parties out of power or opposition parties"—the article states that the CPC works "in tandem" with those parties "to build socialism," that the CPC "governs China," and that it "employs the legal process to make its positions the national will" (China News 1997). That makes the role of the CPC quite clear, even if the Constitution itself leaves it unclear.

No Provisions for Popular Ratification

Because the Chinese Constitution sanctions so vast a program, enabling the government to reach and control virtually every aspect of life in China, and because the Communist Party of China, a small fraction of the Chinese population, plays so central a role in setting the policies of the government, questions about legitimacy loom especially large. How is it that individual citizens are bound to such a program?

One measure of political legitimacy—by no means the only or the most important measure, as will be discussed shortly—is to be found in consent or, in the constitutional context, ratification. If people agree to be bound under a set of rules or rulers, they cannot be heard later to complain about the arrangements they consented to, whatever the scope of those arrangements may be.

But as noted earlier, the Chinese Constitution, with its far-reaching program, contains no genuine provisions for popular ratification—certainly no section dealing explicitly with that issue. At best, the National People's Congress, composed of approximately 3,000 deputies (out of a population of more than 1.2 billion people), exercises the power to adopt and to amend the Constitution by a two-thirds vote of all the deputies (Articles 62 and 64). That is not popular ratification, of course. Moreover, whatever measure of legitimacy a constitutional vote by the NPC may impart—through "representational ratification"—is attenuated by the influence of the CPC. The party is hardly constituted by direct elections; nor, as the "leading" party, can it be said to represent the population as a whole, notwithstanding several claims to that effect in the Preamble of the Constitution.

To be perfectly fair, however, China is not alone in the world in not having solved the problem of establishing formal legitimacy through consent. In truth, the problem is intractable. For if consent is a necessary condition for legitimacy, then even large majorities cannot bind minorities who, by definition, have not consented. Only unanimity will do. But as a practical matter, unanimity is impossible, especially when a vote must run over time and changing populations.

In the end, therefore, one wants to ground legitimacy not simply in formal consent but, more importantly, in substantive considerations, as will be discussed below. Nevertheless, some measure of formal consent will always be needed simply to establish a legal regime in the first place, to get it off the ground. The problem with China is that its measure is terribly thin. Absent anything remotely approaching popular ratification, even a two-thirds vote of the NPC lends little legitimacy, especially when the regime is as far-reaching as the Chinese regime is.[1]

A Transition to Freedom?

But what of the relative freedom that has emerged in China over the past 20 years? How has that happened under so all-encompassing and authoritarian a Constitution? The answers to those questions are complex, but for present purposes a brief response should suffice, especially as it points to the difficulties inherent in the "mixed" situation in China today.

It seems that in the aftermath of the breakdown of authority that followed the so-called Cultural Revolution of the 1970s, quasi-private agricultural arrangements arose "spontaneously" in rural areas—along lines that Hayek discussed—unleashing the productive power of individual self-interest. And the increased productivity that resulted over time did not go unnoticed by local and national authorities. First in the countryside, then later in more urban areas and in non-agricultural affairs, such arrangements came to be tolerated and even encouraged. Thus, by 1993, when the First Session of the Eighth People's Congress met to approve revisions in the Constitution, we find up for approval such phrases as "socialist market economy" (Article 15) and "rural household contracted responsibility system . . . linking remuneration to output" (Article 8). And those changes were approved. Non-socialist arrangements have found their way into a programmatic Constitution dedicated to "building socialism."

Needless to say, that inconsistency creates a certain tension that is resolved only by couching the "market" arrangements in an overarching socialist framework—much as "individual rights" are recognized only insofar as they do not compromise state interests. Thus, the "rural contracted responsibility system" and "cooperative economic forms" recognized in Article 8 are nonetheless "part of the

---

[1]I have discussed the foundations of legitimacy more fully in Pilon (1992; 1992/1993).

socialist economy collectively owned by the working people." And Article 8 also states that members of such collectives have the right to engage in various "private" activities—"within the limits prescribed by law," an important qualification we find throughout the Constitution. More generally, in Article 11 we find that,

> The state permits the private sector of the economy to exist and develop *within the limits prescribed by law*. The private sector of the economy is a complement to the socialist public economy. The state protects the lawful rights and interests of the private sector of the economy, *and exercises guidance, supervision and control over the private sector of the economy* [emphasis added].

Make no mistake, those and a few other such additions to the 1982 Constitution mark important steps in the evolution of Chinese law. They amount to *constitutional* recognition of changes that had already taken place, however "unsanctioned" by the Constitution.

But while granting the importance of those changes, we should also be candid about them: they are anomalies within a vast overarching regime that runs the other way, toward a ubiquitous public sector. More importantly, they are *tolerated* more than recognized. Because they sit within an essentially arbitrary regime of power, dedicated to opposite ends, they can be eliminated with perfect legality. To put the matter in a different idiom, the private economic arrangements that have emerged recently in China, which have contributed so much to the well-being of the average citizen there, are operating more as a matter of "concession" than of right. Those who work under such arrangements are "permitted" to do so—by authorities who can withdraw their permission, if they wish, at any time, as the Constitution repeatedly makes clear.

Such arbitrary power, moreover, can lead only to corruption and self-dealing, as has already happened in many cases. And the issue is not simply the bribery that inevitably arises when officials have such power. More subtly, it relates to the absence in Chinese law of any clear line between private and public, notwithstanding the Constitution's use of the word "private." Thus, it is not entirely accurate to say that over the past 20 years "private" firms have arisen as officials "looked the other way." Rather, the cooperatives and village-based enterprises that have flourished are quasi-public, quasi-private entities. Indeed, Article 17 tells us that, in accordance with the law, "collective economic organizations" (as distinct from the "state-owned enterprises" covered in Article 16) practice "democratic management." A truly private enterprise, of course, would practice whatever management its owners wished. Not here. Instead, collectives compete in market-like settings, but with varying degrees of state "guidance, supervision and control." That is a situation ripe for self-dealing. It affords an opportunity for local officials, who may be managers of local collectives, to use their public power against competitors for private gain (Pomfret 1998: F1).

Corruption will be reduced, however, not by stiffer oversight but by reducing the opportunities for corruption. And the key to that is to reduce or eliminate the official power that enables the corruption in the first place. Thus, just as the key to increasing economic production is to reduce or eliminate the official power that frustrates the forces of individual self-interest, so too the key to reducing corruption is to reduce or eliminate the official power that is the seadbed of corruption.

In the end, all of that should be accomplished through fundamental, constitutional law. To better secure and vastly expand the progress of the past 20 years, what is needed is a constitution that goes about the matter in a very different way. The freedom that the present Constitution "permits," at the pleasure of the government, needs to be taken for granted—as a matter of *right*. What needs to be permitted, by a constitution, is government actions. Those actions need to be "authorized," in the strict sense of that word, and then carefully limited, much like the Chinese Constitution today authorizes, then strictly limits, individual liberty. What is needed, in short, is a constitution that starts at the other end of the matter.

The American Constitution

Nowhere is that other end of the matter more clearly found than in America's Declaration of Independence, which set forth the principles that 11 years later would inspire America's Founders as they sat down to draft the Constitution of the United States of America. The Declaration is not "law," strictly speaking, but its broad principles so illuminate America's fundamental law, the Constitution, as to make it difficult to fully appreciate that law without first understanding its wellsprings. Thus, we begin with the Declaration of Independence.

The Declaration of Independence

In starting at the "other end," the Declaration does not presume government, then carve out areas where individuals are permitted to be free, as the Chinese Constitution does. On the contrary, it presumes freedom, then carves out areas where government is permitted to act. More precisely, the Declaration starts with a situation free of government—a "state of nature"—in which individuals are free by right, then asks how government might be justified under such circumstances.

The reasons for so starting are several, but two stand out. First, as a practical and immediate matter, the Founders wanted to justify to "a candid World" their decision to declare America's independence from Great Britain. Toward that end, they set forth a theory of legitimate government, then demonstrated how far English rule had strayed from that ideal. But second, from a more theoretical perspective, individuals come first, not government—which is constituted by individuals. Thus, the "natural" starting point is a state of affairs without any government. Once that fundamental insight is appreciated, what must be justified is government's power over the individual, not the individual's freedom from government control (Nozick 1974). As we will see shortly, that insight is at the heart of the American Constitution.

Starting from the other end, then, is tantamount to putting morality first, politics second. In fact, that is made clear in the very first phrase of those famous words that have inspired countless millions around the world for more than two centuries. When America's Founders wrote "We hold these Truths to be self-evident," they were saying that the propositions that followed were true and, what is more, "self-evidently" true—true by virtue of being grounded in reason. America government thus springs from moral or natural law—from the idea that there is a "higher law" of right and wrong, discoverable by reason, from which to derive human law and against which to judge human law (Corwin 1955).

Thus, using ordinary reason, accessible to all, the Founders derived the following truths:

> that all Men are created equal, that they are endowed by their Creator with certain unalienable Rights, that among these are Life, Liberty, and the Pursuit of Happiness—That to secure these Rights, Governments are instituted among Men, deriving their just Powers from the Consent of the Governed.

342

We are all created equal, as defined by our natural rights—meaning that no one has rights superior to those of anyone else. Moreover, we are born with those rights, we do not get them from government—indeed, whatever rights or powers government has come from us, from "the Consent of the Governed." And rights to life, liberty, and the pursuit of happiness imply the right to live our lives as we wish—to pursue happiness as we think best, by our own lights—provided only that we respect the equal rights of others to do the same. Drawing by implication upon the common law tradition of liberty, property, and contract—its foundations rooted in "right reason"—the Founders thus outlined the moral foundations of a free society.

Only then, after outlining the basic moral principles, did they turn to government. We institute government, the Declaration says, to secure our rights—our natural rights and the rights we create as we live our lives. But the powers government may need to do that must be derived from our consent if they are to be just. Government is thus twice limited: by its end, which any of us would have a right to pursue were there no government; and by its means, which require our consent.

Notice, then, how fundamentally different this approach to government is than the approach taken by the Chinese Constitution. Government in America is not instituted to undertake a vast, all-encompassing program like "building socialism." To the contrary, its sole function, at least in principle, is to secure our rights—against domestic and foreign threats. As for the rest—"economic, cultural, and social affairs"—that is for individuals and private organizations to "manage," not in any public sense but in their private capacities. Individuals are *free*, that is, to plan and live their own lives—free from the interference of other individuals, if government is doing its job, and free from government interference as well.

The Constitution

In America, then, what must be justified is government power, not individual freedom. Freedom is a given, power is not. And since all power resides first in people—not "the people," in their political capacity, but people as individuals—then the basic political question is how power gets from people to the government. That, of course, is a question about how Americans constituted themselves, which returns us to the issue of ratification.

1. Ratification. Since the Declaration makes it clear that legitimacy is a function of consent—that government derives its *just* powers from the consent of the governed—it is crucial to understand just how consent operates to impart legitimacy to the institutions and actions of government. And the first, primordial consent takes the form of constitutional ratification.

Unlike in the Chinese Constitution, there is a section in the American Constitution that deals with ratification. Article VII provides, quite simply, that "The Ratification of the Conventions of nine States, shall be sufficient for the Establishment of this Constitution between the States so ratifying the Same." Moreover, there is a separate section that deals with amending the document. Amendments can be proposed by two-thirds of both houses of Congress or by a convention called after application to Congress by the legislatures of two-thirds of the states. Ratification of any such proposed amendment requires approval by three-fourths of the legislatures of the states or by conventions in three-fourths of the states, depending on which mode Congress has determined.

Clearly, those methods get us closer to popular ratification than do the methods of the Chinese Constitution, especially insofar as the process takes place not just at the national level—like that of the Chinese Constitution—but at the state level as well. Moreover, ratification in America is not influenced or determined by a party that operates like the Communist Party of China; as noted earlier, in China there are no "parties out of power or opposition parties." And notice too how unanimity was recognized as important as an initial matter: once nine states had ratified the Constitution, it became effective *"between the States so ratifying the Same."* By implication, those states could not have bound other, non-ratifying states to the Constitution. The document was binding only upon those states that agreed to be so bound: thus, among them, there was unanimity.

Still, a number of problems remain if consent is indeed to be the bedrock of legitimacy. At the time of America's founding, for example, the franchise was relatively limited; thus, many had no say in the process, even though they were bound by its result. Moreover, even if the franchise had been much wider, unanimity was required only at the outset and, even then, only with respect to states: at the level of individuals, minorities who voted against ratification—whether of the Constitution originally or of an amendment later—were still bound by the vote of the majority. And finally, the still larger problem of changing populations remains: no American today, except officeholders and immigrants who later become citizens, has consented to be bound by the Constitution. In sum, a basic question any American citizen can ask—Why should I be bound by the consent of others?—remains unanswered for most.

Assuming consent were the only criterion of legitimacy, one can answer, at best, that the American Constitution did and does a better job providing for popular ratification—and thus a better job of achieving legitimacy—than does the Chinese Constitution. That is no small matter, of course, especially when the consent afforded by periodic elections is added in—although that consent pertains primarily to selecting those who exercise the powers of government, not to what those powers should be. But as noted earlier, the problem of achieving legitimacy through consent alone is intractable. And America's Founders understood that, which is why they spoke of government as a "necessary evil": necessary because the problems that arise when individuals try to secure their own rights, outside of common institutions of justice, are themselves intractable; yet evil because those who do not wish to come under common, government rule—those who oppose ratification—are nonetheless forced to be so ruled, as a practical matter. In the end, then, George Washington got it right when he said that "government is not reason, it is not eloquence, it is force" (quoted in Wilstach 1924: 526).

2. A Program for Limited Government. Once we recognize, however, that government is a forced association, that no matter how extensive the provisions for popular consent may be, they will always fall well short of the kind of consent we would expect in, say, an ordinary contractual arrangement, we can look for other, more substantive indicia of legitimacy. In doing so, however, the conclusion drawn from an inquiry into consent has an important implication that needs to be noticed: if government is indeed a forced association—due to the problems of achieving consent—then one wants to do as little as possible through government, through the public sector, where forced association is inescapable, and as much as possible through the private sector, where things can be done voluntarily and thus in violation of the rights of no one. If minimizing coercion and respecting rights are fundamental concerns in the search for legitimacy, that is a profoundly important implication. Government is necessary. But if it is limited in what it does, then the forced association that necessarily characterizes it can be minimized.

That view—that healthy skepticism about government, rooted both in experience and in the theoretical concerns just discussed—imbued America's Founders as they sat down to draft a Constitution 11 years after they wrote the Declaration of Independence. The central problem facing them was to design a government that was strong enough to do the things it needed to do—especially by way of securing rights, its principal function—yet was not so powerful or extensive as to violate rights in the process. Toward that end, the document they drafted, once ratified, authorized government and governmental powers, then checked and balanced those powers through a series of extraordinarily thoughtful measures.

At the heart of the plan, however, was the doctrine of enumerated powers. The Preamble of the Constitution sets the premise for the doctrine: "We the People," for the purposes listed, "do ordain and establish this Constitution." All power, again, comes from the people. But as a reflection of the principles of the Declaration, the power the people give to government, to exercise on their behalf, is strictly limited. In fact, the very first sentence of Article I, following the Preamble, implies as much: "All legislative Powers herein granted shall be vested in a Congress." By implication, not all powers were "herein granted." And that is borne out in section 8 of Article I, where the powers of Congress are enumerated and thus, by implication, limited. But just to make the point clear beyond any doubt, when the Bill of Rights was added to the Constitution two years after the Constitution was ratified, the Tenth Amendment, the final member of that Bill of Rights, recapitulated the point and, with it, the constitutional philosophy of the Founders: "The powers not delegated to the United States by the Constitution, nor prohibited by it to the States, are reserved to the States respectively, or to the people." Plainly, only certain powers were delegated or granted by the people. Those powers were then enumerated in the Constitution. The rest were reserved to the states—or to the people, never having been granted to either level of government.

The contrast between that approach to constitutionalism and the Chinese approach could not be more stark. Both constitutions begin

346

at the same place—with power in the hands of people. But whereas the Chinese Constitution transfers that power, in its entirety, from the people to the government—while maintaining the façade of democratic decisionmaking, to be sure—the American Constitution delegates only certain limited powers to the national government, which are then enumerated, while leaving most with the states or the people. The key to understanding the American Constitution, then, is not through its Bill of Rights, which was added only two years later. Rather, it is through the doctrine of enumerated powers. Americans gave their government only certain things to do. The rest they left to be done by the states—or, far more so, by themselves, in their private capacities. They did not want government managing "economic, cultural, and social affairs," because they knew that that would be the end of freedom. They wanted to manage those affairs themselves, free from government interference.

There were many other restraints on power that the Founders put in the Constitution, of course: the separation of powers among the three branches of government, defined functionally, with power pitted against power; a bicameral legislature, with each chamber differently constituted; provision for judicial review of the acts of the political branches by an independent judiciary, among many such checks; a Bill of Rights; and periodic elections—to name just a few. The important thing to notice, however, is that each of those is in fact a restraint. The American approach was not to facilitate active government dedicated to accomplishing great ends. Quite the contrary, it was to empower limited government for limited ends, and then to check that power as much as possible. The great danger, the Founders understood, lay not in allowing individuals to be free but in allowing government to be free. Individuals were meant to be free; they were born free; *they* were the source of a nation's greatness, not the government.

To return to the question of legitimacy, then, as a formal matter, the American Constitution enjoys such legitimacy as it finds in the fact that it was ratified to the extent that it was: the powers it contains, and only those powers, were thus "authorized" from the outset. As a substantive matter, it enjoys the legitimacy that comes from its leaving individuals free to enjoy their rights to life, liberty, and the pursuit of happiness. (Notice, the Constitution does not "permit" individuals to be free. They already have their freedom.) American citizens pursue happiness in an infinite variety of ways—by working, acquiring property, creating businesses, raising families, and on and on, all without government managing those activities for them. It is a just system of government. And by leaving the productive power of individual self-interest largely free, it is an efficient system, one that maximizes economic productivity.

A Transition from Freedom?

Notwithstanding the manifest virtues of the American approach to government, many changes have taken place in the more than two centuries that have passed since the Constitution was ratified. And many of those changes, especially in the 20th century, have reduced rather than expanded freedom. For the purpose of applying the principles of the American Constitution to the Chinese context, therefore, it would be useful to review briefly a few of those changes.[2]

Without question, the most important change came in the 1930s, during the New Deal Era, in the form of the demise of the doctrine of enumerated powers, the centerpiece of the Constitution, at the hands of the Supreme Court. The impetus for that change came earlier, however, during the Progressive Era at the turn of the century. It was then that many Americans, especially "progressive" Americans, stopped thinking of government as a necessary evil and started thinking of it as an "engine of good"—an institution for solving all manner of social and economic problems. Like the thinking that underlies the Chinese Constitution, Progressive Era thought called for expansive government aimed at accomplishing great things—not by individual initiative, motivated by self-interest, but by government direction, motivated by the "common good." Unfortunately, for that school of thought, the Constitution authorized only limited government, and so the efforts of the progressives to use public power, usually at the state level, to pursue their grand ends were most often frustrated by the courts, especially the Supreme Court, which applied the principles of the Constitution to find those schemes unconstitutional.

With the coming of the Great Depression in the 1930s, however, the focus of the progressives shifted to the federal level. Still, the Court resisted those efforts—until President Roosevelt, early in 1937,

---

[2]I have discussed the issues that follow more fully in Pilon (1993).

threatened to pack the Court with six additional members. Not even Congress would go along with the scheme. Nevertheless, the Court got the message. It started rethinking its conception of the Constitution. And the result was the demise of the doctrine of enumerated powers.

What happened, essentially, was this. Two broadly worded clauses in the Constitution—the General Welfare Clause and the Commerce Clause—were reinterpreted by the Court. Written primarily to be shields against power, they were stood on end by the Court, which turned them into swords of power. Through the reinterpreted General Welfare Clause, Congress was given a vast redistributive power—which has led to the modern American welfare state. Through the reinterpreted Commerce Clause, Congress was given a vast regulatory power—which has led to the modern American regulatory state. Then a year later the Court reinterpreted the Bill of Rights, relegating property and contract rights—the foundations of the free-enterprise system—to a kind of second-class status. With that, the complex web of protections against overweening government that the Founders had established was largely eviscerated from the Constitution.

Not surprisingly, American government has grown exponentially in the wake of those changes. By world standards, it is still relatively limited. But by the standards of the Constitution—as understood by lawyers and laymen alike for some 150 years—it is largely unlimited. It is no surprise either that the problems of corruption and self-dealing that one would expect to find under conditions of ubiquitous government are to be found in America today. Most prominently, the penchant for middle-class majorities to use the political process to provide themselves with benefits paid for by the upper and lower classes has a thousand variations—none more prominent, perhaps, than public higher education, which the upper classes often avoid and the lower classes often fail to qualify for. Less prominent, but more common and more insidious, is the penchant for special interests to work the system to gain concentrated benefits for themselves, the costs of which are widely dispersed and thus little noticed by the many, except in the form of aggregate taxes (Gwartney and Wagner 1988: 19–23).

All of this is the result of the essentially unbridled democracy that followed in the wake of the New Deal court, which is exactly what one should expect when substantive restraints on democratic decisionmaking have been lifted and any subject is a proper candidate for a vote. The tyranny of the majority follows. More commonly, it is the tyranny of special interests who have learned to work the levers of power within the majoritarian system. Independent courts are supposed to restrain such tyranny under the American system of government. But when the tools that would otherwise enable them to do that have been removed from the Constitution, the courts end up deferring to the political branches. Thus, democracy, by itself, is no guarantee of liberty or prosperity. In fact, as philosophers from antiquity to the present have understood, an unbridled democracy may be one of the fastest routes to both tyranny and poverty.

In recent years, however, many more Americans have come to appreciate such issues than seemed to a half-century and more ago. Thus, the Supreme Court today is taking something of a fresh look at the jurisprudence of the New Deal—in a tentative way, to be sure—and the Congress, to say nothing of state governments, is much less enamored of government programs and government planning than it was 20 years ago—to say nothing of 60 years ago. Most importantly, however, the climate of ideas among the general public has noticeably changed in the direction of greater suspicion of government. Whether those recent changes will end America's transition from freedom and head the nation back toward freedom remains to be seen, but the sighs for several years have been pointing increasingly in the direction of restoring freedom.

Applications to China

Thus, in both America and China—and most other parts of the world, for that matter—the trend in recent years has been toward greater freedom. And the reason is obvious. The great socialist experiments of the 20th century have all failed—invariably at tragic human cost. The world has learned from bitter experience the truths that Hayek and a few others, a half-century and more ago, were teaching from reason: that human freedom not only is right but is the wellspring of human prosperity; and that efforts to politically plan and manage a society toward prosperity are doomed to end in tyranny and poverty.

What then is to be done about the Chinese situation? The first thing to be said is that only the Chinese can address their situation,

350

although they can certainly take counsel from others in the process. Yet it is hard to believe that there is anyone in China today who does not understand that the improvements there over the past 20 years are due to anything but the increased measure of freedom that has been allowed. If that is so, then the only question remaining is how to expand that freedom—and the prosperity that follows it— in a secure way, how to insure that the expansion takes root in secure institutions.

On such matters, nothing can be sure, of course. Nonetheless, certain general conclusions can be drawn from the analysis above. The first, and most important, is simply a restatement of what has just been said, namely, that prosperity comes not from government planning but from individual initiative, motivated by self-interest, fairly narrowly understood, but constrained by the rights of others to pursue their own self-interest. Thus, legal affairs must be arranged in a way that both encourages and restrains the individual pursuit of self-interest—the pursuit of happiness. That means that private property must be encouraged by being legally protected. And contracts of all kinds must be allowed and protected, for none of us knows, *a priori*, which agreements will prove beneficial and which not—even if the parties to an agreement inevitably believe that their contract will prove beneficial. With that—property, broadly understood as life, liberty, and estate; and contract—one has the legal foundation of a free market—and of a free society (Epstein 1995).

As noted earlier, China's Civil Law of 1986 and Economic Contract Law of 1993 are already moving in the right direction, even if they are still too heavy with a socialist overlay. The Constitution, however, is another matter. Even after the revisions of 1993, it is a dated relic of a bygone age, a shell that is increasingly ignored in practice— even if its bite remains very real for those who run afoul of it in selected ways.

In thinking about a new constitution, then, one wants to think first not about democracy but about getting the government out of the business of running the business of life. The Chinese people are fully capable of planning and living their own lives, as they have demonstrated for centuries under less officious governments around the world—and as they have demonstrated for 20 years on the mainland. Well more than half the battle would be won if that step alone were taken. There is simply no need to "plan socialism." There is a need to allow freedom.

Beyond that, it is a matter of mechanics—and there, experience is the best guide. Regarding those functions that government must or should perform, in most cases dispersed power is better than central power; but central power can be a check on dispersed power—to insure that it is performing as it should. Similarly, democracy is a check on power; but for all the reasons cited above, it too needs to be checked, especially by limiting the things open to democratic decisionmaking. Such limits will reduce democratic corruption, of course, and they will reduce official corruption as well. But they need to be spelled out in a judicially enforced constitution—and precisely spelled out, as the American experience with broad language should teach.

At the end of the day, then, the answer is, as it has always been, liberty, secured by a constitution grounded in the rule of law, not in the rule of man. If China is to continue on its present course, it will need a constitution of liberty.

References

AWSJ (1998) "China Rediscovers Hayek." *Asian Wall Street Journal*, 12 June.

Chen, K. (1998) "China to Test Waters of Political Reform: President Jiang Approves Study of New Models, Dabbling in Democracy." *Wall Street Journal*, 27 July: A11.

China News (1997) "Political System." *http://www.chinanews.org/China/17e6139p-5.html*.

"Constitution of the People's Republic of China–1993." http://www.quis.net/chinalaw/prccon5.htm.

Corwin, E. (1955) *The "Higher Law" Background of American Constitutional Law*. Ithaca, N.Y.: Cornell University Press.

Epstein, R.A. (1995) *Simple Rules for a Complex World*. Cambridge, Mass.: Harvard University Press.

FEER (1998) "Hayek's Children." *Far Eastern Economic Review*, 14 May: 82.

Gwartney, J.D., and Wagner, R.E. (1988) "Public Choice and the Conduct of Representative Government." In Gwartney and Wagner (eds.) *Public Choice and Constitutional Economics*, 3–28. Greenwich, Conn.: JAI Press.

Nathan, A. (1997) "U.S. Can't Ignore Beijing's Thuggery." *Wall Street Journal*, 27 June.

Nozick, R. (1974) *Anarchy, State, and Utopia*. Cambridge, Mass.: Harvard University Press.

Pilon, R. (1986) "The Systematic Repression of Soviet Jews." *Current Policy*, No. 878. Washington, D.C.: Bureau of Public Affairs, U.S. Dept. of State.

Pilon, R. (1992) "Individual Rights, Democracy, and Constitutional Order: On the Foundations of Legitimacy." *Cato Journal* 2 (3): 373–90.

Pilon, R. (1992/1993) "On the First Principles of Constitutionalism: Liberty, Then Democracy." *American University Journal of International Law and Policy* 8 (2, 3): 531–49.

Pilon, R. (1993) "Freedom, Responsibility, and the Constitution: On Recovering Our Founding Principles." *Notre Dame Law Review* 68 (3): 507–47.

Pomfret, J. (1998) "Chinese Action Sends a Chill: Detention of CEO Causes Investors to Wonder, Worry." *Washington Post*, 24 July: F1.

Ramundo, B.A. (1978) "The Brezhnev Constitution: A New Approach to Constitutionalism?" *Journal of International Law and Economics* 13 (1): 41–108.

U.S. Department of State (1998) China Country Report on Human Rights Practices for 1997. Washington, D.C.: Bureau of Democracy, Human Rights, and Labor.

Wilstach, F.J. (1924) *A Dictionary of Similes*, 2nd. ed. Boston: Little, Brown, and Co.

23. Simple Tax Rules for China

Stephen Moore

Fundamentals of a Sound Tax System

The purpose of this paper is to offer some simple rules for devising a tax system that promotes economic growth and individual freedom. This paper will not discuss the proper level of taxation for China. As Nobel prize-winning economist Milton Friedman has taught us, the real level of taxation in an economy is the amount the government spends. Hence, the only way to reduce the true tax burden—properly defined—in a nation is to cut government spending. There is very little debate that the size of state ownership and public expenditures are well above the level that would maximize the economic well being of the citizens of China—just as is the case in the United States and Europe—and indeed in virtually all nations, today.

The simple tax reform rules outlined in this paper are based on lessons that have been learned across the globe, particularly in the 1980s and 1990s. In many ways the way that economists and policymakers think about taxes has changed quite considerably since the late 1970s. Twenty years ago the conventional wisdom among public finance economists and policy advisers was that taxes are not a key factor in determining the prosperity of nations. Now that view is as outdated as the theory of a flat earth.

We now know that taxes don't just matter—they matter a lot. The spectacular expansion of world trade, the telecommunications and computer-age revolution that is making national boundaries less and less significant, the increasing mobility of human capital, and the growth and sophistication of global capital markets are all factors that are commanding politicians to form a renewed appreciation for the importance of getting the tax policies right.

Stephen Moore is Director of Fiscal Policy Studies at the Cato Institute.

Every nation in the world today can be thought of as being engaged in a frenetic race for global capital. Investment and human capital are the only two truly scarce resource in the world today. These sources of capital are the engines of productive and wealth-creating economies. Investment capital is impervious to national boundaries—capital flows instantaneously across national borders to where it is treated most kindly. The Great Wall of China could be built 100 feet tall and it would be incapable of repelling capital or capturing it.

A nation's tax policies are one key determinant of where investment capital will migrate because capital is in a continuous search for its highest after-tax rate of return. Nations that move aggressively toward adopting pro-growth tax policies will be rewarded with steady inflows of capital as investors vote with their money in affirmation of those tax rules. Similarly, the financial markets can instantly and severely punish any nation—developed or developing—that attempts to adopt confiscatory or anti-capital taxes.

What then are the simple tax rules that China should adopt to continue to attract capital and encourage domestic savings, investment, risk-taking, and wealth creation? Experience from around the world with tax reform suggests the following nine basic rules for success:

1. Tax rates should be low and ideally should be applied at a single flat rate.
2. All income should be taxed once, and only once. Taxes should not punish savings and investment.
3. The tax rate on capital gains and estates should be zero.
4. Taxes should be highly visible to the electorate.
5. The value-added tax should be avoided. It has had disastrous consequences in virtually every nation where it has been adopted.
6. The tax code should be fully indexed for inflation to protect taxpayers against stealth tax increases.
7. The tax system should be stable with voting rules requiring a supermajority to raise tax rates.
8. Tax simplicity should be adopted as a principal virtue of a sound tax system.
9. A sound tax system should be easy to administer and enforce. It should vigilantly protect the rights and civil liberties of the taxpayer.

No nation has adopted a tax system that conforms with everyone of the nine simple rules of reform. Europe and the United States violate many of the simple rules described above. They do not generally have tax systems that are worth emulating.

China's tax system in particular violates many of these nine basic tenets of a sound tax system (see Gao 1997). It does not apply a single low rate; it double taxes certain types of income (particularly foreign-source income); there is no super-majority threshold requirement for raising taxes; the system is not simple; and the system incorporates an European-style value-added tax. To its credit, the Chinese tax system does not tax estates or accumulated wealth. And the administrative costs are not excessive, nor is tax collection overly intrusive. But on balance, China's tax system impedes economic growth. The Chinese government could raise the same amount of revenue with a significantly less distortive tax system.

The place with the most efficient tax system in the world today is probably Hong Kong. Hong Kong has a de facto 15 percent flat-rate income tax system. It is simple—with less than 200 pages to the code. It does not generally tax investment and savings. The average tax rate on middle income families is less than 5 percent. The system has been remarkably stable since it was adopted in 1947. Its tax collection agency is small, but efficient—demonstrating a truism of public finance that low rates and voluntary compliance go hand in hand. This simple, flat rate income tax has been one of the major propellers of Hong Kong's spectacular economic expansion of the past half-century. The low and stable tax rates, coupled with a regime of free and open trade, has been a leading factor in the huge inflow of international capital in recent decades.

The ideal tax reform for China would be to repeal its current tax system in its entirety and adopt the Hong Kong tax model as its own. The flat tax rate that would be required in China to raise as much revenue as the current tax code would undoubtedly need to be higher than the current 15 percent rate in Hong Kong (which is why China needs to couple tax reform with a reduction in the size of government), but the important step is to implement a stable, pro-growth tax system.

One reform model worth consideration would be to adopt the Hong Kong flat tax as an alternative tax. Under this concept, every Chinese worker and business would have the freedom to choose

357

between the standard Chinese tax system or the alternative, simple flat tax on gross income. This approach would have two potential advantages. First, it would neutralize political opposition to reform by allowing powerful special interest groups with a vested stake in the current system to preserve the special deductions and loopholes they benefit from. Second, adopting the Hong Kong system as an alternative, rather than a replacement, would eliminate the complications and economic displacement costs associated with transitioning from one tax system to another.

In summary, to comply with the simple rules for an efficient tax system, China should:

- Establish a Hong Kong-type flat rate tax on consumption, either as a replacement or alternative to the entire current tax code. The current income tax rate of 45 percent plus should be chopped to a maximum of 25 percent. This rate could be achieved by expanding the base through elimination of deductions, credits, and other loopholes.
- Eliminate the 33 percent capital gains tax.
- Immediately repeal the 17 percent value-added tax.
- Enact a taxpayer's bill of rights. This "bill of rights" should include guarantees to investors and workers against future tax rate increases except for times of extreme national emergency; protections against seizures of private (including foreign-owned) property by the tax collection agency; a secure listing of privacy rights for the taxpayer; a presumption of taxpayer innocence in tax disputes; freedom from discrimination in the tax laws against foreign businesses, workers, and investors.

Global Tax Trends: Flatter and Simpler

In their pioneering book on the new global-age economy, *Quicksilver Capital*, economists Richard McKenzie and Dwight Lee (1991) note, "We now see governments acting more like market rivals in their struggle to retain and expand their capital bases. We see them selecting policies more strategically—that is, with greater concern for the international consequences of their actions, with more care, with less abandon, with greater concern for economic efficiency, and with a longer term view." The tax system is unquestionably one of the most critical of these strategic policies that determine whether a nation will successfully attract capital into its borders and promote growth.

The global trend over the past 20 years has been almost exclusively in the direction of lower income tax rates. The confiscatory tax policies of the 1970s, with tax rates of 70, 80, and even 90 percent, are almost nonexistent in developed nations today. Since 1980, corporate and personal income tax rates have been chopped down like dead trees in a forest in almost all industrialized nations and in a growing number of developing countries as well. In the United States, the top tax rate has fallen from 70 percent to 40 percent. In the United Kingdom, the top tax rate has fallen by half: from 83 to 40 percent.

Tax systems have also become much less steeply progressive in terms of the number of tax rates. A 1996 Price Waterhouse tax study (*The Economist* 1996: 106–7) shows that the number of personal income tax rates fell in every OECD nation, except Switzerland, from 1986 to 1995. The implication here is that income tax systems are flattening out over time. Progressivity of the income tax code is increasingly achieved through a generous exemption amount—or what is sometimes called the zero bracket. Price Waterhouse reports that with the exception of the Netherlands, all other OECD nations exempt the first $10,000 to $30,000 in income earned for a typical family.

A 1997 study by the Alexis de Tocqueville Institution in Washington, D.C., has documented that flat rate tax systems are no longer the rarity they once were. Out of a survey of 86 nations, it reported that 80 percent of corporate income tax codes are flat and half of capital gains taxes are flat. Flat tax personal income tax structures, like the Hong Kong model, are still the exception, however. Only about one in five nations has adopted a flat rate personal income tax system. Still, the report's conclusions are worth repeating: "Taking the major economies of the world as a whole, and analyzing how different kinds of income are treated, reveals that progressive taxation is far from dominant. In tax terms, the world is flatter than many people think" (Fossedal and Carey 1997).

How Do China's Tax Rates Compare?

Before we can establish simple tax rules for China, it is worth examining how China's tax system compares to that of other nations.[1]

---

[1]The discussion of China's tax system is based on Deloitte and Touche (1996).

The Chinese tax system was most recently reformed effective January 1, 1994. Is China's current set of tax policies and rates competitive with those of rival nations? The answer is mixed. We have to look at the whole range of taxes imposed in China where we generally find tax rates that are slightly higher than average (Johnson and Sheehy 1996: 132).

Personal Income Taxes

The single most important tax from an economic perspective is the personal income tax. The top personal income tax rate in China was once 55 percent but has recently been cut to 45 percent. The average top income tax rate today for developed nations is between 40 and 50 percent—though many Asian nations' highest tax rate is now well below 40 percent. For developing nations the typical top income tax rate exceeds 50 percent. China has nine income tax brackets—ranging from 5 to 45 percent. Measured in this way, the income tax structure is far more graduated than most competitor nations. On balance, China's income tax system ranks average at best among all nations in terms of capital friendliness and well below the standard of many of its principal Asian competitors.

Corporate Income Taxes

China's corporate income tax rate is 33 percent (30 percent plus 3 plus add-on local tax). Still, a number of nations have corporate income tax rates below 25 percent. Moreover, when considering that China also imposes several other related business taxes, such as a 3 to 5 percent business tax on labor services and the transfer of tangible or intangible assets, business taxes in the PRC appear to be slightly higher than the world average.

Capital Gains Tax

The capital gains tax rate on the sale of property and other assets in China is 20 percent. The average for most industrialized nations (data are hard to come by for the developing nations) is between 20 and 25 percent.

Estate and Gift Taxes

There are no explicit wealth or death taxes in China, according to a recent international comparison study conducted by the Center for the Study of Taxation in the United States. This is a highly advantageous policy with respect to capital flows. In some developed nations, such as the United States and Japan, the death tax rate can exceed 50 percent.

Value-Added Tax (VAT)

The VAT tax rate in China is 17 percent. This tax is imposed on the sale of goods, many services, and most goods imported into China. The VAT tax rate on exported goods is zero. The 17 percent VAT tax rate is above the average for most nations with this consumption tax.

Taxation of Foreign Enterprises and Investors

China has improved its tax code with respect to harmonizing the tax treatment of domestic firms with foreign enterprises, which in part accounts for the boon in foreign investment. But improvement is still needed in creating tax parity between foreign investment and domestic businesses, particularly in industries that compete directly with state-owned enterprises.

On balance, China's personal income tax, corporate income tax, and VAT tax rates are somewhat above average. There are vast opportunities to shift to a simpler and smarter tax system that minimizes the disincentive effects of high rates, but raises the same amount of revenues.

Tax Rules for China: Simple, Flat, and Fair

In this section, we review the nine simple tax rules that increase economic growth and freedom. These rules can be applied to all nations, but this section places special emphasis on their application to China.

Tax Rule 1

Tax rates should be low and ideally applied at a single flat rate. Across the globe, lower tax rates have translated into faster economic growth. The incontrovertible evidence of this favorable tax-cutting effect can be seen with the naked eye. The United States moved from a capital exporting nation to a net capital importer beginning in the early 1980s when income tax rates were cut from 70 percent to 50 percent, and then still further to 28 percent. Since the early

1980s, net capital investment in the United States has exceeded $500 billion. Over that time period the United States has created 20 million new jobs and has reasserted its leadership in many strategic industries. China, too, by privatizing state enterprises and lowering tax rates has had astounding success attracting foreign investment.

High, and in some cases confiscatory, tax rates can have the opposite effect. When a nation's income tax rates exceed 40 to 50 percent they tend to repel the very capital investment that serves as the corn seed for future sustained economic expansion. This has been a problem especially in the welfare-state economies of Europe.

A 1992 study by economist Charles Plosser of the University of Rochester (Plosser 1992) found a strong relationship between tax rates and economic growth from 1960 to 1989 among OECD nations. Plosser discovered a negative correlation (-0.52) between the GDP growth rate in these nations and their average tax rate on income and profits. His study suggests that high marginal tax rates on personal income and corporate profits are a drag on economic development.

Economist Alan Reynolds of the Hudson Institute has updated this research through the early 1990s and derives similar findings. Reynolds (1996) found that of 20 industrialized nations examined, "The economies of countries that reduced tax rates grew at four times the pace (5.1 percent annual GDP growth per capita) of those that did not (1.4 percent)." Reynolds concludes: "Many of the recent economic miracles were in dire economic straits before tax rates started coming down. The economies of South Korea, Mauritius, and Jamaica were falling fast in the early 1980s. And more recent economic basket cases such as Peru and Bolivia have likewise shown dramatic improvement since slashing high tax rates."

Nations with flat tax systems appear to be recording the most impressive economic performance of all. The Alexis de Tocqueville Institution has compared the growth rates of the 11 nations with flat rate income tax systems with non-flat tax nations. The flat-tax countries had per capita GDP growth from 1982 to 1997 of 2.1 percent. The mildly progressive tax code nations had growth of 1.4 percent. The highly progressive tax code nations actually regressed, with a negative with a growth rate of -0.2 percent.

Competition among nations is the natural motivating force behind the decline in tax rates around the world (Moore 1997). As Vito

Tanzi, fiscal affairs director at the International Monetary Fund, has observed, "Highly progressive statutory tax rates have rarely resulted in highly progressive effective tax systems." The nations that have responded most aggressively to the new global reality that low tax rates are conducive to wealth creation seem to be reaping the benefits of more rapid wealth creation and prosperity.

Tax Rule 2

All income should be taxed once, and only once. Taxes should not punish savings and investment. A standard rule in public finance literature is that a well-structured tax system has a broad tax base combined with a low tax rate. The tax base should be neutral with respect to savings and investment. Most income tax systems, including China's, fail on two counts. First, they tend to punish the savings decision vis-à-vis consumption. And second, the tax code tries to pick winners and losers. By exempting some industries or activities from tax, the tax base shrinks and others pay higher rates.

Consider a capital investment that will harvest a 10 percent stream of income over its lifetime. If that income stream is subject to a 40 percent tax rate, then the actual after-tax rate of return on the investment falls to 6 percent. In a competing nation where that same investment may yield only an 8 percent annual return but where the tax rate is 20 percent, the after-tax rate return of 6.4 percent is higher. All other factors equal, the investment will take place in the latter nation. But now assume that the income stream in the first country is taxed twice. The rate of return is lowered from 6 percent to 3.6 percent. With nearly two-thirds of the rate of return diminished through taxes, the investment is foregone.

Most nations today, including China, could realize a huge economic windfall by moving toward a tax system that taxes all income once, and only once. Harvard economist Dale Jorgenson (1991) calculates that incomes would rise by about 9 percent ($2,000 per household) in the United States if it were to shift to a broad-based, low-rate tax system, and the U.S. government could collect roughly the same amount of tax revenues.

Tax Rule 3

The tax rate on capital gains and estates should be zero. Capital gains taxes, death taxes, wealth taxes, and corporate income taxes are all forms of double taxation of saving and investment. They each retard capital accumulation and long-term economic growth.

Taxing capital is economically self-defeating because capital is the engine of a growing economy. It has been estimated that almost half of the growth of the American economy between 1948 and 1980, for example, was directly attributable to the increase in capital formation (with most of the rest a result of increases and improvements in the labor force—that is, improvements in human capital).

Most people think of capital as money—the dollars invested in the stock market or in a new business. But it is wrong to think of capital as just financial assets. Capital refers also to physical investment—the plant, the factory, the forklifts, the computers, the fax machines, and other factors of production that make a business operate efficiently. Capital formation is essential to generating higher incomes for a nation's workers. The world's farmers and manufacturing workers have become more productive and their real wages have climbed as the ratios of capital per worker has risen. Between 1900 and 1990, real wages in Europe and the United States have risen about five-fold. In other words, a worker today earns as much in 12 minutes as a worker in 1900 earned in an hour. What explains this surge in the living standards of the American worker? The short answer is capital and productivity.

Over the past 50 years, 90 percent of the fluctuation in wages in most industrial countries is explained by the capital-to-labor ratio. When the ratio rises, wages rise; when the ratio flattens, wages stagnate. Here is a modern example. If a worker in an industrialized nation works with a computer, his wage is about 20 percent higher than an equally skilled worker without one. The disparity is even higher in developing nations.

Increasing the return on capital via tax reduction often generates misplaced criticism as a tax cut for the rich. But studies have shown that as much as 80 percent of the returns to capital are captured by labor, and only 20 percent go to the owners of capital.

In sum, capital taxes are economically counterproductive. A pro-growth tax policy for China should remove tax penalties against investment. In China this could begin by abolishing the capital gains tax.

Tax Rule 4

Taxes should be highly visible to the electorate. One of the principal functions of a tax system is to "price" government goods and services. The price of government should be readily apparent to the receivers of government services—that is, the taxpaying public. If the price of government is felt by the taxpayers, they can then determine whether they are getting their money's worth from government enterprises. Ideally, taxes should not be hidden; they should be visible to the public.

Corporate taxes are often hidden because businesses simply pass them on to consumers in the form of higher prices. Employer-paid payroll taxes, withholding taxes, and VAT taxes are also undesirable because they are hidden from workers and consumers. Finally, budget deficits are the ultimate form of invisible taxation. James M. Buchanan won a Nobel prize in economics for pointing out that deficits create a "fiscal illusion" whereby voters approve more government than they would otherwise wish to pay for. The absence of a balanced-budget requirement means that taxpayers can purchase $1.00 worth of government for, say 75 cents in taxes.

Tax Rule 5

The value-added tax should be avoided. Another universal tax lesson from around the globe over the past quarter century is the danger of the VAT. Beginning in the mid-1960s many European nations began to experiment with the value-added tax. A VAT is a consumption-based tax that is imposed at each stage of the production of goods and services in the economy. By 1990 the value-added tax had been implemented in 19 developed countries of the world. Ten developed countries did not have a VAT. Subsequently, Japan and Canada have adopted the VAT, as has China.

The arguments commonly made in favor of the VAT are as follows: (1) As a tax on consumption, the VAT may have a positive impact on savings rates; (2) the VAT can raise significant revenues to close budget deficits; (3) the VAT can improve a nation's balance of trade because it is imposed on imports; and (4) the VAT can be used to reduce or eliminate more destructive types of taxes now imposed, such as income taxes.

On balance, experience with the VAT in Europe and Asia has shown these to be false promises. The VAT has had highly adverse economic consequences in most nations where it has been adopted. The problems with the VAT include:

1. *Countries with VATs are virtually all very high-spending nations.* Government spending averages 53 percent of GDP in the OECD nations with a VAT, but only 36 percent of GDP in the OECD nations without a VAT (OECD 1993). In sum, the VAT is the revenue source of choice in those nations with the very largest and most bureaucratic states.

2. *With very few exceptions, the introduction of a VAT has led to subsequent government growth.* Governments consumed 35 percent of GDP on average in countries when VATs were introduced, but by 1988 government consumed 41.1 percent of GDP. In 1970 the average tax burden in EEC countries, where VATs are common, was 30 percent of GDP, but it has grown steadily to 41 percent today (Moore 1997).

It is instructive to compare the growth of government in Europe and the United States since the mid-1960s, when VATs were first implemented in Europe. Although this was a period of rising tax burdens in the United States, the growth of government was half of what it was in Europe (18 percent versus 39 percent).

3. *VAT rates are almost always ratcheted upward from the initial rate.* At the time they were adopted, VAT revenues in OECD countries were about 6 percent of GDP. By 1988, the VAT tax burden was on average 33 percent higher, or 8 percent of GDP. The burden of other types of taxes did not fall in these nations. In fact, total taxes as a share of GDP rose from 35 to 41 percent after introduction of the VAT.

4. *There is no evidence that savings rates have been raised in nations that have adopted VATs.* One of the principal arguments made in favor of a VAT is that it would lift America's very low savings rate. The evidence from abroad does not support this contention. In 1990, economists Ken Militzer and Ilona Ontscherenki published a study in *Business Economics* that documents this non-relationship. Militzer and Ontscherenki compared VAT and sales tax revenues in a nation as a share of GDP versus the national savings rate for 23 OECD nations in 1986. The authors report their findings as follows:

> There is no statistically significant relationship between the relative use of consumption taxes, or of VAT and retail sales taxes, and the rate of savings in these countries. . . . We ran the same regressions for data for 1965, 1970, 1975, and 1985.

> In no case, however, did we find a statistically significant positive relationship between consumption taxes and savings rates, or between VAT and retail sales taxes and savings [Militzer and Ontscherenki 1990: 32–3].

Almost all of these pitfalls of the VAT stem from the hidden nature of the tax. A principle of sound tax policy is that taxes be visible to the taxpayer. Although the VAT is incorporated eventually into the final price paid by the consumer, unlike a sales tax, it is not charged at the cash register. Rather, it is paid at each stage of production by each business that "adds value" to the product or service provided. The taxpaying consumers are not fully aware of the tax they are actually paying when they purchase goods and services.

It would appear that the primary beneficiaries of VATs in Europe and Asia have not been business, workers, or taxpayers. The primary beneficiaries have been politicians and special interest groups who have successfully staked a claim on the money raised from the tax, in order to expand the size of state ownership and control of economic resources. The unfavorable experience of Europe and Asia with a VAT over the past quarter century, to say nothing of the problems experienced by Canada and Japan with the VAT in recent years, indicates that this tax should be repealed in China.

Tax Rule 6

The tax code should be fully indexed for inflation to protect taxpayers against stealth tax increases. Another invisible and insidious tax is the inflation tax. Inflation is a thief that robs workers of the purchasing power of their pay checks. Inflation adds insult to injury when it pushes workers into higher tax brackets. The corporate and individual tax brackets in China are not indexed for inflation. This means that, over time, more and more workers will be unfairly pushed into the 35, 40, and 45 percent tax brackets.

The capital gains tax should also be indexed for inflation, if it is not abolished altogether. To understand how the capital gains inflation penalty distorts investment decisions, consider the following hypothetical case. If an investor made a $100,000 investment in Chinese companies in 1990 and sold the investments in 1997 for $200,000, the reported gain would be $100,000. If the capital gains tax was $25,000 on that investment and the inflation over that period was 80 percent, then the investor actually lost money, because the real gain was only $20,000, or $5,000 *less* than the tax paid. Hence, the tax rate adjusted for purchasing power on the investment is over 100 percent.

Since inflation is the result of the failure of a nation's central bank to properly control the money supply, the government should not collect a tax premium from its own bad policies.

Tax Rule 7

The tax system should be stable with voting rules requiring a supermajority to raise tax rates. Stability in the tax laws are conducive to long-term investment. Investors and business owners want and deserve assurances that the tax rules will not be rigged against them in the middle of the game. In the United States, the tax laws have been reformed or amended hundreds of times in the past decade alone. The only "winners" from such continual tax law changes are accountants and tax lawyers. The lesson: get the tax system right, and keep it that way.

Investors and entrepreneurs especially want assurances that taxes will not be raised on them on a routine basis. The legislature should adopt a rule that requires a two-thirds vote to enact any tax increase. This should apply to all taxes—the VAT, the income tax, the corporate income tax , tariffs, and other business taxes and excises. A two-thirds vote requirement for tax increases would allow the legislature to raise taxes during time of war or national crisis, but not to continuously fund expansions of government programs.

Tax Rule 8

Tax simplicity should be adopted as a principal virtue of a sound tax system. The simpler the tax system, the better. No nation's tax system can compete in terms of complications and special interest loopholes with the U.S. income tax code. It is a textbook case for how *not* to devise a tax policy. It is worth taking a moment to describe the complexities of the U.S. income tax system to demonstrate the deadweight economic loss that arises from layers upon layers of byzantine rules that are typically engrafted onto a tax system over the years.

In a hearing before the U.S. Congress, the chief tax counsel for Mobil Oil Corporation brought to the House office building a six-foot-high stack of bound papers. They weighed 150 pounds. These were Mobil Oil's tax forms for fiscal year 1993. It cost Mobil an estimated $15 million in costs with more than 100 full-time man-years just to figure how much taxes they owed. Mobil is not unique. In 1994 the IRS received nearly 1 billion tax forms as part of the government's effort to track income from dividends, interest, and other forms of business income. According to Robert Hall and Alvin Rabushka (1995: 5), the U.S. tax agency sends out eight billion pages of forms and instructions each year, which if you laid them end to end would stretch 28 times the circumference of the earth.

James L. Payne (1991) has calculated that American workers and businesses spend at least 5.4 billion man-hours a year figuring out their taxes. This is more man-hours than used to build every car, van, and truck manufactured in the United States. Estimates of the economic loss attributable to the complexity of the tax system range from $75–$200 billion a year, or as much as $2,000 for every household in America.

A fast-developing nation such as China should install a simple tax system that mitigates huge compliance costs. This is one of the premier advantages of the flat tax, which allows taxpayers to file their tax returns on a post card. A tax system that is easy to understand, comply with, and enforce constitutes a great comparative advantage for any nation in today's global economy.

Tax Rule 9

A sound tax system should be easy to administer and enforce. It should protect the rights and civil liberties of the taxpayer. Throughout history the tax collector has been the most feared and reviled of all government agents. Indeed, arguably the most troublesome consequence of modern-day income tax systems is that they often confer enormous investigative and prosecutorial powers to the tax agency. Basic rights of citizens are routinely subverted by tax collection agencies in the developed nations. Typically in most nations today, without a search warrant, the tax agency has the right to search the property and financial documents of American citizens. Without a trial, the tax collector has the right to seize private property. No nation can prosper without strict adherence to the rule of law. Often times for the sake of political expediency, politicians allow the rule of law to be compromised when it comes to collecting taxes.

Again, the United States is a model for China of how not to administer and enforce a tax system. The U.S. Internal Revenue

Service now has 115,000 employees. To put the size of this police force in perspective, the IRS has roughly the same number of employees as all other federal regulatory agencies. With the IRS, privacy rights are relegated to secondary status behind compliance enforcement. Fred Goldberg, commissioner of the IRS during the Bush administration, recently stated, "The IRS has become a symbol of the most intrusive, oppressive, and nondemocratic institution in our democratic society."

China evidently has the same kinds of tax enforcement problems and bureaucracies. The International Monetary Fund estimated in 1994 that there were 500,000 tax administrators in China (Tseng et al. 1994: 27). Even for a nation as populous as China, this is a huge workforce devoted to collection. This massive workforce does not create wealth; it is a creature of a tax system that is too complicated and intrusive.

A simple post-card return tax system with few exclusions and exemptions relieves the government tax collection agency of the burden of scrutinizing all of the fiduciary transactions that the taxpayer is engaged in. The invasiveness of the government audit function is substantially reduced—because there is so much less to audit. Moreover, the incentive to cheat or engage in tax evasion is proportionally diminished as the tax rate falls. For, example, the tax savings from hiding a dollar of income with a 40 percent tax rate is twice as high than if the tax rate is 20 percent. Lower tax rates mean greater tax compliance.

The Ideal: The Hong Kong Model

China does not have to look far to find an ideal tax system. Hong Kong's flat tax system—with its low rates, its low compliance costs, its simplicity, and its favorable treatment of capital and investment—is not perfect, but it is hard to beat (Johnson and Sheehy 1996: 162). The tens of billions of dollars of foreign investment in Hong Kong in the post-World War II era has been drawn to the island in no small part because of its adherence to the principles of free trade, its culture of free enterprise, and its simple, pro-growth tax system.

The Hong Kong tax system, first devised in 1947, has many attractive features:

370

- The flat rate tax is 15 percent of gross income with no deductions.
- The system protects the poor from tax by providing a generous "basic allowance" of roughly $8,333, plus a deduction for children, grandparents, and charitable contributions. This adds progressivity into the tax system. More than half of Hong Kong's workers pay no income tax.
- Hong Kong's businesses pay a 16.5 percent flat rate tax with virtually no deductions.
- Hong Kong is able to fund all of the important functions of government with only its flat rate income tax and a property tax. It routinely—15 of the last 20 years—runs a budget surplus. Tax revenues are about 18 percent of GDP in Hong Kong.
- Hong Kong has no withholding tax, no payroll tax, no value-added tax, no capital gains tax, no estate tax, and no tariffs. There is no double tax of saving and investment.
- Hong Kong's tax code is less than 200 pages long. By contrast, the U.S. tax code has more than 8,000 complicated forms and regulations.

As China continues its rapid and exciting transition to a market-based economy, the Hong Kong tax system should not just be preserved for the island, but should be expanded to the mainland as well. China should consider offering Chinese business owners and workers, and foreign investors also, the freedom to choose between the Hong Kong flat tax model and the current Chinese income tax. Many Chinese businesses and workers might even be willing to pay slightly more tax for a system that is taxpayer-friendly. Adopting the Hong Kong model would promote simplicity, efficiency, fairness, and growth. There is an adage in America that advises: don't reinvent the wheel. When it comes to tax reform, China does not have to reinvent the wheel—just borrow it from Hong Kong.

References

Deloitte and Touche (1996) *People's Republic of China. New York:* Deloitte and Touche, LLP.

The Economist (1996) "The Low Tax Guide." 21 December, 106–7.

Fossedal, G., and Carey, M. (1997) "It's a Flat, Flat, Flat Tax World." Alexis de Tocqueville Institution, Arlington, Va.

Gao, P. (1997) "China's Taxation and Tax System under Socialist Market Economic Conditions." *Zhongguo Shuiwo Bao,* 25 April.

Hall, R.E., and Rabushka, A. (1995) *The Flat Tax*. 2nd ed. Stanford, Calif.: Hoover Institution Press.

Johnson, B.T., and Sheehy, T.P. (1996) *1996 Index of Economic Freedom*. Washington, D.C.: Heritage Foundation.

Jorgenson, D. (1991) "Constructing an Agenda for U.S. Tax Reform." Testimony before the Ways and Means Committee, U.S. House of Representatives, 18 December.

McKenzie, R.B., and Lee, D.R. (1991) *Quicksilver Capital*. New York: The Free Press.

Militzer, K., and Ontscherenki, I. (1990) *Business Economics*

Moore, S.J. (1997) "The Global Supply-Side Revolution: A Progress Report." Laffer Associates, San Diego.

OCED (1993) *Taxation in OCED Countries*. Paris: OCED.

Payne, J.L. (1991) *Costly Returns: The Burden of the U.S. Tax System*. San Francisco: Institute for Contemporary Studies.

Plosser, C.I. (1992) "The Search for Growth." Bradley Policy Research Center, University of Rochester.

Reynolds, A. (1996) "It's Supply-Side Economics, Stupid." Hudson Institute Policy Bulletin, October.

Tseng, W.; Khor, H.E.; Kochhar, K.; Mihaljek, D.; and Burton, D. (1994) *Economic Reform in China: A New Phase*. Washington, D.C.: International Monetary Fund.

Comment

Reforming China's Fiscal System

Zhang Shuguang

Importance of Fiscal Reform

Fiscal reform is very important because the government's power to tax and spend affects the allocation of resources. China's fiscal reform is a critical part of overall economic restructuring and has exerted a widespread influence across the country. Since the 1980s, fiscal reform has taken the form of "division of income/expenditure and accounting at different levels"—or figuratively, "cooking meals at different kitchens"—which has led to a system of tax division since 1994. By means of this reform, China's local governments have acquired their own fiscal resources and been enabled to pursue their own interests. In other words, as their revenues grow, they can spend more, thus invest more, and their local economies will expand, which in turn generates more revenue.

For instance, Shanghai has spurred its booming economy thanks to Beijing's willingness to allow Shanghai to retain a larger share of its tax revenues since 1983 and to expand its autonomy since 1992. The rapid development of township and village enterprises, which has significantly contributed to China's prosperous economy, can also find its root in the growth of local financial power.

The success of China's reform does not come out of any intended blueprint. On the contrary, many reform measures have emerged under pressure of financial difficulties. For instance, in 1993, the government set free the price of grain and eliminated grain coupons because of the high cost of subsidizing the grain purchase/sale

Zhang Shuguang is Chairman of the Academic Committee at the Unirule Institute of Economics in Beijing. He is also Senior Fellow and Professor at the Institute of Economics at the Chinese Academy of Social Sciences.

system, which accounted for over 12 percent of government spending. The loosening of controls over the telecommunications sector occurred because the government could not afford to finance the sector's urgently needed expansion. Another example is the reform of state-owned enterprises (SOEs). The government has been grasping the large SOEs, ditching the small ones, and encouraging mergers and acquisitions—not only by solvent SOEs, but also by nonstate-owned enterprises. This is partially because of the rigid management system and heavy loss-making phenomenon of the SOEs, and partially because the central government is too weak to restructure them or even to sustain their survival as its tax revenue dwindles.

The reform of the fiscal system has achieved much progress, but there still remain problems that account for much chaos and misbehavior in the economy. The central government lacks sufficient revenue to maintain a high level of spending and has to allow local authorities the scope to seek extra revenues on their own account. As a result, various types of fund raising or apportionment have emerged that have substantially increased administrative control over economic affairs.

Major Problems in China's Fiscal System

Since the reform, a significant change in the functions of government at all levels has occurred, with the contraction of the traditional role of government in economic planning and the expansion of government's role as a provider of public goods. On the other hand, in order to speed up economic development, government officials, especially at the local level, have been heavily involved in infrastructure development. This fact, combined with dwindling fiscal revenues, has become a major problem and also a key issue in the current fiscal system.

Given that China's total tax revenue accounts for only 10 percent of GDP, plus the headlong pursuance of infrastructure development, many public goods are not able to be funded directly by tax revenue. Ordinarily this situation would result in a fiscal crisis. However, provincial and local governments have been able to mobilize funds from extra-budgetary sources, fund raising, and apportionment. Indeed, these three sources account for nearly one-third of total government discretionary funds.

374

The central government has been collecting revenues by every possible means and, at the same time, shifts its burden onto the banks. The government used to directly draw overdrafts from the banks, but now it asks banks to make loans to SOEs. Many SOEs are losing money, causing a rapid growth of nonperforming loans. The banking system is now shouldering the government's financial difficulties and is very difficult to reform. Financial risks are on the rise. Therefore, China's reform faces three major tasks: securing sufficient financing for public goods, reforming the banking system, and restructuring SOEs. The reform of the fiscal system should include reforming the tax system, creating a unified state budget, and restructuring the fiscal system.

Guidelines for China's Tax Reform

Stephen Moore (1998) suggests that China should adopt a simple tax system with a low rate and a broad base. I firmly appreciate his views. Some problems, however, need further discussion.

At present, China's tax system features a high marginal tax rate and weak enforcement of tax collection. A reduction in the marginal tax rate could possibly increase government revenue. For instance, before 1996 China's average tariff rate hit 35 percent. Yet owing to incidental tariff reduction/exemption and evasion, China actually levied a total tariff amounting to only 5 percent of total import value, somewhat commensurate with that of developed countries. In 1996, China lowered its average tariff rate to 23 percent, yet tariff revenue increased by more than 10 billion yuan compared with 1995.

Moore points out that the value-added tax is a defective tax. Surely, he is right. China needs to change from a value-added tax to an income tax. Presently, the value-added tax is used as the primary source of revenue in China because it can be levied more easily then an income tax, especially an individual income tax. In China, an individual does not declare and pay the income tax, instead the tax is deducted from one's income by the firm or organization to which one is affiliated. In recent years there has been a greater reliance on the individual income tax, but the amount of revenue collected is still a small proportion of the state's overall tax revenue.

Another important factor regarding the reform of China's fiscal system is that there should be an operational standardization and democratization in the financial system. Tax increases, for example, should be subject to taxpayer approval, and government spending should be supervised by taxpayers. Presently, the government's administrative expenditure grows faster than revenue because taxpayers are unable to supervise government expenditures.

Moore claims that Hong Kong's tax system is ideal for China. He argues that China could utilize Hong Kong's model of taxation and benefit from a unified low tax rate and a tax system that is simple to operate, raises sufficient revenue, protects the poor, avoids duplication, and is conducive to economic growth. His suggestion certainly makes sense. Yet, it is somewhat too idealistic. The mainland would like to learn from Hong Kong's tax system, particularly its basic principles. However, the mainland differs substantially from Hong Kong and must consider its own characteristics in implementing tax reform. The formation and evolution of Hong Kong's tax system depended on its unique conditions, many of which have never been experienced on the mainland. Thus, China cannot implant exactly what has been done in Hong Kong, but must create its own fiscal regime along with learning from the outside world.

Reference

Moore, S. (1998) "Simple Tax Rules for China." In J.A. Dorn (ed.) *China in the New Millennium: Market Reforms and Social Development*, chap. 23. Washington, D.C.: Cato Institute.

24. Sustainable Development: A Model for China?

Jerry Taylor

The Alarmists

The mantra of "sustainable development" is constantly on the lips of international agencies and non-governmental organizations engaged in assistance to lesser-developed countries. The concept seems innocuous enough; after all, who would favor "unsustainable development"? But the fundamental premise of the idea—that economic growth, if left unconstrained and unmanaged by the state, threatens unnecessary harm to the environment and may prove economically ephemeral—is dubious. Indeed, the policy prescriptions that are generally endorsed by those concerned about sustainable development are inimical to China's best environmental and economic interests.

This is so for three reasons:

- If economic growth were to be slowed or stopped—and sustainable development is essentially concerned with putting boundaries around economic growth—it would be impossible to improve the environmental conditions of China;
- The bias for central planning on the part of those endorsing the concept of sustainable development will only serve to make environmental protection more expensive, and hence, China will would be able to "purchase" less of it; and
- Strict pursuit of sustainable development, as many environmentalists mean it, would only do violence to the welfare of future generations.

Jerry Taylor is Director of Natural Resource Studies at the Cato Institute and Senior Editor of *Regulation* magazine.

The concept of sustainable development is an important milestone in environmental theory because it posits how society itself should be organized, not simply why environmental protections should be adopted or how best they can be implemented. James Sheehan of the Competitive Enterprise Institute sees it as "an overarching political philosophy merging the twin goals of conservation and controlled economic development" meant by many to be "the central organizing principle for a world of economically and ecologically interdependent nations" (Sheehan 1996: 1). Indeed, many advocates of sustainable development are quite open about the radical implications of the sustainable development. Says Monsanto's CEO Robert Shapiro, a strong proponent of the idea:

> Our nation's economic system evolved in an era of cheap energy and careless waste disposal, when limits seemed irrelevant. None of us today, whether we're managing a house or running a business, is living in a sustainable way. It's not a question of good guys and bad guys. There is no point in saying 'If only those bad guys would go out of business, then the whole world would be fine.' The whole system has to change. There is a huge opportunity for reinvention [quoted in Magretta 1997: 80-1].

Of course, just how much social and economic change is necessary to achieve sustainability depends upon how "unsustainable" one believes the present to be. Many clearly believe the present to be quite unsustainable and thus are prepared for radical change. Even a relative environmental moderate such as William Ruckelshaus, a Republican and two-time director of the U.S. Environmental Policy Agency, says approvingly:

> Can we move nations and people in the direction of sustainability? Such a move would be a modification of society comparable in scale to only two other changes: the agricultural revolution of the late Neolithic and the Industrial Revolution of the past two centuries. Those revolutions were gradual, spontaneous, and largely unconscious. This one will have to be a fully conscious operation, guided by the best foresight that science can provide—foresight pushed to its limit. If we actually do it, the undertaking will be absolutely unique in humanity's stay on the earth [Ruckelshaus 1994: 348].

Others are less alarmed and thus believe sustainability could be purchased as at somewhat less wrenching social and economic price. But one thing most sustainable development advocates agree upon is the tremendous threat that Chinese economic growth poses to global sustainability. Says Shapiro, "If emerging economies have to relive the entire industrial revolution with all its waste, its energy use, and its pollution, I think it's all over" (quoted in Magretta 1997: 87). Douglas Murray, former president of the China Institute and executive secretary of the Committee on International Relations with the People's Republic of China, considers China's environment an international, not a domestic, issue.

> For the health of the planet, and of the United States, China must be judged a vital American interest. The reasons are many and obvious, but still not widely appreciated. Though lacking an immediate, galvanizing crisis—Amazon fires, African famine, Chernobyl—China presents ecological problems so severe that they constitute a collective crisis with global consequences and powerful implications for America [Murray 1993: 1].

Megan Ryan and Christopher Flavin of the Worldwatch Institute agree: "The prospect of one-fifth of humanity suddenly entering the consumer age will force industrial countries. . .to face up to the unsustainability of their current practices. The world cannot afford to have another billion people driving around in big cars or eating fast food hamburgers" (Ryan and Flavin 1995: 129). The Chinese, it is widely agreed, cannot be allowed the luxuries of today's Western consumers.

Fortunately, those alarmists are wrong. It is the current Western system of (more-or-less) free markets that is the best hope for environmentally sustainable development. The agenda forwarded by the sustainable development lobby would ironically usher in the very environmental destruction that they hope to avoid by central planning.

What Is Sustainable Development?

Despite its institutionalization, sustainable development is rather difficult to define coherently. The United Nations Commission on Economic Development (UNCED), in its landmark 1987 report titled *Our Common Future*, defines sustainable development as that which "meets the needs of the present without compromising the ability of future generations to meet their own needs" (United Nations 1987: 8). But that definition is hopelessly problematic. How can we be reasonably expected to know, for instance, what the needs of people in 2100 might be? Moreover, one could point out that one way people typically "meet their own needs" is by spending money on food, shelter, education, and whatever else they deem necessary or important. Is the imperative for sustainable development, then, simply a euphemism for the imperative to create wealth (which, after all, is handed down to our children for their subsequent use)? True, there are human needs—such as the desire for peace, freedom, and individual contentment—that cannot be met simply by material means, but sustainable development advocates seldom dwell on the importance of those nonmaterial, non resource-based" psychological needs when discussing the concept of sustainable development.[1]

Thus, sophisticated proponents of an environmentally sustainable development path are forced to discard as functionally meaningless the UNCED definition. Otherwise, the UNCED definition can be read as a call for society to maximize human welfare over time. An entire profession has grown up around that proposition. They are known as "economists," and maximizing human welfare is known to them not as "sustainable development" but as "optimality." Few sustainable development advocates would be comfortable with the idea that Adam Smith's *The Wealth of Nations* was the world's first call for sustainable development.

Economists David Pearce and Jeremy Warford, two of the world's more serious thinkers about sustainable development, thus disclose that many advocates mean sustainable development to describe "a process in which the natural resource base is not allowed to deteriorate" (Pearce and Warford 1993: 8). This is generally known as the "strong" definition of sustainability. The "weak" definition allows the natural resource base to deteriorate as long as critical biological resources are maintained at a minimum critical level and the wealth generated by the exploitation of natural resources is preserved for future generations, who are otherwise "robbed" of their rightful inheritance. Natural resources are considered just another form of

---

[1] For a summary of the various economic, ecological, and socio-cultural conceptions of sustainable development, see Munasinghe (1993: 3).

capital. Weak sustainability, then, can be thought of as the amount of consumption that can be sustained indefinitely without degrading capital stocks.

Given varying assessments about how unsustainable the present is, how rigorously various resources ought to be sustained, and what sustainable development should actually entail, it is not surprising that a multitude of policy agendas have been advanced to promote this governing concept. Unfortunately, both "strong" and "weak" definitions of sustainable development pose problems. As Robert Hahn (1993: 1750) points out, the narrower the definition of sustainable development, the easier it is to determine, but the less satisfactory the concept.

The Chimera of Resource Scarcity

A constant refrain from the sustainable development lobby is the importance of not "drawing-down" the natural resource base. Underlying much of the concern about the importance of sustainable development is the belief that, if the world's economy continues to grow unchecked, economic growth will, in the not-too-distant future, consume natural resources beyond a critic minimum threshold and lead to a major collapse of the world's economy with dire consequences to human and ecological health.[2] While there is much about this theory to criticize, the most important criticism relates to a fundamental misunderstanding of the nature of natural resources.

Resources are simply those assets that can be used profitably for human benefit. "Natural" resources, then, are a subset of the organic and inorganic material we think of as constituting the biological "environment," since not all of that material can be used profitably for human benefit. But what can be used productively changes with time, technology, and material demand. Waves, for example, are not harnessed for human benefit today and thus cannot really be thought of as a "natural resource." But the technology to harness the movement of waves as a means to generate energy certainly exists, and the day when the cost of doing so is lower than the cost

---

[2]While a veritable mountain of important books and essays have been written expounding on this theme, perhaps the best two representatives of the "resource-crash" genre are Donella Meadows et al. (1972), *The Limits to Growth: A Report for the Club of Rome's Project on the Predicament of Mankind,* and Meadows et al. (1992), *Beyond the Limits: Confronting Global Collapse and Envisioning a Sustainable Future.*

of alternative energy sources is the day when waves become a natural resource. Uranium, to cite another example, would not have been considered a resource a century ago but is most certainly thought of as such today. Petroleum was not an important resource 100 years ago but today is thought of as perhaps the most important resource to modern society. And if cold fusion technology had panned out, coal would be another example of yesterday's resource but tomorrow's relatively useless rock.

Thus, the "natural resource base" is itself a relative thing and its components vary greatly with time due to technology and material demand. The composition of the natural resource base of a century ago is substantially different than the natural resource base of today. Conserving today's natural resource base does not ensure that tomorrow's natural resource base is secure, and drawing down today's natural resource base does not necessarily mean that tomorrow's natural resource base is in jeopardy.

More importantly, the relative abundance of a society's natural resource base can change dramatically with technological advance. This, of course, is counterintuitive for many, who continue to think of resources as fixed and finite. Monsanto's Shapiro, for example, speaks for many when he posits that:

> We are encountering physical limits. You can see it coming arithmetically. Sustainability involves the laws of nature— physics, chemistry, and biology—and the recognition that the world is a closed system. What we thought was boundless has limits, and we're beginning to hit them. That's going to change a lot of today's fundamental economics, it's going to change prices, and it's going to change what's socially acceptable [quoted in Magretta 1997: 82].

This sentiment is reflected in discussion about China's long-term economic potential. As Ryan and Flavin (1995: 113) assert, "China's dilemma is that it has a huge population but a far smaller slice of the world's resources. . . . With 22 percent of the world's population, China has only 7 percent of the [planet's] fresh water and cropland, 3 percent of its forests, and 2 percent of its oil." While other nations have overcome their relative lack of natural resources by importing them from abroad, Ryan and Flavin, like much of the sustainable development community, believe that "China's size precludes this option. Recent projections cast doubt on the ability of the rest of the world to supply all the oil or food that this country may require in the decades ahead" (p. 113). If China's per capita oil consumption were that of Japan, for example, Ryan and Flavin note that China "would need 61 million barrels daily—nearly equal to the current world production" (p. 124). Moreover, "even with yield increases (in cropland, through the year 2030), production is likely to fall by at least one fifth, due to loss of cropland, leaving a deficit to be made up by imports of nearly 400 million tons. It is not at all clear who would supply this. Since 1980, annual world grain exports have averaged just 200 million tons" (p. 120).

The problem with the finite-resource theory is nicely illustrated by recent trends in oil production. There are 6,784 trillion fewer barrels of oil in the ground today than there were in 1981, the year in which relative oil scarcity was greatest.[3] At first glance, then, one might think that the natural resource base has deteriorated. Yet oil is relatively more abundant today than it was 17 years ago. After adjusting for inflation, the price of a barrel of Saudi crude has declined by 62 percent and U.S. crude by 64 percent since 1980. The reasons for this increased oil abundance are several-fold. First, new technologies have emerged that have made oil discovery and production far more efficient and thus less costly. Second, greater efficiency of resource use (a reaction to previous run-ups in petroleum prices as well as ongoing technological advances) has contributed to reducing the amount of oil necessary to produce a unit of goods or services and, hence, the relative abundance of the energy resource base. Indeed, the amount of petroleum and natural gas necessary to produce a dollar's worth of gross domestic product has declined by 29 percent since 1980. The story is not unique to petroleum; all resources have become far more abundant—not more scarce— throughout the 20th century (and indeed, throughout recorded history).[4]

If sustainable development, then, is understood as an admonition that the aggregate size of the natural resource base (absent any consideration of demand) should "not be allowed to deteriorate,"

[3]The data on the petroleum industry cited in this paragraph are from the U.S. Department of Energy (1998).

[4]For a quick review of the pertinent data and the debate over this matter over the last 40 years, see *The Economist* (1997: 19–21). For a more comprehensive summary of the data, see Simon (1995: 279–442).

then sustainable development is not particularly helpful as a policy device. First, it posits wrongly that absolute (as opposed to relative) scarcity is the primary threat to the economy and human society at large. Second, the theory is oblivious to the ongoing process of resource creation. As Harold Barnett and Chandler Morse (1963) explained in their classic work *Scarcity and Growth*, as resources become more scarce, people will anticipate future scarcities, prices will be bid up, incentives will be created for developing new technologies and substitutes, and the resource base will be renewed. Indeed, Barnett and Morse's ideas are now widely excepted in the world of resource economics and are not even particularly controversial among those who specialize in that field within academia.[5]

Is Barnett and Morse's optimism regarding "just in time" delivery of new technologies and resource subsidies justified? Well, historical experience—as noted earlier—would certainly seem to justify their optimism. Those who find Barnett and Morse's theory counterintuitive betray a fundamental misunderstanding of the genesis of resources. Natural resources do not exist independent of man and are not materials we simply find and then exploit like buried treasure. Natural resources, on the contrary, are created by mankind. As resource economist Thomas De Gregori (1987: 1243,1247) points out, "Humans are the active agent, having ideas that they use to transform the environment for human purposes. Resources are not fixed and finite because they are not natural. They are a product of human ingenuity resulting from the creation of technology and science." Political scientist David Osterfeld (1992: 99) thus concludes, "Since resources are a function of human knowledge and our stock of knowledge has increased over time, it should come as no surprise that the stock of physical resources has also been expanding." Obsessing nearly exclusively on conserving present natural resources is akin to a farmer who obsesses over conserving eggs rather than the chickens that lay them.

Even so, natural resource scarcity is simply not a binding constraint on economic growth in lesser-developed countries. In a classic study, Joseph Stiglitz (1974) found that exogenous technological

---

[5] For additional texts that have built upon Barnett and Morse's work, see V.K. Smith (1979), Gordon (1996, 1967), and Adelman (1995).

advances lead to long-run gains in per capita consumption in lesser-developed countries under conditions of exponential population growth and limited, exhaustible stocks of natural resources. Edward Barbier (1996) found that even in an endogenous growth economy, technological change is resource augmenting. As Barbier and Thomas Homer-Dixon (1996: 3) put it, "Sufficient allocation of human capital to innovation will ensure that resource exhaustion can be postponed indefinitely, and the possibility exists of a long-run endogenous steady-state growth rate that allows per capita consumption to be sustained, and perhaps even increased, indefinitely."

Unfortunately, the entire question of whether resource availability will or will not constrain Third World development is muddied by a fundamental misunderstanding of Western economic history. Ye Ruqiu, an advisor to the Chinese government regarding sustainable development, asserts that "the high economic growth and wealth of Western nations were built upon their low-price use of natural resources, tremendous pollution emissions, and excessive consumption, which was in reality an unsustainable production and consumption pattern" (Ye n.d.). China, he says, must not—indeed, cannot— follow the West's lead. Yet growth in the advanced industrialized world was built not by low-cost exploitation of natural resources but by economic liberty and the rule of law.[6]

What does all this mean for China? Well, it means that as long as economic liberalization continues, China will begin to create more natural resources than it consumes, just as is done by more economically advanced Western economies. Indeed, even the World Resources Institute (WRI)—a prominent alarmist about sustainability trends—acknowledges that "the trend is toward increased sustainability" in China (Hammond et al. 1995: 25).

Other Theoretical Problems of Sustainable Development

Other important problems cripple the utility of sustainable development theory, at least in its "strong" variant. Among them is an unwarranted bias for "natural" as opposed to "man-made" capital, the presumption that the ecology is well-served by "sustaining" resources in the first place, the idea that sustainability ought to be

---

[6]See, for example, Landes (1969), Osterfeld (1992), Rosenberg and Birdzell (1986), Raico (1994), Bauer (1981: 185–90), and North (1988).

a driving concern for commercial or industrial undertakings, and the belief that intergenerational equity is a useful idea for public policy.

Natural versus Man-Made Capital

While advocates of sustainable development argue that natural capital is in most cases more desirable than the "man-made" capital created from its exploitation, the wealth created by exploiting resources is often more beneficial than the wealth preserved by "banking" those resources for future use. Otherwise, there would be little point in exploiting resources for commercial use in the first place.

The Unnaturalness of Resource Equilibrium

There is growing doubt within the ecological community about whether stocks of natural capital are naturally constant at all. "Strong" sustainability assumes that ecosystems naturally evolve toward some equilibrium and eventually stabilize. But within the academic community, lack of empirical evidence supporting the theory has led to a wholesale questioning of the equilibrium paradigm.[7]

- If ecosystems do not tend toward stabilization, then policies that are intended to promote "sustainable" capital are unnatural and without ecological merit;
- If resource stocks are not functionally and structurally complete, then "sustainable management" of those stocks will prove suboptimal; and
- If ecosystems do not tend toward stability, then calculations about the economic or ecological value of natural capital are impossible on a macro level.

Uncertainties surrounding the nature of ecosystem evolution and the means by which resource stocks can best be maintained have two main implications for policy analysts. First, conclusions about whether or not certain economic activities are "sustainable" are more problematic than some would like to think. Second, preserving indefinitely certain ecological states is less a matter of ecological necessity than social preference.

[7]See, for example, Kay (1991); Pickett, Parker, and Fiedler (1992); Walker (1992); and Noss (1990).

The environmental benefits of sustainable resource use are often oversold while the environmental costs of unsustainable use are frequently overblown. "Sustainable development" is a concept that looks good on paper but is built upon a shaky ecological foundation indeed.

Sustainability über Alles?

While it is certainly true that sustainability can be an important consideration for certain economic or social arrangements, it does not necessarily follow that sustainability should be elevated to the status of some overriding criterion for public policy. After all, there are innumerable human activities and undertakings that are highly desirable—even necessary—but, unfortunately, not indefinitely sustainable. We must make a distinction between sustainability as a purely technical concept and optimality, which is a normative concept. Many economic activities that are unsustainable may be perfectly optimal and many that are sustainable may not be desirable, let alone optimal (Beckerman 1996: 145).

The Incoherence of Intergenerational Equity

It is fashionable in certain intellectual circles to go even further and argue, as does Georgetown Professor of International Law Edith Weiss (1989), that future generations have as much right to today's environmental resources as we do, and that we have no right to decide whether or not they should inherit their share of those rights.[8] Indeed, this concept of "intergenerational equity" is rife throughout environmental literature.

Yet the concept of tangible rights to resources for those not yet even conceived is dubious, to say the least.[9] First, it is philosophically inconsistent. Those disincorporated beings not yet even a glimmer in someone's eye are said to have "rights," yet the moment they are conceived, they are legally held to have no rights whatsoever. Leaving aside the ethics of abortion, in order to be consistent, those who defend the rights of future generations must by the same logic oppose abortion (a position few environmentalist activists hold,

[8]For a summary and a sympathetic critique of Weiss, see Barresi (1997).
[9]For a thorough review of the theoretical and practical difficulties in defining and assigning rights to future generations, see Baier (1984), Barry (1997), and Golding (1972).

387

given their allegiance to population control). And once individuals are conceived, we do not maintain that they have a "right" to all the resources of the parent.

The concept of intergenerational equity is hopelessly incoherent. If the choice to "draw down" resources is held exclusively by future generations, then are we not some previous generation's "future" generation? Why is the present generation bereft of that right? If the answer is that no generation has the right to deplete resources as long as another generation is on the horizon, then the logical implication of the argument is that no generation (save for the very last generation before the extinction of the species) will ever have a right to deplete any resource, no matter how urgent the needs of the present may be. If only *one* generation (out of hundreds or even thousands) has the right to deplete resources, how is that "intergenerational equity"?

Compounding that problem is the fact that the entire discussion of intergenerational equity is bereft of any acknowledgement that future generations will almost certainly be far, far better off economically than present generations. If one were serious about equality between generations, then, we might take economist Steven Landsburg's advice and "allow the unemployed lumberjacks of Oregon to confiscate your rich grandchildren's view of the giant redwoods." The math is actually quite simple. If U.S. per capita income manages to grow in real terms by 2 percent a year (a conservative assumption), then in 400 years, the average American family of four will enjoy an income of $2 million *a day* in 1997 dollars (roughly Microsoft's CEO Bill Gates' current income). If per capita income grew a bit faster—say, at the rate reported by South Korea over the past couple of decades—it would take only 100 years for an average family of four to earn $2 million daily. "So each time the Sierra Club impedes economic development to preserve some specimen of natural beauty," writes Landsburg, "it is asking people who live like you and me (the relatively poor) to sacrifice for the enjoyment of future generations that will live like Bill Gates" (Landsburg 1997).

Furthermore, the notion of resource rights for future generations is premised on the argument that one has a "right" to forcibly take property from someone else in order to satisfy a personal need. Although that is an argument best left unexplored here, suffice it to say that such a claim is so expansive and fraught with peril that few philosophers have taken it seriously (see, for example, MacCallum 1967 and Pilon 1979).

Finally, the belief that future generations are more likely to be protected by political rather than market agents strikes one as incredibly naïve. The failure of central planning around the world points to the absurdity of placing the future in the hands of government rather than in the hands of profit-seeking entrepreneurs who stand to gain by increasing the future value of resources to consumers and who will lose their wealth if they fail. Indeed, any clear-eyed survey of government versus market decisionmaking finds that market agents are far more likely to invest for the future than governmental agents (see Stroup 1991 and Smith 1993).

Since advocates of sustainable development rely upon governmental action to ensure the success of their agenda, it is unlikely—no matter how well intentioned their efforts or successful their political campaign—that their goals will be realized via state intervention in the economy.

In sum, it is hard to overemphasize the wrongheadedness of sustainable development as a useful policy construct. Society has managed to "sustain" development for approximately 3,000 years without the guidance of green state planners. The result is not only a society that is both healthier and wealthier than any other in history, but a society with more natural resources at its disposal than ever before. Experience has taught that the best way to sustain development—or to maximize human welfare—is to protect economic liberty and proscribe the boundaries of state authority to protecting life, liberty, and property (Gwartney and Lawson 1997).

As an all-encompassing governing philosophy, sustainable development is a dubious pipe dream. Even promoters of the concept are increasingly in agreement that sustainable development must ensure that economic and social considerations are balanced with environmental concerns and are not trumped by them (Munasinghe and Cruz 1995: 7). As a policy admonition, it might well have its uses, but sustainable development (intelligently considered) is but one consideration in the quest to maximize public welfare.

Wealth = (Human + Environmental) Health

China's present environmental problems are those typically encountered by nations transitioning from early-industrial to late-industrial stages of development. First, as a lesser-developed nation,

China's obsolescent machinery, dated production techniques, and top-heavy, centralized industrial structures are highly pollution-intensive. Meanwhile, China's fantastic economic growth has been accompanied by newer forms of pollution, particularly those associated with the automobile, urban congestion, waste disposal, and sanitation. In essence, China is today experiencing the worst of both the developed and underdeveloped worlds (Beckerman 1996: 31).

Is this state of affairs environmentally "sustainable"? If Chinese statistics can be believed, the answer is "yes." An official 1994 report on the state of the environment in China notes that, just as in the West, air quality is not worsening despite continuing urbanization, water quality is slowly improving, and discharges of industrial and toxic wastes are slowing (Ye n.d.). Rural Chinese, for example, have seen access to "improved water supplies" increase from 50 percent in 1985 to 75 percent by 1990 (Riskin 1996: 364).

What China is experiencing is nothing short of what the West experienced a century ago. As the WRI (1998: 8) observes:

> Just a century ago, health conditions in Europe, North America, and Japan were similar to those of the least developed countries today, as was environmental quality. Conditions in London and other major centers were squalid; sewage-filled rivers, garbage-strewn streets, and overcrowded and dank housing were the norm. Much of the population lacked access to fresh water or adequate sanitation. Epidemics of typhus, cholera, tuberculosis, and measles swept these cities. Indeed, in the world's most prosperous cities at the time, the infant mortality rate—the number of children who die before their first birthday—was more than 100 per 1,000 live births, and in some places it exceeded 200. Diarrheal and respiratory diseases and other infections were the main cause of death.

The environmental plight of cities such as London might not have been indefinitely "sustainable," but industrialization—even when accompanied by heavy pollution—contributed to improvements in human welfare. Industrialization was accompanied by an increase in life expectancy and an improved standard of living. Incomes rose so that people were able to afford more environmental amenities, better health care, modern sanitary investments, and an improved diet. Economic growth spawned new manufacturing technologies that were more efficient, less resource intensive, and, hence, less polluting. Moreover, these gains in human welfare accelerated over time.

Indeed, it is the *lack* of economic growth—not the pollution spawned by growth—that is the root cause of most health-related problems in the lesser-developed world today (Pritchett and Summers 1993). As the WRI (1998: 14) notes:

> Of all the factors that combine to degrade health, poverty stands out for its overwhelming role. Indeed, WHO [the World Health Organization] has called poverty the world's biggest killer. Statistically, poverty affects health in its own right: just being poor increases one's risk of ill health. Poverty also contributes to disease and death through its second-order effects; poor people, for instance, are more likely to live in an unhealthy environment.

While this argument is generally accepted throughout academia, sustainable development advocates counter that industrialization in the developing world today is proceeding in a far more compressed time frame than it did centuries ago (Krustifm 1997: A14). Moreover, it is thought, rapid population growth compounds the pollution problem so dramatically that the various pollution sinks of the Third World are being exceeded far more rapidly than they ever were in the industrialized West while also exposing more people to those harms (WRI 1998: 51). Others doubt whether the development experience of the West can translate into the Third World because, as Pearce and Warford (1993: 263) argue, "A great many environments in the developing world are ecologically fragile. They are capable of sustaining certain levels of activity and certain levels of population, but exceeding that carrying capacity may well lead to growing poverty." The data suggest that the skeptics are wrong. Observes the WRI (1998: 14), "As the disproportionate burden of ill health in the poorest countries shows, a clear correlation exists between health and wealth. By and large, the wealthier a country becomes, or the higher its average per capita income, the healthier its population becomes."

In the case of China, after two decades of robust economic growth:

- The occurrence of infectious disease is only slightly higher in China than in the advanced industrialized West (WRI 1998: 10, 261);

391

- Life expectancy in China now stands at 69 years, far higher than other economies of similar size or wealth (p. 247);
- The infant mortality rate has declined from 52 per 1,000 births in the period 1975–80 to 38 per 1,000 births today (p. 259);
- Although China has added 200 million people since 1980, less land is required to feed China's population today than was required 18 years ago (p. 299). Cereal yields alone have increased 17 percent per hectare over the past 10 years (p. 289);
- Average daily per capita calorie and protein consumption increased 13 percent between the periods 1982–84 and 1992–94 (p. 289); and
- Only 17 percent of those under five years of age experience malnutrition, a far better situation than in most other countries of comparable wealth (World Bank 1996: 198).

The Environmental Kuznets Curves: Empirical Support for Growth

Empirical data support the argument that economic growth initially worsens environmental quality in underdeveloped nations but eventually contributes to environmental improvements. Numerous economists have studied the relationship today between economic growth, population, and industrialization and environmental quality (known in the economics community as "environmental Kuznets curves," or EKCs, because the inverted U-shaped relationships discovered when per capita income and environmental indicators are put in graph-form bear a striking resemblance to the relationship between income inequality and economic development discovered by economist Simon Kuznets in 1955 and found that, beyond a certain point, economic development does indeed reduce the burden of pollution. Data compiled by the World Bank for example demonstrates an unmistakable correlation between per capita income and access to safe drinking water, sanitation, and declining urban concentrations of particulate matter and sulfur dioxide (El-Ashry 1993: 18).

Will China, however, prove an exception to the rule? Almost certainly not. Not only are major indicators of human health trending in a positive direction, but experts from the Harvard School of Public Health and the World Health Organization predict continuing improvements in life expectancy in China over the next several decades (Murray and Lopez 1997: 1499). The most harmful pollutants in China are by-products of poverty, and as that problem is alleviated so too will the problem of Chinese pollution. Moreover, the lack of even the most rudimentary pollution control devices is due not to a lack of desire for those devices, but to an inability to pay for them. Since China's per capita income in 1991, adjusted for domestic purchasing power, stood at about $3,000, the country is on the positive side of virtually all the environmental Kuznets curves and continuing improvement of environmental quality is almost inevitable.

Economic growth will also help alleviate the pressures on China's natural resource base. For instance, a large percentage of the energy used in rural households comes from traditional biomass sources such as straw or firewood. A modern energy infrastructure—a natural byproduct of economic growth—would not only alleviate a major source of indoor air pollution but would also replace rural reliance upon the land for energy.

That is but one example of the larger point that must be made about economic growth and resource conservation. Lesser-developed economies, lacking the most modern technologies and production practices, are relatively inefficient and consume more natural resources per dollar of economic output than Western economies. According to one estimate, China's major industries consume 30 to 90 percent more energy than similar industries in developed countries (Huang 1992: 3). Economic growth leads to industrial modernization, which leads to resource efficiency, which, in turn, results in a reduced burden on natural resources. The increasing efficiency of Chinese energy use shows that this phenomenon is already occurring.[10]

Leapfrogging the Industrial Revolution?

A standard prescription for sustainable development in the developing world is for preindustrial economies to "leapfrog" the industrial revolution altogether. Since businesses now have access to advanced pollution control technologies and new "green" technologies to minimize emissions at their source—technologies not available to the West when it industrialized the more than a century

---

[10]According to the WRI (1994: 68) only 1.03 kilograms of oil-equivalent energy was required to produce a dollar's worth of goods in 1988 compared to 1.44 kilograms of oil-equivalent energy per dollar's worth of production in 1980. Worldwatch Institute analysts confirm that China reduced its energy intensity by one-third between 1978 and 1990 (Ryan and Flavin 1995: 126).

ago—why shouldn't lesser-developed economies skip the old industrial stage of development altogether and move directly into a 21st century economy?

To some extent, of course, "leapfrogging" is exactly what is happening in various industrial sectors today. China's rapid adoption of cellular phones in lieu of common wire-based telephone system is but one example of this phenomenon. India's rapid advance in computer software programming is another. Still, China's living standard is so low compared to the West that some industrial development is vitally necessary for simple human comfort. For example, the typical Chinese household uses only 0.03 percent of the energy consumed by the typical American household, a shortfall largely due to a lack of even the most basic modern household appliances (Chandler, Makarov, and Zhou 1990: 121).

No matter how energy efficient new appliances might prove, per capita energy consumption is bound to rise dramatically along with demand for electricity. An industrial "energy revolution" will be required irrespective of advanced technology. Even if the world market share of nonfossil fuels doubled by 2020 (about all that is technically feasible even if economic considerations were discarded), coal and oil were the fossil fuels that were the primary market "losers," and energy efficiency investments were maximized, fossil fuel consumption in China would still increase substantially, as would world carbon dioxide emissions (Leffler and Karlin 1993: 11–12).

Given the necessity of industrialization in the developing world, the decision whether to embrace advanced technological practices or industries must be made by market agents, not by government planners. When it makes economic sense to do so, the private sector will adopt "leapfrog" technologies without the need of government encouragement. It is important to remember that prices are for a large part reflections of relative scarcity, and if the price of solar-fired electricity, for example, is greater than the price of coal-fired electricity, it means that greater resources are necessary to deliver solar power than coal power. Unfortunately, many of the enthusiasms of the environmental community—such as renewable energy—are far more expensive than conventional alternatives, which is the main reason why the West has yet to widely adopt them. Not only could China scarcely afford to embrace what Western economies find prohibitively expensive (for the time being, anyway), but to do so would deplete the very resource base sustainable development is supposed to protect.

A few opportunities to leapfrog old technologies indeed exist. Most cars sold in China, for instance, lack even the most basic emission controls and continue to rely on leaded fuel. While Beijing has only one-eighth the number of cars on the street as does Tokyo, the two auto fleets emit the same the amount of carbon monoxide (Johnson 1997: 2A). The undoubted increase in auto prices that would result from banning leaded gasoline and requiring basic tailpipe pollution controls would help to achieve an internalization of the costs of auto emission (the legitimate goal of making polluters pay for pollution) while achieving a relatively large amount of pollution reduction for a minimum public cost.

Still, the amount of regulatory "low-hanging fruit" in the environmental arena is less than meets the eye. China must be careful to minimize state regulatory action so that the engine of economic growth is not too greatly damaged, for it is economic growth that must ultimately occur for China's environment and human health situation to improve.[11]

Population Growth and Urbanization

Much has been made by the sustainable development crowd about the declining amount of land devoted to agriculture in China. From 1961 through 1990, the amount of land devoted to crops fell from 105.2 million hectares to 96.6 million, and some think those figures underestimate actual cropland losses by 20–30 percent. That 30-year decline has meant cropland dropped almost 50 percent on a per capita basis (WRI 1994: 70–71). The Chinese Academy of Sciences estimates that net cropland area is shrinking by 333,000 hectares per year (Chada 1992: 32). For Ryan and Flavin (1995: 120–21), this is largely a sign of environmental degradation (but also, it is conceded, a fact due to changing land use patterns driven by economics rather than environmental degradation), primarily from soil erosion, which harbors ill for China's ability to feed itself. Accordingly, they propose

---

[11] While it is true that only 0.7 percent of China's GNP is spent on environmental protection compared to over 3 percent in most Western nations (Ryan and Flavin 1995: 130), increases in that expenditure must be done carefully so that economic growth is not unduly constrained.

rigorous centralized land planning and national zoning controls to protect valuable farmland from other sorts of use.

Yet Chinese agricultural productivity gains have more than offset cropland retirement (WRI 1994: 71). While soil erosion is a natural product of low-intensity, subsistence agriculture on marginal lands, advanced high-intensity agriculture substantially reduces soil erosion and more than offsets the loss of soil with spectacular increases in yields (Avery 1995: 367–93; Gardner and Schultz 1995: 416–24). Thus, there is no reason to believe that the maintenance of the natural resource base is the key to agricultural sustainability in China (Crosson 1994: 45). Furthermore, the "right" mix of cropland versus industrial land is more a matter of comparative international advantage than it is a domestic engineering or scientific consideration. How much food China should produce domestically can only be answered by consideration of international grain and foodstuff prices.

Yet, as noted earlier, some scholars believe that the world would be hard stretched to provide the grain necessary to feed the Chinese people in the 21st century. Such concerns, however, are unwarranted; the planet's agricultural capacity is far greater than most non-specialists realize and is not even close to peek capacity.

Roger Revelle of Harvard—a scholar often cited glowingly by Vice President Al Gore as one of the scientific giants of this century—demonstrated convincingly that simply increasing the efficiency of water use outside the humid tropics in Africa, Asia, and Latin America would produce yields capable of feeding 18 billion people (Revelle 1984: 185–86). Extending those calculations to the arable parts of the tropics results in yields capable of feeding 35–40 billion people (Osterfeld 1992: 83). Moreover, there are promising strategies beyond increased water efficiency—such as crop hybridization, advances in cloning and bioengineering, advances in transportation of foodstuffs and storage efficiency, and simple use of productive cropland that has been allowed to go fallow due to recent declines in food demand—that can radically improve global yields (Avery 1995). And that doesn't even begin to address the increasing ease by which agricultural science can turn nonarable to arable land if the demand is sufficient to justify the investment.[12] Only about 1 to

[12] For an excellent summary of the state of agricultural science, see Osterfeld (1992: 64–72).

3 percent of the ice-free earth is occupied by humans, and less than one-ninth is used for agriculture. Concerns that increasing yields will cause more human health problems (from chemical contamination of the environment) than it solves are unpersuasive.[13]

Another common concern is that population growth will inevitably lead to an accelerated depletion of natural resources, such as timber. But a study of 64 lesser-developed countries in Africa, Asia, and Latin America found that deforestation had little to do with population growth but had much to do with lack of private property rights over forestland. Moreover, once per capita incomes exceeded $4,760 in Africa and $5,420 in Latin America, deforestation rates actually moderated slightly (Cropper and Griffith 1994: 250–54). Nor is the "footprint" of a burgeoning population as great as one might think. "The proportion of the world's land surface used for farms and pastures has remained constant at about 35 percent since mid-century. Though much of the land surface has been altered by human action, buildings and roads and other human artifacts actually cover less than 1 percent" (Ausubel, Victor, and Wernick 1995: 9).

Nor has population growth in China led to excessive crowding. Despite both general and urban population growth, the amount of living space per person has increased 215 percent in rural areas and 100 percent in urban areas since 1980 (Riskin 1996: 363).

There is also general concern about whether China (and other nations) can sustain "megacities" given the widespread belief that human health and the environment are natural casualties of rapid Third World urbanization. While it's certainly true that governmental interventions in lesser developed countries often indirectly fosters the growth of megacities at the expense of the agricultural economy and the efficiency of the economy as a whole (see Powelson and Stock 1990), megacities are, as a general matter, an important component of economic growth, particularly in the lesser developed world (Montgomery 1988). Their emergence is a sign not of demographic disaster but of economic development. Urban growth is so important to the developing world that scholars believe restricting urbanization to combat pollution will do more economic harm than good (Shukla and Parikh 1992: 425). Moroever, there is good reason to believe that restricting city size would actually increase overall national

---

[13]For a brief discussion of the issue, see Bailey (1994) and Ames (1995).

pollution rates by fostering resource-costly inefficiencies and increasing overall transportation costs and attendant fuel-based emissions (Mills and Graves 1986).

Finally, there is certainly little to the argument that population growth somehow in and of itself impedes economic progress. A dozen statistical studies, starting in 1967 by Kuznets, have found no negative statistical relationship between population growth and economic growth.[14]

Conclusion

The most important step China can take to protect human health and the environment is to protect private property rights, ensure that markets remain as free from government intervention as possible, and protect the resulting engine of economic growth. Since poverty is also a major cause of environmental destruction, economic growth serves both a social and ecological function.

China would be well advised to cease paying lip-service to the international sustainable development agenda as forwarded by the United Nations and the host of mostly Western environmental NGOs (non-governmental organizations). Agenda 21—an action plan for sustainable development signed by China at the UN "Earth Summit" held in Rio de Janeiro in 1992 (see United Nations 1992)—is by-and-large an ill-considered call for massive state intervention in the economy that would only undercut the very market forces necessary to secure economic growth. The official white paper on *Population, Environment, and Development in China in the 21st Century*, otherwise known as "China's Agenda 21," is a 20-chapter document calling for massive centralized environmental planning to implement the UN's Agenda 21 at home (National Environment Protection Agency 1995). The white paper found its way into the ninth five-year plan for national economic and social development that was adopted by the 14th National People's Congress in March 1996. There is, however, widespread suspicion that the white paper is actually more with appeasing Western NGOs and foreign loan agencies than it is with guiding China's policy in the future.

---

[14]For a comprehensive review of the population literature, see Osterfeld (1992: 104–35).

Sustainable development is a kind of socialist subterfuge, an attempt to reimpose state planning of the economy—which, in reality, means state planning of people's lives—under a new rationale: the protection of the environment. Such an agenda would not only exacerbate poverty and human suffering in China, it would harm the environment and injure future generations as well. China should ignore Western entreaties to undertake this project and stick with the liberal reform path it embarked upon two decades ago. The best way to ensure that development is sustainable is to ensure the protection of economic and personal freedom.

References

Adelman, M. (1995) *The Genie Out of the Bottle: World Oil Since 1970.* Cambridge: MIT Press.

Ames, B. (1995) "Pesticides, Cancer, and Misconceptions." In J.L. Simon (ed.) *The State of Humanity,* 588–94. Cambridge, Mass.: Blackwell.

Ausubel, J.; Victor, D.; and Wernick, I. (1995) "The Environment Since 1970." *Consequences* 1 (Autumn): 2–15.

Avery, D. (1995) "The World's Rising Food Productivity." In J.L. Simon (ed.) *The State of Humanity,* 367–93. Cambridge, Mass.: Blackwell.

Baier, A. (1984) "For the Sake of Future Generations." In T. Regan (ed.) *Earthbound: New Introductory Essays in Environmental Ethics.* New York: Random House.

Bailey, R. (1994) "Once and Future Farming." *Garbage* (Fall): 42–51.

Barbier, E. (1996) "Endogenous Growth and Natural Resource Scarcity." EEEM Discussion Paper 9601, Department of Environmental Economics and Environmental Management, University of York (U.K.).

Barbier, E. and Homer-Dixon, T. (1996) "Resource Scarcity, Institutional Adaptation, and Technological Innovation: Can Poor Countries Attain Endogenous Growth?" American Association for the Advancement of Science.

Barnett, H., and Morse, C. (1963) *Scarcity and Growth: The Economics of Natural Resource Availability.* Baltimore: Johns Hopkins University Press.

Barresi, P. (1997) "Beyond Fairness to Future Generations: An Intragenerational Alternative to Intergenerational Equity in the International Environmental Arena." *Tulane Environmental Law Journal* 11(1) (Winter): 59–88.

Barry, B. (1977) "Justice Between Generations." In J.M.S. Hacker and S. Raz (eds.) *Law, Morality, and Society: Essays in Honour of H.L.A. Hart.* Oxford: Clarendon Press.

Bauer, P. (1981) *Equality, the Third World, and Economic Delusion.* Cambridge, Mass.: Harvard University Press.

Beckerman, W. (1996) *Through Green Colored Glasses: Enviromentalism Reconsidered.* Washington, D.C.: Cato Institute.

Chada, K. (1992) "China's Grim Challenge." *Far Eastern Agriculture* (July/August).

Chandler, W.; Makarov, A.; and Zhou, D. (1990) "Energy for the Soviet Union, Eastern Europe, and China." *Scientific American* (September).

Cropper, M., and Griffith, C. (1994) "The Interaction of Population and Growth and Environmental Quality." *American Economic Review* 82(2): 250–54.

Crosson, P. (1994) "Sustainable Agriculture." *Environment* 36(1) (February).

De Gregori, T. (1987) "Resources Are Not; They Become: An Institutional Theory." *Journal of Economic Issues* 21(3) (September): 1243–7.

The Economist (1997) "Plenty of Gloom." 20 December: 19–21.

El-Ashry, M. (1993) "Balancing Economic Development with Environmental Protection in Developing and Lesser Developed Countries." *Journal of the Air & Waste Management Association* (43) (January): 18–24.

Gardner, B., and Schultz, T. (1995) "Trends in Soil Erosion and Farmland Quality." In J.L. Simon (ed.) *The State of Humanity,* 416–24. Cambridge, Mass.: Blackwell.

Golding, M. (1972) "Obligations to Future Generations." *The Monist* 56(1): 85–99.

Gordon, R. (1966) "Conservation and the Theory of Exhaustible Resources." *Canadian Journal of Economics and Political Science* 32(3) (August): 319–26.

Gordon, R. (1967) "A Reinterpretation of the Pure Theory of Exhaustion." *Journal of Political Economy* 75(3) (June): 274–86.

Gwartney, J.D., and Lawson, R.A. (1997) *Economic Freedom of the World : 1997 Annual Report.* Vancouver, B.C.: Fraser Institute.

Hahn, R. "Toward a New Environmental Paradigm." *Yale Law Journal* 102(7) (May): 1719–61.

Hammond, A.; Adriaanse, A.; Rodenburg, E.; Bryant, D.; and Woodward, R. (1995) "Environmental Indicators: A Systematic Approach to Measuring and Reporting on Environmental Policy Performance in the Context of Sustainable Development." World Resources Institute, Washington, D.C.

Huang, Y. (1992) "Strategic Alternatives for Coordinated Development of Energy and Environment in China." Recommendations to the China Council for International Cooperation on Environment and Development, Paper No. 5, Beijing.

Johnson, I. (1997) "Beijing Ends Roast Mutton Smog." *Baltimore Sun,* 7 January: 2A.

Kay, J. (1991) "The Concept of Ecological Integrity, Alternative Theories of Ecology and Implications for Decision-Support Indicators." In P.A.Victor,

J.J. Kay, and H.J. Ruitenback (eds.) *Economic, Ecological, and Decision Theories: Indicators of Ecological Sustainable Development*, 23–58. Ottawa: Canadian Environmental Advisory Council.

Krustifm, N. (1997) "Across Asia, a Pollution Disaster Hovers." *New York Times*, 28 November: A14.

Landes, D. (1969) *The Unbound Prometheus*. Cambridge: Cambridge University Press.

Landsburg, S. (1997) "Tax the Knickers Off Your Grandchildren." *Slate*, 6 March.

Leffler, W., and Karlin, R. (1993) "Energy and the Environment: Is a Sustainable Energy Path Possible?" Paper presented at the Global Tomorrow Coalition: 21st Century Dialogue, 25 February.

MacCallum, Jr., G. (1967) "Negative and Positive Freedom." *Philosophical Review* (76) (July): 312–34.

Magretta, J. (1997) "Growth Through Global Sustainability: An Interview with Monsanto's CEO, Robert Shapiro." *Harvard Business Review* (January/February): 80–1.

Meadows, D., et al. (1972) *The Limits to Growth: A Report for the Club of Rome's Project on the Predicament of Mankind*. New York: New American Library.

Meadows, D., et al. (1992) *Beyond the Limits: Confronting Global Collapse and Envisioning a Sustainable Future*. Post Mills, Vt: Chelsea Green.

Mills, E., and Graves, P. (1986) *The Economics of Environmental Quality*. New York: W.W. Norton.

Montgomery, M. (1988) "How Large Is Too Large? Implications of the City Size Literature for Population Policy and Research." *Economic Development and Cultural Change* (36): 691–720.

Munasinghe, M. (1993) "Environmental Economics and Sustainable Development." World Bank Environmental Paper No. 3. Washington, D.C.: World Bank.

Munasinghe, M., and Cruz, W. (1995) "Economywide Policies and the Environment: Lessons from Experience." World Bank Environment Paper No.10. Washington, D.C.: World Bank.

Murray, C., and Lopez, A. (1997) "Alternative Projections of Mortality and Disability by Cause 1990–2020: Global Burden of Disease Study." *The Lancet* (349) (24 May): 1498–1504.

Murray, D. (1993) "America's Interest in China's Environment." National Committee China Policy Series No. 6, National Committee on U.S.-China Relations.

National Environmental Protection Agency (1995) *Agenda 21 for Environmental Protection in China*. Beijing: China Environmental Science Press.

North, D. (1998) "Institutions, Ideology, and Economic Performance." In J.A. Dorn, S.H. Hanke, and A.A. Walters (eds.) *The Revolution in Development Economics, 95–107*. Washington, D.C.: Cato Institute.

Noss, R.F. (1990) "Indicators for Monitoring Biodiversity: A Hierarchical Approach." *Conservation Biology* (4): 355–64.

Osterfeld, D. (1992) *Prosperity versus Planning*. New York: Oxford University Press.

Pearce, D., and Warford, J. (1993) *World Without End: Economics, Environment, and Sustainable Development*. New York: Oxford University Press.

Pickett, S.; Parker, V.; and Fiedler, P. (1992) "The New Paradigm in Ecology: Implications for Conservation Biology above the Species Level." In P.L. Fiedler and S.K. Jain (eds.) *Consevation Biology: The Theory and Practice of Nature Conservation Preservation and Management, 66–88*. London: Chapman and Hall.

Pilon, R. (1979) "Ordering Rights Consistently: Or What We Do And Do Not Have Rights To." *Georgia Law Review* (13): 1171–96.

Pritchett, L., and Summers, L. (1993) "Wealthier is Healthier." Working Paper Series 1150. Washington, D.C.: World Bank.

Powelson, J., and Stock, R. (1990) *The Peasant Betrayed: Agricultural and Land Reform in the Third World*. Washington, D.C.: Cato Institute.

Raico, R. (1994) "The Theory of Economic Development and the 'European Miracle.' " In P. Boettke (ed.) *The Collapse of Development Planning, 37–58*. New York: New York University Press.

Revelle, R. (1984) "The World Supply of Agriculture." In J.L. Simon and H. Kahn (eds.) *The Resourceful Earth*, 185–86. New York: Basil Blackwell.

Riskin, C. (1996) "Social Development, Quality of Life and the Environment." In *China's Economic Future: Challenges to U.S. Policy*, 361–80. Study papers submitted to the Joint Economic Committee, 24–960cc (August). Washington, D.C.: U.S. Government Printing Office.

Rosenberg , N., and Birdzell, Jr., L.E. (1986) *How the West Grew Rich*. New York: Basic Books.

Ruckelshaus, W. (1994) "Toward a Sustainable World." *The Environmental Ethics and Policy Book*. Belmont, Calif.: Wadsworth.

Ryan, M., and Flavin, C.(1995) "Facing China's Limits." In L. Brown (ed.) *State of the World 1995*. New York: W.W. Norton.

Sheehan, J. (1996) "Sustainable Development: The Green Road to Serfdom?" Unpublished manuscript, Competitive Enterprise Institute.

Shukla, V. and Parikh, K. (1992) "The Environmental Consequences of Urban Growth: Cross-National Perspectives on Economic Development, Air Pollution, and City Size." *Urban Geography* 13(5): 422–48.

Simon, J.L., ed. (1995) *The State of Humanity*. Cambridge, Mass.: Blackwell.

Smith, F. (1993) "The Market and Nature." *The Freeman* (September): 350–56.

Smith, V.K. (1979) *Scarcity and Growth Reconsidered*. Baltimore: Johns Hopkins University Press.

Stiglitz, J. (1974) "Growth and Exhaustible Natural Resources: Efficient and Optimal Growth Paths." *Review of Economic Studies* 41:123–38.

Stroup, R. (1991) "Political Control vs. Sustainable Development." Paper presented at the Cato Institute Conference on Global Environmental Crises: Science or Politics? 5–6 June.

United Nations, World Commission on Environment and Development (1987) *Our Common Future.* Oxford: Oxford University Press.

United Nations (1992) *The Global Partnership for Environment and Development: A Guide to Agenda 21.* Geneva: United Nations Conference on the Human Environment, April.

U.S. Department of Energy (1998) Energy Information Administration, *Annual Energy Review* (http://tonto.cia.doe.gov/aer).

Walker, B.H. (1992) "Biodiversity and Ecological Redundancy." *Conservation Biology* (6): 19–23.

Weiss, E. (1989) *In Fairness to Future Generations.* Dobbs Ferry, N.Y.: Transnational.

World Resources Institute, WRI (1994) *World Resources 1994–95: People and the Environment.* New York: Oxford University Press.

World Resources Institute, WRI (1998) *World Resources 1998–99.* New York: Oxford University Press.

Ye, R. (n.d.) "Sustainable Development in China and International Trade." (http://iisd1.ca/trade/cciced/agenda21.htm.)

Index

Gao, P., 357
Gao, S., 319, 325
Gardner, B., 396
Garnaut, R., 179
Gelb, A., 55
Gellner, E., 271–72
General Agreement on Tariffs and
  Trade (GATT)
  China's effort to rejoin, 178–82
  potential for China's membership in,
    191–92
  See also World Trade Organization
    (WTO)
Gordon, R., 50
Gore, Al, 242
Government
  limits and powers specified in U.S.
    Constitution, 345–48
  military power centralized in, 12
  role specified in U.S. Declaration of
    Independence, 343
Government role
  in adjustment of economic growth,
    57–61
  in civil society, 242
  controls in foreign exchange markets,
    215
  effect of limited, 106
  under first five-year plan, 43–46
  in laissez-faire system, 111
  under market-liberal regime, 110–11
  in sale of small SOEs, 84, 89–90
  in telecommunications sector, 194–96,
    200–203
Gradualism
  China's approach in trade
    liberalization, 181–82
  of China's economic reform, 37,
    87–89, 91–92
  defined, 75
  of move to current-account
    convertibility, 217–18
  of ownership reform, 82–83
  See also Competition; Economic
    reform; Nonstate sector
Graves, P., 398
Griffith, C., 397
Gross domestic product (GDP)
  estimates for China (1997–2015),
    14–16
  estimates of China's per capita
    (1997–2015), 16–17
Groves, T., 50
Gu, B. C., 284

Gwartney, J. D., 164t, 166f, 170f, 349,
  389

Hahn, R., 381
Hall, R. E., 369
Hammond, A., 385
Harrold, P., 55
Havel, Václav, 101, 104
Hayek, F. A., 6–7, 99, 107, 115, 238,
  242, 333; 165
Health care system, China, 327–28
Heavy industry. *See* Industrial sector.
Hegel, G. W. F., 269
Heston, A., 171
Hoffman, D., 230
Homer-Dixon, T., 385
Hong Kong
  bank branches in China, 131
  Basic Law, 135
  China's partnership in trade and
    investment with, 134–35, 151–52
  as free port for intangibles, 124
  free trade policy of, 121–28
  government's resistance to
    intervention, 122
  investment in China, 154
  lack of trade barriers in, 123–25
  manufacturers moving to China
    from, 131
  model applied to China, 2, 152–58
  partnership with China in trade and
    investment, 134–35, 151–52
  real estate opportunities in China,
    133–34
  services to manufacturing in China,
    15
  standard of living and opportunities
    in, 158
  Stock Exchange, 132–33, 135, 154
  tax system, 357–58, 370–71
Hong Kong Trade Development
  Council, 154
Hou, L., 295
Household responsibility system,
  49–50, 70, 79
House-Midamba, B., 277
Howell, J., 245
Hu, J., 109
Hu, X. L., 61
Huang, G., 215
Huang, J., 50
Huang, Y., 179, 393
Human capital
  in banking system, 144–45

ABOUT THE EDITOR

James A. Dorn is Vice President for Academic Affairs at the Cato Institute and Editor of the *Cato Journal*. He also directs Cato's annual monetary conference. He has lectured at the Central European University in Prague and Fudan University in Shanghai, and currently is a Professor of Economics at Towson University in Maryland. In 1998, the Board of Regents of the University System of Maryland presented Dorn with its highest honor, the USM Regents' Faculty Award for Excellence in Research/Scholarship.

Dorn has written widely on public policy issues and has edited or coedited 10 books including: *The Revolution in Development Economics; The Future of Money in the Information Age; From Plan to Market: The Future of Post-Communist Republics; Economic Reform in China: Problems and Prospects; Economic Liberties and the Judiciary; The Search for Stable Money;* and *Money and Markets in the Americas*. His articles have appeared in the *Financial Times*, the *Asian Wall Street Journal, El Economista, Forbes Digital Tool,* the *Journal of Commerce,* and in scholarly journals.

From 1984 to 1990, he served on the White House Commission on Presidential Scholars. Dorn is a member of the Mont Pelerin Society. He holds an M.A. and Ph.D. in economics from the University of Virginia.

Cato Institute

Founded in 1977, the Cato Institute is a public policy research foundation dedicated to broadening the parameters of policy debate to allow consideration of more options that are consistent with the traditional American principles of limited government, individual liberty, and peace. To that end, the Institute strives to achieve greater involvement of the intelligent, concerned lay public in questions of policy and the proper role of government.

The Institute is named for *Cato's Letters*, libertarian pamphlets that were widely read in the American Colonies in the early 18th century and played a major role in laying the philosophical foundation for the American Revolution.

Despite the achievement of the nation's Founders, today virtually no aspect of life is free from government encroachment. A pervasive intolerance for individual rights is shown by government's arbitrary intrusions into private economic transactions and its disregard for civil liberties.

To counter that trend, the Cato Institute undertakes an extensive publications program that addresses the complete spectrum of policy issues. Books, monographs, and shorter studies are commissioned to examine the federal budget, Social Security, regulation, military spending, international trade, and myriad other issues. Major policy conferences are held throughout the year, from which papers are published thrice yearly in the *Cato Journal*. The Institute also publishes the quarterly magazine *Regulation*.

In order to maintain its independence, the Cato Institute accepts no government funding. Contributions are received from foundations, corporations, and individuals, and other revenue is generated from the sale of publications. The Institute is a nonprofit, tax-exempt, educational foundation under Section 501(c)3 of the Internal Revenue Code.

CATO INSTITUTE
1000 Massachusetts Ave., N.W.
Washington, D.C. 20001

DATE DUE
